3702602544

FRANCIS CLOSE HALL
LEARNING CENTRE

**FRANCIS CLOSE HALL
LEARNING CENTRE**
Swindon Road Cheltenham
Gloucestershire GL50 4AZ
Telephone: 01242 714600

UNIVERSITY OF
GLOUCESTERSHIRE
at Cheltenham and Gloucester

WEEK LOAN
WEEK LOAN

16 APR 2002

23 APR 2002
-4 MAR 2003

28 MAR 2003

WITHDRAWN

D1350152

Charismatics and the New Millennium

*The impact of Charismatic Christianity
from 1960 into the new millennium*

Nigel Scotland

FCH LEARNING CENTRE
UNIVERSITY OF GLOUCESTERSHIRE
Swindon Road
Cheltenham GL50 4AZ
Tel: 01242 532913

eagle

Guildford

Copyright © 1995 Nigel Scotland
This edition © 2000 Nigel Scotland
First published by Hodder & Stoughton Ltd. A division of Hodder
Headline PLC, 338 Euston Road, London NW1 3BH.
This edition published by Eagle, an imprint of Inter Publishing Service
(IPS) Ltd, PO Box 530, Guildford, Surrey GU2 5FH.

The right of Nigel Scotland to be identified as author of this work has
been asserted by him in accordance with the Copyright, Design and
Patents Act 1988.

British Library Cataloguing in Publication Data. A catalogue record for
this book is available from the British Library.

All rights reserved. No part of this publication may be reproduced or
transmitted in any form or by any means, electronic or mechanical,
including photocopying, recording or any information storage and
retrieval system, without either prior permission in writing from the
publisher or a licence permitting restricted copying. In the United
Kingdom such licences are issued by the Publishers Licensing Society
Ltd, 90 Tottenham Court Road, London W1P 9HE.

Unless otherwise indicated, Scripture quotations are taken from the
HOLY BIBLE, NEW INTERNATIONAL VERSION, copyright © 1973,
1978, 1984 by International Bible Society. Used by permission of
Hodder & Stoughton, a Division of Hodder Headline.

Typeset by Eagle
Printed by Cox & Wyman, Reading
ISBN No: 0 86347 370 9

CONTENTS

Acknowledgements

This volume is a revised version of what was originally titled *Charismatics and the Next Millennium*. It has been thoroughly updated and extended with a new chapter added on, 'Charismatics and Theology'. Many people have generously taken time to discuss and debate the issues contained in the chapters which follow. Their names are listed separately among the sources at the end of the book. I am particularly indebted, however, to Bishop David Pytches for his friendship and encouragement with this project and for his careful scrutiny of the manuscript of the first edition. Wynne Lewis very kindly read the text of this second edition and graciously took time from his busy schedule to write the Foreword. Desmond Cartwright helped me with advice on many details of Pentecostal history and practice. Frank Booth, Arthur Champion, Lori Lee, Keith Hitchman and Bryony Benier all gave me valuable advice and points of information along the way.

Thanks are also due to Sarah Shailer who helped me with the revivion of the text of the second edition and also to Rebecca Halifax and Lyn Goodwin for word processing. Finally I would like to thank Lynne Barratt and Sue Wavre for setting and correcting the text and David Wavre, Editorial Director at Eagle Publishing, for his warm encouragement in the publication of this book.

Nigel Scotland
Cheltenham

FOREWORD

The outstanding feature of church life in the twentieth century has been the thrust and outpouring of the Holy Spirit, with scenes reminiscent of what happened on the Day of Pentecost. Thousands of believers have prayed, 'Do it again, Lord'. He has. Some 500 million Christians have been filled with the Holy Spirit in our day.

Classic Pentecostalism is a spiritual phenomenon. In the United Kingdom there are over 350,000 worshippers who belong to a Pentecostal church. However, that is not the full story of the workings of the Holy Spirit in our day and age. We have seen the Holy Spirit leaping over denominational walls and making dramatic inroads into the life and witness of all historic churches. That which seemed impossible has come to pass.

This book introduces us to these greater works of the Holy Spirit. It is an exciting story. We are indebted to the author for his painstaking research to give us a very vivid picture and an accurate account of events. Nigel Scotland has given us a very useful book. He is very well qualified to do so; with his academic theological background allied to his practical understanding through hands-on leadership of a fast-growing church.

He traces the birth of the modern charismatic movement and examines the emergence of various groupings. He agrees with Professor Andrew Walker that 'Restoration charismatics belong both theologically and sociologically to classic Pentecostalism'. He is not afraid of dealing with the emerging problems and difficulties. He paints a realistic picture, warts and all. He tackles a large number of questions in an honest manner. Glossolalia has not only blessed the church, but in some instances has polarised matters. Analysing Toronto, while believing that it has benefited the church with its cathartic element, he concludes that it is a mixture of the divine and human. While the author is bold and fearless in handling thorny issues and not afraid to give his assessment, he is at all times objective and kind.

The book will help readers appreciate the tremendous

impact that the charismatic movement has made on the church in general. The pre-charismatic church was pretty lifeless and cerebral and was experiencing the greatest falling away in membership. The author contends that the 'renewal' arrested the decline and reversed the trend. The Anglican Renewal Ministry strongly impacted the Church of England, the Dunamis Renewal Group influenced the Methodist Church while 50 per cent of Baptist churches were affected. He believes that the charismatic renewal has helped the wider church to think more carefully about worship and what exactly it is that the church is attempting to achieve by singing. 'In very general terms, the music, the culture and the buildings used by charismatic churches are very much closer to the level at which ordinary people have their daily lives'. He believes that many people find in the worship of a charismatic church, a much greater depth of love and acceptance.

He takes a close look at the house church movement, its Restoration Kingdom teaching, Apostolic authority and authoritarianism, the shepherding issues with potential dangers and consequential damage. His views on the emergence of prophetic leadership, the issues of unfulfilled prophecies, John Wimber, spiritual warfare and demonism are invaluable. Dealing with the issue of when does 'baptism in the Spirit' occur, his quote of Nigel Wright's view of those who believe that it happens at conversion is a beauty: 'If you got it all at conversion, where is it?'

This book is a mine of information, giving us excellent historic and background information. It also shows the grace and love of God in using 'vessels of clay'; God uses ordinary people to achieve the extraordinary. I believe you will enjoy reading it.

Wynne Lewis
General Superintendent,
Elim Pentecostal Church.
January 2000

1

INTRODUCING
THE CHARISMATIC MOVEMENT

By far and away the world's largest church is Yoido Full Gospel Church in Seoul, Korea, with a seating capacity of 25,000. Led by Paul Cho (b 1936) it had 600,000 members and 90,000 house groups in 1994. It is an avowedly charismatic church.[1] By the close of 1999 its membership had increased to 734,077.[2] Yoido Church reflects the fact that charismatic Christianity is dominant in parts of the Far East and Latin America. In the developed West it is still marginal but its influence is growing rapidly. In 1981 Peter C Wagner, a church growth expert from Los Angeles, California, calculated that there were 90 million charismatic Christians in the world. In 1994 he estimated their number at 400 million. David Barrett reported that in 1992 there were 207 million professing charismatic Christians and 204 million denominational Pentecostals. Together they made up 24 per cent of Christians worldwide.[3] In 1999 the combined total of charismatics and Pentecostals was just under 450 million. The 1991 report, *Christian England,* showed an almost identical trend in this country. Charismatic Christians had increased in number by 9 per cent during the previous ten years whilst all other categories of Christian declined 5 per cent or more in the same period.[4] Another statistic in the same volume showed the highest proportions of growing churches occurred among charismatic evangelicals. The picture since 1995 has been one of decline at least in terms of official statistics. One estimate is that the number of charismatic Christians in the UK has dipped steeply since 1995 which means an overall decline of 16 per cent in the last ten years.[5] One reason for this drop is that since the

9

Toronto Blessing phenomenon many churches who formerly described themselves as 'charismatic' now prefer to be designated 'mainstream evangelical'. This of course does not necessarily mean that their members have rejected their initial charismatic experience but simply that they either eschew the Toronto phenomenon or are uncomfortable with it. On the world stage, however, Pentecostalism is expanding rapidly. It is the fastest growing religion in the Third World and in some South American countries Pentecostals are approximately 10 per cent of the population.[6]

The word *charismatic* derives from the Greek word *charismata*, which means gift of the Holy Spirit. Peter Hocken asserted that Harald Bredesen (b 1918) and Jean Stone (b 1924) 'have the distinction of coining the term "charismatic" to denote the new movement of the Holy Spirit within the older churches. At the end of an article entitled "Return to the Charismata" they stated, "we call this movement 'the charismatic revival' " .'[7] The charismatic movement is a worldwide phenomenon of the Holy Spirit which is rooted in the experience of the Day of Pentecost. It emphasises such gifts as speaking in tongues, prophecy and healing, but also sees the importance of other gifts mentioned in the New Testament. It is characterised by its 'free' expressions of worship, most often with untraditional words and music. From small beginnings in England in the 1960s this movement expanded rapidly and widely across all sections of the church in England. Attitudes to it have changed and become quite strongly polarised at times. In the mid 1960s some Anglican Theological College principals questioned the fitness of charismatic students for ordination. By the 1990s there were bishops, archdeacons and Theological College principals who were committed card-carrying charismatics. Despite this growth in all denominations there have been, and are, prominent Christian leaders who voice great anxiety about the movement. One former Cheltenham vicar for example likened speaking in tongues to the incantations of the witch doctor. In contrast, others, reflecting on the steep decline in traditional church-going and the financial crisis in the established church saw charismatic Christianity as the only hope in an otherwise bleak future.

Part of the reason for these strongly held differences of opinion about the charismatic movement is the phenomena which it generates. For some, the Holy Spirit experience has come like a dove in a gracious and gentle manner and has brought a deep sense of peace and the presence of Jesus. For others, the charismatic movement has been enthusiastic, heady stuff. It has come with hyper ecstasy, raucous foot stamping worship and unrealistic faith claims. For this reason critics say it has more the appearance of a 'wild goose' than a 'gracious dove'. It is this movement, and the strongly held but differing views which Christians have about it, which the book seeks to examine.

Origins

In one sense, of course, movements of the Holy Spirit have always been in evidence in the church's life and work. In the very early period there were a number of spring-like periods in which the Christian faith burst out into new life. This was followed by the long winter of the Middle Ages in which the Holy Spirit seems to have been largely dormant. Since the Reformation in the sixteenth century, however, there have been a growing number of renewal movements.

In the early period of Christian history there was a remarkable movement which began in AD 157 in the Roman province of Phrygia (modern Turkey). It was known as Montanism after its leader Montanus who announced a fresh outpouring of the Holy Spirit and called for a reform of the church.[8] Montanus was assisted by two prophetesses, Maximilla and Priscilla. Together they practised speaking in tongues and prophecy and preached the imminent second coming of Jesus and the need for strict asceticism. Montanism became more widespread when Tertullian (AD 160–220), one of the church's leading theologians, joined their ranks in about AD 206. The movement only came to an end in AD 381 when the Council of Constantinople refused to recognise the validity of their baptism services.

A little later, Irenaeus (AD 130–202) who was Bishop of Lyons in central Gaul, wrote at the end of the second century of those who 'through the Spirit do speak all kinds of language and bring to light for the general benefit the hidden things of men and declare the mysteries of God'.[9] Justin Martyr (c.100–165), a contemporary of Irenaeus, declared: 'It is possible now to see among us women and men who possess the gifts of the Spirit of God.'[10] Gregory Thaumaturgos (c.210–c270)

11

became bishop of his native town of Neo-Caesarea. 'Thaumaturgos', meaning miracle worker, was a nickname given to Gregory on account of the remarkable power which attended his ministry. According to his biographer, he could move the largest stones by a word. He healed many sick people and the demons were subject to his every word. He is also reported to have stopped rivers overflowing their banks and to have dried up mighty lakes. On one occasion he spent a night in a heathen temple and banished its divinities by his single presence. Tradition says that when he became bishop there were only seventeen Christians in the city, but when he died thirty years later there were only seventeen pagans.[11] However, by the time of Augustine (AD 354–430) and Chrysostom (AD 345–467), the main view seems to have been that the gifts had been given to authenticate the preaching and teaching of the early Christians and then had been withdrawn. Augustine himself taught that the sign of tongues for the individual believer had been replaced by Christian love.[12] Later however he came to believe in miracles and healing through a number of such incidents in the closing years of his life.

From this time on, particularly through the long medieval period (800–1500), the wider church seems to have lost touch with the Holy Spirit. There were only very occasional shoots of new spiritual life in what was otherwise a 'dark age'. Such was the movement inspired by John Wycliffe (1328–1384) in the late fourteenth century and the period of the sixteenth-century Reformation in Europe. The seventeenth century witnessed the emergence of the Jansenists. Like their leader Cornelius Jansen (1585–1638), Archdeacon of Paris, they practised speaking in tongues and rigorous Christian living. A little later the Camisard Huguenots were also known for their practice of glossolalia and prophecy.[13]

The eighteenth century in the United States witnessed truly remarkable happenings under the preaching of Jonathan Edwards (1705–1758) at Northampton, Massachusetts. News of this 'great awakening' was networked to England in reports and letters[14] and helped to fan the flame of the revival which broke out under George Whitefield (1714–70) and John Wesley (1703–91). In this Methodist movement it is estimated that possibly as many as 100,000 people became 'born-again' believers and were organised into societies. As Wesley preached, people often sank to the ground as though dead and called to God for mercy. John Wesley stressed what he termed the 'witness of God's Spirit' in the individual Christian believer. Wesley was convinced of the necessity of spiritual gifts. He maintained that 'the cause of their decline was not as had been vulgarly supposed because there is no more need of them because all the world were become Christians . . . the real cause was the love of many, almost all Christians, was waxed cold.'[15] Glossolalia seems not to have featured significantly in early Methodism although Thomas Walsh recorded in his diary for 8 March 1750: 'This morning the Lord gave me language that I know not of, raising my soul to Him in a wonderful manner.'[16] Significantly, however, Methodism's fourfold pattern of Christ as Saviour, Sanctifier, Healer and coming King is the same pattern adopted by Pentecostals except that they substitute Baptiser for Sanctifier.

A generation or so after Wesley's death, Edward Irving (1792–1834) was appointed Presbyterian minister of Cross Street Chapel, London, in 1822. His dignified bearing, athletic appearance and fiery pulpit eloquence drew large crowds including Members of Parliament to his church. Irving gradually came to the view that apostolic gifts had been lost to the church for no other reason than people's lack of faith. Tongues and prophecy became a regular feature in the worship of Irving's congregation. The London Presbytery however felt that such 'excesses' could not go unchecked and in 1833 Irving was expelled from the ministry. He subsequently became the moving spirit in a new sect, the Catholic Apostolic Church, but died in 1834, probably saddened and broken by his conflict with the presbytery.[17]

Twentieth Century Pentecostal Outpourings in England and America

In 1904 Joseph Smale (1867–1926), pastor of 1st Baptist Church, Los Angeles, returned from Wales. He had seen the revival under Evan Roberts (1878–1951) and was on fire to have the same visitation in his own church. Although Smale's congregation were deeply moved by his reports, it was at Azusa Street that things began to happen. In 1906 William Seymour

(1870–1922), a black preacher, began to hold services in an abandoned warehouse in Azusa Street. Soon there were reports of tongues-speaking and walls covered with canes and crutches of those who had been miraculously healed. Frank Bartlemann wrote: 'Few events have affected modern history as greatly as the famous Azusa Street revival 1906–1909 which ushered into being the world-wide twentieth-century Pentecostal revival.'[18]

From Azusa Street, the Pentecostal flame spread right across America and into Canada. The 'Apostle of Pentecost' to Europe, Thomas Ball Barratt (1862–1940), a Norwegian Methodist, was influenced and from his ministry the torch spread to England. One of those drawn to hear Barratt was Alexander Boddy (1854–1930), vicar of All Saints, Sunderland. His church and vicarage became a centre for those who sought the baptism of the Spirit in the early years of the twentieth century. A memorial plaque in the entrance of the parish hall witnesses to the extraordinary move of God's Spirit: 'September 1907. When the fire of the Lord fell it burned up the debt.' As a result of the revival considerable building deficit was paid off almost overnight.

Among those who were powerfully touched by the Spirit at All Saints was Smith Wigglesworth (1859–1947). In a letter dated November 1907, Wigglesworth related that Mrs Boddy had laid hands on him: 'The fire fell and burned in me till the Holy Spirit clearly revealed absolute purity before God . . . when I could not find words to express then an irresistible power filled me and moved me till I found to my glorious astonishment I was speaking in other tongues clearly.'[19]

Smith had a truly remarkable ministry of preaching and healing and travelled the world. He kept in close association with the newly emerging Pentecostal churches and his own Bowland Street Mission merged into the Elim Alliance which had been formed in 1915 by George Jeffreys (1889–1963). The name 'Elim' is taken from Exodus chapter 15 verse 27. While Smith was visiting South Africa in 1936 he met with a young Pentecostal minister. He apparently propelled him firmly against the wall of the room and looking into his eyes he prophesied:

I have been sent by the Lord to tell you what he has shown

14

me this morning. Through the old line denominations will come a revival that will eclipse anything we have known throughout history. No such things have happened in times past as will happen when this begins . . . Then the Lord said to me I am to give you warning that he is going to use you in the movement. [20]

Charismatic Beginnings

So it proved. The young minister in question was David du Plessis (1905-87). He became internationally known as Secretary of the World Pentecostal Fellowship. In 1954 he attended the Second Assembly of the World Council of Churches. He provided the link between the early Pentecostal stirrings of the first three decades of the twentieth century and the so called 'second wave' of the 1960s in which the charismatic experience began to move into the historic denominational churches. It was the coming of the Pentecostal experience into the historic denominational churches which resulted in the use of the term 'charismatic renewal'.[21] Among the first of those to be touched in the Protestant Episcopal Church was Dennis Bennett (1917-1991), rector of fashionable St Mark's Church, Van Nuys, California. His morning sermon on Passion Sunday, 1960, created no small stir among his congregation. He related how he had been filled with the Holy Spirit and spoken in tongues just as the disciples did on the day of Pentecost.[22] Another significant influence was the Full Gospel Businessmen's Fellowship International. Founded in 1951 in Southern California by Demos Shakarian (b 1913), it was an organisation for all people committed to evangelism in the context of the charismatic renewal.[23]

In a fairly short space of time these developments began to reach England. Philip Hughes, the scholarly editor of *The Churchman*, wrote very positively of his visit in 1962 to witness the impact of the charismatic renewal in California. Not one readily given to mindless emotional enthusiasm, Hughes' assessment was: 'Dare we deny that this is a movement of God's sovereign Spirit?'[24] It made a profound impact. Hughes' endorsement helped to put the newly emerging charismatic movement as a serious issue before many British Pentecostals and Church of England evangelicals.

One of those who was touched by this new current of the

Holy Spirit's activity was Michael Harper (b 1931), curate to John Stott (b 1921) at the evangelical mecca of All Souls, Langham Place, London. In September 1962, Harper was at a conference in Farnham where 'I was filled with all the fullness of God and had to ask God to stop giving more – I couldn't take it'.[25] In July 1965 Harper left All Souls after six successful years in order to devote his time to sharing this message of spiritual renewal. He became secretary of The Fountain Trust which was formed in September of the same year. This was an interdenominational organisation which aimed to encourage 'local churches to experience renewal in the Holy Spirit'. To this end conferences were organised and tapes and literature circulated, especially *Renewal* magazine. Although the Trust closed down in 1980, *Renewal* magazine, now edited by Dave Roberts, has continued to exert a significant influence.

American impact on the English scene grew steadily. Dennis Bennett[26] and two of his parishioners, Mrs Jean Stone and her husband Don, were among those who came to England in the early 1960s to share their experience and to minister in churches and at conferences. Jean Stone, who was editor of *Trinity*, an American Episcopal magazine, spoke at Caxton Hall and the City Temple. These were the first large-scale meetings of the new movement held in Britain.

It is clear that this movement of charismatic renewal had emerged from classic Pentecostalism of the earlier years of the twentieth century and was in fact an extension of Pentecostalism into the historic Christian denominations. Professor Andrew Walker refers to the charismatic renewal as 'the gentrification of Pentecostalism'.

In the 1970s men such as Derek Prince (b 1915), Ern Baxter (1914–1993) and Bob Mumford (b 1930) also visited England to minister. Soon after this, several controversial teachings began to surface. Derek Prince published a book on 'Believers' Baptism' and words such as 'covering', 'submission' and 'authority' became common currency. 'Covering' meant placing each individual Christian under the personal supervision and guidance of a church elder or leader. Submission required individuals to 'obey' their elders even if, on occasion, they were wrong or unwise. During the Lakes Bible Week Baxter's teaching on 'covering' met with sensational responses. 'The audiences went "wild" every time he came on stage.'[27]

From the outset the charismatic movement straddled the entire denominational spectrum. Vatican II, which concluded in 1965, had created a new openness and humility in the Catholic Church as she sought to discover what the Holy Spirit was saying to her. Pope John 23rd composed a special prayer to be said daily throughout the world during the council which asked the Holy Spirit to 'renew your wonders in this our day, as a new Pentecost'.[28] From about 1967 Roman Catholics became significantly influenced by the charismatic renewal. On the occasion of the Pope's visit to England in 1982, Roman Catholics were heard singing the same choruses which were familiar in charismatic circles generally! Numbers of Roman Catholic charismatics were influenced by David Wilkerson's book *The Cross and the Switchblade* which spoke so forcefully of the power of the Holy Spirit in the lives of New York street kids. In 1969 Kevin and Dorothy Ranaghan spoke of the move of the Holy Spirit in Catholic America having become a 'raging flame'.[29] This was no more clearly visible than at an International Charismatic Conference organised in Rome in 1975. Ten thousand charismatic Roman Catholics gathered in St Peter's Basilica to celebrate the Pentecost season. The charismatic renewal took early root among English Roman Catholics. The first Catholic sponsored conference was held at Roehampton in July 1972. Another was held at Guildford the following year. A 'high proportion' of the delegates to the National Pastoral Congress in Liverpool in 1980 were 'either actively involved in, or had more than a passing contact with charismatic renewal'.[30] Another influential book was John and Elizabeth Sherrill's *They Speak with Other Tongues* published in 1965. Sherrill, an Episcopalian writer, began a journalistic investigation which became a personal experience. The book saw tongues as opening the door to fuller spiritual life. Once you go through that door 'you are surrounded by the thousand wonders of light and sound and form that the architect intended'.[31]

In the mid 1970s Terry Fullam, rector of St Paul's Episcopal Church in Darien, USA, was becoming a familiar figure in England. His gifts lay in teaching and testifying and he demonstrated wide pastoral skills and leadership in his home parish. He encouraged Michael Harper and his friends to plan an

Anglican Charismatic Conference in 1978 to coincide with the Lambeth Conference of that year. Over three hundred Anglican leaders, including thirty bishops, gathered at Kent University. Archbishop Donald Coggan attended a packed Cathedral for a festival of praise and spoke in glowing terms of the renewal in England. One very positive outcome of the conference was the creation of SOMA (Sharing of Ministries Abroad). This organisation, whose director is Donald Brewin, still actively seeks to maintain fellowship and promote spiritual renewal among Anglicans worldwide.

Touching the Denominational Churches

Over the years, charismatic renewal took root in several of the mainline denominations in Britain. It was sometimes called 'neo-Pentecostalism' to distinguish it from the early Pentecostal denominations (*neo* meaning new). In the Church of England it is fostered by Anglican Renewal Ministries and based in Derby, and the ever-widening ministry of Bishop David Pytches (b 1931) at St Andrew's Chorleywood in Hertfordshire and more recently, since his retirement, through travel and conferences, most notably the highly successful New Wine and Soul Survivor summer gatherings on the Bath and Wells showground. Barry Kissell has directed 'Faith Sharing Ministries' from St Andrew's. Teams continue to be sent out to spread charismatic renewal not only in the UK but in many other European countries. Archbishop George Carey signalled his endorsement of the charismatic renewal by his presence on the platform at the opening night of the Brighton 1991 Charismatic Conference. Indeed he has publicly expressed his own personal indebtedness to the charismatic movement on several occasions. Among Church of England bishops who currently identify themselves as charismatics are John Perry (b 1935), Bishop of Chelmsford, Graham Dow, Bishop of Willesden, David Gillett (b 1945), Bishop of Bolton and Cyril Ashton (b 1942), Bishop of Doncaster.

The Methodists were early inspired by one of their ministers, Charles Clarke (1903–1984), a Staffordshire circuit superintendent, who was baptised in the Spirit in 1963 and edited *Quest* to promote the experience among British Methodists. The Methodist Revival Fellowship (MRF) was launched in the 1950s and 'CJ', as he was affectionately known, became an active leader. In 1970 Clarke and others[32] founded the Dunamis Renewal Group with the specific aim of promoting charismatic renewal in Methodist circuits. In areas where ministers were unsympathetic, local members organised circuit 'celebrations' and practical encouragement was given through their magazine *Dunamis Renewal* which was first published in 1972. It regularly contained articles and teaching about renewal in the Holy Spirit. Circulation was about 6,000 in 1986. Five hundred Methodist ministers were on the *Dunamis Renewal* mailing list in 1993. A leading inspiration in the movement was the Reverend Dr Bill Davis who was Principal of Cliff College until 1994. His successor, the Reverend Howard Mellor, has continued to encourage the charismatic renewal. In April 1995 the Dunamis Renewal Group combined with Headway, another Methodist renewal group with similar objectives which had been running since 1995. *Dunamis Renewal* ceased publication and the group shared the quarterly magazine *Headline* which in 1999 had a circulation of 2,500 of whom about 500 were Methodist ministers. Headway also organise an annual prayer conference which in 1999 was led by a team from the revival church in Pensacola, USA.

A parallel movement was also established among the Baptists with the founding in 1980 of Mainstream. Mainstream organises an annual conference for Baptist Union ministers and other leaders. With the passing of the years it came to exert considerable influence within the denomination. Leading figures included Paul Beasley-Murray, who was Principal of Spurgeon's College until 1992, and David Coffey, the Baptist Union General Secretary. Both are very much personally committed to charismatic renewal. There is a general perception that charismatic renewal has changed the whole tenor of the Baptist Union during the last decade. Mainstream links many Baptists who are active in charismatic renewal. It estimated that the life and worship of 50 per cent of Baptist churches is influenced by renewal in the Holy Spirit. Douglas McBain writing in 1997 suggested that 'the majority of Baptist ministers in Britain who began their ministry in the middle to late 1970s onwards appear to be willing to identify themselves with whatever they perceive as the positive attributes of renewal'.[33] Significantly, Douglas

McBain who was President of the Baptist Union 1998–1999 and his successor Michael Bochenski were both charismatics.

Restoration and the House Churches

In the 1970s the so-called 'house church' movement began to establish itself in England. Groups of Christians who had been 'baptised in the Spirit' became increasingly disenchanted with the rigid formalism and the lack of warm fellowship within the denominational churches. They started initially to meet together in each other's homes and then, as numbers grew, they began to hire schools, community halls and even cinemas. The house church movement is a loose umbrella title covering a variety of independent charismatic groups which are not linked with any historic denomination. Few of them now meet in houses.

House churches which later came to be known as 'new churches' are by no means uniform in their ethos or aspirations. Different strands and factions are discernible. In the 1970s and 1980s a large sector operated under the banner of 'Restoration'. The term arose out of a commitment to 'restore' to the contemporary churches the pattern of ministry and structure of the New Testament churches with emphasis on all the ministries of Ephesians chapter 4 verse 11. This included oversight and direction by 'restored' apostles with prominence given also to the ministry of the prophet. In his classic text *Restoring the Kingdom,* Andrew Walker distinguished (not altogether helpfully in my opinion) between Restoration 1 and Restoration 2 (R1 and R2).[34] Although Restorationists recognised that the Kingdom of God would not fully come until the return of Christ they began to believe that through their work and worship people would experience its power and reality now. R1 Restorationists were those who exercised much stricter control over their followings and expected much greater commitment from them.

R1, which was the more rigorous of the two groups initially clustered around the swashbuckling ministry of Bryn Jones (b 1939) who early located in Bradford. In 1977 they purchased the former Anglican diocesan Church House headquarters and transformed it into offices, a coffee shop, lounge and worship area for 500 people. They later moved in 1990 to a new purpose-built site at Nettlehill near Coventry. This complex is replete with offices, a conference centre and Covenant College where there were year-long in-depth Bible study courses. R1 was a highly structured national network whose leaders formed a hierarchy to whom the local leaders submitted, often in the early days without question or discussion. Under their aegis thousands of people met each year for a jamboree of worship and seminars at The Dales in Yorkshire. Numbers of Elim, Baptist and other independent churches affiliated with Jones' outfit after testing the new wine of The Dales. The venue was subsequently moved to Builth Wells in Mid Wales and later to Stoneleigh. Another similar conference known as The Downs began in 1981 at Plumpton Racecourse in Sussex.[35] In addition to Bryn and his brother Keri, the leaders of this R1 group included Arthur Wallis and, for a brief period, Terry Virgo, a former London Bible College student of Baptist origins. They produced a glossy periodical under the caption *Restoration* which from 1978 disseminated the movement's central doctrines and Virgo authored an influential book under the same title.[36] Virgo later separated from R1 but continued to exercise apostolic responsibility for a cluster of churches in the South East known as 'Coastlands'. They were later re-named 'New Frontiers' in 1986 and had their base at Hove in Sussex. New Frontiers progressively aligned themselves with the less authoritarian stance of the R2 clusters.

In 1984 Jones and his associates made energetic thrusts into Birmingham, Leicester and Leeds. Andrew Walker estimated that by 1985 the Jones' segment of R1 had between 12,000 and 15,000 members although others put this figure considerably higher.[37] By the early 1990s, however, increasing numbers of his churches and individuals were transferring their allegiance to the calmer waters of R2 and some of the renewed denominational churches.

R1 now operates under the banner of 'New Covenant Ministries International' with three recognised apostles, Bryn and Keri Jones together for a time with Michael Godward of Thurrock. The circulation of *Restoration* magazine dropped from 13,000 to 6,000 and was eventually replaced by *Covenant News* magazine which was distributed free of charge. In the mid 1990s CMI underwent a number of changes. Mike Godward was recognised by Bryn as an apostle and commissioned in the early 1990s for independent work. In 1997 Alan Scotland, Andy

Owen and Paul Scanlon were also all recognised as apostles simultaneously by Bryn in a public meeting and released to form their own networks. They were all men whose ministries had emerged 'in-house' and had been given churches under Bryn and Keri's oversight. Paul Scanlon is perhaps the most notable of the three. He was an unchurched lad who was led to Christ by Keri at the age of sixteen and his whole Christian life had been spent within CMI. He was given the largest and oldest church in the network, Abundant Life, in Bradford. By 1999 Paul Scanlon was making a name in satellite TV and Andy Owen was one of the moving forces behind the popular Christian magazine *Power for Living*. Alan Scotland had established his network under the title Lifelink at South Wigston in Leicestershire. Covenant Ministries International had a membership of 6,250 in 1995 and were projected to increase to 6,900 by the year 2000.[38]

In the early days at least, R1 were noted for their extremes of authoritarianism and 'heavy shepherding'. I personally encountered individuals who were not allowed to move jobs and sell houses and, in one case, go out to supper with their college tutor until they had their elders' say so. Other examples of authoritarian leadership from within this group included the way in which R1's headquarters were uprooted from Bradford, together with Harvest Time Ministries, and resettled at Nettlehill near Coventry. Numbers of those who made the move did not find work easily and were left somewhat disillusioned and stranded by the high level of unemployment in the West Midlands. Some of these extremes of authoritarian teaching emanated from a Chinese Christian, Watchman Nee (d 1972), who taught that even to criticise those in authority is tantamount to rebellion against God.

Restoration 2

Originally the leaders of the major house churches enjoyed good fellowship and in 1974 they covenanted to work together. However in 1976 the movement divided into two separate factions. Gerald Coates and the so-called 'London Brothers' enjoyed the cinema, popular music and other aspects of contemporary culture whereas individuals such as Wallis and Jones regarded them as 'worldly'. Arthur Wallis (1922–1988) used to refer to the R2 leaders and their following as 'the hairies' because numbers of them grew their hair long. Wallis felt this to be dishonouring to the gospel. Bryn and Keri Jones worked in harness supported initially by Dave Tomlinson who devoted his energies to the Midlands. R1 grew rapidly in the 1980s but declined thereafter. Covenant Ministries had only fifty congregations in their fellowship in 1994. Part of the reason for this demise may have been Dave Tomlinson and his churches transferring their allegiance to R2 in 1983. That same year proved to be a good year for R2 with their first summer camp on the Staffordshire Showground and the publication of Gerald Coates' book *What on Earth is this Kingdom?*

Gerald Coates, a former postman, lived for a time in a historic mansion once owned by Clive of India before moving to another more modest Surrey residence. He emerged as a gifted teacher and lucid writer. A number of other prominent leaders of this group, which operated under the title of Pioneer, such as John and Christine Noble and Peter Lyne were close and longstanding friends of Coates. 'Team Spirit', led by John and Christine Noble, entered into a closer working relationship with Pioneer in 1991. John believed the Lord gave him a 'word' while he was out jogging! 'This is not a time for independence or fragmentation, but for togetherness and inter-dependence.'[39] Pioneer's membership was reckoned at 7,400 in the year 2000.[40]

There were several other clusters of house-church style fellowships. One such looked for teaching and input to Pastor George (Wally) North who ministered to Holiness Church in Bradford from 1952–1965. It was sometimes humorously and erroneously designated as 'the North circular'. Wally adopted Wesley's teaching on holiness and perfection. Generally speaking fellowships and groups which were linked with him tended to keep themselves to themselves. Much of the oversight of this group in recent years was taken over by Norman Meeten, a former Church of England clergyman. Another group was based on a small community at South Chard in Somerset. Founded by Sid Purse, formerly a member of the Brethren, it is associated with the practice of re-baptism. According to their teaching, baptism in the Acts of the Apostles was always in Jesus' name and this was the only correct formula. Those who have already been baptised, but in the name of the Trinity, are encouraged to seek re-baptism.

Britain's largest church, affectionately known as 'KT', short-hand for Kensington Temple, belongs to the Elim denomination. Like many charismatic churches it has been wholly committed to planting satellite congregations. KT's pastor until June 1990, Wynne Lewis, had a vision to set up fifty satellite house-style churches. In 1994 there were more than seventy-five, some of them meeting in halls, pubs and wine bars. By the close of 1999 there were 160 listed in the Elim Church Year Book. Over 3,500 worshippers attended the main Sunday service. At the beginning of 2000, Kensington Temple had 6,000 attending the Central Church each Sunday with another 10,000 in its satellite congregations. Another Pentecostal church, Kingsway International Christian Centre, led by Matthew Ashimolowa, has regular Sunday congregations of 5,000.

In 1974 in South East London, Roger and Faith Forster, assisted by musician and leading song writer, Graham Kendrick, developed the Ichthus Fellowship. By 1999 they had established some twenty-seven area congregations in schools, halls and disused church buildings. In addition there are 120 Ichthus Link Churches in the UK and Europe.[41] They have demonstrated an impressive social concern which includes literacy classes and training for the long-term unemployed and they readily co-operate with Christians of other denominations. Ichthus' total membership was probably in the region of 5,000 at the close of 1999. Among other groups there is Salt and Light, a large cluster of new churches and some denominational churches, including one or two Church of England churches which look to Barney Coombs for 'apostolic oversight' and input. 'Apostle' is a term which house churches used to describe their top level of leadership who oversee their churches countrywide. Salt and Light hold an annual conference at Swanwick in Derbyshire. Their membership was estimated to reach 9,000 by the close of the year 2000.[42] Another recognisable strand are the Faith Churches under Kenneth Hagin, an American fundamentalist pastor who claims to have been to heaven and back on at least two occasions. Kenneth Hagin (b 1917) and his followers are categorised as 'positive confession charismatics'. Converted to Christ in 1933, Hagin was guided by a steady stream of visions to an itinerant travelling ministry in 1949. In 1974 he founded the Rhema Bible Centre in Tulsa, Oklahoma. By 1988 more than 10,000 students had graduated, many going on to establish faith churches a number of which are in England.

Some of these more recent house church groupings witnessed staggering growth in the 1980s. For instance in 1994 Barney Coombs 'apostled' 105 churches in the Salt and Light ministries, and a Bible school in Scotland. In the same year Terry Virgo had 96 fellowships under his oversight. By 1999 NFI had 143 congregations in the UK with a membership of about 25,000. Other new church groups include Cornerstone led by Tony Morton with a membership of 5,000 and Ground Level with about 3,000.[43] Ian Boston, writing in *Renewal* in 1990, estimated the total number of house church members at 200,000.[44] This figure was probably reasonably accurate and was certainly endorsed by figures from the Evangelical Alliance.[45]

Charismatic Communities

The charismatic movement brought a number of religious communities into being. One such group is the Jesus Fellowship and later the Jesus Army which was based initially at Bugbrooke in Northamptonshire. It emerged from the local Baptist church under the inspirational ministry of its pastor, Noel Stanton (b 1926), and his fellow leaders. The community provides a stable base for many people who find difficulty in coping with life in the outside world. Beginning in a small way in 1974 with the purchase of Bugbrooke Hall for £6,700, it grew to the extent that in 1999 there were some seventy-six communal houses in the British Isles each with between twelve and thirty adults.[46]

Members are bonded together by a covenant pledge. This involves joining with others in the community in 'the mutual confession of faults, recognising that there must be a full openness in the brotherhood and all must be accountable to one another'.[47] The covenant also includes a lifetime commitment to the church which is expressed in the following declaration: 'My desire is that all my earthly life I shall be a Covenant Member of this church and a soldier in the modern Jesus Army.'[48] As with Bryn Jones' Harvest Time ministries, the Jesus Fellowship/Jesus Army is strongly patriarchal in its stance. The New Christian Community has a large number of celibates and strong emphasis is placed on celibacy. According to Katz in 1991 'around half the single members have taken vows of celibacy'.[49] NCC women 'dress simply and modestly' and 'don't go in for fashions which provoke sensuality'.[50] Women are seen as subservient because 'man was not made from woman but woman from man'. The implication of this is that 'women accept the leadership of strong godly men'.[51]

The New Creation Community established a number of businesses which it owns. These included House of Goodness Ltd which operated Goodness Foods and had a turnover of £18 million in 1995. The Community is also responsible for the farming operations which encompass some 280 acres of land at New Creation Farm and Plough Farm near Stockton in Warwickshire.

The Fellowship and Army have a strong leadership and engage in effective evangelism particularly among the poor and disadvantaged. By 1999 total membership was around 2,000.[52] Members live a simple lifestyle with a common purse, eating plain whole foods and all helping with the children. Members are distinguished by 'virtue' names such as John Gentle or Susan Peaceful rather than by their second names. Radio, television and other aspects of worldly culture are avoided. The leadership in the Community Houses is generally authoritarian and members must refer many decisions to their elders, including becoming friendly with the opposite sex.

Bugbrooke spawned the Jesus Army in June 1987,[53] an updated 'young look' version of the Salvation Army. Jesus Army soldiers wear combat jackets and live under a fairly strict regime reflective of the military image. There are 2,000 core members in more than seventy household churches in the UK. It should be emphasised that the Jesus Fellowship/Jesus Army have differing styles of membership and many live in their own accommodation. Worship at Jesus Fellowship/Jesus Army celebrations and in Noel Stanton's communities is a high octane charismatic experience. There are often fierce and intense spiritual battles with the powers of darkness and the demonic. Exorcisms and outbursts of screaming in worship are not infrequent occurrences.

Other early charismatic communities included one at Post Green near Lytchett Minster in Dorset which was well-known in the 1970s because a musical group known as the Fisher Folk were based there. In 1971 Reg and Lucia East left their parish of East and West Mersea in Essex and set up Whatcome House (closed in 1989), a Georgian mansion, near Blandford in Dorset. They were able to accommodate a community of ten and about thirty guests. They welcomed anyone who was open to the will of God and wanted to know the Spirit's power in their lives.

A major influence in the charismatic movement has been Colin Urquhart. Formerly incumbent of St Hugh's Church, Luton, he moved to establish a conference centre at the Hyde and later moved to Roffey Place, a substantial building complex in rural Sussex, which his organisation purchased for £585,000 (a large sum for that time). Through his many books and summer conferences Colin has drawn out for large numbers of people the practical application of charismatic Christian experience.

Other similar ventures have included Lamplugh House in Yorkshire, Blaithwaite House in Cumbria and Fellowship House near Brentwood. The German evangelical community known as the Sisterhood of Mary established a branch at Radlett in Hertfordshire. The sisters soon created a deep impression on British Christians because of their transparent Christlikeness. In 1983, inspired by the vision of Canon Arthur Dodds, a group of Anglicans established a trust and purchased Harnhill Manor which has since become Harnhill Centre for Christian Healing. Under the direction of its first warden, Hugh Kent, and his wife Hilary it became and continues to be a prominent retreat house and centre for ministry and renewal in the Holy Spirit.

Ellel Grange in Lancashire directed by Peter Horrobin opened its doors in 1987.[54] It organises healing retreats and offers counselling and deliverance ministry. In its first three years of work over three thousand people had received ministry.[55] Ellel Ministries also have centres at Glyndley Manor near Eastbourne and at Pierrepont in Surrey.

John Wimber and the Third Wave
One of the foremost influences on the modern charismatic movement was the Californian-based evangelist John Wimber. A former secular band leader with Quaker roots, Wimber (1934–1997) taught at Fuller Theological Seminary where he met with Canon David Watson, a Church of England evangelist. Resulting from this encounter, Wimber came to England in the

early 1980s and addressed gatherings and ministered in churches at Chorleywood and York.

John Wimber always appeared relaxed and easy going. 'I'm just a fat man trying to get to heaven' he somewhat modestly used to say. His style of ministry was laid back and involved inviting the Holy Spirit to come and then allowing him time to act in people's lives. Despite what appeared to be a casual atmosphere there were often 'remarkable occurrences'. Nigel Wright of Spurgeon's College related how John Wimber lectured to a gathering of British pastors and Christian workers. Just at the point when people had nearly had enough of his 'pseudo academic' style of teaching, he stopped and said, 'Now we're going to have some fun!' He put his notes to one side and asked people to stand with their hands outstretched. What followed in Nigel's own words was indescribable 'holy carnage'.[56] Many, including Nigel Wright himself, found themselves on the floor amid shaking, laughing and tears. The Wimber approach is that the words of Jesus must be validated by the works of Jesus. What the Holy Spirit does when he comes is to confirm the message by signs and wonders. In the Wimber jargon this is 'power evangelism'. It is seen as part of the great commission of Matthew chapter 28, where Jesus commanded the disciples not only to preach the gospel to all nations but to do 'all that I have commanded you'. This includes all manner of signs and wonders including healing the sick and casting out demons. John Wimber and his Vineyard aimed to release this ministry not just to a few but all the people of God. Replete in a new complex at Canyon West, purchased in 1991 at a cost of $20 million, the Vineyard rapidly grew into an established denomination with regional supervisors and a hierarchy of senior and junior pastors. Michael Mitton wrote:

> During the 1980s the renewal of the Church of England was profoundly helped and encouraged by the ministry of John Wimber and his teams from California. Thousands of Anglicans, clergy and lay, will testify to profound experiences of God at Wimber conferences which have changed their ministries.[57]

During the later 1990s the Vineyard denomination has expanded rapidly in England under the leadership of John Mumford, formerly curate of Holy Trinity, Chester Square. By 1999 there were fifty-nine Vineyards in the British Isles.

The fresh impact which John Wimber brought to the charismatic movement has been designated the 'third wave'. One of its more important aspects was the releasing of the laity into ministry of the Holy Spirit and his gifts. No longer was it just the anointed few who could pray for others to be filled with the Holy Spirit. John Wimber showed that ordinary congregational members could 'do the stuff'. Additionally 'third wave' put particular emphasis upon the evidence of the miraculous 'signs and wonders' and 'spiritual warfare' as important factors for promoting church growth.

In very general terms it can be said that charismatic Christians fit into one of four categories. There are the 'Restoration' type who emphasise the kingdom and seek to restore the fivefold New Testament ministry to the contemporary church. The 'Positive Confession' charismatics teach guaranteed health, wealth and prosperity. 'Signs and Wonders' charismatics stress the importance of 'power evangelism' and miraculous occurrences as aids to confirm the preaching of the Christian message. 'Historic Denominational' charismatics are those who feel called to remain within their mainline churches and to bring renewal to their life and worship. The charismatic movement is an extremely broad and diverse phenomenon. It straddles the entire denominational spectrum from Roman Catholic and the Church of England at one end to the smallest independent house churches at the other. The charismatic experience is found among people of all theological persuasions, Catholic, Protestant, Liberal, Conservative and Fundamentalist. The ethos and style of charismatic worship also shows a great deal of variation from place to place. Yet for all its wide diversity it is possible to discern a common core at the heart of charismatic Christianity.

Baptism in the Holy Spirit
The majority of charismatics emphasise the need for some sort of overwhelming experience of the Holy Spirit which is generally speaking subsequent to conversion. For this reason it is sometimes called the 'second blessing'. Many charismatics, but

by no means all, believe that this experience is authenticated by speaking in tongues.

Some charismatics are not happy with the terminology of 'baptism in the Holy Spirit' and feel that 'filling of the Holy Spirit' is preferable. Others emphasise the need for a conscious felt experience but are unhappy with a two-stage terminology. Such, for example, is Peter Lawrence, vicar of Canford Magna in Dorset. Once asked: 'When does the second blessing take place?' he replied: 'Between the first and the third!' In many instances baptism of the Spirit takes place when people lay hands on the seekers and pray for them to be filled.

Those who have been influenced by John Wimber's teaching emphasise other signs as evidence of the Spirit's filling beside speaking in tongues. Some of these phenomena are more after the style of early gatherings of the Society of Friends in which individuals literally tremble and shake. Others experience heat sensations and literally become very hot to touch in a sort of baptism of fire. Some fall, usually gently, to the ground.

Leaving aside the validity of these experiences many of those who have them testify to a renewed relationship with Jesus and a growing thirst for God and spiritual reality in their lives.

Lively worship

Charismatic Christians have, from the very first, emphasised the importance of renewed worship. It is hard to be precise in articulating exactly what this means in practice. Generally speaking however there is a high level of congregational participation and the whole atmosphere is vibrant. There is frequently a move away from traditional hymns to twentieth-century language and more chorus-orientated singing which calls for guitars, flutes, keyboards and drums rather than organ and piano.

Charismatics from all backgrounds have been rediscovering the value of Holy Communion or the Lord's Supper. In the independent new churches there is often an atmosphere of complete informality with members joyfully serving the bread and wine to each other in small circles. Even in 'renewed' Anglican and Roman Catholic congregations there is often a decidedly relaxed atmosphere with the greeting of peace and individuals contributing prayers, readings, words and sometimes dance. Charismatic Christians have come to regard the eucharist as not merely high octane spiritual fuel for the few but spiritual power to enable all God's people to grapple with and overcome the forces of darkness.

Fellowship

A very striking feature of the charismatic movement has been its emphasis on 'fellowship'. Charismatic churches and communities are invariably characterised by an atmosphere of warmth, friendliness, mutual support and care. Christian names tend to be the rule and members frequently greet one another with a loving embrace. There is the feeling of belonging to a close-knit family.

Much of this fellowship is sustained by house groups which consist of anything from a dozen to twenty members meeting on a weekly basis in homes. A group meeting will normally include a time of worship, a Bible study or sometimes a video, a sharing of experiences and needs, prayer and social enjoyment. In some of the independent congregations house groups are 'heavily shepherded' by male leaders who are supervised by one of the elders. In general terms it is the case, as with early Methodist class meetings, that these groups are the nerve centre of church life.

Spiritual gifts

Up until the charismatic movement established itself, many Christians held what is known as the 'cessationist' view that the gifts of the Holy Spirit were intended only for the initial period of the church's history to validate the ministry of the apostles. Charismatic Christians hold the view that the gifts of the Holy Spirit were intended for the entire history of the church until the return of Jesus. They only ceased to be in evidence because of their neglect or misuse at certain periods of time.

Although the charismatic movement has sometimes been dubbed 'the tongues movement', it has emphasised other gifts just as much. In fact at different points since the 1970s particular gifts have been emphasised, notable ones being healing, exorcism and prophecy. Revelational gifts such as 'the word of knowledge' and 'the word of wisdom' are also emphasised and fostered.

During times of congregational worship in charismatic churches there will often be times when members in good standing will be permitted to speak out prophecies. Usually these are short inspirational messages. In some congregations such as St Nicholas, Nottingham, members were required to give the substance of the word to the church leadership before going to the microphone. In others, for example the Solihull Christian Fellowship, prophecy could be initiated freely from the congregation.

Wholeness

Healing is one of the spiritual gifts which receives frequent reference in the New Testament. Prayers for healing feature in the life of all charismatic churches. Frequently this is done informally in homes or at house groups or at the close of worship services. Those praying simply place their hands on the head or shoulders of those who are sick and pray in the name of Jesus for their healing. In some Anglican and Roman Catholic churches healing services take place in a more sacramental environment and people may be invited to kneel at the communion rail and are anointed with oil.

Every member ministry

To some extent the charismatic movement is a reaction to clericalism, not just the Anglo-Catholic variety but also evangelical brands. Along with the renewed interest in the gifts of the Holy Spirit, charismatic churches have rediscovered the church as the body of Christ. Charismatics see the church not as spectator entertainment, provided by colourful ritual, a well read Protestant Prayer Book service or brilliant preaching but rather as a fully participant activity. The teaching given in passages such as Romans chapter 12, 1 Corinthians chapter 12 and Ephesians chapter 4 is taken very seriously and individual members are encouraged to discover their role as teachers, evangelists, carers, healers, administrators, discerners, prophets, exorcists and whatever other roles are felt to be needed within their fellowship.

The Kingdom of God

From the earliest days of charismatic revival there was a strong emphasis on the Kingdom of God. A renewed church was crucially important but the Kingdom was something of altogether greater concern. It was God's rule breaking out into both church and society. The Kingdom also involved the assertion of God's justice and gradually during the 1980s, possibly prompted by the influence of John Wimber, groups such as Bryn Jones' Harvest Time, later Covenant Ministries, and Gerald Coates' Pioneer became more focussed on issues relating to the poor and disadvantaged. In the heady days of the early 1970s the Restorationists had a very futuristic focus and believed that they, the Spirit-filled church, were going to restore and bring in the end-time Kingdom. They saw the ministry of restored apostles as being a crucial arm of the restoration process. By the early 1990s, however, most Restorationists were beginning to see the importance of the Kingdom as a present reality and were concerning themselves with issues of practical care and social justice in the local community. In his most recent book, *The Radical Church*[58] Bryn Jones still sounds a note of the old Restorationist triumphalism, 'Christ is not coming to save a beleaguered church . . . but for a triumphant church that has overcome all its enemies, advanced His Kingdom across the earth and reaped the greatest worldwide harvest of lost souls that the world has ever seen'.[59] Nevertheless, in a later section entitled 'The Kingdom and Social Justice' he writes, 'The question of human justice cannot be pushed aside or relegated to the socio-economic or political spheres as something of no interest to the Christian community'.[60] 'God's restoration purpose,' he asserts in a later paragraph, 'not only gives us a concern for the soul of the man in the gutter, but also provokes a response to seeing his external conditions changed'.[61]

The spiritual battle

Charismatic Christians find that the experience of baptism in the Holy Spirit has given them a new awareness of unseen spiritual realities. In general terms charismatics have a heightened awareness of the presence of evil and the personal devil and powers of darkness. They are conscious that life is a spiritual struggle against Satan and his demon hosts. They frequently engage in what they term 'spiritual warfare'. This involves 'putting on the armour' in the way that Paul urges in his letter to the Ephesians. It also involves 'intercessory prayer', fasting, deliverance and exorcisms.

Emphasis on the end times

As with many revivalistic movements before them, charismatics have tended to see the outpouring of the Holy Spirit with which they are associated as a sign that their generation is the last age of history. Such a notion not only gives self-affirmation to their members, it is also a powerful agent to recruitment and expansion. Bryn Jones warned the house churches as early as 1974 not to get carried away with the thoughts of the second coming.[62] The doctrine has however remained high on the charismatic agenda.

Evangelism

The baptism of the Holy Spirit brought greater power and impetus to evangelism. Throughout the history of the Christian church many individuals and movements which have stressed Holy Spirit experience have been powerful proclaimers of the Christian message. Prominent instances are the early Methodist churches in England, the Church of God in America and the Pentecostal churches in South Africa.

The Aim of this Book

It will be clear by this stage that charismatic Christianity is not only a wide-ranging movement but also a very important one. It is without doubt the most significant influence in church life today. Like the proverbial curate's egg, however, the charismatic movement is only good in parts. It has many strengths but also great weaknesses.[63] A recent book on the church in America pinpoints the charismatic movement as being of major significance. The authors commented as follows:

> Everywhere one looks throughout the Anglican Communion the ranks of the renewed are swelling. Reading the statistics and monitoring the vitality, there is

little doubt this is the predominant trend within world-wide Anglicanism, and it is conceivable that by the next century renewal Christianity will be on the verge of becoming the mainstream of the Episcopal church.[64]

What they feel to be the trend for worldwide Anglicanism will also be true for the wider church. The purpose in what now follows is to offer an appraisal which is both empathic and yet objective. This is done in the hope that what is positive and potentially strengthening for church life will be drawn out and affirmed. Conversely, those aspects which are spurious and lack substance or reality will be highlighted and underscored in the hope that they will be discarded. At the very least it is to be hoped that what is written here will cause all believers to reflect on their Christian life, faith, experience and worship.

2

THE CHARISMATIC EXPERIENCE

The late Canon David Watson of York went to preach at a public school chapel service. At the start of his sermon he asked which boys present believed in God? Quite a number raised their hands. Then he asked who believed in Jesus? There was a smaller, but noticeable response. Finally he said, 'Hands up all those who believe in the Holy Spirit.' Not a single hand was raised but a little voice said: 'Please Sir, the boy who believes in the Holy Spirit is away this week!' The incident was reflective of English Christianity in the late 1960s and early 1970s. The Christian faith had become a cerebral affair. The Holy Spirit was beyond the experience of the great majority of Sunday worshippers. To the Church's theologians he was part of the irrational theological conundrum otherwise known as the doctrine of the Trinity.

During the period immediately before the charismatic movement, the church had become very sceptical about the reliability of the New Testament. Many of its leaders were doubtful whether the Gospels could really be believed. In 1963 Bishop John Robinson produced *Honest to God*[1] in which he questioned the whole notion of a personal God who relates to men and women and who intervenes in human affairs. Small wonder therefore that this period saw the biggest falling away in church membership in this century. Christians were losing their nerve. There was, with hindsight, a growing desire to rediscover biblical experience to offset this cold cynical rationalism.

The 1960s witnessed to this hunger for spiritual reality in a number of ways. They saw the emergence of the hippie culture which was a reaction to the materialism of the 'never had it so good' post-war years under Harold Macmillan. Prompted by Timothy Leary, people began to take drugs in the hopes of getting in touch with some deeper level of reality. Others followed the example of the Beatles and began to look East for meaning. The Maharishi and the practice of meditation became the focus of many hopes in a country which was losing its way spiritually.

The charismatic experience which began to emerge in England in the 1960s was to some extent part of this environment. On the one hand, it was a reaction away from enlightenment thinking. On the other, it reflected the widespread quest of the time for the exotic and the culturally new. Western evangelicalism was very much a one dimensional affair in which the middle classes, reinforced by Intervarsity paperbacks, looked for 'sound' teaching. But for most, there was little in it beyond a certain satisfaction of having been able to bend one's mind round a 'good word'. At the same time existentialist thinking which emphasised the importance of the present moment prompted people to seek new experiences and the growing popularity of television increased their desire for deeper emotional and spiritual satisfaction.

Baptism in the Spirit

The aspect of the charismatic experience which emerged in the 1960s was generally speaking termed 'baptism in the Spirit'. This phrase was lifted from earlier or 'classic Pentecostalism' and possibly explains why some church leaders sought to move away from it. In essence, this baptism is a repeat of the Day of Pentecost described in Acts chapter 2. On that occasion the Holy Spirit came on the disciples and the inner circle of their followers in a remarkable way. It was a deeply-felt emotional experience in which numbers of them were so overcome that they staggered like partygoers who have had too much to drink. There was also much joy which surely would have included laughter as they praised God and spoke in new languages (the gift of tongues).

The actual outworking of this experience in individual people varies according to the church, context and the person concerned. Nevertheless, in almost all cases there is a new awareness and consciousness of the presence of God and in many instances speaking in tongues begins either at the same moment or subsequently. Peter Hocken has helpfully analysed the experience of baptism in the Spirit. By his definition it exalts

Jesus Christ. It makes him known, loved, praised and adored. In its corporate aspect it touches every dimension of the church's life including worship, preaching, ministry, evangelism, prayer, service and spirituality. Clearly, he says, 'there is a link between baptism in the Spirit and spiritual gifts'.[2] He makes the point that this baptism cannot be reduced to the reception of spiritual gifts but there is a close relationship between them. Hocken stresses that 'without an openness to the reception of, and practice of the spiritual gifts, it would not be charismatic renewal'.[3] Hocken regards baptism in the Spirit as 'the foundational distinguishing feature of the charismatic movement'.[4] Andrew Walker observed that as an experiential phenomenon, baptism in the Spirit 'has shown itself capable of considerable adaptation and mutation taking root not only in churches of non-evangelical persuasion, but outside Protestantism altogether'.[5] Despite these variations, Walker, like Hocken, regards baptism in the Spirit as the '*sine qua non*' of their Pentecostalism. 'Take away the experience,' he wrote, 'and there is no charismatic movement.'[6]

The experience of baptism in the Spirit clearly links the charismatic movement with the Pentecostalism of the earlier years this century. Jesse Penn Lewis noted baptism in the Spirit to be a feature of the earlier Welsh Revival of 1904.[7] The subsequent Elim and Assemblies of God Churches followed suit. Clearly without their influence the charismatic movement would not have happened in the way that it did.[8] Andrew Walker has demonstrated that Restoration charismatics belong both theologically and sociologically to classical Pentecostalism.[9]

When Does Baptism in the Spirit Occur?

James Packer over-simplified the issue when he wrote that 'charismatics view Spirit baptism as a necessary post-conversion experience which God always models on the apostles' experience recorded in Acts 2 verses 1–14, and identifies to its latter day recipients the gift of glossolalia'.[10] Even an earlier report entitled *The Charismatic Movement in the Church of England* had noted a good deal of variation in the practice and teaching of charismatics on this particular issue.[11] It asked among other things, 'Is the crisis event of this "baptism in the Spirit" always a second event following conversion?' Later it raised a further question: 'Does "baptism" require an experienced crisis at all? Or are there ways in which people may become Pentecostal by slow change?'[12]

The crux of the problem in the early days was in the use of the term 'baptism' to denote a second experience at some point after conversion. Baptism, it seemed to many, both charismatics and others, was about initiation or a beginning experience. John Stott argued for this position very clearly in his *The Baptism and Fullness of the Holy Spirit*[13] and a number of early charismatics accepted his analysis of the biblical material.

Part of the reason for this difficulty and confusion was the fact that most of the early leaders of the charismatic movement had come from evangelical backgrounds. Conversion for them had been largely on the basis of intellectual assent to biblical teachings. No one had taught them about the power of the Holy Spirit. So in their case this had to follow their conversion at a later stage. However, the second generation of charismatic Christians began to bring people to commitment to Christ and pray for them to receive the Holy Spirit at the same moment. With this teaching and approach 'baptism' in the Spirit came to be seen as an initiation experience in many charismatic circles. David Pawson in *The Normal Christian Birth*[14] made the case that in the early days of Christianity the new believers were immediately baptised in water and then prayed for to receive the baptism of the Holy Spirit.[15] In a later volume Pawson wrote that 'charismatics must stop thinking and talking in two stage terms'. Significantly, both David Wilkerson in New York and Jackie Pullinger in Hong Kong were brought to this position. They found that when the drug addicts they were caring for turned to Christ they would often pray in tongues quite spontaneously without any teaching or Christian contact.

Pawson was clear that the single reception/baptism/filling is an integral part of the first blessing, not a later one. It should normally come right at the beginning of the Christian life.[16] Another Baptist, Paul Beasley-Murray, explained in an article in *Mainstream* how this thinking had caused many Baptist churches to review their baptismal practice. Numbers of them are returning to the earlier form of laying hands on candidates immediately after they come out of the baptistry. 'Needless to say,' he commented, 'this "filling" is not a one-off event to be associated with baptism.'[17]

Tony Higton was vicar of the parish of Hawkwell in Essex. He was an influential charismatic leader in the Church of England and made a powerful stand on many issues in the General Synod. In 1984 he founded the Association for Biblical Witness to our Nation (ABWON). This organisation, which continued until 1999, had several hundred link churches in England and its teaching materials made a wide impact. ABWON's *Towards 2000 Radical Anglican Manifesto* stated categorically that 'conversion/new birth includes being forgiven through the blood of Christ and being baptised with the Holy Spirit'.[18] Higton's organisation deliberately set out to avoid 'the errors which some charismatics have fallen into'.[19] He specifically singled out those who peddled with a 'second blessing theology' and 'the insistence that everyone must speak in tongues'.[20]

Perhaps it may be helpful to reflect that while baptism does have to do with initiation or beginnings it is also a continuous experience. A person is immersed in water at a particular moment in time but the sacrament is intended to be continuous in its effect. Baptised people must live out their baptism every day. The same should be true where the Holy Spirit is concerned. The first experience of his coming on a Christian believer is designated 'the baptism of the Holy Spirit' but that baptism is intended to be a continuous every-day experience. The apostle Paul wrote: 'Go on being filled with the Holy Spirit' (Ephesians 5:18). It has also been pointed out by charismatic teachers that in the New Testament the terms to be 'baptised', to 'receive', to 'be filled', to be 'sealed' and to have had the 'Spirit poured' out are used interchangeably.[21] For this reason, most contemporary charismatics tend not to spend too much pen and ink debating terms, they simply get on with the experience. Michael Mitton, the former director of Anglican Renewal Ministries commented:

I am perfectly comfortable with the phrase [baptism in the Holy Spirit] myself. It's useful and I think it's Biblical, but I think it's not an issue that is actually uppermost in the minds of the Anglican charismatics I move amongst. They want to see the experience happening but it's not the kind of thing they want to spend hours debating.[22]

Michael Mitton is wise to counsel charismatics to avoid unresolvable arguments about baptism in the Spirit. On the other hand if charismatics do not teach what is biblical there will be nothing for the next generation when the experience is taken for granted or forgotten.

Speaking in Tongues

When the Holy Spirit came on the first Christians on the Day of Pentecost, as related in Acts 2, they spoke in languages other than their own. These languages were those of the hearers who were in the city for the festival celebrations. It has been argued that the languages spoken on the Day of Pentecost were unique for this reason. On all other occasions, when the gift of tongues is mentioned in the New Testament, the language is unknown to the hearers. Nevertheless, the fact remains that the coming of the Holy Spirit in power was accompanied by the gift of speaking in tongues. The same thing happened when the Holy Spirit came on those who were gathered in the house of Cornelius (see Acts 10) and on a small company of believers in Ephesus (Acts 19).

For these reasons a major focus of the teaching on baptism in the Holy Spirit by the present charismatic movement has been the gift of speaking in tongues. For many in the early days the experience just happened. Attempts were made to theologise it later. Tom Walker, a former archdeacon of Southwell, for example, received the baptism in the Spirit while driving to Brighton in 1964:

There and then there was an overwhelming, flooding, filling, wholly absorbing, penetrating experience of joy and praise. Words were inadequate to express a proper response of gratitude to God; and I found myself praying and praising in tongues, shouting aloud in the car and almost leaping in the driver's seat with worship and gladness.[23]

Gerald Coates who these days is leader of the Pioneer group of churches was riding along on his bicycle one day singing one of Wesley's hymns. As he did so he says, 'I began to sing in another language.' Because he'd been brought up in the Brethren he'd never heard speaking in tongues before. It was not until a month or two later that a friend said to him, 'Oh, you've been baptised in the Holy Spirit.'[24]

Tongues became a focus of controversy in the early days for several reasons. Many evangelicals held to the 'cessasionist' view of the gifts of the Spirit. They believed that the gifts had been strongly in evidence in the period of the apostles' lifetime in order to validate their preaching and teaching. After their generation had passed away, however, the New Testament was put together. This was the complete revelation through which God could now speak decisively and finally. The gifts of the Spirit were no longer needed to back up the spoken word because the Church now had the written word. Some of the early opponents of spiritual gifts even taught that the New Testament was 'the perfection' which had come to replace the imperfection of spiritual gifts (1 Cor 13:10).[25]

A number of Christian leaders were concerned about the emphasis on speaking in tongues because of their use by groups such as the Latter Day Saints. Joseph Smith (1805–1843) and Brigham Young (1801–1877) regarded the gift of tongues as a means of praising God.[26] Joseph exhorted his followers: 'If one of you will rise up and open your mouth, it shall be filled, and you shall speak in tongues.'[27] Of greater concern still, as some church leaders saw it, was their conviction that tongues belonged exclusively to the realm of voodo and the witch doctor. To indulge in such a practice was a recipe for madness and might well lead the participants to insanity or worse.

Others disliked what they took to be an insistence that speaking in tongues was required as the initial evidence that a person had been baptised in the Holy Spirit. This was the line which had been taken by some of the earlier Pentecostal leaders in the 1920s and 1930s such as the brothers George and Stephen Jeffreys.

Without doubt there is a close relationship between baptism in the Holy Spirit and the spiritual gifts. To say that baptism in the Spirit is the release of one of the spiritual gifts is an oversimplification. Nevertheless, without the use of spiritual gifts the charismatic renewal would not be worthy of the name. Some of the early leaders were insistent in following the official line of the Assemblies of God that speaking in tongues was the initial evidence of the Spirit's filling.[28] Not only did this result in tension among charismatics it was also a cause of contention between charismatics and those who stood aloof from the movement.

Among the early charismatic leaders who took the view that tongues were not necessarily a sign of the baptism of the Holy Spirit was Wally North. North, who emerged as a prominent house church leader, had himself been baptised in the Spirit in the early 1940s.[29] For him the experience was 'memorable, clear-cut and of infinite sweetness to this day'. At the time he knew nothing of Pentecostal things. Possibly for this reason it wasn't until some months later he first spoke in tongues. He recalled: 'One morning when kneeling by my bed in prayer and worship, strange words rose within . . . I started to speak in another tongue. What then began has remained, increasing in volume and range.'[30]

Despite valuing the gift and using it on occasion in public meetings, North was adamant that it 'is scripturally uncon-firmed that speaking in a certain tongue is the initial evidence of baptism'.[31]

The charismatic movement has seen distinct phases in which one particular phenomenon, gift or ministry has been empha-sised. Often in the initial stages of the phase there has been a degree of overkill which has soon levelled out. This appears to have been the case with speaking in tongues. Some, such as David Pawson and Michael Harper in the early days, stressed tongues as the evidence of the Spirit's filling.[32] Now, however, their position is less rigorous. 'To regard tongues as "the initial evidence" (a common, but unbiblical phrase),' Pawson wrote in 1993, 'seems to go beyond the Biblical data.'[33] He continues, 'It is one thing to say that tongues may accompany the reception of the Spirit (and may do so often), and quite another to say they must.'[34] This distinction between may and must is one which most charismatics now seem to be comfortable with. David Pytches wrote in 1984 that he did not believe the gift of tongues to be necessary as the sign of being filled with the Holy Spirit.

He does however maintain that everyone wanting it can have it.[35] Michael Mitton feels similarly that it is normal for tongues to accompany baptism in the Spirit but not essential.[36] Like David Pytches he sees it as a gift which is available to all Christians. Probably it is the case that these days speaking in tongues is so widely practised that people no longer think anything of it. In the words of Barry Kissell it's just something we do 'like having a cup of tea after the service'.

When all has been said, it is very important to be clear that speaking in tongues is not the filling or baptism of the Holy Spirit. Rather, it is only at most a sign of it. To be filled with the Holy Spirit is nothing less than to be filled by the very presence of God himself. The General Synod report, *The Charismatic Movement in the Church of England*, expressed the matter with lucidity: '. . . the central feature of the movement is an overwhelming sense of the presence and power of God not previously known in such a combination of otherness and immediacy.'[37] Michael Mitton more recently commented in *Anglicans for Renewal*, 'At the heart of the charismatic renewal is a personal experience of the Holy Spirit bringing an awareness of the love and holiness of our Father, and equipping us to serve our Lord Jesus.'[38]

Assessing Charismatic Experience

Charismatic experience opens up individuals to a heightened spiritual awareness. This often produces an increased vitality and feelings of power. Of course, as with any new insight or experience some may be thrown off balance and lose their sensitivities or sense of proportion. John Charles Ryle, first Bishop of Liverpool, made reference to this aspect of the filling of the Holy Spirit. He wrote: 'There are few people who can hold a full cup with a steady hand.' One of the consequences is a wide range of strange stories or extremes of behaviour. The following are one or two representative examples. *Renewal* magazine carried an advertisement which stated: 'Helpers wanted for charismatic riding stables'. Did the horses neigh in tongues I wondered? I even read of a lady who taught her dog to praise God in an unknown bark! Charismatic organisations abound with inappropriate nomenclature and use religious terms in a way which marginalises their capacity to relate to secularised society. Thus we find Antioch Ministries, Mercy Ministries, Green Pastures Healing Ministry, Canaan Hotel, Berean Books and the Kerith Centre to name a few. A book which has been circulating among Kenneth Hagin churches in this country is Roberts Liardon's *I Saw Heaven*.[39] Liardon is an American 'positive faith charismatic' who was born in Tulsa and named after the Christian healer, Oral Roberts. In his book Roberts Liardon relates how in 1974 at the age of eight he went on a guided tour of heaven with Jesus as his guide:

> All I knew that afternoon in 1974 was that suddenly I was flying through the heavenlies at an unbelievable speed. I passed many things in the first heaven, then zoomed through the second heaven, and landed outside the biggest gate I had ever seen – or have ever seen since.[40]

On his arrival Roberts met with Jesus. 'I remember,' he says, 'that he looked about six feet tall, with sandy brown hair, not real short and not too long.'[41] Jesus said to him, 'I want to give you a tour of heaven because I love you so much.'[42] At the start of his tour Jesus took Roberts to visit one of the residents. A little gentleman stuck his head out of the door and said, 'How are you doing, Jesus? And how are you doing Roberts?'[43] Roberts still recalls the ease with which he reclined on the sofa:

> The couches in heaven are different than here. Earth furniture sometimes becomes uncomfortable. In heaven, comfort finds you. I sat down on a black velvet couch, and comfort reached up and cuddled me. I was so comfortable, I never had to move once.[44]

Later Roberts visited one of heaven's storehouses. He gives the following account of his experience:

> We walked a little farther – and this is the most important, and perhaps the strangest part of my story. I saw three storage houses 500 to 600 yards from the Throne Room of God. They were very long and very wide. There may be more, but I only saw three. We walked into the first. As Jesus shut the front door behind us, I looked around the interior in shock!

On one side of the building were exterior parts of the body. Legs hung from the wall, but the scene looked natural, not grotesque. On the other side were shelves fitted with eyes; green ones, brown ones, blue ones and so forth.

This building contained all the parts of the human body that people on earth need, but Christians have not realised these blessings are waiting in heaven. There is no place else in the universe for these parts to go except right here on earth; no one else needs them.

Jesus said to me: 'These are the unclaimed blessings. This building should not be full. It should be emptied. You should come in here with faith and get the needed parts for you, and the people you will come in contact with that day.'

The unclaimed blessings are there in those storehouses – all of the parts of the body people might need; hundreds of new eyes, legs, skin, hair, eardrums – they are all there. All you have to do is go in and get what you need by the arm of faith, because it is there.[45]

In addition to this visit, Roberts enjoyed the beauty of the birds, the animals, the grass (which never has to be mowed) and the trees. He also went swimming with Jesus in the River of Life. Jesus dunked him and they had a water fight. Before he left heaven Roberts says Jesus ordained him to the Christian ministry. He said 'Roberts, I am calling you to a great work. I am ordaining you to a great work. You will have to run like no one else and preach like no one else. You will have to be different from everyone else.'[46]

Many charismatic Christians find it hard even to be reverently agnostic about such accounts. In some circles the mere suggestion of suspending your judgement on such matters is taken to indicate a lack of openness to the Spirit. There is a need however to recognise that the Holy Spirit's coming with intensity on a person's life can readily generate a capacity to receive mystical visions of angels, Jesus and heaven. Such experiences can also however be projections from within the human psyche. They must therefore be weighed carefully and in the light of biblical teaching. The lack of critical assessment on the part of charismatics is humorously illustrated by the story of a man who went to purchase a new Christian brain, possibly from a Liardon type storehouse! The first one he came to was priced at $2,000. It was labelled Baptist. A little further he came to one at $4,000 which was identified Presbyterian. Finally he came to one at $10,000. On querying the very high price tag he was told it was a charismatic brain and therefore unused!

The New Testament constantly urges believers to 'test all things', to be wise and to renew their minds. The fact has to be faced that some of Liardon's stories are fanciful and seem well beyond the scope and imagery of the book of Revelation.

The Charismatic Pushover

Another aspect of charismatic experience which has caused some concern has been the issue of 'falling under the Spirit'. This has been a particularly observable phenomenon of Wimber-style ministry, but was fairly widely known before-hand. Falling has also been a feature of the Toronto experience and this is discussed more fully in Chapter 10. Allegations of pushing, hysteria and hypnosis have all been advanced in criti-cism. I encountered one individual who admitted falling from time to time to gain attention and ministry. Others believe it is expected of them when prayed for and do a courtesy fall.

Frank Booth was active for many years in the Cheltenham chapter of the Full Gospel Businessmen's Association. He recalled that it was fairly normal for people to be 'slain in the Spirit' after FGB dinners! 'Those ministering often put two fin-gers on people's foreheads,' he recalled, 'it was almost a sub-conscious aid to "going down" '. Frank attended an FGB Conference at a Hotel near Bromsgrove in the early 1990s. At the end of the last meeting the speaker got everybody to line up at the front so that he could pray for them. As he ministered he put one hand on the forehead and the other in the small of the back and 'pushed hard'. Incensed by this Frank Booth tried an experiment on his return home. He found that if he stood still, his young daughter standing on a chair could with one hand on his forehead and one in the small of his back push him over quite easily. Frank Booth subsequently parted company with the FGB.

Undoubtedly all of these criticisms contain at the very least a substance of truth and charismatics do well to acknowledge the fact. Having said that it must be recognised that there are biblical instances of a positive nature where people fall down in the presence of God. Paul fell to the ground when confronted by the risen Lord on the Damascus Road (Acts 9:4). The apostle John wrote of his encounter with the risen Jesus on the island of Patmos: 'When I saw him I fell at his feet as though dead' (Rev 1:18). The disciples on the Day of Pentecost appeared like people who had too much drink (Acts 2:13). The phenomenon of people falling was widely observable in the ministry of John Wesley in the eighteenth-century revival in England. For example, when Wesley preached at Newgate Prison in April 1739 he reported 'one, and another, and another sunk to the earth: they dropped on every side as thunderstruck'. It was also observed in some of the early breakaway Methodist offshoot groups in the early nineteenth century. For example, John Benton (1775-1856) was a virtually illiterate Primitive Methodist evangelist who was active in the West Midlands in the second decade of the nineteenth century. A local preacher once remarked to him, 'You are bringing a scandal to the cause of Christ, you have no learning and you do not understand grammar.' Sometime later on a Good Friday while Benton was preaching on the text 'It is finished', rough colliers started to shriek and fall from their seats. Benton, chancing to see the same local preacher who had criticised him, was unable to resist the temptation to say with emphasis: 'This is grammar.' Similarly a Bible Christian preacher in Devon noted in his diary in 1816 somewhat passingly that 'three fell while I was speaking. We prayed, and soon some more fell; I think six found peace.'[47]

Hugh Bourne (1772–1852), one of the co-founders of Primitive Methodism 'sank down' before the presence of God.[48] Julia Werner in her study of Primitive Methodists noted that it was not only the pious who were afflicted with the 'falling exercise' but even some of those who came to scoff at it![49]

Some recent studies of falling in Methodism have interpreted the falling phenomena as instances of exhibition or hysteria. The fact remains however that the falling phenomena didn't have any overall damaging impact on Methodist congregations or the movement as a whole. John Wesley himself recorded an instance of a young man who 'was suddenly seized with violent trembling all over'. In a few moments he was 'sunk to the ground'. After some little while Wesley reported he got up 'full of peace and joy in the Holy Ghost'.[50]

Some critics regard 'falling' as a fail safe response for those with no capacity for a spiritual dynamic. David Pawson and some other charismatic leaders have expressed the view that in certain cases, falling can be a reaction against the Spirit. Put another way, a psychological black-out to resist the Spirit's ministry. In the contemporary charismatic movement there are undoubtedly individuals who have fallen to the ground 'under the Spirit' seemingly without positive benefit. The present writer encountered an instance of one individual who had gone down on several occasions and then had to seek extended counselling from a Christian medical doctor.[51] Even here however it might be countered that the Spirit experience highlighted the problem and opened up the way into in-depth counselling.

A survey of 100 individuals who had gone down under the Spirit indicated that for the great majority the experience was beneficial. Respondents testified to the release of hurts, freedom from fears, a new found peace, a more positive self-image, a new sense of wholeness and self-love, together with a deeper consciousness of God in their lives.[52] Similar replies were given by others who had experienced trembling, shaking and palpitations in the chest area following invocations of the Holy Spirit at the close of church services, house groups or other gatherings. Thirteen medical doctors responsible for first aid at a recent New Wine Family Conference attended by over 7,000 people where there was a frequent falling and shaking reported no ill effects at all. Clearly, although there is a 'downside' in some cases to being overwhelmed in these sorts of ways, for most there is a catharsis or healing release.

A Confusion of Tongues

The same is clearly true of speaking in tongues. It can be a dysfunctional practice in some instances. Tongues can be psychologically induced and they can also be demonic. Regarding the former, David Pawson reported the case of a travelling evangelist laying hands upon people's heads and telling them to say 'banana' backwards and that this was evidence that they had been baptised in the Spirit![53] There are similar stories of people being 'ministered to' urged to say first slowly, but then with quickening pace, 'She come on a honda' or for variation, 'shish kebab on a calor gas stove'!

Instances of what are manifestly demonic tongues appear to be few within the present charismatic movement. In most cases the person concerned had prior involvement in some form of spiritism or magic. According to Michael Mitton demonic tongues are readily discernible by the impact they have on hearers. Demonic tongues leave those who witness them 'terribly disturbed' much in the same way as people are disturbed when they listen to tape recordings of Hitler's speeches.[54] On the other hand, Spirit-inspired tongues which are 'most beautiful' leave a sense of peace and well-being.

There is a danger in some circles of over-using the gift of tongues to the point where it becomes a fetish or form of fanaticism. In one of the new churches, those setting up the school for Sunday worship were told not to put out chairs until they'd prayed in tongues for fifteen minutes. Kenneth Copeland gave the following instruction in a prophecy:

> Pray in tongues. Pray in the Spirit. Not only just your hour a day that you surely spend praying in tongues, but all during the day, all during the day, even when it's under your breath or like you say, 'to yourself' because I'm in your self. I'll hear you in your self. I'm in your self and you're in myself. We are one in Spirit, saith the Lord.[55]

The problem here is both in trying to 'systematise' or 'ritualise' the Holy Spirit's ministry as well as in 'excessiveness'. Paul exhorted the Ephesians to pray in the spirit on all occasions with all kinds of prayer (Eph 6:18). The danger of excessive use of tongues is that it can heighten an individual to new levels of consciousness to the point where 'dysfunctional' mystical experiences more readily occur. Wynne Lewis, the General Superintendent of the Elim Church, has wisely warned that 'there are too many charismatics hissing, going tick, tick, tick, under their breath and muttering in wakistani!'[56]

Faith Teaching

For some, charismatic experience has led them into overconfident assumptions. In particular Kenneth Hagin and others of 'positive confession school' have overplayed the extent to which God will answer prayers and grant healing and prosperity. Much of this teaching is based on Mark 11 verses 23 and 24: 'Whatever you ask for in prayer, believe that you have received it, and it will be yours.' People are encouraged to live on the basis of four steps; say it, do it, receive it and tell it. A positive frame of mind and outlook on life is clearly a good thing. However, to tell someone in need of something they simply have to name it and claim it will sooner or later lead to disappointment. God's provision is not on a coin in the slot machine basis. Some people will remain unhealed or without work or sufficient funds. While it is clearly God's will that no one should lack the basic necessities of food, clothing, shelter and employment, this does not mean to the level of middle-class 'dincies' (double income, no children).

It needs to be said that 'faith teaching' as expounded by Colin Urquhart and Wynne Lewis and other charismatics also has much to commend it. Some acceptable aspects of the faith teaching of Kenneth Hagin and Kenneth and Gloria Copeland have been unjustly put down, particularly by rival American fundamentalists who have tended to equate faith with 'doctrinal belief'.

Early 'faith teaching' in the 1960s was in many ways a positive reaction against 'failure acceptance', self-pity and the wimpish Christianity found in many places. In the developing nations 'faith teaching' represented a positive reaction against the acceptance of poverty on the part of indigenous Pentecostals. It also aimed to counteract the gap between saying one thing and doing another. People prayed for healing but did not expect anything to happen 'unless it be thy will'.

For Kenneth Hagin, faith was not quite as automatic as some of his critics have implied. He emphasised the need for a two-way dialogue with God in healing prayer. The purpose of this is to pray according to the 'living word of God' before claiming his promises. He coined the Rhema/Logos concept to show this principle. 'Rhema' is God's active word for the particular situation of need, whereas the logos is God's written word.

'Faith Teaching' has helped Christians to grasp the authority which has been delegated to believers. Many began to have a positive understanding of their responsibility to put their faith into action. People were enabled to develop a positive image of themselves and to grow in self-respect. This in turn generated a capacity to affirm and encourage others. All of this was a healthy reaction against negative teaching by groups of evangelicals in the 1960s which stated that the self must be crucified. Some of the Rwanda teaching on open confession denigrated the individual's sense of his or her own worth.

It has also been rightly observed that certain kinds of charismatic churches have shown distinctly introversionist traits. Concentration and focus on their own experience of God has led, in some cases, to a diminished concern for evangelism and the needs of the world beyond. On the other hand, some of the most effective evangelising churches in the nation are charismatic. Cobham Christian Fellowship, Kensington Temple, Holy Trinity Brompton, St Michael-le-Belfrey, york, Millmead Baptist Church, Guildford, St Thomas Crookes, Sheffield and Clarendon Church in Hove immediately come to mind. Taken as a whole, the statistics demonstrate conclusively that charismatic churches are the most effective evangelisers.

Peter Hocken in his book, *The Glory and the Shame*, suggested that part of the 'shame' is the divisiveness of charismaticism. He commented: 'Each decade of pentecostalism has experienced divisiveness and seen further schisms. New denominations have continued to proliferate at an astonishing rate.'[57] It is perfectly true that on occasion some charismatics have given the impression that 'the Spirit filled' are a superior breed of Christians and have thereby created division. In all probability however, charismatic experience has been no more responsible for division than certain forms of fundamentalism or liberalism. In any event it must be doubtful whether charismatic experience is the villain of the piece. More often, it is people or structures rather than experience that prompts the increase of sects and breakaway groups. Many of the so-called new charismatic churches separated from the historic denominations over issues of structure, church government, fixed liturgy, patterns of ministry and pastoral care. In fact, almost anything except charismatic experience. Hocken discusses the ecumenical flavour of the charismatic movement and concludes on a note of discouragement. 'In the 1990s,' he wrote, 'it is impossible to be so optimistic as in the early 1970s.'[58]

Some charismatics would probably take issue with Hocken on this point. In the first place, he sees ecumenicity in somewhat institutional terms. In the early 1970s a significant feature of the charismatic movement was the links which developed between Anglicans, Baptists and Roman Catholics. The charismatic movement led many Protestants to an acceptance of Roman Catholics because of their common experience. In the 1990s most charismatics in England passed increasingly easily across denominational boundaries partly because their leaders adhered to them much less rigidly. John Wimber's impact and emphasis on loving the whole church has affected Baptists, Anglicans, Roman Catholics and the newer churches, bringing their members together in national conferences and local events. One of the positive spin-offs of the revivalist influences from Toronto which began to reach England in June 1994 was the significant breakdown of barriers in particular localities.

Some Positive Aspects of Charismatic Experience

The Trinity becomes a reality

In very general and broad terms there is a good deal that is positive in charismatic experience. Christianity is meant to be an experiential religion. In the words of its Founder: 'Now this is eternal life: that they may know you, the only true God, and Jesus Christ, whom you have sent' (Jn 17:3). To 'know' in this context is to know by experience. At heart the Christian faith is the experience of a personal relationship rather than knowledge or commitment to a set of doctrines. Historic Christianity is a trinitrian experience. The charismatic movement has made the Trinity a reality in daily Christian living. The Holy Spirit brings to the believer an awareness of the love of God the Father. He makes the person of Jesus a reality. He strengthens Christian people with his presence which is the presence of God within. Put more simply, charismatic Christians know the reality of coming to the Father, through the Son in the Holy Spirit. This full experience of God as Father, Son and Holy Spirit motivates the church to reach out in mission. The charismatic experience does justice to the book of Acts. Throughout its early chapters Luke relates again and again how the Holy Spirit came repeatedly on the life and work of the early Christian leaders.

Spiritual resources

Baptism in the Spirit opens up the possibility of a growing faith. Many traditional denomination churches have asserted that the entire Christian package is received at conversion. If this is the case we do well to ask Nigel Wright's question: 'If you got it all at conversion, where is it?'[59]

Speaking in tongues has been found to be refreshing, invigorating and therapeutic. David Du Plessis, the Pentecostal pioneer of the 1950s and 1960s, testified as follows:

> Often I have to get my night's sleep sitting up in a Greyhound bus or jet plane . . . The minute I close my eyes I begin to pray in the Spirit. I pray all night that way, waking up and drifting back to sleep, always praying. I don't get much sleep, but I get a lot of rest. The next morning I'm fresh and strong and ready for a day's work.[60]

Jackie Pullinger is well known for her work amongst the drug addicts in what was the Walled City in Hong Kong. In the early years of her time there she met with Jean Stone who made her promise to speak in tongues for fifteen minutes every day. After keeping her word for nearly two months she noticed something remarkable. She found that those she talked to about Christ believed. It wasn't that her Chinese had suddenly taken a turn for the better. Rather: 'I had let God have his hand in my prayers and it produced a direct result.'[61]

Speaking and singing in tongues has opened up a new dimension of worship and prayer for many charismatics. At Glenfall Fellowship in Cheltenham one of the congregational leaders, Lori Lee, was singing in tongues during a time of worship. Another of the leaders, Grace Booth, who had been brought up in Argentina and is fluent in Spanish, was standing close to her. She distinctly heard Lori, who had no knowledge of the language, singing 'I love you O God' and other similar expressions of praise in beautiful Spanish.

Many charismatic Christians relate that their own personal prayers have taken on a new depth as they have prayed quietly in tongues in their private devotions. Others have found that the 'love language' has deepened their awareness of the presence of Christ and made their relationship with him a living reality.

A sense of wellbeing

From the beginning of January 1994 onwards, what were termed 'times of renewing' came to a small cluster of churches in Toronto near the city's International Airport. Among them, what was then the Airport Vineyard. The Spirit of God began to impact on the lives of this congregation in quite remarkable ways. Meetings for worship, prayer and openness to the Spirit were held six nights of the week. Revivalistic phenomena including trembling, weeping, laughing and, more unusually, shaking and jumping up and down were in evidence. In early May and June, leaders of English congregations, including Eli Mumford of South West London Vineyard and Sandy Millar of Holy Trinity Brompton, visited Toronto. By the close of 1994 it was estimated that people from as many as 700 churches in the UK had visited Toronto Airport Vineyard. Returning visitors soon found that they were able to pass on what they had received. Other churches came into the 'Toronto Phenomena' through the ministry of Rodney Howard-Browne. Special times of waiting and openness were organised in many UK churches.

The so-called 'Toronto Blessing' is treated in much greater detail in Chapter 10. Brief mention of it is necessary in the present context since much of it is basic charismatic experience. A prominent feature at these waitings was and is the phenomenon of laughter, some of it lasting for half an hour or more. Many fell to the ground, and others swayed, staggered and shook.

How are we to assess this particular kind of charismatic experience? In the first place we must recognise that these kinds of phenomena are no new thing. On the Day of Pentecost (see Acts 2:12, 15) many were staggering like drunkards under the power of the Spirit. The New Testament draws this same parallel between drunkenness and Spirit fullness, urging us not to be drunk with wine but filled with the Spirit (Eph 5:18). Aspects such as falling, weeping, trembling and even laughter all find a positive place at some points in the biblical record. Shaking and trembling also featured in the early Quaker gatherings. The 'falling' and the 'laughing exercise' were common among the early followers of Wesley and the revivalistic Primitive Methodists. Falling, rolling and even somersaulting were frequently noted at holiness meetings organised by William Booth's Salvation Army.

A general feeling which I gleaned from attending 'Toronto' meetings and the worship of the charismatic churches in general is that there is a strong cathartic element to them. A number of people with whom I spoke felt profoundly cleansed and released from sins, bondage and pains. People who had 'gone down' under the Spirit testified to release from fears and stress. Laughter can be, though of course not always, a very powerful form of release therapy. Psychologist Robert Holden, for example, runs laughter clinics on the NHS in Birmingham. He finds that laughing has a very positive effect physically on the body. 'One minute of sustained laughter is equivalent to ten minutes of any mainstream aerobic activity such as jogging, cycling or rowing.' Laughter, he finds, is contagious. He plays a tape with infectious laughter on it. At first one or two will almost always succumb to it. Then, he says, it's only a matter of time before everyone in the group gives in.

New life and vigour

Inevitably, within the charismatic experience there will be instances of someone trying to start something by laughing deliberately and exhibitionism will become intertwined with experience that is genuine. Probably however little harm, if any, will be done and the potential for the positive would seem to outweigh the risk of any extremes. We do well to underscore the words of Canon Michael Green that 'it is better that our churches have the excesses of life than the quiet of the graveyard'. A key lesson which needs to be learned from the past is the importance of supplementing experience with biblical teaching. The Welsh Revival of 1904 brought this same range of experiences to thousands of believers and unbelievers alike. Yet many received no instruction on the basics. Within four years thousands who had been touched were no longer within the churches. We need to follow the lead of Peter on the Day of Pentecost. 'This is that,' he said, 'spoken of by the prophet Joel in the Old Testament.' He then proceeded with detailed instruction. On the whole, however, the present signs are good. I was impressed when I attended a revival meeting at Queens Road Baptist Church in Wimbledon on 20 June 1994. Forty-five minutes of biblical teaching were given before the pastor invited the Holy Spirit to come. It seemed all so matter of fact and low key. I counted nearly ninety people down on the floor and observed people laughing and others shaking and weeping. It was clear that many were being released from emotional wounds and hurts.

The charismatic experience has enabled Christian people to express their feelings both by word and by touch in an open way which has not been the case in the traditional churches. Possibly this is why friendship and commitment appears to run at a much higher level in charismatic churches. One member of a charismatic church with whom I spoke said, 'At my local church if you have a disagreement you have to bury it. In this congregation you have it out straight away, you pray together, have a hug and that's the end of it!' The renewal experience has empowered individual lives and produced evangelising and outgoing congregations. The charismatic experience has resulted in the recovery of spiritual gifts and a vital emphasis on every member ministry and service. Many charismatics would want to echo Barney Coombs when he wrote: 'We are finding that each person's need for love, security, recognition and adventure (the four basic needs of the human personality) is being met within the kingdom life of the body of Christ.'[62]

3

WORSHIP

James Boswell, the diarist, once made the following entry in his journal as though it were something strange: 'I have been to church to-day and am not depressed.' Many churchgoers in historic denominational Christian churches would find more than an echo in his words. For them traditional worship is con-trolled, sedate, dull and predictable. If there should be anything of a spontaneous nature it will happen at paragraph 4 in the ser-vice book or when the vicar structures it.

A.W. Tozer once warned of the danger of evangelical religion becoming more doctrinal idolatry without heart experi-ence. He also spoke of worship as 'the missing jewel in the evan-gelical church'. Charismatic Christians have made it their business to re-insert it into its rightful place. In fact worship is one aspect where charismatic Christianity is most immediately apparent to an outsider.

The Nature of Charismatic Worship
Anyone attending a service in a charismatic church would immediately be struck by an atmosphere of informality. Probably the majority of worshippers would dress down, although casual clothes in themselves are not a sign of being a charismatic. The clergy or leaders would usually not be clad in gowns or dog collar. The singing is unlikely to be from a traditional hymn book or accompanied by a robed choir and organ. The music would generally be in 'folk' style and led by a small band with an electronic keyboard, guitars and possibly drums, sup-plemented perhaps by a violin or flute. The songs would be simple in content and for the most part uncluttered with religious ter-minology. The words of the songs and prayers would probably be displayed on the wall or a screen using an overhead projector.

A particular feature is the amount of time devoted to singing. This is likely to be considerably greater than in a non-charismatic church. Times of singing may last for anything from fifteen minutes to an hour. Often the chorus or indeed the whole song is repeated before moving on to the next one. Most often too there is a flow from one song to another. As the music plays, many worshippers will raise their hands with palms lifted upwards as a sign of openness and surrender to God as was the custom in the New Testament churches and in early Catholic Christianity. Congregations use their bodies a good deal to express their devotion to God. There may be clapping, dancing and movement of all kinds. Most stand, some sit, and at times people feel free to kneel during quieter and more worshipful songs.

Buildings are often decked with brightly-coloured banners and other visual material. Use is made of performing arts. Sketches and dramatic pieces are quite frequently a feature in services as a way of communicating religious truths.

In charismatic churches there is not the rigid distinction between clergy and laity which is found in the historic churches. In most congregations, whether from the established denominations or the newer fellowships, the leaders regard themselves as doing in a full-time paid capacity what the rest do on a part-time basis alongside their daily work. For this reason, worship is democratic in style. Individuals contribute prophecies, which are usually brief words to encourage, comfort or inspire others' prayers and praises (see 1 Cor 14:3). There are often interviews, testimonies or reports and updates on matters which concern the congregation.

In historic churches where it is the custom to have a liturgy or fixed written order of service, charismatics tend to be less slavishly attached to it. As Bishop Colin Buchanan once remarked in a discussion on the new Church of England Alternative Service Book: 'It's a framework for your local happening.' In many places the charismatic movement has brought a renewed valuing of Holy Communion or Breaking of Bread. The form in which this is taken varies a good deal from place to place, but generally speaking, the atmosphere is informal and relaxed.

Most charismatic churches offer some kind of prayer or ministry to any individual present who has a particular need or concern. Usually this takes place at the end of the worship, although it may be during the time of taking Communion, perhaps at the altar rail or in a side chapel. People coming for prayer often stand quietly at the front of the building or in the sanctuary area where one or two specially appointed individuals will place their hands gently on their head or shoulders and pray for the Holy Spirit to come and for healing to be ministered if that is requested. This too represents a return to the practice of the early Christian churches.

It has often been suggested that charismatic churches undervalue the need for teaching but this does not seem to be the reality of the situation. Most charismatics find their experience has made the Bible a new book for them. This is particularly true of Roman Catholics who have been renewed. They come to worship on Sundays expecting a 'substantial feeding' from the word of God. Sermons are frequently taped and circulated among those who are unable to attend. Many charismatics give a good deal of time to the presentation of their sermons, which are often quite lengthy affairs. Half an hour or forty minutes might be the sum extent of the dose at St Andrew's Chorleywood or St Aldate's Oxford. On the other hand, when I attended Woodgate Church on the outskirts of Birmingham, Mike Price's sermon lasted for an hour and thirty minutes with most of the 500-strong congregation still actively attentive at the end!

Attitudes to the Bible are generally uncritical and range from conservative to fundamental. In some groups of churches like Gerald Coates' Pioneer, or Roger Forster's Ichthus, women are in leadership and allowed to preach and lead in worship. In other new churches such as 'Covenant Ministries' and the 'King's Churches', which are rather more patriarchal, women have a role which is quite clearly subservient to the men. The basis for this view of women's role is a very literal reading of texts such as 1 Corinthians 14 verse 34 and 1 Timothy 2 verse 11. 1 Corinthians 14 verse 34 says that 'women should remain silent in the churches. They are not allowed to speak, but must be in submission, as the Law says.' In 1 Timothy 2 verse 12 Paul states that he does not permit a woman to teach or have authority over a man.' In both cases no attempt has been made to recognise that these instructions were given by Paul at a particular time and in a particular culture in which women had no rights or status either in Roman or Jewish law. Those charismatics who do allow women to have leadership roles believe that the contemporary situation is very different from that which the New Testament writers addressed. We live in a society in which women are now as equally well educated as men and do have equal rights and do teach.

One example of a very literal approach to the biblical text about women being in submission to men is the Bath City Church, which was under Bryn Jones. Here there was until 1994 a pass-the-veil ritual. At any time when a woman wanted to pray or give a prophetic word, they had to raise a hand and the veil was passed to them. Only when it was firmly planted on their head were they permitted to speak out. This was done to comply with Paul's injunction in 1 Corinthians 11 verse 5 that every woman should have her head covered when she prays or prophesies in the church meeting. Interestingly, there was a certain degree of inconsistency because the leaders of the church didn't force the same women to follow the apostle's instruction to attend worship with uncut hair (see verses 15–16). The veil passing ceased at about the same time as the church severed its link with Bryn Jones' Covenant Ministries.

At Living Waters Church in Clevedon, led by Charles and Joyce Sibthorpe, the congregation are often invited to stand immediately before the sermon and, holding their Bibles in the air, make the following pronouncement:

> This is my Bible. I am what it says I am,
> I have what it says I have, I can do what it says I can do.
> I boldly confess, my mind is alert, my heart is receptive.
> I'll never be the same.
> I am about to receive the incorruptible, the indestructible,
> ever-living seed of the Word of God.
> I'll never be the same, never, never, never.
> I'll never be the same in Jesus' name, Amen.

This credo struck me as being close to bibliolatry when I first heard it. It does however illustrate very well the deep commitment to the Bible and to a fairly literal interpretation of it by many of the newer charismatic churches. On the other hand, the attitude to the Bible found among the leaders of the Bristol Christian Fellowship or at St Thomas Crookes is academic almost to the point of being scholarly. John Osborne, for example, prepared a paper 'Women in Leadership' on behalf of the elders of the Bristol Christian Fellowship. In it he discussed the 'context' of 'household codes' and the different meanings of Greek words such as *Kephale* translated as 'head'. He also considered the 'cultural context', the New Testament 'backdrop' and cited and footnoted an academic paper on 'Women, Authority and the Bible'.[1] All of this is a very different approach to the biblical text than that of 'Covenant Ministries', 'Salt and Light' or the King's Churches.

Robert Warren wrote in 1991 about the now defunct Nine O'Clock Service having taken a conscious step to 'distance itself from a narrow view of things charismatic'. He went on to relate that it had opened itself to the challenge of rational engagement with the world, and dialogue with the liberal tradition. He also stated that it was exposing its practices and theology to the rigours of critical scholarship.[2] All this represented a huge departure from earlier attitudes to the Bible and indeed to the charismatic movement.

The Character of Charismatic Worship

The worship of the English churches in the early 1960s, immediately prior to the emergence of the charismatic movement, reflected the rational enlightenment culture of the time. It was very cerebral and appealed primarily to the mind. The ultimate in Anglican worship was reckoned to be a choral eucharist replete with Latin anthem and intellectual sermon. Even the experimental Church of England Communion rites of the 1960s were still lengthy theological recitations with an extended capacity to put the inattentive and daydreamers under guilt and condemnation.

The 1960s, however, witnessed a movement of peoples' interests towards the religions of the East. As a result of this, some were hit for the very first time with the realisation that truth was more than simply a mind-bending exercise. Truth was also something you can 'just know'. Its reality can quite simply be experienced in the human spirit. As some have said: 'You can know it in your knower.' This desire for an immediate experience of truth has become very much a part of our current Western ethos. We still see it in the burgeoning of New Age practices. It was also visible in Fergie's visits to Madam Vasso of the perspex pyramid and perhaps even in the benefits which the Prince of Wales says he gets from talking to plants.

Charismatic worship which is rooted in openness to the Spirit represented and still represents something more than the cerebral. The heart of charismatic worship is not about mentally accepting the presence and forgiveness of Jesus and then doing one's darndest to live by his teaching. It's something altogether more spontaneous but which gives people the inspiration and desire to stay close to God throughout the week ahead. In charismatic worship, God's Spirit comes on individuals and touches their spirits. Their worship is a welcome to this and a response to this. People's emotions and feelings are brought into touch with the presence of God. Many charismatics testify to the warmth of a presence within. They feel edified, built up and affirmed by God's love and by the close-knit fellowship of other worshippers. Many testify to being freed from emotional hurts or the baggage of past memories during times of worship. Individuals find the immediate presence of God as they are released through tears. In short, charismatic worship is worship in spirit. It opens up a person's spirit and emotions to the presence of God in a new way. In the words of A. W. Tozer, 'Worship is to feel God in your heart.'

Intimacy and Flow

One of the distinctive contributions which the charismatic movement has brought to worship is a strong note of tender intimacy. This has been reinforced in recent years by the teaching of John Wimber and the Vineyard Christian Fellowship. From early days it was pointed out that the Greek *'proscuneo'* which is commonly translated 'worship' is a very intimate word. Literally translated it means 'to come towards and kiss'. It's almost a shocking concept. John Wimber wrote that the early Vineyard Fellowships learned that 'worship is the act of freely giving love to God'. Indeed, he continued, in Psalm 18 verse 1 we read; 'I love you, O LORD, my strength'. To truly worship God is therefore to meet and experience the Lord in an intimate and tender way. It's something akin to the physical union between a husband and wife. Paul in fact says as much in Ephesians 5 verse 31: 'For this reason a man will leave his father and mother and be united to his wife, and the two will become one flesh. This is a profound mystery – but I am talking about Christ and the church.' John Wimber articulated this objective as follows: 'We are headed towards one goal: intimacy with God. I define intimacy as belonging to or revealing one's deepest nature to another (in this case to God), and is marked by close association, presence and contact.'[3]

Many charismatic churches therefore structure their worship in such a way that at some point the congregation are enabled to make this intimate contact with God. A distinction is frequently drawn between 'praise' and 'worship'. Praise is seen as jubilation and declaration of God's greatness and power. In short, praise is proclamation *about* God – who he is, his holiness, his majesty and his mighty acts. Worship, on the other hand, is to sing *to* God. More than that it is to bow down, to kneel before him. It is to express love and gratitude to him and to surrender the whole of life to him. Charismatic church services often start in joyful praise and later move into more reflective periods of quieter worship.

It is the case that traditional worship as reflected by the BBC is anthropocentric. It frequently focuses on themes such as pilgrimage, suffering, the family, education, the poor, reconciliation, peace, with poems, readings and prayers all to match. In contrast, charismatic worship is Christocentric and always has a strong upward aspect.

In the early days of charismatic renewal there was much stress, particularly in the Restoration churches, on the importance of praise. Congregations were often 'hyped' from praise to what was termed the 'high praises of God'. In this upper phase the powers of darkness could be dispelled and there was a breaking through into the presence of God. Latterly there has been rather less exuberance in the singing of praise. The 'Dales two step' and stampeding of raucous 'warfare' songs which marked the honeymoon phase of the early 1970s have been much less in evidence even in the charismatic churches of the 1990s.

Moments of intimacy require personal intimate words. This

is why 'spiritual songs' are regarded as so important by charismatic congregations. As one church leader put it: 'If a husband wants to express love for his wife in a personal way, he doesn't stand at the kitchen door and exclaim "Praise my soul my wife for ever, to her feet thy tribute bring." No, he says "I love you", "You're marvellous", "You're wonderful", "You're excellent".' This distinction can be illustrated well enough with reference to some of the songs which have enjoyed popularity in recent years in charismatic circles. 'The Servant King', 'Great is the Lord', 'All you angels around the throne, praise him!', 'Glory in the highest' and 'The Lord is marching out in splendour' would primarily be regarded as praise. In contrast, 'I bow down before you Lord', 'I love you my Lord', 'I only want to love you' and 'I am coming back to the heart of worship' are seen as songs of worship, vehicles for making the intimate contact with God. Bishop David Pytches emphasised the need for worship to move to such an encounter in the following lines of his widely-read book *Come Holy Spirit*: 'The Old Testament seems to indicate a "gradual" in worship. There were Psalms of invitation to worship, of ascent – going up to the city of God, entering the Temple gates, coming into the courts of the Lord and delighting in the very presence of God, seeking his face.'[4]

Mark Stibbe in a slightly later book entitled *A Kingdom of Priests* articulated the same point. 'The greatest of all spiritual petitions,' he wrote, 'is neither for gifts nor for fruit but for deeper intimacy with Jesus Christ.'[5] He goes on to point out how Jesus had 'taught the importance of intimacy' when he commanded us to abide in the Vine (Jn 15:1–8).[6]

Freedom

Richard Hare, a former Bishop of Pontefract, once referred to a well-known cartoon. It showed a sour-faced clergyman looking over the pulpit at his suitably respectful congregation. The words which flowed from his mouth were: 'I don't know who it was interrupted our worship last Sunday with the words "Praise the Lord", but in future will he kindly remember that this is the House of God and not do that again!'[7] 'We take it for granted,' said Bishop Hare, 'that it was an Anglican church!'[8]

Bishop Hare's story leads on to one of the positive aspects of the charismatic movement and that is the freedom to make mistakes. Where any congregation is going to allow its members the freedom to actively contribute by, for example, sharing a word of encouragement, speaking out a prophecy, starting a song or offering a spontaneous prayer, there will inevitably be the odd blunder! Many charismatic churches have displayed a willingness to take that risk and allow their members to make mistakes. Often there are moments of awkwardness and perhaps occasional embarrassment. However people learn and grow by being able to make mistakes. It is often the case that the preaching in a charismatic church is enriched by someone in the congregation being given an impromptu invitation to tell their story or share a relevant personal experience.

Charismatic worship in which there is freedom for the regular members to spontaneously take part also makes much greater demands on the minister or leader. He or she may need to be firm and yet gracious when one of his resident prophets is off again with a 'Yea my people I have something to say to thee . . .!'

When Bishop David Pytches was at St Andrew's Chorleywood he was given freedom by his congregation to make mistakes and I have encountered other charismatic leaders who have the same benefit. Many positive outcomes result from such freedom. Worship can still be sensitive, balanced and from the heart but it no longer needs to be a polished theatrical performance. The corporateness of such worship reflects the pattern of the New Testament churches and is in keeping with the biblical doctrine of the church as the body of Christ. Individuals are likely to be more committed to come prepared if they know that they have a part to play.

In the report *The Charismatic Movement in the Church of England* the authors listed five key features which the charismatic churches displayed in their worship.[9] The third of these was freedom. Their focus was primarily on the freedom made 'for contributions, for personal devotion, for singing and for seeking counselling'. By 'counselling', they referred primarily to various forms of ministry and prayer with the laying on of hands which is frequently on offer either at the time when Communion is received or at the close of the service.[10]

Yet the freedom which the charismatic movement has brought to worship is considerably wider than the authors of the report suggested. It is seen in less slavish attachments to fixed written orders of service (liturgies). It is frequently visible in the ways in which people feel free to express their worship by movement, by clapping or raising their hands, by dance or by speaking out words of praise and declaration or by contributing short extempore prayers.

The new churches came into being primarily because many of the congregations in which they had come to experience renewal proved stubbornly resistant to change in their Sunday worship. Non-conformists stuck rigidly to their hymn sandwich menu. Clergy of the establishment feared letters to their bishop if they didn't read every word of the liturgy. In Anglican circles, however, David Watson began to move his congregation at St Michael-le-Belfrey in York away from slavish attachment to the Prayer Book. He was already widely known as a preacher, speaker and writer and his influence led to many others following suit. Worship at the Belfrey, as at other major Anglican churches such as Holy Trinity Brompton, soon began to combine the new with the old.

Appreciation of the Traditions of the Past

In the early phase of the charismatic movement the new churches shied away from liturgy altogether. In more recent times many of them have come to see that there is value in some structure. They have also realised that liturgy must constantly be updated and re-shaped if it is to be a living thing. Noel Richards, a worship leader with the Pioneer team, wrote: 'We must take the wonderful expressions of truth in our liturgies and update them. There must be a way to re-work liturgy so that its content can be appreciated by a new generation.'[11] Perhaps Paul Yongi Cho's church in Korea is a pointer to the way forward. Healing and clapping are the norm together with a robed choir and the Nicene Creed.

Power in Praise

In the emphasis on praise among charismatics in the 1970s several books enjoyed wide circulation. Among them were Merlin Carother's *Power in Praise* and Judson Cornwall's *Let Us Praise*. Praise was seen as the best medicine for the individual to overcome the bad situation or negative circumstances. The basic teaching was that by praising, the focus of attention could be moved away from the problem to the God who could bring help. In the context of worship which is the present concern, some charismatics saw praise as having two functions. One was to bring God's presence close to the worshippers. The other was to dispel the forces of darkness from the immediate environment and certainly from the worshippers. Two texts were often expounded in this connection. The Lord 'inhabits the praises of his people', taken from Psalm 22 (AV), was understood to mean that if a congregation could really lift up a great panoply of praise to God, he would come in a very personal way so that his presence would be known and experienced by them. The other passage, also from the Psalms, speaks of worshippers with 'the high praises of God . . . in their mouth . . . binding kings with chains and their nobles with iron' (Ps 149:6, 8). This aspect is considered in more detail in the chapter on spiritual warfare. At this stage we need simply to note that this particular understanding of combating the forces of darkness led to many congregations, particularly in the early days of renewal, deliberately setting out to lift their worshippers up into the 'high praises' of God.

The theology which underlies this commitment to praise is derived from the book of Acts. At the Council of Jerusalem in Acts 15 the apostle James made the point that God had rebuilt the tabernacle of David. This was the tabernacle which David pitched on Mount Zion and to which he had brought the ark with great rejoicing and celebration. Ron Trudinger of the Salt and Light group of churches, along with other Restoration leaders, saw this as being fulfilled in the 'restoration to the churches of "open worship and the presence of God".'[12] Trudinger further commented:

> In striking contrast to the tent in the Wilderness, Mount Zion was characterised by continual free celebration and worship, often noisy, around the ark. Similarly, in striking contrast to most traditional settings, a Spirit-led congregation today engages in open praise and worship.[13]

This theology has much to commend it. Not only is it biblical, it is meeting a clearly felt need. Historically it is the case that in most periods when the Christian Church has undergone periods of awakening there has been a revived interest in creative music. In the revival under John and Charles Wesley in eighteenth-century England there was a huge output of songs and hymns. The eighteenth-century revival was marked by singing. The Wesleys introduced simple repetitive choruses so that those who were unable to read could still imbibe Christian truth. *Wesley's Hymns* were a unique collection. Instead of being grouped around Christian doctrines or the Church's year, they were categorised according to Christian experience. Wesley claimed that his hymn book was 'a little body of practical divinity'. A few of Wesley's hymns (2–5 per cent) have an enduring quality which has stood the test of time.

In the nineteenth century the revival meetings led by Moody and Sankey were also accompanied by new music. Sankey's *Sacred Songs and Solos* sold between 50 and 90 million copies worldwide. Just while Sankey was in England with Dwight L. Moody, the book earned the evangelists £7,000 in royalties.[14] Sankey's hymns were sung in mines and on the factory floors. They even proved popular at some of the early trade union meetings. Sankey's hymns were great favourites with many agricultural labourers whose union marches through the streets were accompanied by songs like 'God speed the plough' and 'God save Joseph Arch' sung to the tunes of *Sacred Songs and Solos*.[15] The revivalism of the Salvation Army and the renewal of spiritual life in the wake of the Oxford Movement also produced words and music which were vitally alive.

Distinctive Singing

A distinctive characteristic of charismatic worship is its singing. The movement gained rapid popularity in its early phase on account of its music and singing. The years 1970 to 1975 saw the songs of the Christian road show *Come Together* supplanted by the altogether more charismatic *Sounds of Living Water* (1974) and *Fresh Sounds* (1976), both of which were edited by Jean Harper and Betty Pulkingham. These two collections made a particular impact on Anglican churches because they not only acknowledged the liturgy, but they actually produced music specifically for the Holy Communion service. The early music which emanated from the Restoration churches and their Dales and Downs Bible weeks was contrastingly raucous in tone. Many of their first creations were stampeding warfare songs such as 'The Battle Belongs to the Lord', 'It's God who makes my hands to war', 'An army of ordinary people' and 'The Lord is marching out in splendour'. Another feature of early charismatic worship was the use of Jewish songs, some of which started slowly and gradually got faster and faster. With the passing of the years however there has been a general mellowing in the singing of charismatic churches. The Vineyard songs which began to emerge in the early 1980s also helped to reinforce this trend. In fact John Wimber (1934–1997) was undoubtedly a major influence in British charismatic worship in the later 1980s and 1990s. The simplicity of what has been termed his Adult Orientated Rock Songs (AOR) resonated with Radio Two's 25–40s culture. A post-graduate student researching gospel and culture recently informed me that almost all the churches which were proclaiming the Christian message in a relevant idiom in the later 1990s were influenced in some degree by Wimber's style. Vineyard Songs and Vineyard music, particularly that of Brian Doerksen and Andy Park, have continued to enjoy widespread popularity both in public worship and for home listening on tapes and discs. Churches and worship leaders began to recognise that God could be personally encountered just as readily in the quieter gentler songs and even – and this was a revelation to some – in total silence.

In the 1990s, charismatic singing in many congregations continued to become more relaxed and leisurely in style. Worship as a whole was increaingly more informal in its ethos and structure. Song writers such as Chris Bowater, Noel Richards and Dave Bilborough continue to write songs with Richards in particular emphasising the role of music in evangelism. These three, together with Graham Kendrick, really belong to the earlier phase of the charismatic movement. From the mid-1990s the two most influential charismatic songwriters were Martin Smith and Matt Redman.

Martin Smith, who based himself in Littlehampton, became highly influential in the wider Christian scene and beyond. His group, Delirious, signed a huge record label with a secular company in the USA. Smith's major thrust has been to reflect strong Christian values in the wider world beyond the church. Matt

Redman's songs on the other hand are much more God-focussed and Christocentric in character. Perhaps this is nowhere better illustrated than in his song 'When the music fades' with its refrain, 'I'm coming back to the heart of worship, and it's all about You, all about You Jesus'. In this, Redman's central concern still resonates with Wimber's stress on intimate worship, although he is undoubtedly producing a very contemporary sound. Two aspects which do not appear to have changed in any significant degree are the simplicity of the word forms and the repetitive singing of shorter devotional songs.

Mainstream evangelicals and other advocates of traditional hymnology frequently make harsh pronouncements against what they see as contentless charismatic ditties and what they regard as mindless repetition. On the other hand, as advocates of renewal have pointed out, many older hymns require a dictionary to understand them and they are etymologically, musically and lyrically out of date. 'Crown him the Lord of life/The potentate of time/Creator of the rolling spheres/In ineffably sublime'[16] may be part of a classic hymn but it barely meets the requirement of the Church of England that public worship should be in 'a language understood of the people'. Charismatics recognise that people are not readily blessed by hymns such as 'Immortal, invisible, God only wise/Unresting, unhasting hid from our eyes'. Nor are the average worshippers on a Sunday able to meet with Jesus in the tongue-twisting words of John Mason Neale's 'Christ is made the sure foundation'. What meaning for example do the words 'consubstantial co-eternal while unending ages run' have for any except those familiar with the Arian controversy and the Council of Nicaea?

Many people who have worshipped with charismatic choruses find that their very simplicity is the key to their depth. Whether it be the gentle melodic tones of a Taizé chant like 'Jesus Remember Me' sung forty times, or a Vineyard chorus such as 'Jesus I love you/I bow down before you/praises and worship/to our King' sung perhaps six or eight times, the capacity is there to carry the worshipper into the very presence of God. Part of the explanation is seen to be that because the words are few and short, it isn't necessary to bend the mind round archaic or theological language. Repetition eventually focuses the attention and enables the worshipper to worship in spirit as well as in truth. One well-known worship leader explains it like this. If a person is always thinking about the steps on the dance floor, strictly speaking they are learning to dance. If, however, they can dance without thinking, they're dancing! Similarly, if worshippers continuously have to think about the words they are singing, they are like the person who is learning to dance. If, on the other hand, the words are totally familiar, they can readily be a vehicle for truly expressing love, bowing down, or offering their lives to God. It is of course true that repetition can become mindless but it can also be anointed by the Spirit of God and immensely healing and worshipful. The same dangers and benefits are also both inherent in the repetitive nature of the Church of England's Prayer Book services and a canticle such as the 'Benedicite' with its refrain of 'Praise Him and magnify Him for ever' which recurs some thirty-two times in thirty-two verses.

Charismatic songs have met with criticism both from people within the movement as well as those outside. A frequent comment is that the lyrics and the words are often cobbled. They lack enduring poetic quality. For this reason Michael Mitton, formerly of Anglican Renewal Ministries, feels that many of them are disposable. In a sense this could be seen as both a strength and a weakness. Many of the most recently produced hymn books still contain many hymns which reflect a music, culture and theology which is out of keeping with the contemporary situation. Hosanna, Vineyard and Kingsway Renewal Music may be as someone remarked 'MFI as opposed to Chippendale', but probably it's more generally user-friendly for that very reason. One possible exception to this pattern has been the prolific output of the song-writer, musician and worship leader, Graham Kendrick, the quality of whose work shows every sign of standing the test of time.

There can be no doubt that the music of the charismatic movement has profoundly influenced the music of the whole church including the mainstream evangelical and Catholic traditions. A number of examples bear testimony to this fact. The Archbishop's committee on worship included Mrs Jackie Webb who was the director of worship at St Andrew's Church Chorleywood. When Graham Dow was consecrated Bishop of Willesden, one of the songs which was sung by the congregation was a Vineyard chorus. Prominent churches like All Souls, Langham Place, in London and Holy Trinity in Norwich, while rejecting the validity of charismatic experience, nevertheless supplemented their diet of traditional hymns with some of the songs which had emerged from the charismatic movement.

Charismatics have helped the wider church to think more carefully and critically about worship and what exactly it is that they are attempting to achieve by singing. I sense, too, that numbers of charismatic churches are also moving back to rediscover the riches of some of the great and the better hymns of the past. In churches such as the Kensington Temple for example there are both the more doctrinal hymns and the shorter songs and choruses. This would seem to be in keeping with the apostle Paul's injunction to sing 'psalms, hymns and spiritual songs' (Col 3:16).

Its Multi-Dimensional Aspect

Much traditional worship, particularly in the late 1960s, was unidimensional. In the Anglican tradition it had the appearance of 'a stately masked ball'.[17] Everything was carefully planned and diligently carried out to the letter of the book. The primary appeal was to the intellect. While it may well be true that charismatics have to some extent underplayed the rational aspect, they have given full acknowledgement to the fact that people have spirits and bodies as well as minds. Charismatics have certainly helped the church to recover some of the art forms of the pre-Reformation era. They have recognised that the visual dimension can speak directly and powerfully into the human psyche.

Even the smallest independent charismatic fellowship meeting in a village hall or school will quite probably have decorative banners and texts. Possibly line drawings or images may be put on screen or a wall with an overhead projector. The individual members will feel free to use their bodies to express their worship of God. As we have seen, they may clap, dance, kneel, raise their hands in the air or stretch them out in front of them with palms upturned.

In some charismatic churches a real effort is made to utilise visual forms to convey the Christian message. This is what Bishop Colin Buchanan termed an 'inchoate sacramentality'. In this process music, artwork, movement and colour all help to draw out into experience the ever-present Spirit of God. Stoke Baptist Church in Coventry, for example, ran a monthly service for young people on a Sunday evening. Use was made of video extracts and visual imagery. There was a dry-ice machine, special lighting and a good deal of dancing. An Anglican church in Long Eaton ran a monthly Seekers Service using a multi-media approach. Nationally speaking, the best example in recent years was the early days of the Nine O'Clock Service at St Thomas Crookes in Sheffield. In 1993 this moved away to a separate location at Pond's Forge in the centre of the city. The presentation there drew on a wide range of traditions with a great deal of use of dance and large-screen visual imagery. Shortly before the service was closed down in consequence of its leader's scandalous behaviour there were experiments with incense and Gregorian chants. Much of this emphasis represented a very positive step forward and needs not only to be commended but reinforced and developed. The best educational research constantly reminds us that we learn through all our senses. In fact the point has been made that if all the human senses are brought into play a truth will penetrate much more deeply into the human psyche. This is something which Eastern religions and Orthodox Christianity have grasped in a way that Protestants in particular have not.

The Eucharist and Charismatic Worship

In some churches, particularly those belonging to the historic denominations, there has been an increased valuing of the eucharist. Indeed some have come to see the sacrament for the very first time as the central act of Christian worship. Numbers of charismatics have come to the realisation that Holy Communion can involve all the elements of Christian worship. The style of these occasions varies a good deal but often the atmosphere is informal with folk-style liturgies, and time for quiet and waiting. Many charismatic conferences, particularly in the early days, were marked by a concluding eucharist in which members from all denominations delighted to share. Larger-scale charismatic gatherings like New Wine and the semi-charismatic Spring Harvest often culminate in Communion services. Holy Communion has also been seen by some in the charismatic renewal as the appropriate context in which to minister healing. At the Harnhill Centre for Christian Healing, near Cirencester, Communion services are held every Friday with prayer for healing at the conclusion. A similar emphasis was observable at the London Healing Mission led by Andy and Audrey Arbuthnot.

The renewal of interest in Communion is not totally uniform and varies a good deal from one denomination or group of churches to another. The so-called new churches tend to be less focused on the Communion or breaking of bread than the renewed denominational churches. This is well reflected in Noel Richards' new Pioneer perspective volume entitled *The Worshipping Church*. In all the eleven chapters on worship there was no mention of Holy Communion or sacramental worship.[18] Bath City Church which was part of Covenant Ministries until 1994 typifies this position. In their Sunday worship they share in breaking of bread roughly once every four to six weeks. In one sense this is to be expected since the majority of their leaders came from Non-conformist backgrounds.

Some Weaknesses of Charismatic Worship

As with most things in life, charismatic worship has both strong and weak moments. In fact it has many good things going for it. This is borne out by the ever-growing appeal that it is making to so many people. Having said that, there are areas which are cause for concern and need adjustment and correction. One area which was particularly in evidence in the early days and is still featured to a degree is hype and stereotype.

Hype and stereotype

'Hype' is a term which first emerged from the drug culture of the 1960s. It's an experience something akin to a shot in the arm from a hypodermic syringe. To 'hype' is to stir up or artificially contrive to raise the intensity level of worship or prayer. In times of worship this is often achieved by leaders turning up the volume to a higher pitch and demanding the worshippers 'to sing it over, loud, because God likes to really hear it'. Hype is also often generated by clapping and feet stamping. At Woodgate Church near Birmingham, on Sunday 5 May 1994, Mike Price boomed down the microphone 'Devil this is for you'.

Almost immediately the congregation were up on their feet jogging on the spot, pounding the floor and slapping their legs above the knees. A close friend attended worship at one of the King's Church off-shoot congregations. She described the worship as 'manic'. It was as though the musicians were clockwork toys who had suddenly all had their buttons pressed. Two of Clifford Hill's associates reported a visit to a large charismatic church in Brighton to witness something of the Toronto phenomena. Heavy triumphalist choruses bellowed forth for the best part of an hour.

The reason for 'hyping up' is the belief that it will bring an increase of the power and presence of God into the meeting. The problem with this is that the atmosphere becomes contrived and some of the happenings become 'forced' as certain more suggestible individuals will do what they feel is expected of them. This can result in psychologically induced experiences and spurious emotional phenomena generated by group expectations. Meetings and phenomena which have been hyped up often leave the participants feeling flat and drained.

Charismatics need to learn to distinguish between 'hype' and the genuine 'anointing' of God's Spirit which is evidenced by his power and his presence. Often a real anointing of God's Spirit takes place when the 'hype' factor is low. When human input is low the 'anointing' is often at its most powerful. God can move when men and women give him the room to do so.

Stereotyping is another aspect of charismatic worship which needs to be attended to. It occurs not just among the historical churches with their fixed orders of service, but it can happen just as readily in the newer churches. There's a feeling on the part of some that God won't show up unless particular types of songs are used or a certain length of time is spent in worship choruses. Vineyard churches for example have a very fixed order in which they always sing at least thirty continuous minutes of Vineyard songs. There is on occasion an almost hidden paranoia that unless it is done in precisely this way God won't show up and there won't be a powerful time of ministry at the end. Other groups almost have a fetish about getting into 'real' praise or dancing. There is a danger here that congregations may lose sight of the fact that God is the sovereign Lord. Ultimately, spiritual renewal is not something the church manufactures. Rather, it is God coming as he wills.

Charismatics, and indeed the whole church, need to rediscover the very wide resources which the New Testament churches had at their disposal. Up until AD 70 when the early Christians planted a new congregation, they had the temple model with its rich heritage of priestly ritual and liturgy. The temple also had the traditions of psalms and their exhortations to shout, dance, clap, make processions and sing with a joyful noise and many instruments of praise. Alongside, there was also the pattern of the Jewish synagogues with their elders and deacons and emphasis on praise, prayer and preaching. With all of this there was little danger of the early Christians trying to meet with God in a stereotyped fashion. Relationships are kept alive by variety and Christian worship will need that same variety and freshness if it is to avoid becoming dull and boring.

Undermining the rational

In some quarters of the charismatic movement there has been an unbalanced undermining of the rational. Some fellowships reflect an almost 'Gnostic' strand which is urging that the mind be bypassed so that God can be fully reached. This kind of thinking is epitomised by Kenneth Hagin urging his hearers to 'Open the spirit-man to receive special revelation'.

Charismatic worship contains a number of high risk elements which need to be assessed thoughtfully. 'Words' are often given out 'as from God' and people invited to respond. Directional prophecies are also spoken on occasion, to groups as well as to individuals. There needs to be the opportunity to reflect and assess them. A particular danger emerges when individuals preface the words they bring with a 'Thus saith the Lord' or 'The Lord says to you today'. Such words do not leave much room for manoeuvre. Worshippers need to be taught to begin by saying something along the lines of 'I have the following words. Would you listen carefully and judge if its from God or applicable to your situation.' Wynne Lewis, Director of Elim Home Mission, said on one occasion: 'Whenever I hear someone begin to speak with the words, "Thus saith the Lord my children", I think, God help us!' Some churches are better than others at managing these kinds of contribution. Their congregations are invited to sit and reflect on what they have heard.

Others keep a written name check on everyone who gives out a word during a service. If what they bring on several occasions is judged to be unhelpful or irrelevant the matter is discussed with them.

Sometimes these words are put on too high a level even to the point of their being set over and against the written biblical revelation. Proponents of this teaching have noted that there are two Greek words translated 'word'. '*Logos*' is the objective, historic, written word of the Bible and '*rhema*' is God speaking directly to the individual at their point of need. The all important thing is that God by his Spirit speaks a personal 'rhema' into a person's situation. All charismatics would be happy with that. A danger which has sometimes resulted is that the 'rhema', or immediate word from God, has been followed even when it is out of line with the written biblical word. David Watson and others pointed out that the New Testament doesn't in fact make such a marked distinction between 'rhema' and 'logos'.[19]

Some congregations have, like the Corinthian church of the New Testament times, misused the gift of tongues. David Pawson has helpfully questioned the unintelligible use of this gift without interpretation in the presence of unbelievers.[20] A much misunderstood text in this context as he further pointed out is 1 Corinthians 14 verse 22 which speaks of tongues as 'a sign for the unbeliever?'[21] The key question is what do they signify to the unbeliever? When the context of the quotation from Isaiah 28 which follows is studied, it's clear that they are a sign of their rejection and exclusion by God. The New Testament repeatedly urges that Christians are to test all things, particularly in public worship; they are to assess and judge what they hear, including the public use of interpreted tongues (1 Cor 14:29).

There is a danger in some circles that people who question or have doubts are regarded as 'unspiritual'. Everything must be measured against the yardstick of what Apostolic New Testament teaching says. Martin Luther's '*Sola Scriptura*' (the Scripture alone) as the final court of authority is vital in this context. John Stott wisely cautioned against separating the mind and the spirit. He made the point that the fact that 'man's mind is fallen is not an excuse for retreat from thought into emotion, for the emotional side of man's nature is equally fallen'.[22] The

Christian must therefore constantly grapple with the meaning of the biblical text as the basis of all life and worship.

It is a significant fact, which must however be underlined at this particular point, that the charismatic movement has brought large numbers of Christian people to a real love for the Bible. The testimony of many is that it has become alive in a new way and that they have an ever-growing appetite to read and study it and hear it expounded. Many evangelicals believe that God is present in the very words of Scripture and that simply to teach them is to bring the hearers into his presence. Charismatics believe that God also speaks directly to individuals by his Holy Spirit, although always in keeping with the teaching of Scripture. Their view is that it is the Holy Spirit who takes the words of Scripture and brings them alive in preaching and teaching. Charismatic Christians pray particularly for the Holy Spirit to come and make the word alive and relevant to the situation of everyday living and church life and worship.

The Strengths of Charismatic Worship

Having acknowledged that there are clearly weaknesses and potentially dysfunctional features to charismatic worship, it is important to recognise that it also has many positive aspects. When St John's Church, Harborne, was first touched by the charismatic movement in the early 1970s they saw their worship transformed 'in quality in answer to prayer and through the release of gifts of music, art and dance'.[23] Their mid-week prayer time grew from about 20 to 300 at its peak and nearly 500 were attending prayer or house groups of some kind. This picture could be replicated many hundreds of times over since that time.

Culturally relevant

One of the reasons for this burgeoning success is the very positive fact that charismatic worship is in touch with the ethos of the contemporary post-modern culture. The priestly and the ritualistic belong essentially to the old order. They reflect the hierarchical structure of the ancient regime and the class-ridden society. In contrast, the democratic spirit of the charismatic movement which allows individuals and groups free rein to participate and on occasion make their own personal contributions in worship is altogether much more in keeping with the way things are in present Western society. Even in management structures people work together in teams and leadership is exercised from behind. Decisions are often worked on the basis of open discussion and consensus. All of this is much closer to the New Testament. The ideal of God's people as a body doesn't sit comfortably with the traditional church in which the priest or pastor calls all the tunes or conducts public worship as if he or she were on a rostrum in front of an orchestra. Individual members often therefore feel a much closer bond with their leaders who are not put on a pedestal and addressed as Father, Canon, Rector or Pastor. Charismatics in general have done more than other sections of the Christian Church to stress the servant model of Christian ministry as outlined by Jesus in Matthew 23 verse 11.

In very general terms the music, the culture and the buildings used by charismatic churches are much closer to the level at which most people live their daily lives. Large numbers of charismatic congregations, particularly those of the newer churches, meet in community centres, wine bars and public halls. For many ordinary and 'unchurched' people it's much easier to walk into a worship service in a familiar local school than to darken the doors of a gloomy edifice that has the appearance of a Victorian Workhouse and offers a priestly ritual resembling a masonic lodge. Equally, a congregation who are casually dressed, chatty and informal are much less of a barrier than the stiffly suited and hatted middle-classes who patronise the establishment. There is also a sense in which charismatic worship is more universal in its appeal. It has a distinctly multicultural aspect. In inner city areas in particular, many more individuals from black and Asian communities find themselves at home in charismatic churches. The opportunity to be free and to express oneself in clapping, movement and dance is an instinctive aspect of many non-white cultures. Sadly it is the case that even the charismatic movement has not completely brought about an integration of blacks and whites in the same churches. Kensington Temple in London is one of the bright exceptions to this and there are often more than a hundred different nations represented at their Sunday services.

Its cathartic aspect

Many people find in the worship of charismatic churches a much greater depth of love and acceptance in the more tightly-knit fellowship of renewed worship. There is frequently the chance to be hugged, affirmed, encouraged and prayed for. For many who live in a harsh environment with brokenness and pain in their home or family situation, this is a very attractive and healing aspect.

In charismatic services of worship it is commonplace to see people cry or unburden themselves and find care and emotional support. It is for this reason, as the General Synod Report observed, that 'many inadequate and emotionally crippled people are being tended within this movement'.[24] Numerous national and local prayer counselling ministries have been developed by charismatic churches and groups of charismatic individuals. Churches have sponsored Pastoral Care courses and organised conferences on themes such as 'Restoring Personal Wholeness through Healing Prayer' with teaching from individuals such as Leanne Payne and Clay and Mary McLean. Mary Pytches has introduced many Christians and churches to some of the important basics of prayer counselling through her teaching at the New Wine summer conference and by her seminars at Chorleywood and elsewhere. Many organisations such as the Harnhill Centre for Christian Healing, Salem Court and Ellel Grange offer residential care and help. John Leach who followed Michael Mitton as director of Anglican Renewal Ministries in 1997 shared something of this concern and organised a conference in 1999 under the title of 'Healing the Wounds of Ministry'.

All of this amounts to a catharsis or healing aspect. Attenders are coming to experience the shalom or wholeness which is the essential aspect of Christian salvation. One interviewee explained it as follows. She said that she had many sandy areas in her life's experiences. She could cope with them provided she didn't contemplate them for too long. But now as a result of attending worship in the Oxford Vineyard, concrete had been poured in to replace this sand. The areas of pain and weakness had become solid and firm and she could look at them without fear or anxiety.

Increased giving

Giving has always been an aspect of charismatic worship from the earliest times. Generous giving has been a prominent feature of charismatic churches since the very beginning of the renewal movement in the late 1960s and early 1970s.[25] St Philip and St Jacob's Church (Pip and Jay), Bristol came into the baptism of the Holy Spirit in 1968. Up to that point they gave away money in hundreds of pounds. From 1969 onwards they were able to give in thousands. If they gave away £93,000 in 1993 they would have given away £1 million in thirty years. 'However,' Canon Malcolm Widdecombe commented, 'God enabled us to give away £97,000 in that year!' A new target has now been set to give away a second million by the first Sunday in December 2003.[26] St John's, Harborne for example reported in 1981 that since the charismatic movement had come to the parish weekly giving had risen from an average of £50 a week to about £1,500 per week. When the renewal movement touched Holy Trinity, Hounslow, the majority of the congregation were soon observed to be tithing their gross income. St Andrew's, Chorleywood which has been in renewal for thirty years has always aimed to give half of its income to needs beyond its own. The diocesan quota and the cost of the staff are all paid for out of the 50 per cent it spends on its own needs. A £600,000 church extension at St Thomas Crookes was characterised by 'hilarious giving' with Securicor once attending an evening service in 1989 at which £50,000 had been pledged and given. At Ashtead in Surrey where Chris Hughes was rector, the giving rose by 20 per cent in the years 1989–1993 to £350,000.

At the present time many charismatic congregations have remarkable testimonies to tell about their growing capacity to give to Christian work. St Philip and St Jacob's Church (Pip and Jay), Bristol, recently reached a point where they had given over a million pounds to missions over a thirty-year period. Holy Trinity Brompton not only supports a large church and staff, but have been able to finance the re-opening and re-furbishment of a number of redundant and disused churches in the south-west London area. The giving at Holy Trinity Church, Cheltenham, where the incumbent is Mark Bailey, increased by 500 per cent in the period 1994–1999 to £250,000 per annum. In 1996 they installed a PA and closed circuit television and in 1999 they purchased outright for £500,000 a warehouse and substantial property close to the church. St Paul's, Ealing, where Mark Melluish is vicar had a total income of £26,000 in 1993 with £12,000 from hall lettings. By 1999 their giving had climbed to £200,000 with £20,000 from hall lettings.

These achievements have come about because charismatic congregations have either been taught to tithe 10 per cent of their income, or made to understand the blessings and benefits of generous giving.

Postscript on Charismatic Worship

Sociologists of religion have observed that many religious movements which are vibrant in their initial stages show a capacity to run out of steam. The early 'charisma' and spontaneous vitality begins to drain away in a process which is termed 'routinisation'. This happens as the enthusiastic leader begins to run out of energy or tire with the passing years. Often this shows in the worship of the institution concerned. It is possible to see the beginnings of such a trend in certain quarters where the charismatic movement has been active. Michael Mitton commented in 1994:

> We actually feel, I think, that it's running out of steam ...
> there's a feeling of being left empty. I think that is because
> there is a real need for ritual, the need for liturgy, the need
> for a connectedness with roots and I think we will find that
> the music of Taizé, the worship style of Taizé, will long
> outlive charismatic worship.[27]

Michael Mitton saw these roots in the Jewish, Celtic and Orthodox traditions. ARM held a symposium to examine Celtic roots in March 1994 and a further one in 1995 focused on Jewish roots. They had hoped in the following year to do the same with the Orthodox tradition but with the Toronto Blessing impacting the Bristol scene the DOG (Deposits of Glory) Conference was held in its place. Clearly there is a rich culture and learning in all of this inheritance, but there is also a danger of fossilising what is a vital living reality. No relationship will continue to be alive and well if it becomes stuck fast in one way of doing things or hidebound in a particular spirituality or static culture. If the experience of a charismatic relationship with Christ is to be a daily living reality there will need to be continuous, adaptive and fresh ways of going about it.

There is a wide variety of style and music in use in charismatic churches. It ranges on the one hand from gentle Taizé chants and unaccompanied singing which is pensive in mood, to hour-long 'knees ups' resembling spiritual aerobics. In these cases singing is often raucous and even manic in its mood. There is danger, particularly in the latter style, that the majesty and 'otherness' and the holiness of God can get lost in the informality and camaraderie of the close and intensive fellowship. It is true of course that immanence, the sense of God's nearness, is an essential ingredient in Christian worship. Nevertheless the difficulty is that an overstress on this may result in losing the sense of a God who is altogether greater than his creation, who controls the universe and who is able to act on behalf of his people.

The charismatic emphasis on 'ministry' times and ensuring that the individual is 'touched' is another positive side to charismatic worship. The converse of this, however, is that the focus is increasingly on God within us to the detriment of God over us. He is 'Emmanuel, God with us', but he is also 'the Everlasting Father, the Mighty God, who holds the universe in his hands'. Christopher Cocksworth has pointed out in a lucid paper that 'we tend to think of the Holy Spirit as God in his immanence, and the worship of the charismatic movement is often criticised for so majoring on God's immanence that it has lost sight of God's transcendence'.[28] In his paper Cocksworth went on to show clearly how an overstress on the closeness of God which features in so many charismatic worship services can be counteracted by a full and proper understanding of the doctrine of the Trinity.

For some, charismatic worship has brought a growing appreciation of sacramental worship. Charismatic Christians have recognised the presence of the Holy Spirit in sacramental acts which they had not previously appreciated. As we have seen, many Anglicans have testified to their growing appreciation for a more Catholic eucharistic liturgy. Baptist Union ministers who have experienced renewal in the Holy Spirit have begun to lay hands on baptismal candidates as they come out of the baptistry and to pray for the Holy Spirit to fill them.

An important aspect of all Christian worship, be it Catholic, Protestant, evangelical, charismatic or that of other strands of the Church, is the ethical consequences which result from it. It is the Holy Spirit's function to change God's people into the likeness of Christ. The apostle Paul talks in Corinthians about the Lord who is the Spirit transforming us into his likeness (2 Cor 3:18). In his letter to the Romans he speaks of worship keeping us from 'conforming ourselves to the standards of this world' (Rom 12:2). This is an aspect which was certainly neglected in the earlier phase of the charismatic movement. In recent times, however, there have been more conscious efforts to generate positive ethical outcomes to Christian worship. Perhaps charismatic clergy and Christian leaders have come to imbibe Bishop Michael Marshall's saying: 'The worship is over, let the service begin.' Robert Warren, writing under the title 'Maturing Christian worship' was able to comment: 'Again I can certainly testify that renewal has brought real and substantial change in people's lives.'[29]

4

LEADERSHIP AND MINISTRY

One of the most marked features of the traditional churches is their dependence on a clerical ministry. A typical Church of England parish church for example has a rector and possibly a curate. The clergy are a race apart, most often wearing special clothes and on Sundays sitting at special big oak desks looking down over their congregations, in much the same way that Victorian school teachers towered over their cowering charges. Generally speaking, not much happens in the church unless the vicar initiates it, chairs it and effects most of it himself, later writing about it in the church magazine or bulletin if he or she still has any surplus creative energy. One of the major achievements of the charismatic movement has been to question and seek to change much of this. Charismatics tend not to regard the church as being like a train with the driver and the guard doing all the work and the rest going for the ride. They see it rather as being like an ocean-going liner where everyone from the captain to the newest recruit has a vital role to play. Visit a traditional church for the first time and you will observe what is usually a one-person-roadshow. Go to a charismatic church and before long some sort of contribution will emerge from the congregation itself.

When the charismatic movement began in the 1960s the image of traditional clerical ministry was at a low ebb. It was lampooned in the satirical reviews like *Gas and Gaiters* and *Beyond the Fringe* and blasted mercilessly by literary critics such as Malcolm Muggeridge, who reflected:

In an average village today Anglican worship has become little more than a dying bourgeois cult. A small number of motor cars may be seen outside the parish church. When a service is in progress the bells still ring joyously across the fields and meadows on Sunday mornings and evenings, but fewer and fewer heed them, and those few predominantly middle class, female and elderly.[1]

Muggeridge commented that 'in such circumstances it was not surprising that the ministry should attract crack pots, eccentrics and oddities'. 'Scarcely a day goes by,' he reflected, 'but some buffoon in holy orders makes an exhibition of himself in one way or another.'[2]

In the light of this kind of imagery, charismatics set themselves steadfastly against the notions of clerical caste (male or female). In the older denominational churches which had been touched by the Spirit the vicars and pastors came to see themselves in much less establishment terms. They were one of a team. They appointed elders or congregational leaders to assist them in the decision-making and caring. They saw their ministry as 'priestly' only in the sense that all believers are priests and have a calling to bring people into the presence of God. There was a much greater emphasis on lay ministry in charismatic Anglican and Roman Catholic circles. Charismatics generally rejected the idea that church leadership should be confined to those who had been trained in university or Bible college. They stressed the importance of using people's 'giftings' to the full.

Changing the Structures

The problem for most charismatics was the question of changing the structures. Many were mindful of Jesus' saying that new wine was not to be put into the old wineskins. The question was, could this new wine of the Spirit be contained in the old denominational wineskins? Some were aware that it is possible on occasion to stretch old wineskins by soaking them in water and rubbing them with oil (both symbols of the Holy Spirit). They therefore felt that they should try to extend the structures of their existing denominational fabric. However, it proved no easy task. In a 1977 *Renewal* article, a Church of England cleric, John Gunstone, reviewed Michael Harper's book *Let My People Grow*. 'Yes,' he wrote, 'I agree with practically everything, but how are we going to change the structures?'[3] For Anglicans this was often particularly hard. They had been nurtured on the Prayer Book teaching that 'it is evident unto all men diligently reading the Holy Scriptures and ancient authors that from the apostles' time there have been these orders of ministers in Christ's Church: bishops, priests and deacons'. Others felt that the task of putting the new wine into an ancient system was an impossible one and that a more radical solution was called for. Dave Tomlinson, for example, wrote: 'Some of us have . . . been disillusioned with trying to put new wine in old wineskins.' He, like many others, advocated 'restoration principles of church structure'.[4]

For men like Tomlinson and his fellow leader, Bryn Jones, 'restoration' meant replacing the threefold order of ministry inherited from the Emperor Constantine's church with the five-fold ministry of Ephesians 4. In 1978 Bryn Jones looked for 'a move of God that will restore the apostles, prophets, evangelists, pastors and teachers into the Body of Christ'.[5] Much more recently Gerald Coates, the leader of Pioneer, is still sounding the same clarion call. 'In all charismatic strands,' he asserted, 'there is a decisive move away from the one man leadership to shared leadership.'[6] He pointed out that many of the local fellowships which are affiliated with his organisation 'look to four-fold ministry of pastors, teachers, elders and prophets'. He continued:

The house church movement doesn't have any ordained 'ministers' as such in the accepted sense of the word, we believe that we are all priests. There is not a special breed and class of priests. We certainly don't believe in setting people aside with peculiar clothes and titles.[7]

All of this is relatively easier to effect in new fellowships which meet in an informal manner in leisure centres, community halls and local schools. It's considerably harder to achieve in a local parish church with hundreds of years of tradition and a history dominated by the Squire and his relations. This said, by no means all charismatic Anglicans have given up on the task. Tony Higton, for example, maintained that the fivefold ministries 'are in the church today'.[8] The problem is that 'some leaders have such gifts and some don't'.[9] Higton suggested that all

Church of England incumbents should have at least one of the ministries listed in Ephesians 4 verses 11-13. Baptist minister, Alastair Campbell, also stressed the need for the contemporary Church to be 'apostolic, prophetic, evangelistic, pastoral and educative'.[10]

Wynne Lewis, formerly pastor of Kensington Temple, now director of Elim Church's Home Mission used to believe that there should be an apostle for an area and a prophet for an area. More recently he has come to a different view that in every local fellowship there should be an apostle, a prophet, an evangelist, a pastor and a teacher. He believes that it should be possible to recognise these giftings in each church. 'We've done it in London,' he says, 'and it released hundreds and hundreds into their God-given spiritual giftings.' Perhaps this is a factor in the remarkable growth of Elim congregations in greater London.

Who Are Today's Apostles?

Traditionally, there have been three models of church government: Episcopal or direction by bishop, Presbyterial or oversight in the hands of a group of elders, or Congregational with power invested in the democratic vote of the members. In addition, in pre-Reformation times, some churches were under the control of monastic communities. To these options, Restorationist charismatics have added a further alternative: rule by apostles.

The first man to really stress the importance of recovering the ministry of 'apostles' for the contemporary Church was Arthur Wallis. In 1972 he called together a group of those he felt to have leadership and other skills. On that occasion 'we entered into a covenant relationship, agreeing to be committed to each other's welfare in every way.' The aim was 'to cover each other by bringing encouragement, direction and where necessary correction to each other's lives'. There were seven in this group: Arthur Wallis, Peter Lyne, Bryn Jones, David Mansell, Graham Perrins, Hugh Thompson and John Noble.[11] They jokingly referred to this group as 'the magnificent seven'. Some further get-togethers were held as a result of which they more or less appointed themselves as the new apostles. Later, their number was augmented by a further seven to become the 'fabulous fourteen'.[12] Quite where the 'idea' of 'apostle' initially came from isn't clear. Andrew Walker speculated that the group were influenced by the Welsh-based Apostolic Church with its headquarters in Penygroes.[13] In fact Bryn was a leader in the Apostolic church at Aberdare.

At this early point in the story there was a considerable power struggle between John Noble, 'a man of the mind who had always wanted to be a barrister', and Bryn Jones who felt and spoke from the heart. These two were always locking horns and Arthur Wallis felt the whole country was going to be kept from God's blessing because of it.

By this time both Wallis and Bryn had contact with a group of American Bible teachers in Fort Lauderdale. These men, Bob Mumford, Charles Simpson, Derek Prince, Don Basham and Ern Baxter became known as the 'Fort Lauderdale Five'. They taught a pyramid form of church government which placed the individual congregational members at the bottom. Over them the next layer of the pyramid, were the house group leaders. Next above were elders and at the very top was the chief or over-shepherd. The Lauderdale group tended to deal in 'shepherds' rather than 'apostles' although in practice there often wasn't a great deal of difference.

Arthur hoped that these American brothers could get matters in England sorted out. They duly hit on a plan that Bryn and John Noble should submit to Arthur, he being the senior and more fatherly figure. Arthur would then submit to the Fort Lauderdale group. When they arrived back in England, however, the plan was more or less laughed out of court. It was felt that Arthur would never be able to keep tabs on either Bryn or John. John himself later went out with Maurice Smith to the Fort Lauderdale brothers who tried to convince them to submit to the original plan. It all proved to be to no avail.

Although the Fort Lauderdale men rarely spoke of 'apostles' and their speech was always of 'shepherds', the English leadership began to use the term 'apostle' and to speak of apostolic ministries. The concept which they developed owed much to the 'big shepherd' notion coming out of Fort Lauderdale. The apostle's job was to structure the outfit and help with the practical problems. In Maurice Smith's somewhat cynical words, he had to deal efficiently with the real issues that bugged local fellowships, 'dreary teachers, fiery evangelists, dull worship leaders and the lovey dovey pastors'.

Some of these apostles demonstrated extremes of authoritarianism. Particularly was this so in earlier heady days but there is still evidence of it in more recent years. Bryn Jones, the dominating Welsh leader of Covenant Ministries, now based at Nettlehill, was dubbed by ITV as one who required 'unconditional submission to leadership'.[14]

Apostolic brothers are still emerging in the charismatic world, although in more recent times a few more safeguards appear to have been built into the system. The role of apostles is still seen as 'confirmed by prophets and other ministries' and 'evident through their work'.[15] Wally North emphasised this point in his book on the subject. He pointed out that as the New Testament churches grew, 'men of apostolic stature emerged from among them and were acknowledged as such without causing any undue stress among the original eleven'.[16] He did however point out that 'a spiritual church is quite capable of judging whether or not a man is an apostle of Christ'.[17] Even Bryn Jones declared, 'We are wise if we prove all things, including the claims of those who set themselves forth as apostles in the church of God.'[18]

What Do Apostles Do?

In 1981 Arthur Wallis wrote a lengthy article for *Restoration* magazine entitled 'Apostles Today? Why Not!'[19] He suggested that the view that apostles have passed away was based on 'the faulty premise' that the completion of Scripture rendered them obsolete.[20] Although the Church has the inspired writings 'we still need the men of revelation'.[21] In another piece under the title 'Getting Your Thinking Straight', Wallis distinguished three classes of apostle. The first is 'our Lord himself, the apostle and high priest of our confession'. Second are the Twelve. 'The Apostleship of the twelve, like that of our Lord terminated with their earthly course.' Third are the 'post-Pentecost apostles' of Ephesians 4 verse 11. These were given to the church 'until we attain to the measure of the stature of the fullness of Christ' (v 13).

Bishop Lightfoot had written in his celebrated essay, 'The Christian Ministry', that the word apostle is 'not so used as to lend any countenance to the idea that it is in any way restricted to the twelve'.[22] The main problem from a historical perspective, however, is that the evidence for the office of an apostle in the early Catholic Church is fragmentary. Nevertheless Hermas in the second century referred to the seventy-two as 'apostles' and Eusebius, the church historian, spoke of 'numberless apostles'. This would appear to support the main Roman Catholic and Anglican claim that the apostles appointed bishops as their successors. But even when this is said, the available sources are sparse and mostly written by representatives of the Catholic hierarchy.

Apostles are seen primarily as 'foundational men', missionaries and church planters. Restorationists point out that in the early days post-Pentecost apostles such as Paul, Apollos, Andronicus, Junias and Titus engaged in a variety of pioneering tasks. These included church planting, laying of foundations, leadership, oversight and problem solving. Terry Virgo, the pastor of Clarendon Church in Hove and the director of New Frontiers International churches, suggested that one of the distinguishing features of the apostle is that he is 'a master builder' (1 Cor 3:10).[23]

Dave Tomlinson while still with Bryn Jones saw an apostle as 'a man of revelation, a man of strategy, a man of ability and a man of fatherhood'.[24]

When the issue is looked at practically, it can be seen as sensible and inevitable that emerging independent churches will seek to form a relationship with senior, competent and tested ministers who can care for and pastor their leaders. In fact where historic churches fail to give it, some of their clergy seek it from the apostolic men of the newer churches. Even some Church of England incumbents are receiving 'covering' and input from the Salt and Light and Ichthus leaderships.

In the last analysis it is the ministry not the office which is important. The fact that there are a significant number of 'apostolic men' whose services seem to be sought and appreciated witnesses to a substantial pastoral need from among local church leaders. Dave Tomlinson expressed the view that some churches have benefited from the ministry of 'apostolic men who haven't used the label' without actually realising it.[25] As Tomlinson saw it, terms such as apostle are simply job descriptions, not titles or status, so 'going under the right name is not the most important thing in the world'.[26]

To date, house church apostles have resisted pressure to organise their covering into neatly packaged geographical areas approaching an Anglican diocese or a Methodist district. This has kept the focus on the congregation and people rather than on a local area or territory. In practice this means that churches in Bath and Swansea, for example, are 'covered' by leadership in the Midlands and fellowships in Liverpool are 'related' to leadership teams based in Surrey. One advantage of this translocal pastoring of congregations is that churches in an area get support and input from several different perspectives and locations. They are then able to share these among themselves at area meetings and celebrations.

Danger: Apostles at Work

One of the dangers of this system of translocal apostles 'covering' churches is the possibility that some develop a taste for power. Stories abound about American apostles bragging over who was 'covering' the most churches. Maurice Smith, one of the 'fabulous fourteen' recalled that one's success as an apostle was judged by the number of churches that one had relating to oneself. He recalled, for example, that in the early days Graham Perrins and John MacLaughlan were thought to be the least successful because they had so few churches relating to themselves.

In the latter 1970s and early 1980s there was considerable rivalry between Bryn Jones' northern outfit grouped around Bradford and some of the groups in the southern counties. Keith Fyleman of Stroud Community Church also recalled the highly competitive spirit and rivalry with other similar groups in the earlier days of charismatic renewal.

Several of the men who made up the 'fabulous fourteen' continued their link with Christian leaders based in Fort Lauderdale and began to go along with their authoritarian views on leadership and submission. Most of them became fairly dictatorial and domineering. Bryn Jones and Arthur Wallis were much influenced by Ern Baxter, and Barney Coombs developed close links with Bob Mumford. As a result all three began to run particularly tight ships. Baxter for example drew heavily on Watchman Nee's book *Spiritual Authority*. In one passage Nee maintained the following:

93

If God dares to entrust his authority to men, then we can dare to obey. Whether the one in authority is right or wrong does not concern us since he has to be responsible directly to God. The obedient needs only to obey; the Lord will not hold us responsible for any mistaken obedience, rather he will hold the delegated authority responsible for his erroneous act. Insubordination, however, is rebellion, and for this the one under authority must answer to God.[27]

Despite the fact that Nee was making a nonsense in denying an individual's personal responsibility before God, his teaching was still enthusiastically taken up both in America and in England. At the Dales Bible Week, for example, Baxter declared:

God is restoring spiritual authority as against democratic ecclesiastical authority. Men are rising up with a dimension of delegated authority imparted to them by the sovereign Christ of apostolic, prophetic, evangelistic and shepherding power of anointing. God is bringing His Kingdom in not run by democratic appointment but by King Jesus.[28]

Astonishingly, Derek Prince, another of the Lauderdale men, stated, 'We do not obey those in authority because they are right, we obey them because they are in authority.'[29] This appears to be nothing less than a surrendering of God-given human rights!

Nigel Wright observed that charismatic house churches 'eschew democracy (rule by the people) in favour of theocracy (rule by God) but their version of theocracy is in fact oligarchy (rule by a few)'. In this context we might even go further and suggest that their version of it is in fact autocracy, rule by one man. As the situation emerged in the later 1990s most of the Restoration charismatic groups were still presided over by one dominant overall leader. With Covenant Ministries it is Bryn Jones, Salt and Light is still directed by Barney Coombs, New Frontiers is under Terry Virgo and Pioneer is led by Gerald Coates. Other less successful individuals have small clusters of churches which 'relate' to them. There is still a good deal of rivalry between these major groups who can be observed planting out new fellowships in the same small commuter towns in the south-east of England and elsewhere. No one would want to suggest that any of these leaders are anything approaching dictators or absolute monarchs, although some gave that appearance, or came close to it in earlier days. The fact is all of these men are 'up front', dominant, high-profile people who may 'delegate' but they keep a strong grip on the reins. They are people of 'charisma' who take the central platform seats, give key note speeches, have their name and picture at the centre of the brochures and are editor-in-chief of their magazines and journals. People respect and revere them. Andrew Walker described Bryn Jones as 'the top man in his segment'. Gerald Coates, according to Maurice Smith, 'always wanted to be a household name'. What is it that you get by being a part of New Frontiers? I asked one church leader. 'We get Terry Virgo,' was the reply.

Many of the new breed of apostles were 'men on the move' who were, as Jesus urged, 'forceful men', laying hold of God's 'kingdom' (see Mt 11:12). For them, democracy was never going to be anything other than emotionally draining and frustratingly inefficient. They therefore set out to justify autocratic rule. They did it in terms of 'anointing'. 'When there is no anointing,' wrote Terry Virgo, 'democracy is probably the safest form of church government, but when God befits to give anointed leadership, democracy must make room for God to have his way.'[30] Clearly God and democracy don't mix, at any rate not in Restoration charismatic churches!

Virgo went on to state that 'the appointment of elders is an important part of the apostle's foundation laying ministry. Without it we resort to man-made structures'.[31] Autocratic rule might work out satisfactorily in the hands of a Virgo, but for lesser mortals there are always going to be problems. At one end there is the difficulty of handling newly acquired power and the dangers of 'spiritual abuse'. At the other end of the scale there is the temptation just to make a name for oneself or to earn a good living. When some of the 'fabulous fourteen' first met the Fort Lauderdale group they were impressed at what could be done with the tithe! Certainly Bryn Jones lived in flamboyant style in a spacious mansion. To his followers he was a genuinely charismatic leader utterly loyal to his king. To his opponents he was 'the big bad wolf of Britain's booming new church

95

movement' or 'the nearest British equivalent to a US televangelist'. It seems to be the case that these men were probably a good deal more domineering in the early 1980s than they became in the mid 1990s. Public opinion, television documentaries and widespread press reports all helped to refine their apostolic behaviour patterns.

In earlier times there was some fairly ruthless behaviour. Churches were shut down, moved and their local leaders disciplined and dismissed. Bryn Jones, for example, appeared in Cheltenham in September, 1985 and closed the doors on the Cheltenham Christian Fellowship in Charlton Kings. Up until that point the group had been led by Steve Apelle but he had experienced something of a faith crisis and wanted to stand down. Others in leadership who had left jobs and moved to Cheltenham to work with the church were happy to assume the reins but to no avail. Needless to say they soon cut their links with Covenant Ministries.

Graham Perrins moved the majority of his church in Canterbury to Petersfield in Hampshire. Having got them there he dismissed Brian Johns from leadership and replaced him with a Welshman, David Hopkins, who subsequently fell into serious moral problems.[32] John MacLaughlan's church in Camberley, Surrey, was similarly manhandled. MacLaughlan, also a prophet, ordered them to move lock, stock and barrel to Yeovil in Somerset. He then specified which locations and neighbouring villages were acceptable. Once settled in their new surroundings, MacLaughlan dismissed Ted Rotheram from leadership leaving him hurt, isolated and unemployed. MacLaughlan's teaching was heavy stuff:

> Submission involves submission to leaders and principally to whoever is taking responsibility for his life . . . the primary area in that thing of submission is to emphasise the thing of submission to leaders. I don't think an individual can have a real corporate experience of the body of Christ unless he is experiencing submission to leadership.[33]

The question is what do you do when you have someone who just will not submit? MacLaughlan answered by referring to one of the local congregation he was 'dealing' with:

I think all you can do within that situation is put the person under pressure, step up the pressure, step up the pressure, step up the pressure until something gives. And what we've insisted on is a framework of weekly discipline with her. She has to give an account of everything she's done during the week. She has to keep a diary of everything. We're just gradually stepping up the pressure until something has to give.[34]

Clearly these circumstances are from the rather more extreme end of Restorationism and significantly they relate to two of the least successful of the 'fabulous fourteen'. It has in fact been observed that the more insecure the leader the greater the attempt they make at gaining and keeping control. Nevertheless there are dangers in the lone ranger style of leadership. In theory, it is said that apostles 'cover each other'. But the question is, do they? or how well do they do it? Part of the problem is that the apostles covering a particular group often know each other too well to be able to assess one another or the situation with objectivity. Some churches relate to only one apostle or overseer and in such a case there may be no one to keep check on the situation. In reality of course the situation is probably no worse than the gay Anglican clergy who live with their partners in their vicarages, or the case of Bishop Peter Ball of Gloucester who was eventually forced to resign on account of his act of 'gross indecency'.[35] David Sheppard, the former Bishop of Liverpool, reflected on the case as a breach of trust and it was noted that there was a lack of accountability on the part of diocesan bishops.

Raising an Important Issue

The apostolic covering system is manifestly not without its faults. Clearly these were much more discernible in the earlier years of the movement. Nevertheless, the fact that so many fellowships sought for the 'covering' and input of individuals such as Terry Virgo reveals that in many churches this is an area of lack and present need. It is my observation that in general the newer churches have learned quickly from some of their earlier mistakes. Many of their top leaders provide personal quality support, input and prayer. Bill Bates, the minister of New Life

Church, Cheltenham, visits his covering, Derek Brown, at least once a month for a meal, prayer and discussion. Sometimes Derek Brown will come over from Aldershot. On other occasions 'we will meet for breakfast at a halfway point or whatever'.[36] The English Vineyard pastors get together on a regular basis with their director, John Mumford, for prayer, teaching and encouragement.

Tony Higton in his *The Challenge of the House Churches*[37] drew out a number of aspects of the leadership from which the historic churches should be learning. He instanced an Anglican clergyman who wrote to the *Church of England Newspaper*:

I went to the Dales weary after nearly two years as an incumbent. During that time I have received little support through the diocesan structures. In the past week there was Biblical advice on leadership in a church, personal fellowship and encouragement; and people were concerned enough to pray for me without any preconditions![38]

'Such support,' Higton comments, 'is provided regularly to leaders within the house churches, not least through the apostolic ministry.'[39]

The same writer went on to outline a number of other key roles of the New Testament apostle which are also evidenced by their modern counterparts in the new churches. The following are particularly relevant in the present context. The apostle 'sees the overall picture and strategy of church building' (planting!). He also offers an objective assessment of a local church's condition (see 1 Thess 3:10). The apostle deals with disciplinary matters. He is responsible for a network of local churches and he 'breaks new ground with the gospel'.[40] All too often it happens that the church's bishops or district chairmen or area superintendents are bogged down with circuit administration or oiling the diocesan machine so that there is little time for the primary task of caring for the local church leaders. When did a bishop last call round on each of his clergy to check out any particular needs, to give some advice and pray with his local leadership? When did an area superintendent or rural dean last make a telephone call and pray with his fellow clergy or ministers?

In the last analysis of course it's not the office which is

important but the ministry. As Dave Tomlinson so clearly saw even in his days with Bryn Jones, 'terms such as apostle, prophet and teacher are job descriptions, not titles or symbols of status'.[41] The popularity and growing influence of 'apostolic leaders' among Restoration charismatic and house church groups is witness to a felt need.

Charismatics have learned the need for and practised much higher levels of pastorally supportive leadership in the church in recent times. Bishop David Pytches for example pastored clergy and congregations from across the whole country by arranging for a number of years monthly Saturday teaching days at St Andrew's, Chorleywood. The church was often jam packed with 500 visitors for regular leadership training days on five or six occasions in a year. These training days have been continued by Barry Kissell and Mark Stibbe. Britain's largest annual Christian conference, Spring Harvest, which attracts upwards of 50,000 participants, is organised and run by the charismatic wing of the church. The New Wine conferences hosted by David and Mary Pytches and John Coles represents one of the largest summer conferences with teaching on many practical aspects of Christian living and ministry. Up to 800 churches were represented by their leaders and congregations in 1999, three quarters of which are Anglican. Charismatics are also prominent in organisations which are ministering to the needs of wider society. Both the director of Care Trust, Lyndon Bowring, and the Evangelical Alliance, Joel Edwards, are prominent leaders from the charismatic wing of the Church.

Apostolic Ministries

Terry Virgo wrote: 'Like Paul, the modern apostle will find he cannot work alone. As the work multiplies he will draw colleagues to his side. We have coined the phrase "apostolic team" .'[42] With the passing of the years, leaders like Terry Virgo and Gerald Coates have developed 'apostolic teams' to assist them in their work. In his leadership of Pioneer, for example, Gerald Coates has a team consisting of John and Christine Noble, Phil Vogel, Peter Lyne, Mike Pusey and a dozen or so others. Such groups have helped leaders and individuals at the local level to develop their own gifts and ministries. Indeed from the very outset, one of the major benefits the churches have received from the charismatic movement is the emphasis on every member ministry. In one of his early books, *Let My People Grow*, Michael Harper wrote, 'If the church is to grow, every member must be released to minister.' Working from Ephesians 4 verse 11 as his starting point he highlighted four key areas for development: the apostolic, the evangelistic, the pastoral and the didactic.[43]

This same emphasis has been a continuing emphasis in charismatic churches of every denomination. Tony and Patricia Higton launched 'Time Ministries International' in 1991. In its first four years of operation it resourced over five hundred churches. Its vision was a simple one: 'We wanted to encourage churches to be united in the vision of every member ministry and evangelism, based on corporate prayer.'

One of the most positive helps in developing every member ministry in the charismatic churches has been David Pytches' publication, *Come Holy Spirit*,[44] a handbook on learning how to minister in power. The book briefly outlines in turn each of the major ministries with suggestions on how to learn to use them. The book, wrote David Pytches, 'is not a rule book – more a set of guidelines offered to any who want basic material to adopt or adapt for teaching the local church to minister in power'.[45] The whole range of gifts are dealt with, including the prophetic and speaking gifts, the healing and helping gifts and miraculous signs. One major context for operating these gifts, he suggested, is at times of public worship. Another place in which to begin is the house or cell groups.

Women Too!

In the early days of the charismatic movement, women tended to play a subservient or secondary role in leadership and ministry. This was particularly the case in the R1 house churches which held to rigidly fundamentalist interpretations of the passages about women in Paul's first letter to the Corinthians and to Timothy. Stephen Waterton, a Restoration church member, asserted, 'God has placed men to be the head of households, to cover their wives and bring security to their home, ruling and reigning in situations and making decisions'.[46] In the early days of the Bradford Harvestime Church women wore head coverings in house groups as a sign that they were under their husbands' authority. It was reported that the women of the King's Church, Aldershot are attractive and outgoing, and that 'they willingly embrace the teaching on submission and seem to flourish under it'.[47] Andrew Walker observed that while women in the main were subservient and submissive, there were some who could persuade apostles and elders that they had a role to play. These were in the main 'women who have established careers'.[48] This suggests that the women who do not achieve a position of leadership in the new churches have to fight to gain recognition. It also suggests that there is still reluctance on the part of the male leadership to entertain the possibility of women in positions of authority.

Notwithstanding these instances, by and large it is true to say that charismatic churches have encouraged women to take active roles in developing their gifts and ministries. They have also come to take a growing part in the life and worship of all categories of charismatic churches. Faith Forster, for example, has become one of the prominent national leaders of the Ichthus Christian Fellowships in London. Two women, Maggie Ellis and Christine Noble, featured in the 1994 Pioneer Leadership Team.[49] The Bristol Christian Fellowship group of churches have recently produced a thoughtful study entitled *Women in Leadership – A Biblical View*.[50] Its author, John Osborne, endorsed by the whole leadership, writes:

> After careful thought we have come to believe a woman can take any leadership role in the church . . . scripture does not support the notion that a woman must be under male authority in exercising her ministry in the church.[51]

The document is clear that Scripture does teach that a husband is the head of his wife but believes 'different views are possible on how this is to be interpreted'.[52] In the Bristol Christian Fellowship Foundation Course it is clearly stated that 'scripture places no restraint whatever on the role or ministry a woman may exercise in the church today, including teaching and having ultimate responsibility for leading a church'.[53] Tony Higton, whose wife Patricia co-directed ABWON, wrote shortly before the first Church of England General Synod debate that he did 'not think scripture is quite so clear on the ordination of women as some Christian leaders do'.[54] He felt it was possible to argue that 'because of its unusual nature, 1 Timothy 2 verse 12 is a command for the Ephesian church rather than for every church'.[55]

I sense that we're beginning to see a gradual but growing recognition by charismatics that women have a role to play in the leadership of the church. My perception is that charismatic Anglicans were much more active supporters of the ordination of women than the evangelicals of the Proclamation Trust and Reform. There is a gradual but slow recognition of the role of women in Pioneer and Ichthus. On the other hand, the Vineyard churches, New Frontiers, Covenant Ministries and Salt and Light still seem to be strongly dominated by male leadership. There are still many charismatics who slavishly adhere to David Pawson's view that 'leadership is male'. If the Church is ever to reach the women of this nation, let alone the men, there needs to be a much fuller recognition of the underlying principle that in Christ there is neither 'male nor female'. Furthermore, that Christians are a 'priesthood of all believers' that is men *and* women.

Charismatic Leadership and Ministry under the Spotlight

Clearly the charismatic teaching about and practice of leadership and ministry has been a major factor in the success of their churches. The concern and dedication of many charismatic leaders has generated deep and growing fellowships where people are not afraid to bring things out into the open in a healthy way and to offer one another down to earth practical support.

It was Oliver Cromwell who once said, 'he could not abide so anti-Christian and divisive a thing as the distinction between clergy and laity'. Again, he declared: 'I had rather have a plain russet-coated captain, that knows what he fights for and lives what he knows, than what you call a gentleman, and is nothing else'. Very much in keeping with Cromwell's views, Bryan Wilson, the Oxford sociologist of religion, observed that in charismatic churches worship 'may be conducted just as effectively and more authentically without the service of priests or professional men'. He also noted that the effect of such leaders on the church organisation and activities as well as on the wider society was no less profound.[56] Charismatics have grasped that the late twentieth century is a rationalistic age in which 'priests' and ecclesiastics are regarded as belonging to an authoritarian and bygone era. The charismatic approach to leadership which has put the stress on the lay man and lay woman and every-member ministry has rightly caught the mood of the time and proved vitally effective.

All this is not to say that there haven't been problems and mishaps along the way. Clearly there have, as noted in the first part of this chapter. The early excesses of apostolic ministry need to be avoided, particularly the domineering and controlling aspects. In recent years there do appear to have been positive changes in emphasis. In the 1970s the talk was of 'submission' and 'coming under' apostolic covering. In the 1990s it was spoken of in terms of which leader or apostle the fellowship 'relates to'. Whereas in the early days the apostolic brethren visited the churches under them, nowadays they tend to be invited by the local leadership. The initiative and tune seems to come from the grass roots level rather than from the top.

People still speak of the damage done by some of the early Restoration leaders and there was plenty. Nevertheless, lessons have been largely learned and defective teaching and practice has for the most part been corrected. It needs to be recognised also that the leadership in other sections of the wider church has not been without its damaging aspects. Anglican clerics who deny the existence of a personal God and New Age sympathisers who occupy the pulpit in denominational churches have also given Christianity a very confused public image.

When I lived in Aberdeen, I once heard it said with cynicism that if the date of the sounding of the last trumpet were to be announced from heaven, the Church of Scotland would set up a committee to ensure that it was blown at the right time, in the proper manner and by a suitably qualified person. One of the positive spin-offs from the charismatic movement is that it has helped the church's leaders to free themselves from this stranglehold of committees. Too many positive visions and thoughtful forward plans have died a death at Parochial Church Councils and Circuit meetings. Many of the new churches, however, have steered away from a surfeit of open democratic meetings and set up small leadership teams to put their strategies into operation. This has proved its effectiveness and resulted in many charismatic denominational churches appointing eldership and pastoral helpers to assist the vicar or minister in their role.

Some of these churches developed what they termed 'shared leadership' and this produced other problems. There were instances where clergy relinquished too much to their assistant leaders and were then unable to regain full control. I witnessed this to some extent in my own parish in Cheltenham in the late 1980s. The same problem surfaced in a slightly different form in the church of St Michael-le-Belfrey in York under David Watson. David began by inviting a number of people to share the life of the rectory. They all had the run of the home with the exception of David's study which was sacrosanct and they operated on the basis of a common purse. David outlined three rules for communal living. First, everyone must support the ministry of the house. Second, everyone must support the children. Third, everyone must support one another 'expressing this by serving each other in practical and specific ways'.[57]

At one time there were no less than seven such community households in York. With the passing of time, however, these experiments in communal living began to collapse. It was realised that strong overall leadership was demanded but David was away too much on university missions and church teaching weekends. The other houses began to encounter problems. Some found they were ill-equipped to deal effectively with some of their more needy members.[58] A distinction needs to be drawn out between 'shared' leadership and 'delegated' leadership. The leader who delegates doesn't surrender his overall authority to others of his team. When Canon Michael Green was at St Aldate's Church, Oxford, he operated on this principle. He saw the different areas of the church's life and work as small circles, each with its own leader or co-ordinator. But all of these different areas or small circles were within a much larger circle of his overall authority. People who worked with him at St Aldate's, regardless of how much leeway they appeared to have, always acknowledged that he was the real leader. Tom Marshall, a ubiquitous New Zealander and charismatic, taught widely that churches are best run by elders but with one overall leader. That leader demonstrates his effectiveness by his ability to convey his vision to the group and his ability to motivate his core elders to help him effect or manage it.

I have the impression that charismatic churches are concerned to give adequate support to their paid leaders. Information received from questionnaires and personal interviews at the beginning of 2000 indicated a considerable diversity of salary. Whereas the standard Church of England clergyman's basic salary was £16,420, the minimum for an Elim Church minister was £18,500. A number of Salt and Light pastors received around £22,000 and Vineyard pastors above that figure. This must be one of the very positive aspects of the charismatic movement. Many church leaders are not able to give of their best in service because they are overly concerned about the financial needs of their family and making ends meet. This means that they may have to supplement their income by additional part-time work or spend their time writing begging letters to grant-making trusts.

Charismatic churches are much more aware of the need to train, equip and help their leaders. This is done by regular teaching days with speakers coming to lecture and organise seminars and discussion. In general terms, it would be true to say that the leaders of charismatic churches are more in tune with their surrounding culture and more involved with the community needs than their counterparts in other sections of the church. In short, the leadership of the charismatic churches is one of their major assets.

5

AUTHORITY AND PASTORAL CARE

One of the issues for which the charismatic movement became infamous in the later 1970s and early 1980s was shepherding. Shepherding is a system in which each member of a congregation is given another person by their church elders or leaders to give them Christian teaching and direction. The guidance aspect often includes every aspect of their daily living. It was put about that house church elders in particular were a sinister breed who wore sandals, sported bushy beards and kept tropical fish. It was rumoured that some of the more extreme of their number stood outside the supermarket entrances and checked out the baskets carried by members' wives. It was even reported to Dave Tomlinson that the elders of one particular fellowship required a duplicate front door key before allowing people into membership!

I personally encountered some specific instances in the first flush of enthusiasm for shepherding. Two students at Cirencester College of Agriculture in the early 1980s were invited to supper by their tutor. He was a member of the local Baptist church. They said: 'Would it be all right if we let you know tomorrow?' He replied, 'Fine.' They came to supper and he thought nothing more of it. The next term he asked them again. They said they would love to come but would it be all right if they confirmed the arrangement the next day. All was well and the students duly came. The lecturer was a trifle disconcerted by the incident, but on making a discreet enquiry he found that they had had to check out their socialising with their shepherds before committing themselves.[1]

Cheryl was a student at the college where I lecture. She obtained a first teaching post in the West Midlands, joined a Restoration fellowship and attended the course for prospective new members. She enjoyed the sessions and signed membership forms which included submission to the church's leaders. She subsequently became desperately unhappy in her job and wanted to move to another post. She put the matter to the elders but they said, no. The result was that she was forced to stay where she was. She had in fact surrendered her freedom to make her own decision. In later interviews I encountered individuals who had to submit their holiday plans, discuss their rent payments and electricity bills, and even reveal their romantic intentions. Some of these incidents are not without their moments of humour however. Simon, an eligible bachelor in his late twenties and with a prospering business behind him, arrived at a Covenant Ministries church in Bath. The elders took him on one side and said, 'Now while you're here, Simon, we should like you to feel free to take out any of the young women in the church.' In the words of his close friend: 'It was like giving a box of matches to a pyromaniac and telling him to get on and enjoy himself!'[2]

Stories of 'heavy shepherding' and the casualties resulting from them were commonplace in the mid 1980s and in fact still linger on to the present time in some places. Even allowing for exaggeration we are bound to acknowledge that such shepherding churches produced a high level of commitment, some of which has had very positive results in terms of evangelism and church planting. This is not to say however that there hasn't been a cost in terms of emotionally damaged, hurt and exploited people.

The Background to Authoritarianism

The shepherding movement emerged against a backcloth of extreme libertarianism in the mid 1960s. This was the time when traditional values were being challenged and generally accepted norms were being thrown to the winds. The caption lines on the cover of one issue of *Nova* magazine said it all:

I've taken the Pill
I've hoisted my skirts to my thighs
Dropped them to my ankles
Rebelled at University
Abused the American Embassy

Lived with two men
Married one –
Kept my identity
And frankly
I'm lost.

In England, *The Obscene Publications Act* of 1959 and *The Theatre Act* of 1968 more or less removed the last restraints on censorship. This soon led to increased immorality and permissiveness on stage, screen and ultimately in society. The 1960s saw the performance in London of the rock musical *Hair* with the tabloids reporting 'the nudity is stunning'. 1965 saw the abolition of the death penalty and 1967 witnessed *The Abortion Act* which cheapened the value set on human life. Nearly three million abortions took place in the first twenty years following the Act. The 1970s and 1980s saw the breakdown of marriage as a social institution. There was a steep rise of 11 per cent in the divorce rate in 1985. The number of one-parent families rose from 570,000 in 1971 to 940,000 in 1984.[3] The 1987 Conservative National Conference served only to reinforce this trend when a self-confessed adulterer was given a four and a half minute standing ovation on his return to government after a brief period on the sidelines. Twenty years previously, John Profumo, another government minister involved in a sex scandal, had resigned immediately and retired from public life altogether. Recent years had seen the continuing and steady rise of 'condomania' with the accompanying message to the nation that sex is the only reality. Alongside all of this there was a growing licence in the established churches with homosexual vicars banging their drums against a background of anti-credal liberal theology.

The most likely explanation for the sudden enthusiasm for authoritarianism on the part of some churches was as a reaction to this growing wave of lawlessness. As one widely influential charismatic teacher put it: 'People needed to belong, to be a part of something. There was a widespread cry for personal discipline; people hungered to get their lives together.'[4] Dr Haddon Willmer of Leeds University interpreted this 'enthusiasm for authoritative eldership'[5] in slightly broader terms. He regarded it as the religious form of 'conservative, security-seeking authority' which was sweeping through Britain and North America in the early Thatcherite years.[6]

But however we regard it, the fact is that the charismatic movement attracted 'a disproportionate number of young adults into its ranks'. Here were people who lacked self-direction and were looking for a strong source of authority to provide a solid basis for their daily living.[7] Whatever the origin of this rigorous pastoral care, the fact remains that it has become a significant part of the charismatic story. It was adopted with most enthusiasm in the so-called house churches but it also found a place among Anglicans, Baptists and Roman Catholics.

The Origins of the Shepherding Movement

The beginnings of the doctrines which underlay the shepherding movement are traceable to two individuals in particular, Watchman Nee and Juan Carlos Ortiz. Watchman Nee was a Chinese Christian who taught a system of answerability in the 1920s and 1930s. His books, particularly his devotional volumes, are still prized and read in charismatic circles. In *The Body of Christ* Nee taught complete submission to God's ordained authority in the church.[8] He declared that 'to reject delegated authority is an affront to God'.[9] Nee even ventured the view that Christians who were unwilling to submit their lives to God's ordained leaders would be separated from Christ.[10] Their lack of submission, he maintained, was evidence that their union with Jesus was a sham. They would be cut off from the body of Christ because they had failed to be committed to its head.[11]

It was Carlos Ortiz, an Argentinian Christian, who pioneered the teaching of 'covering' of 'shepherding'. He wrote in his much read book, *Call to Discipleship*, of the need to 'control your disciples'. He described a disciple as 'one who obeys commands'.[12]

This teaching was as music to the ears of the 'Fort Lauderdale Five', Bob Mumford, Charles Simpson, Derek Prince, Don Basham (1926–1989) and Ern Baxter.[13] Andrew Walker has clearly outlined how these 'independent American Pentecostals, Bob Mumford and his associates, were big hits with British Restorationists during the years 1975 and 1976'.[14] Ern Baxter was greeted with rapturous stampeding applause at the Harvestime Dales Bible Week in 1976, and others of the Fort Lauderdale brothers addressed differing strands of the house churches. A large and similar style conference was held at the Exeter Showground with 2,000–3,000 people present. Mostly they were those who were 'relating to' Barney Coombs. During the main meetings the biblical basis of shepherding was outlined. The foundational material was drawn from the book of Exodus. Moses' father-in-law impressed upon him that the people were too many for him to handle. Moses eventually broke them down into companies of hundreds, fifties and tens. In this way everybody came to have a shepherd.

It is the placing of each individual member of the people of God under one man and accountable to that one man which became known as 'shepherding'. Different charismatic teachers and leaders both in the new churches and, in some cases, in the established churches, adopted and refined this basic idea. For example, in 1980, Dave Tomlinson, who was then part of the Harvestime leadership team, set out the biblical principles as he understood them. Discipling, he wrote, requires 'a level of personal involvement such as we see in the life of Paul'.[15] For three years the apostle never ceased 'to admonish, advise and exhort' the Christians at Ephesus.[16] 'That,' wrote Tomlinson, 'is discipling!'[17] Moving on to look at Paul's words to Philemon, Tomlinson noted the distinction between 'advising' and 'ordering'. Although Paul would rather always appeal on the basis of love, the fact remains 'that he did claim the right "to order" another brother' (Philem 8). Tomlinson added weight to this view by quoting Paul's instruction to believers 'to obey and submit to those over them in the Lord' (1 Thess 5:12; 1 Cor 16:15–16; Heb 13:17).[18]

Although some sections of the shepherding movement were demanding absolute obedience of individuals in their charge, Tomlinson did put in some qualification. 'No leader can rightly expect obedience if that obedience contradicts the revealed Word of God.' 'This aside however,' he wrote, 'we cannot avoid facing up to the apostle's statement, "obey your leaders and submit to their authority".'[19]

'Will church leaders tell me what to do?' is one of the questions on a commitment course used by some of the King's Churches. To which the answer is 'when necessary, yes'.[20] The paragraph which follows draws a parallel between a father and a young child and new Christians and their shepherd. Just as a father gives a three-year-old plenty of directive input, says the pamphlet, 'so in the church the new-born babe is helped in the formative stages by being led quite decisively by a godly under-shepherd'.[21]

Some speak positively of their experience of being shep-herded. Brian and Anne Murgatroyd who were in membership with Salt and Light churches in Witney and Cirencester for a number of years look back on their shepherds with gratitude. Brian commented: 'It was almost like a propagator. It really grew you quickly.' They emphasised that submission to the elders as they experienced it was 'a purely voluntary thing'. Nevertheless there was a tacit assumption that you would do it. They recalled, 'you submitted the whole of your life'. This meant you were then asked to account for how you had done. Help of a very practical kind was often given. 'If you couldn't pay your electricity bill you went to your shepherd and you said "there's no way I can pay my electricity bill . . .".' The money would be provided without strings but 'they would expect bet-ter management next time round'. Holidays were submitted for approval. Brian recalled: 'If you were going to go on holiday you would say, "Look I'm going to go on holiday." If you were very timid you would say "Would it be all right if I went on hol-iday?"' Courting was another area which was 'very tightly con-trolled' with a 'big heavy hand'. If you wanted to go out with a young lady you asked. 'You didn't go alone, you were chaper-oned not by your shepherd but by another from the young peo-ple's group who would be organised for you.'[22]

The shepherding system in the Salt and Light churches under Barney Coombs was well organised. Normally each shepherd had about ten people. Fifteen was a maximum. The demands on shepherds were quite high as they were encour-aged to try and make contact with each one of their charges at least once a fortnight. Keith Fyleman who shepherded in the Stroud Community Church also looked back on the system as being well organised and positive in its effects.[23] Sissel Harrison however recalls that shepherding in Salt and Light was 'unhealthily tight' in the early 1980s. 'It got very prying into pri-vate areas.' Buying cars and almost any major expenditure had to be submitted to the shepherds. 'I felt it was almost reaching the stage,' she says, 'where if I wanted to buy knickers from Marks and Spencers I had to ask!' Looking back on it all now she is of the opinion that 'the whole thing so very nearly went over the top'. But by the grace of God they were spared because in the nick of time Barney Coombs saw the dangers and the authoritarian screws were lifted.[24]

The shepherding pattern in Bryn Jones' Covenant churches presents a rather more varied pattern. Generally speaking, there was a much tighter system in the northern fellowships which were closer to the Bradford headquarters. Here there was 'rigid shepherding' and closed communities. Further south in affiliated centres like Bath, Newent and South Wales there was a generally looser system with house groups usually pastored by married couples.[25]

At Bryn's Bradford church, for example, ex-member Julie Bradford was subjected to 'heavy psychological pressure' by shepherds. They would ring up and tell her she was unloving and unsubmissive and that she was a bad wife. In the end the pressurised regime of fear to which she was subjected led to the loss of her baby.[26] Doris Fellows who had been part of the Yeovil Fellowship reported that leaders' advice intruded into every area of their private lives, their homes, their finances, and in the end their married life. 'Everything in married life,' she recalled, 'was dealt with, if it was a problem, sexual or whatever.'[27]

Others of the apostolic men were into 'discipling' rather than 'shepherding'. In practice, however, there was often little to choose between the two. Disciplers tended not to have specifically appointed individuals to oversee particular people whereas the shepherding movement did. Maurice Smith recalls that John Noble with his Team Spirit was 'very strong on discipling' as was Gerald Coates. The 'shepherding' system was more intense than discipling. In 'shepherding', individuals were often seen on a one to one basis. Not only were their personal and private lives reviewed, notes were often made afterwards and passed up to the area leaders. In discipling, it was more a case of house group leaders being instructed to keep a firm hand on the people placed in their groups. Clear guidelines were laid down about such things as relationships, spending and tithing into the church. Individual counselling on a one to one basis didn't feature in the same way.

Terry Virgo's New Frontiers churches were possibly more easy going about discipling. Donna Woodman who was part of Virgo's Clarendon outfit recalls only relaxed friendly house groups such as one would find these days in almost any evangelical church.[28] Virgo himself wrote 'People are happy to join churches where there is a sense of involvement which includes genuine discipleship with plenty of checks and balances to safeguard from error and excess.'

Instances of shepherding featured in Noel Stanton's Jesus Fellowship/Jesus Army. In 1974, during a time at Ashburnam in Sussex, a number of small groups were formed and new leaders were commissioned by laying on of hands.[29] A 'senior brother' was to be supported by two others who were given pastoral responsibility. Groups of about ten 'sheep' were placed in the care of one 'shepherd'. This all-male membership was publicly recognised and on occasion proved to be quite authoritarian. Permission was needed to leave the premises. Celibacy is actively encouraged. According to Katz in 1991, 'around half the single members have taken vows of celibacy'.[30] Writing in 1995, MacDonald-Smith suggested that 'about a quarter of the members, including Noel Stanton, had made a lifelong vow'.[31] The Jesus Fellowship themselves attach value to both marriage and celibacy. Both are seen as callings from God. Families are needed to 'provide the essential base of homeliness and security'. Celibates on the other hand, are free to engage in pioneering and evangelistic work. If a fellow 'fancies' one of the young ladies of the community, the leaders approach her to find out whether her feelings are reciprocal. In fact, in the early days, permission had to be asked before engaging in quite a number of activities.[32] Those joining the community are actively encouraged to commit themselves to it for life. The Jesus Fellowship Covenant includes the following declaration: 'My desire is that for all my earthly life I shall be a Covenant Member of this Church and a soldier in the modern Jesus army'.[33] Mrs L. Mackinney who lived for some months in one of the community houses felt strong pressure to remain in the movement.[34] My own view is that in more recent times the atmosphere is much more relaxed and members can disengage relatively easily.

Dangers of Shepherding

Shepherding[35] was and is always going to be a system with potential for abuse.[36] In the hands of wise and good leaders, people clearly flourished, learned quickly and matured. Often, however, particularly at the local level, the shepherding system attracted individuals who lacked any previous experience of being responsible for others. For some it was their first taste of power and, in the words of Moriarty, it led to them becoming 'the power abusers'.[37]

One of the most immediate problems is that under close-knit 'shepherding', individuals did not find the opportunity to learn to hear God for themselves or to make their own mistakes. Only with a reasonable degree of latitude is it possible for a person to mature. 'Wally' North was one of the few house church leaders, along with Sid Purse of Chard, who at an early point saw the dangers of the movement. In 1980 North wrote:

> Personal responsibility to make decisions before God is both a basic freedom and a basic necessity in the churches. To rob a man of that in the name of eldership is abuse of office.[38]

He spelt the matter out in more precise detail. 'Eldership,' he insisted, 'does not involve organisation of people's private lives, disposal of their properties, direction of families and control of individual's finances.'[39]

Submission, as North and others were aware, cannot be forced. Where the attempt is made, 'submission' becomes 'subversion' and will result, in North's words, 'in submersion'.[40] Hebrews 13 verse 17 urges believers to obey leaders and submit to their authority. This does not however give a mandate to make obedience obligatory or to enforce it by excommunication procedures. There is a clear difference between ordering and advising.

Perhaps one of the greatest dangers of 'shepherding' is that is makes congregations more dependent on their leaders rather than more responsible as individual Christians before God. One of the techniques employed by cults, or New Religious Movements as they are frequently termed, is to create 'leader dependency'. Once this reaches a certain point, members begin to feel that they cannot do without their leader. It is then only a short step for the leader to assume total control of the individual or movement and a new cult will have been birthed. This same phenomenon has been observed in the life of some monastic communities. Members are only allowed to confide personal problems with the abbot or mother superior, not with their fellow monks or nuns. For that reason they sometimes come to be totally dependent on their order and unable to make their own decisions even in the most trivial domestic matters.

'Shepherding' has also meant that erroneous doctrines and other wrong emphases are unlikely to be challenged. There was, in general terms, in the early days of the house churches a downward chain of command. As in the army it was considered out of order to question a higher authority. If Martin Luther had subscribed to this view of authority he would never have challenged the Pope!

A less obvious danger inherent in the shepherding procedures is that of substituting the system for God himself. Nigel Wright helpfully drew a parallel with the introduction of kingship to the people of Israel under Samuel. 'We need to be careful,' he suggested, 'that in setting up men as authorities and powerful figures we are not thereby rejecting God who desires to rule directly over his people.'[41]

There can also be a tendency towards party spirit and competitiveness. A question which is still common among newer churches is whose, i.e. which leader's, 'covering' are you under? Despite generally good relationships between the 'apostolic men' there has often been a good deal of rivalry at the local level. For example, there was strong contention between John MacLaughlan and John Noble as to which of them was 'covering' the fellowship in Yeovil.[42] In the last analysis, the churches, and their leaders in particular, must take the words of Jesus about servant ministry seriously. He urged his apostolic group 'not to lord it over' those in their charge (Lk 22:25–26) but to serve them.

A Loosening of Attitudes

With growing criticism being voiced in the Christian press and at public meetings the brakes were applied to the teaching on shepherding and pastoral care. This loosening up was particularly apparent among the Restoration house churches. There were hints that change was in the air in the early 1980s. For example, in Salt and Light fellowships periodically they would withdraw shepherding maybe for a week or for a fortnight. In the words of one member, 'It sounds childish but it wasn't . . . it was, OK folks, go and do it yourself. Stop leaning on us.'[43] About this time the requirement that the ladies who had had to wear head coverings as a sign that they were being covered by male authority was lifted.

For Salt and Light churches things came to a head in 1982. Present members still recall 'Barney' arriving at a Sunday meeting and saying, 'Right folks, today we stop.'[44] It was just as simple as that. 'It was very radical teaching to us. It said, do you know you're allowed to hear God for yourself!' The teaching was no longer that people were on a journey relating upwards through their shepherds but a journey along with God speaking directly into the situation rather than through the shepherd. It was also in 1982 that Dave Tomlinson severed his contacts with Bryn Jones over the shepherding issue. It is not altogether clear why this sudden change in shepherding policy took place at this point. Possibly there was an order from the Fort Lauderdale group who had been so influential in the mid-1970s. Certainly the group parted company in the mid-1980s.[45] But by this point the damage in England had already been done. The question of discipleship, as Andrew Walker has shown, had already proved the crunch issue. Indeed Walker wrote that if R1 had not insisted so rigidly on discipleship there would have been no R2. The fact was, however, that Dave Tomlinson, John Noble and Gerald Coates could no longer 'relate' to men like Bryn Jones and Barney Coombs on the matter.

To his credit, in November 1989, Bob Mumford, one of the so-called 'famous five', issued a public statement concerning discipleship which was circulated both in America and among church leaders in England. He also published a statement in *Christianity Today*[46] in which he apologised 'to anyone who was hurt by leaders who were oppressive or authoritarian or even self-aggrandising, and who justified their practices with my teaching and my name'.[47] Mumford's circular revealed both his sadness and his humility. He wrote of having 'offended the

Lord himself' and went on to repent of the consequences of his teaching:

> Accountability, personal training under the guidance of another and effective pastoral care are needed biblical concepts . . . These biblical realities must also carry the limits indicated by the New Testament. However, to my personal pain and chagrin, these particular emphases very easily lent themselves to an unhealthy submission resulting in perverse and unbiblical obedience to human leaders. Many of these abuses occurred within the spheres of my own responsibility. For the injury and shame caused to people, families and the larger body of Christ, I repent with sorrow and ask your forgiveness.[48]

Committed Church Membership

The term 'shepherding' is no longer in use in the vast majority of charismatic churches. The practice has been largely replaced by a modified procedure known as 'covering'. 'Covering' also indicates spiritual protection. It's more than a church having a respected person over them, it is seen as the means by which God preserves that congregation from evil and harm. People joining a fellowship for the first time follow an introductory course and then sign their commitment to the particular church concerned. They are then under the 'covering' or perhaps, better, 'authority' of that particular church or leadership. The main difference in emphasis between shepherding and committed membership is in the focus of the commitment. In shepherding, commitment was to the leadership and to individual pastoral advisors. In committed membership commitment is to the whole church, leaders and other members together.

Some typical instances of what committed membership means in practice can readily be seen in the Ichthus and King's churches and in the Bristol Christian Fellowship cluster which now relate to Pioneer. Forster wrote of their determination at Ichthus 'to commit ourselves to one another and share our lives as fully as we could'.[49] A particular aspect of this was 'a determination to avoid rampant backbiting and mistrust, so we simply made a commitment to love one another and to build relationships of trust and forgiveness'.[50] At the King's Church in

Aldershot led by a former lawyer, Derek Brown, potential members were taken through a course entitled Committed for Life. Derek's view is that when sheep come in through the door they need to feel secure in the church. 'They do,' he says, 'thanks to the commitment course.'[51] At the Bristol Christian Fellowship there is a Foundation Course.[52] The section on membership urges that 'all members are expected to be committed to one another, to love and serve one another and to mutually care for one another'. There is a section on pastoral care which states that prospective members must be willing to 'make ourselves accountable in areas of need'.[53] There is also mention in the same paragraphs of 'shepherds' and the need 'to be open and teachable'.[54] However, there is no suggestion that individuals are expected to give unquestioning obedience.

In the 1980s, Tony Higton, Vicar of Hawkwell in Essex and a local member of the Church of England's General Synod emerged as a leading exponent of the 'committed membership' principle within the Church of England. Tony's Association for Biblical Witness to Our Nation (ABWON) had at one point more than 1,000 affiliated churches. A major way by which the movement sought to achieve its end or goal was by restoring the churches 'to biblical principles and structure'.[55] This involved establishing an authoritative leadership and a committed membership.

The ABWON committed membership style emerged out of their Committed Membership course. This was followed by as many of the congregation as were willing. At the completion of the course, members were asked to commit themselves to the vision of the church, including a willingness to serve God within it. When the church council or its equivalent was appointed, it was suggested that only committed members be encouraged to stand for office.

There were a number of Church of England churches who established a committed membership by these means. In most cases this took place without serious friction resulting although, for example, there was a lengthy fracas at St Silas, Cheltenham, over the matter. The nub of the problem was that the vicar introduced a commitment course. No one was allowed to hold any official position from Sunday School teacher to PCC member unless they had completed this and made an open commitment to the church. This procedure was clearly out of keeping with the Church of England and the Bishop of Gloucester at the time, John Yates, had to be brought in to mediate in what became a fairly intense dispute. Committed membership brings with it some real and positive benefits. The most significant is that a membership develops which is not only active in service but which shows much greater concern for holiness, prayer and Christian living. Some difficulties have also surfaced. Often an ecclesiola or mini church within a church, develops. This can develop into a kind of spiritual elite and result in tension and conflict. Some feel that individuals should be committed to God alone and that there is a danger of people becoming enslaved to human rules and regulations. Others have maintained on the basis of parables such as the wheat and the weeds that compromise will always be a feature of church life.

Covenant Relationships

An important aspect of committed church membership is making a covenant. Andrew Walker likened the covenant to a Red Indian pact made between tribes in North America. Bryn Jones in his book *Joined in Covenant* likened 'covenant' to marriage. 'Covenant,' he wrote, 'demands that we don't quit on each other.' He also asked the question 'If we were to quit easily on covenant, how many women would walk out on their husbands?' The same commitment he urged must hold good within the church.[56] In the words of Ron Trudinger of Salt and Light, 'true church membership is a covenant relationship'.[57] He went on to state that when a person becomes a member of a fellowship they not only bind themselves to God, they have also 'made a compact in the sight of God with that body'. Keeping covenant or being faithful to one's word is regarded as very important indeed. Trudinger instances a testimony given by someone before their baptism at Basingstoke Baptist Church. His word was 'outstanding in terms of what he had entered into' with regard to co-operation with leadership, obedience (i.e. true covenant membership of the body) and the Lordship of Christ.[58] Yet only a year later this man began to defect and later broke covenant. 'The last I heard,' Trudinger recalled, 'he was trying to commit suicide.'[59] Clearly the full circumstances of this incident may never be known. It does appear however that this particular man had possibly been allowed, albeit voluntarily, to place himself under too much psychological pressure. Trudinger doubtless wanted to warn people of the dangers of breaking covenant with God. Nevertheless, the incident also has overtones of emotional blackmail. 'Woe betide any other reader who breaks the covenant with his church!'

The beginning of these covenant relationships goes back to the Fort Lauderdale group in America who pledged themselves to support one another. One of their number, Don Basham, printed and circulated a decorative sheet entitled *Covenant Community*. It stated the following:

> A covenant community . . . is a community of God's redeemed people bound together in covenant love, submitted to compassionate authority and rulership . . . A community where loving correction and instruction produces healthy growth and maturity . . .[60]

A year to two after this there was a gathering of some of the Restoration leaders from churches in England, Canada and the USA for a 'covenant conference'. The crowning point of this holy pow wow was a Communion service lasting several hours. Each leader present 're-expressed and renewed his personal covenant with each other man there. It was a "till death us do part" pact which the brothers believed would be unbroken by geographical separation or any other factor'.[61]

This was a very high degree of commitment. It seems to be the explanation as to why Bryn Jones stood so vehemently behind Dave Mansell when his private life 'was not totally glorifying to the gospel'.[62] In short, he had been 'womanising' and it was not just one isolated slip. Although Andrew Walker suggested that the split in the Restoration house churches occurred over discipling and lifestyle issues,[63] the crunch seems to have been Bryn Jones' unwillingness to discipline Mansell for his moral lapses. In fact Mansell, who Maurice Smith described as 'a barrow load of monkeys', meaning he was always into some mischief, subsequently became a prominent member of the Covenant Ministries leadership team though he did not reach 'apostolic' status.

Shepherding – the Good and the Bad

Perhaps the biggest downside of shepherding occurs in the area of power abuse. Indeed the word 'spiritual abuse' has gained common currency in the United States as a result of so many individuals controlling others in unhealthy and emotionally damaging ways. Since the time in the 1960s when Jim Jones persuaded more than 900 of his followers to exterminate themselves by drinking Koolade laced with cyanide there has been a steady stream of autocratic leaders right down to David Koresh and his Branch Davidian tragedy at Waco in 1993. It is true to say that the authoritarianism and domination of some charismatic leaders is not far removed from control exercised by some of these cultic leaders. Many charismatic Christians, and particularly those from newer fellowships, have a hefty involvement in church activities. Often these people have no real friends outside religious circles. They are therefore trapped within a very confined community with the result that their horizons and perspectives are limited. In fact, they have no individual purpose in life. Their whole life is bound up with the vision of the group. Their early joy and freedom have been substituted by structures and strategies.

Dave Tomlinson who joined the Church of England after severing his links with Bryn Jones' Covenant Ministries, contributed an essay to Andrew Walker's book, *Harmful Religion*, entitled 'Shepherding: Care or Control?'. He made the point that 'the line between care and control, between service and exploitation, is extremely thin and the time to start worrying is when we have convinced ourselves that we are safely ensconced on the right side of that line'.[64] He further urged that all in positions of leadership 'never tire of searching our hearts and motives' because 'shepherding in some form crouches at the door'. In his chapter, Tomlinson pointed out that women have frequently been the victims of abuse resulting from charismatic shepherding, counselling and control. He cited the example of Sonia who worked in the City of London and was well accustomed to holding her own in a male-dominated work environment. On one occasion she spoke her mind to the church leaders. One day Tom, her husband, was taken aside by his shepherd and informed he was 'good leadership material'.

However, there was a problem; he had to bring his wife into 'proper submission' if he wanted to advance in the church. Like a fool he attempted to follow this advice and his relationship with Sonia quickly took a nose-dive. Two years of painful conflict ensued, during which time Sonia was variously told she was 'rebellious', possessed of 'the spirit of Jezebel' and 'living in disobedience to Scripture'. 'Given the circumstances,' Tomlinson wrote, 'it would have been a miracle if their marriage survived'.[65]

Instances of excessively 'heavy shepherding' even in Restoration charismatic churches were probably not frequent in the 1990s. Where they did and do occur, the victims are often afraid to speak out. There seems to be a latent fear either of reprisals from the leadership or that God will mete out Ananias and Sapphira style reprisals on them for their disloyalty.

One instance which I encountered in the 1990s concerned the Havering Christian Fellowship in Hornchurch, a town in which I lived myself for a while. The leaders of this congregation exerted a control which was extended into every aspect of members' lives. This ranged from the choice of a marriage partner to the area where they should live. Total submission was required and failure to obey the leaders produced dire consequences.

A young lady, who wishes to have her identity protected, gave details of her five-and-a-half-year involvement. She eventually became a member of the 'elite' on the pastoral team and discipled and shepherded other young girls, bringing them words of prophecy, guidance and instruction. She submitted written weekly reports on those she cared for to the leaders. 'Non-conformism was not tolerated. If you did not believe and act as the leaders did you were going against God. If the leader said "dance" you danced.' This kind of unsubtle control was accepted as it was believed to be God's will.

At one point she became so desperate to have some time alone with her husband that she requested to have one evening free of church commitments. She vividly recalls, 'I was rebuked for being insolent and answering back. I was treated like a child.' Later she was removed from the church's pastoral team for three months for talking to her brother-in-law after he and his wife were expelled from the fellowship. She had to publicly repent and confess her wrongdoings to the pastoral team before being re-admitted. Earlier, her marriage had been carried out under the authority and direction of the pastoral team. It was reported to me that her family (themselves charismatic Christians) had tried to remove her from the influences of the fellowship. She was forcibly brought back to the fellowship and issued with an ultimatum that she married the young man showing interest towards her. She was twenty-two at this stage and had never had a relationship with anyone before. The fellowship threatened an 'injunction' on the girl's father for abducting her from the fellowship. Not wanting to implicate her family she remained with church members, talking only to those the fellowship permitted. She married one week later. Her family contacted the police to ascertain her whereabouts and were informed she was on honeymoon! Within this fellowship elders and shepherds pried into every detail of the members' lives including sexual matters. They even on occasion intercepted and censored mail.[66]

I have highlighted this particular area at some length because it so clearly shows the darker side of pastoral care that can occur in Restoration and other charismatic fellowships. There was a pyramidal structure which allowed only a downward chain of command and permitted no questioning or dialogue.

Indeed, to question the system was designated as insolence. As Joyce Thurman in her early study of the house church movement observed, 'To rebel against the leaders was to rebel against God.' The incident recounted above amounts to an almost cultic degree of submission. It reveals a system which scrutinises people's lives and occupies their time to a point where there is no room for private thoughts, personal space or private living. The hazard warning lights are clearly flashing with great intensity at this point. There are important lessons which must be drawn from this incident and others like it. Those in authority need to be made accountable for the way they handle their charges. Most important, great care must be taken that people's basic freedom of opinion, movement and choice are not taken from them.

The Dangers of Church Pastors

The dangers of church pastors and leaders having no accountability was graphically highlighted by the case of Chris Brain (b 1957) who led The Nine O'Clock Service (NOS) which was closed down in 1995. Most of the justifiably savage attacks by church press and Christian leaders damned Brain's charismatic experience and rave services, but the real villain of the piece was the complete lack of accountability.

Mark Stibbe, who was curate at St Thomas Crookes between 1990 and 1993, stated that 'it would be fair to say that accountability was not the first characteristic of the NOS leadership'.[67] He continued, 'In spite of strenuous efforts by Canon Robert Warren between 1991 and 1992, it would be fair to say, we never really succeeded in bringing the NOS leaders into line with the overall leadership of St Thomas''.[68] When the NOS finally left St Thomas Crookes in 1992 it was apparently not because they had become too big for St Thomas's but rather, in the words of one staff member, 'they had become too big for their boots'.

On their move to Pond's Forge, a major conference centre in the centre of Sheffield, the Bishop of Sheffield, the Rt Revd David Lunn, took overall responsibility for NOS making it an independent parochial place. After a short period he gave complete charge to his Archdeacon, Stephen Lowe. In October, 1994, Lowe informed the congregation who were attending a planetary mass that he had originally been instructed by the bishop 'to police them', but that he saw no need for it.[69]

To the general public, NOS life and worship seemed a thriving spiritual concern, but beneath the surface all was far from well. Brain was living in style in a Victorian town house with an upmarket interior design with no expenses spared. He invariably wore designer clothes and ate at restaurants several days a week. In 1994 he was given a £200,000 farmhouse in the Pennines by two members of the congregation. Its features included a stainless steel spiral staircase and televisions suspended from the ceilings of several rooms. It later emerged that approximately 25 per cent of all the congregation's donations went into Brain's personal account. Some of this was used by Brain and his team to take a £23,000 holiday in the Canaries.

In addition to his extravagant lifestyle, Brain experimented with what he described as post-modern non-genital sex in which the boundaries between friendship, sex and romance became totally blurred. Sarah Collins summed up the feelings of many of the victims when she said: 'All the stuff about sexual ethics was just clever language; basically it was about one bloke getting his rocks off with forty women.'[70] One of the arenas in which this took place was in the 'home base team', a small group of 'post-modern nuns' initiated by Brain. They dressed in black lycra and mini skirts and their duties included massaging Chris and, on occasion, putting him to bed. On top of all this Brain frequently crushed and humiliated his leadership team and inner corps helpers with violent and abusive language.

While all this was emerging, nobody kept tabs on his leadership. The diocesan authorities were so impressed with the success of the NOS Sunday worship that he was given a fast track to ordination in 1991. Chris himself later commented: 'It seems utterly ridiculous that I was made a priest. I had stood there with a group of other ordination candidates and thought, "What am I doing here?" It changed everything. Everyone became dependent on me'.[71]

Tragically, the Archdeacon and the Bishop of Sheffield, Professor John Rogerson, Head of Biblical Studies at Sheffield University and scores of other senior clergy and theologians endorsed Brain's ministry at a time when he needed to be brought to book and held accountable for his abusive and disreputable behaviour.

The Dangers of Becoming a Cult

It has been said with justification that the greater the degree of control which is exercised the more insecure is the leadership. For others, leadership of one of the new charismatic churches has given them their first experience of spiritual power. Once leaders develop a taste for power there is always the danger that it will corrupt. There will be the temptation to misuse power for sexual, financial or other forms of gain which will be too great to resist. A number of groups who have been led by individuals who have been part of the charismatic renewal have become cultic. This means the leaders have adopted a God-like, dictator status. They have used manipulative persuasion techniques, taken absolute control over their followers and separated them from the world. Some obvious examples are the Jonestown Community led by Jim Jones, Chris Brain's Nine O'Clock Service and 'The Family' founded by David Berg. Although this latter movement originated in America, it is active in this country. David Berg (1919–1994) began life as an evangelical charismatic preacher in the Jesus Revolution of the 1960s. He established a small community calling themselves 'Teens for Christ'. Later, however he took total control styling himself 'Moses David' or 'Dad'. His movement became known as the 'Children of God' but was subsequently renamed 'The Family'. It was then that Berg demanded that all the sisters, married or single, were the property of any man in the community. They could be visited without right of refusal for sexual intercourse. Berg went even further. He introduced his 'Flirty Fishing' (ff) edict by which the women in his communities were expected to offer sex to interested men as a way of drawing them into the movement and to faith in Christ. A 1994 television documentary showed small groups 'dressed for the kill' and ready for a night of steamy evangelism. One of them clad in a revealing dress, seduced her subjects with 'hot tongues'. Berg communicated with his followers by means of Mo letters. 'Mo' was short for Moses and indicated his messianic status. Although these and other Children of God tracts were punctuated with biblical references, orthodox Christians found them blasphemous in the extreme.

Some people have observed that the charismatic renewal experience has a tendency to give birth to cultic groups such as Waco or the Solar Temple. The danger, however, lies not in the experience but rather in the lack of proper accountability. Cults can in fact be high in religious experience or lack it all together. It is in fact the degree of the leader's control over his following which results in the group becoming a cult. The more the membership's time and energy is monopolised, the more dependent they become on the leadership and the group. Eventually they reach a point where the movement is everything and, because they are totally reliant on their leader (who may by this time be 'God' or the 'Messiah'), they are prepared to do whatever she/he asks. After all if she/he's God, she/he must be right.

It is at this point that many churches or communities have the potential to become 'cultic'. It is vital that charismatic churches, especially those which are independent of any form of oversight or relational links with umbrella organisations, keep open to the outside world and allow their members the space to move and the freedom to question and discuss matters. They should also know how the church's money is spent and what their leaders are paid. It is significant that many of the small cults which are known to form began as small independent charismatic fellowships.

When all of this has been said, the fact that people abuse their pastoral roles and turn pastoral care into a form of religious terrorism is no reason to give up on it. People do need some kind of guidance and structure for their living. Provided this is done in a gentle manner with proper forms of answerability and supervision, it could enhance the effectiveness of the churches' pastoral care in the future. It has been said with a certain amount of justification that the measure of a person's commitment to Christ is their commitment to his people. Clearly the New Testament indicates that a commitment to Christ, the Head of the Church, involves some form of commitment to the members which are his body. Nevertheless such a commitment or submission is to be voluntary and not a legal bondage (Gal 5:1). In addition, obedience to any authority is relative. Christians are only bound in absolute obedience to Christ. New Testament obedience is always 'in the Lord'. In the last analysis it must be remembered that the church is called to make disciples of all men. Furthermore, the New Testament picture seems to be that elders oversaw churches (1 Tim 3:5) in general rather than the lives of particular individuals in those churches. It seems to have been only major matters such as immorality which were dealt with on a personal basis (Mt 18:17 and 1 Cor 5:2).

Having made these points, it is clear that discipline is an integral part of Christian discipleship. The very word disciple implies it. A disciple is one who lives under 'discipline'. Charismatic churches have made strong endeavours to try to restore this essential ingredient to the church's life. Everybody knows that the Church of England warns in its prayer books of 'the dangers of this naughty world' and that there is an instruction to repel 'notorious evil livers from the communion table'. One rarely hears however of either matter being taken seriously. In fact, when the future head of the established church admitted to marital unfaithfulness,[72] who among the church's bishops publicly stood out against it? The Church of England report on the charismatic movement was spot on target when it stated 'The Church of England appears almost indifferent to the ordering of spiritual oversight'.[73]

It is undoubtedly true that in general terms the charismatic churches have a much higher level of commitment to one another among their members. They also value and support their leaders in a greater and more wholehearted way than is the case in the majority of the historic churches. Furthermore, they provide a higher level of instruction and correction to their people. Perhaps it is for this reason that many of their fellowships are growing rapidly and reaching out into their local communities in significant ways including schools, youth initiatives and homeless projects.

Among the denominational churches which have been influenced by the charismatic movement there is also a general perception of a much closer sense of fellowship and mutual caring. The Reverend John Williams, for example, did a small research project which illustrates the point well enough. He studied the influence of the charismatic renewal on six parishes near London of varied churchmanship and in contrasting social areas. He found several common threads, one of which was a new sense of care and support. He wrote: 'From the corporate point of view, church members seem to have a new sense of belonging to one another as fellow members of Christ's body.'[74]

One of the major problems in English Christianity is that converts do not last. It has been estimated that 80 per cent of new Christians have left the active life of the church within five years. Charismatic churches have at least made a genuine attempt to rectify this trend and to teach, instruct and disciple their converts. Generally speaking, they have been far more successful in holding them than the older churches,

Despite some obvious mistakes and wrong emphases in charismatic pastoral care, it has drawn the attention of Christian leaders to the importance of providing proper instruction for those who are new to the Christian faith. John Wesley, in his generation, consolidated the work of the Holy Spirit through his preaching by placing his members in small groups called 'Class Meetings'. Here they were instructed and grew in the understanding of their faith. Charismatic pastoral care has made a similar very positive impact in that it has put Christian nurture back on the agenda of many churches.

6

SPIRITUAL BATTLE

A more controversial aspect of the charismatic movement is the whole issue of spiritual warfare. It only takes a glance or two at the shelves of a Christian bookshop to realise that the devil and all his works are big business for the Christian booksellers. The books themselves run from semi-scholarly volumes like Michael Green's *I Believe in Satan's Downfall* down to fundamentalist endeavours like Bill Subritzky's *Demons Defeated* and populist scare stories like the Frank and Ida Mae Hammond's *Pigs in the Parlour*.

In one sense this preoccupation is readily understandable. The charismatic movement emerged at a time when the occult was burgeoning: 1959 witnessed the repeal of *The Witchcraft Act*; 45,000 witches were reported to have been active in the UK at the time. Pop groups like Black Sabbath and Electric Lucifer were suddenly all the rage. Films such as *Rosemary's Baby* and *The Exorcist* were a sell-out.[1] Newspapers in the late 1960s blatantly proclaimed it was the 'Age of Aquarius'. In 1962 the New Age Christ was said to have been born. Indeed, in this very same year, the celebrated New Age Community was set up at Findhorn in Scotland by Peter and Eileen Caddy. Findhorn came to see itself as co-operating with the Devas (Hindu gods) and the nature spirits who inhabited their flower and vegetable gardens. From the 1960s to the present time New Age shops, courses and therapies have enjoyed ever-growing popularity. By the early 1990s the tabloid press were regaling the public with lurid accounts of child sacrifice, sexual abuse and blood-chilling accounts of barbaric rituals. Typical of many was the *Sunday Mirror*'s graphic report of Caroline Marchant's initiation into a coven at the age of thirteen with a perverted sex orgy in a Norfolk graveyard.[2] By the close of the decade the *Daily*

Telegraph was happy to print a full-length obituary of Doreen Valiente (1922–1977) who was one of Britain's most influential witches. Her obituary spared no blushes and detailed Doreen's penchant for smoking 'skunk', a strong variety of cannabis, and indulging in tantric sex.[3]

Shortly before her death, Diana, Princess of Wales and Dodi Al Fayed had consulted a medium concerning their future.

Coinciding with these developments, East started to come West with the arrival of many immigrants from parts of the Indian and Asian continents. Hindu and Buddhist temples and Sikh gurdwaras began to emerge on the industrial skylines of towns and cities like Bradford, Birmingham and Huddersfield. No longer was it considered quite so irrational to think of the world populated by evil spirits. For many of our new settlers this was precisely where they were at!

Christian Sceptics

Yet despite this differing world view brought to our shores from the furthest parts of the Empire, the British middle-class have remained sceptical. To most of them Satan and his hosts are simply the beliefs of the ignorant and unlettered of a pre-rational age. David Jenkins, a former Bishop of Durham, spoke for most in October 1990 when he said, 'I do not believe in the Devil. The tendency of a number of religions, including Christianity to some extent, to have a quasi independent centre of evil just adds to the mythological picture of things. It's an attempt to cope with the problem of evil which does not cope with it.'[4] In the popular mind, exorcism is still largely associated with the tele-vangelists sensationalism of Maurice Cerullo's 'end time' healing crusades. The 'anointed giants' who yell 'come out' down their tennis-ball sized microphones are regarded as part of the razzmatazz of show-biz religion. Many have a suspicion that somewhere at the bottom of it all money is being made, if not through prayed-over clothes and bottled holy water, perhaps in bills for counselling and prayer.

Part of the problem is that there are some charismatics who have clearly 'gone over the top' in this realm of the demonic. Many speak as if the whole atmosphere is just thick with principalities and powers. Not only do these myriads of demons interfere with every aspect of life, they also have the capacity to add to their number by breeding.

In 1986, five years of hard work came to fruition for a new American author, Frank Peretti, with the publication of his first novel *This Present Darkness*. It proved to be a blockbuster with more than half a million copies in print in 1989.[5] The book deals with the struggles and conflicts in the church and community of Ashton, a place of no importance, in fact 'just a name on the map'. The reader is soon made aware that the tensions and battling in this locality are not merely of the inhabitants' own making. They have been brought about by advancing hosts of wickedness who have been summoned to wreak havoc and destruction. Tal, the captain of the angelic warriors, is summoned to make a stand against the encroaching tide. The book makes much of the power of the wicked demonic beings. It reaches a climax with a battle for the control of the town with the good angels eventually coming out on top. The story, though gripping, has one or two less than helpful aspects to it. It invests a great deal of power in the evil angels and the good angels only seem able to get into the action in response to the prayers and intercession of Christians here on earth. In places the book leaves the reader with an almost fatalistic feeling that what happens in this world is simply dependent on angelic warfare in the heavens.

Peretti's book is certainly a good read, ideal for a plane ride and we can be thankful that Sheila Walsh saved her marriage by reading it.[6] Could it be however that it has left Christian people overdosed with the demonic and spiritual warfare and not enough aware of the power of Jesus' victory on the cross? It is of course true that Ephesians 6 makes the point that Christians wrestle 'against demonic principalities and powers in the heavenly realm' but this particular text can be and has been overplayed. Does it mean that in every situation, in every place, in every church, that Christians are wrestling against principalities and powers? Might they not in some circumstances be grappling with their own selfishness or stubbornness, greed or pride?

Some charismatics seem to think not on this point. There is a fringe, quite articulate in some places, which is forever talking demonic hierarchies and will do 'deliverance ministry' on just about anything which moves. It will name demons of lucozade and cream buns down to attachment to the 1662 Church of England Prayer Book! In fact Ben Davies, minister of Bracknell Family Church, told me of a lady he'd been counselling who had been informed by a well-meaning maverick ghost buster that she had a spirit of chocolate eating which must be cast out. A national newspaper reported in February 1998 the case of a man who was delivered from an addiction to peppermint by a full-scale exorcism at a conference centre which specialises in deliverance ministry.[7] A New Testament conference was held at Northampton in February 1994 to consider the biblical teaching on 'Spiritual Powers'. One of the participants, a Baptist minister, related how he had recently cast out of a man a spirit of complaining.[8] Frank Hammond recalled having asked his congregation to minister deliverance to him 'and cast out a demon of heart attack'. His father had died of a heart attack and his mother was dying of the same, but after ministry all his worries about his health were lifted.[9] Dave Matthew, sometime editor of *Restoration*, reported on a friend of his who 'was casting out evil spirits from a man who, though not a Christian, attended many meetings'. One of the spirits revealed itself as a religious spirit. Matthew's friend asked it what it did. The reply was: 'I make him shout hallelujah very loud, then everybody turns round and looks at me.'[10] Frank and Ida-Mae Hammond in their widely-read book *Pigs in the Parlour* reported that they had never met anyone who didn't need deliverance.[11]

In the light of these kind of incidents it's little wonder that many people see charismatics as those who are given to extreme views. For example, it was James Packer's perception in 1990 that charismatics hold 'a firm belief that some, if not all, disturbed people with addictive enslavements (bondages) are under the influence of demons who must be detected and exorcised'.[12]

Charismatic Demonology

In reality, of course, there is no one 'charismatic' demonology. On the ground, 'charismatics' are probably as diverse a bunch as, say, the clergy of the Church of England or the members of the Liberal Democrat Party. There are nevertheless some threads which are common in the thinking of many of those who are part of the renewal movement. Almost all charismatics, for example, are agreed that the devil is a personal being intent on damaging and destroying the lives of Christian people and the churches to which they belong. Most also seem to be of the view that the devil is not omnipresent and therefore accomplishes much of his work by means of demonic spirits. These evil beings are held to be active agents for ill in the social, political and economic affairs of peoples and nations.

Most charismatics are of the opinion that even Christians can have a demon. Frequently the state of the temple in Ezekiel's time is used as a model. Although the temple had a Holy of Holies there were also rooms in the walls of the building where terrible occult practices took place (see Ezek 8:12). In a similar way, Christians can have the Holy Spirit dwelling in their hearts while there may still be some closed-off area inhabited by a demon (though they would not say possessed). Charismatics would also believe that a demon can only be exorcised by the power of God. No medicine, drug, spell in hospital or prison sentence can deliver anyone from a demon.

One aspect where differences begin to appear is in the matter of the hierarchies and sphere of influence which Satan's demonic hosts are said to occupy. Some charismatics, usually those of a more fundamentalist disposition, hold to elaborate systems with principalities holding sway over particular nations and powers over cities with other lesser beings appointed to local areas and churches. Most of this teaching is worked out from passing references in Ezekiel 28 verses 11–19, Daniel 10 verse 13 and Ephesians 6 verse 12. Ezekiel's lament for the King of Tyre is taken to be a description of the creation, fall from perfection and expulsion of Satan from Eden. The Daniel passage speaks of a heavenly messenger coming to minister to him and being hindered from doing so for twenty-one days by the Prince of Persia. From this, charismatics often deduce a doctrine of 'territorial spirits' which maintains that each nation and area is controlled by particular wicked spirits. Thus, Peter Horrobin asserts: 'Demons are strategically involved in the affairs of nations via ruling princes whom Satan has positioned in control of specific territories throughout the world.'[13] This means, for example, that if the situation suddenly gets out of hand in Pudsey, Brighouse or Merthyr Tydfil, the immediate need is for intercession to dislodge the hold of the spirits of wickedness

which are over them. These malevolent creatures 'will' says
Horrobin, 'do all they can to attack God's children (Satan's enemies)'.[14] Their strategies 'may include sickness, accidents, financial problems, relationships and breakdown'.[15]

An indication of the perceived magnitude of the threat posed
by these demonic hosts is given by John and Ida-Mae
Hammond. They have identified fifty-three clusters or demon
groupings. Cluster number eleven for example, is 'escape' and
number forty-eight is 'sexual impurity'.[16] Number eleven
includes 'spirits of stoicism, sleepiness, alcohol and drugs' and
number forty-eight includes 'spirits of fantasy, lust, masturbation, exposure and frigidity'.[17] Each local church has, say the
Hammonds, a 'prince demon attached to it'. For this reason
many churches 'have a history of certain types of problem'. In
fact the identity of the prince spirit over a church 'can readily be
identified by a church's specific type of problem'.[18] Some local
churches are believed to be controlled by doctrinal demons and
others by the demons of rebellion or adultery.

Belief in the controlling and harming influence of territorial
spirits spreads itself quite widely across the charismatic denominational spectrum. At one end, Arthur Wallis wrote an article
entitled 'End Time Conflict'.[19] This conflict 'will intensify as the
time of the end draws near'.[20] Christians are called to assist the
forces of light in this struggle with the spirits of darkness which
hover over the nations. 'The staggering fact is,' Wallis declared,
'that the prayers of the saints release these glorious beings to
perform the will of the throne.'

Territorial Spirits

Bryn Jones, Wallis' close associate in the early heady days of
Restoration, saw 'powers and evil personages' behind the
events, politics and happenings of human history. Their aim 'to
obtain their control over mankind'. This teaching Bryn had earlier derived from Ern Baxter, one of the Fort Lauderdale heavy-
weights. He had spelt it all out in great detail in a series of
evening addresses at the Dales Bible Week in Yorkshire. David
Carruthers vividly recalled Bryn Jones ending a major Dales
gathering by taking authority over the Prince of Great Britain.[21]
Bill Subritzky, who acknowledges his great debt to the
American Bible teacher Derek Prince, also spelt out his belief in

an elaborate network of Satanic potentates spanning the world. 'Satan,' he wrote, 'places unseen princes and powers of the air over every nation and city with descending order of authority all the way down to demons which walk on the ground and seek a home.' These beings have 'a craving to live in an unclean body . . . not necessarily a human body, it can be the body of an animal'.[22]

On the opposite side of the spectrum, Church of England charismatics also hold views about territorial spirits which are not greatly dissimilar from those of the Restorationists. Graham Dow, Bishop of Willesden, spoke of a thirteenth-century legacy of darkness over Coventry.[23] In another place he wrote of 'spiritual powers . . . operating in a hierarchy from Satan' and seeking 'to exercise controlling authority over human life'.[24] Tony Higton wrote in the *ABWON Radical Anglican Manifesto* of being 'unconvinced by some of the teaching on territorial spirits'.[25] He and his wife Patricia nevertheless found that 'a demonic spirit of criticism' had entered the church.[26] They also encountered 'a destructive influence of rebellion'.[27] Later they were able to rectify the situation, on Good Friday 1983 when with the elders 'they travelled around the parish proclaiming God's rule and victory over it'.[28]

Another Anglican, Canon Ken Gardiner, contributed an article on spiritual warfare to *Renewal* in 1990 in which he outlined a doctrine of territorial spirits. 'There are,' he wrote, 'Lords or rulers who wield great authority and power.'[29] He suggested that this may have been the prize which Satan held out to Jesus if he would bow down and worship him. Using the Daniel 11 passage Gardiner drew the conclusion that each nation has its angel or prince. Michael, for example, is the prince of the Jews.[30] Ken was later able to put this theology to the test. When the German evangelist, Reinhard Bonnke, held a mission in their local area, he and his parishioners visited every road in the parish claiming them for God. As they went they called out the following declaration: 'We come against every spirit in the heavenly realm that would seek to hinder the spread of the Kingdom and we remind you that you have been disarmed by Christ and command in his name that you yield and depart from this place.'[31]

Part of the theology behind the March for Jesus movement

has been rooted in a similar conviction that the landscape is in the grip of demonic powers. Marchers 'reclaim the ground' by taking authority over territorial spirits. Graham Kendrick, in his introduction to the *Make Way Song Book and Instruction Manual* explained it in the following way:

> Satan has the real estate of villages, towns and cities overshadowed by ruling spirits which work untiringly at his command to bring about his malevolent will fostering fear, violence and deception and successfully ruining lives which God intended for joy, happiness and true worship.[32]

He went on to maintain that they will continue their work of deception until God's people rise up and take hold of the victory which Christ has already won for them on the cross. The one offensive weapon which God has given to make this a reality, he maintained, is 'the word of God'. It is 'as we take it to our lips and sing or speak it out in faith by the power of the Holy Spirit that the powers of darkness will have to make way for the King of Kings'.[33]

A number of the songs and responsive calls which are shouted out by the marchers while they're on the move illustrate the point very clearly. A typical instance is the song 'I will build my church'. It has the chorus

> So you powers in the heavens above, bow down
> And you powers on the earth below, bow down
> And acknowledge that Jesus
> Jesus, Jesus is Lord, is Lord.[34]

English Christians have long held beliefs about territorial spirits. In fact the venerable Bede recounted how Cuthbert drove out spirits from part of the Island of Lindisfarne. When he had done this, trees and corn apparently started to grow in that part and the island became quite habitable.[35] Clearly it is common Christian experience that certain areas or buildings do seem to be gripped by the presence of evil in a way which can be felt. But having said that, it needs to be recognised that the notion of angelic hierarchies and evil angels ruling over towns and territories is in the last analysis a surmise. It is well beyond the most generous interpretation of the Daniel and Ephesians passages. Christians and charismatics in particular must guard against investing Satan with more power than the Scriptures accord him.

Having recognised the dangers, the Church owes a real debt to the charismatics at this point. It is the charismatics who have begun to take people's experiences of the presence of evil with genuine seriousness. They have not tried to explain it away with nihilistic liberal platitudes. Furthermore, charismatics have actively attempted to grapple with the acute sense of evil which people feel to be present in parts of our towns and inner city areas in particular. This has been done not just in terms of declaration and worship but also by challenging the social hierarchy and political and economic structures. Bishop Graham Dow provides a wholesome counterbalance by stating that spiritual warfare is not merely engaging in praise and prayer but also idividual Christians 'making life more wholesome, justice, being the kingdom of God because the kingdom of God is in you'.[36] In the same vein, Graham Cray, Principal of Ridley Hall Theological College, Cambridge, emphasised that the agenda for advancing the kingdom of God 'may validly be summed up as the restoration of justice and peace'.[37]

The Charismatic Battle Strategy

Although charismatics may differ regarding the finer details of Satan's organisational strategies, they are fairly unanimous as to how to counteract them. High on the list of successful tactics is the use of 'warfare praise'. This practice is based on Psalm 149 verse 8 which promises that with 'the high praises of God . . . in their mouth . . . [they] bind their kings with chains, and their nobles with fetters of iron'.

In many charismatic churches, particularly those on the Restoration wing, praise is strongly emphasised. Often it is accompanied by declaration, dancing and clapping, all very much in the Old Testament Jewish tradition. The aim is to move up a gear from praise into what is termed 'the high praises of God'. People who have been part of this say that you can often sense the powers of darkness and oppression lifting. It is for this reason that many charismatic congregations have regular 'celebrations', perhaps monthly on a Saturday or Sunday evening.

These are not merely excuses for a big 'knees-up'. Their organisers frequently see them as part of the spiritual battle for the local community. The objective is to so uplift the name of Christ that the principalities and powers which are opposed to his kingdom will disperse. Judson Cornwall's influential paperback *Let Us Praise* articulates this kind of thinking clearly. He wrote:

> Praise not only works as a foil for men, whether heathen or Christians, it is also a most effective weapon against the evil spirit world . . . It is when we come into the high praises of God that God will bind the Satanic, put limitations on it, so that you and I have true deliverance and freedom.[38]

Doubtless there are occasions when charismatics have gone over the top with their stampeding praises. Complaints directed against mindless repetition may also have been justified on occasion. However, what matters most is that worship should lift the tide of oppression and free the participants from the burdens and pains they bring. In the end exuberance of charismatic praise may well be less damaging that the sedate predictability of the rational Broad Church or the cerebral Protestantism of the evangelical fraternity.

Demon Possession and Exorcism

One of the 'hot potatoes' of the spiritual battle is the issue of exorcism and the extent to which Christians can be influenced or gripped by the demonic. In the early period of the church's history few questioned either demon possession or exorcism. Origen (AD 185–254), the great Bible teacher of Alexandria, for example, testified to the fact that Christians could still 'expel evil spirits and perform many cures . . . and also take away diseases'.[39] Hippolytus (d 236), another early Christian leader from Rome, described the baptism services of his day. Each candidate was prayed over for deliverance by the bishop the night before the service took place. Even in England right up until the sixteenth century it was customary for there to be an exorcism immediately before the baptism took place.[40] In the period following the Reformation, however, people became rather more sceptical. It was a critical age and things which couldn't be rationalised tended to be discounted. Even at the present time many evangelicals regard demon possession as 'witch doctor stuff' which might possibly be encountered in darkest Africa but not in England's green and pleasant land.

It wasn't until the advent of the charismatic movement in the 1960s that a wider circle of English Christians began to question the traditions which they had received. Even then by no means all charismatics were prepared to acknowledge a Christian could be taken over by an evil spirit. Wynne Lewis, the director of Elim Home Mission, said, 'We teach our people that they cannot be possessed by an evil spirit. Influenced, yes, possessed, no.' In fact most charismatics these days are quick to point out that strictly speaking the word 'diamonizomenos' means 'to be demonised' or 'to have demons'. It should not be taken to mean 'possession'. They are happy to say that Christians can be 'demonised', that is gripped or influenced by a demon, but not 'indwelt' by one.

Others, however, see this as mere playing with words. They are quite happy to assert that Christians can be possessed. The Hammonds, for example, in their book state: 'We have taken the position in this writing that Christians can be and are indwelt by demons.'[41] Graham Dow is of the opinion that 'there's plenty of deliverance which needs to be dealt with in ordinary stable Christians'.[42] He writes elsewhere: 'From my own experience I am quite certain that a Christian can have an evil spirit.' 'Perhaps,' he says, 'the wrong use of the word "possessed" has been the trouble here.'[43] Michael Harper wrote: 'If by "possession" we mean the complete "take over" of the personality so that it comes entirely under the control of Satan then we can say without hesitation that no true Christian can experience such a thing.'[44] He goes on to point out that this is not however what the New Testament is describing. 'But,' he says, 'in the sense of having an evil spirit, then no Christian is immune.'[45] John Richards in his lengthy treatise, But Deliver Us From Evil, suggests that for the Christian 'having an evil spirit' is a real possibility, being 'owned' by an evil spirit is not.[46] Canon Michael Green held a similar view.[47]

One of the problems, according to Graham Dow, is that the English churches 'have lost the capacity to deliver people from the grip of evil spirits as a matter of routine'.[48] At the other extreme there are too many well-meaning extremists demanding 'come out in Jesus' name' the moment anyone coughs or sneezes at a prayer group or house meeting.

Michael Mitton, formerly of Anglican Renewal Ministries, bemoaned the fact that 'we're almost at the point where some people want to deliver just about anything which moves'. Nigel Wright, possibly in reaction to this extremism, countered: 'It is wise to be highly reluctant to conclude that a person is demonised. Therefore every previous avenue normally needs to be explored before coming to this conclusion.' Certainly there is some weight of opinion behind this rather more cautious approach. A psychiatrist with wide experience in the area of possession and deliverance put the number of his patients needing exorcism at around four per cent.[49]

Knowing Your Enemy

'Discerning of spirits' is one of the gifts listed by the apostle Paul in his letter to the church at Corinth (1 Cor 12:10). Unfortunately it's not always very wisely used. In fact too many charismatic ministry team leaders who lack it jump in with a demon diagnosis where angels fear to tread. The great danger, as has already been noted, is 'putting demons on people when in fact they have nothing of the kind'. A radio programme in February 1993 discussed the problems of schizophrenia. It was reported that a serious school of thought has come up with a new theory about the origin of the illness. It has apparently been caused in some patients by a counsellor intimating that they have the symptoms of the illness. In a similar way the mere suggestion to someone that they have a demon can cause them to roll their eyes, shake or cry out. The enthusiastic counsellor may then think they're on to a winner and launch into exorcising that which they have just put on their unsuspecting victim. At the end of the ministry time, the counsellee then professes to feel no different which is hardly surprising since there was no demon in the first place! Matters can be made even worse by the counsellor telling the person concerned that they haven't fully repented or they lack faith or that futher deliverance sessions will be necessary. It has also been shown that 'bonding' often occurs between counsellee and counsellor. As a result, counsellees will sometimes come up with the explanation that their counsellors are looking for.[50]

The crucial question in all of this is how do we recognise whether or not a person is 'demonised' and therefore needs exorcism. At the looney end of the spectrum the diagnosis is, 'if there's a problem there's a demon!'. Thankfully, in the majority of charismatic churches and fellowships this view is not widely entertained. Bishop Graham Dow, for instance, says: 'When some difficulty in a person's Christian life does not respond to the normal processes of growth that is one of the clues that there may be a spirit.'[51] He also lists out a number of symptoms which may indicate the presence of a demon. These include such things as reaction to Jesus, reaction to worship, prayer and holy things, occult practices, paranormal phenomena, and blatant evil or immoral practices.[52]

John Richards in a lengthy section lists a number of other telling signs which may indicate possession. Among them are abnormal strength, supernatural knowledge and what he terms 'lesser manifestations' such as perversions of spiritual truth, delusions and false doctrines.[53] Discerning charismatics such as the late John Wimber and Graham Dow are quick to point out that cries or screams may not necessarily demonstrate the presence of the demonic. They may simply indicate the release of emotional pain or suppressed memories. Ron Trudinger also helpfully distinguished chronic insomnia, depression, migraine and sickness, for example, as forms of satanic oppression rather than 'straight out possessions'.[54] The Hammonds, on the other hand, possibly reflecting their holiness background, describe how they cast the 'demon of worldly dancing' out of one particular man they encountered.[55]

Dow perceives the sexual arena as one in which lustful spirits are 'extremely common'. It may simply be heterosexual lust. 'Try addressing a spirit of lust,' he suggested, 'if people have struggled and struggled and struggled with temptation and not got far, it may be there's a spirit there.' He sees them as very common, especially among men.[56] On the other hand, Gerald Coates of Pioneer maintains that the act of 'masturbation for the purpose of self-control' as and of itself is 'not wrong'.[57] Ben Davies of New Frontiers, refers to it as often arising out of indiscipline and watching television after 9.30 pm in the evening[58] when the more explicit sex encounters are screened.

One particular problem area in identifying the demonic is

the equating of the generational curse with the presence of the demonic.[59] The Scriptures do not explicitly equate the two. The teaching is frequently given at Ellel Grange that demons ride down the moral and personality weaknesses of particular families.[60] John Wimber also suggested that demons can be passed down the generation line although he was less explicit about it. He cited the book of Exodus: 'I, the LORD your God, am a jealous God, punishing the children for the sin of the fathers to the third and fourth generation ofthose who hate me.' Wimber commented, 'While this does not mean that demons are always passed from one generation to another, in some cases they may be.' Whilst some see this as the explanation for several generations of adulterers, drunkards or football hooligans, it's not a doctrine explicitly taught in either the Old or the New Testament. In fact there is no place where the Scripture teaches that demons are transferred in the act of conception.

Entry Points

A potentially dangerous doctrine associated with exorcism is that of 'entry points'. This teaches that evil spirits enter into people through particular points in the body such as the eyes, the mouth, the ear and even the genitals. Release, according to some exorcists can only come as the entry point is prayed over, signed with the cross or anointed with oil. Roland Howard in his book *Charismania* charted the tragic case of the former leader of the London Healing Mission, Revd Andy Arbuthnot and his wife who ministered to Mary at their Notting Hill centre. In a chapter entitled 'The Nottinghill Sexorcist', Howard underlined the fact that 'the Arbuthnots took the concept of "entry points" and "exit points" seriously, interpreting Mary's coughs, sneezes or even yawns as demons leaving her'. Over a two-year period a number of marathon sessions took place in which her private parts were anointed with consecrated Dubonnet. The whole case ended in tragedy with police intervention and a court case for abuse.

Other charismatic centres offer teaching on entry points. For example, in July 1995 the Ellel Ministries course at Glyndley Manor offered a seminar on 'Demonic Entry Points'.

Handle with Care

It has become increasingly recognised that in the ministries of deliverance and exorcism some form of accountability and pastoral supervision are essential. Much damage has been, and still is being done, by groups and individuals who are going it alone Robinson Crusoe style. Graham Dow wisely counsels that deliverance needs to be the work of a specially appointed team under the church leader's direction. There needs to be training, practice and learning together on the job. When he was an incumbent in the diocese of Coventry, Graham Dow had an agreement to consult with the bishop over any cases which had 'the feel of a major deliverance about them'.[61] Peter Lawrence, when Vicar of Christ Church, Burney Lane, kept the bishops of the Birmingham diocese 'informed of developments in the deliverance ministry within our parish'.[62]

Charismatics are increasingly seeing the need to get to the root of the problem which gives the demonic a hold in people's lives. Thus, for example, a person may be totally gripped by a demon as a result of alcohol or drug addiction but the underlying cause is seen to be something which is quite possibly entirely different, a trauma or child abuse for example. Once this is dealt with, deliverance becomes much more of a possibility. John Wright, pastor of the Nottingham Trent Vineyard observed 'most demonised people have a lot of emotional problems relating to the reason why they're demonised'.[63] In other words, the starting point needs to be prayerful, sensitive counselling which enables a person to come to terms with the wrong, the hurt or pain which has happened to them. On this understanding, for example, once sexual sins have been acknowledged and repented of, it is much easier to expel a demon of lust. John Wright summed it up as follows: 'Dealing with [the emotional] garbage is how to get rid of demons.'[64] Bill Subritzky at the end of his book *Demons Defeated* pointed out that all deliverance depends on genuine repentance. Without repentance, deliverance may not last, with repentance, deliverance may not even be needed.

Generally speaking, charismatics of most persuasions seem to be broadly agreed as to the method by which demons should be expelled. Graham Dow, for instance, underlines that following the counsellee's repentance it should be done in the power of the Holy Spirit by commanding the spirit to leave in Jesus' name.[65] Dow also counsels that on occasion it is better not to use words like 'demon'. 'More judicious words should have been used,' he suggests.[66] Nigel Wright wrote similarly: 'It is the name of Christ alone which . . . drives out demons.'[67] John Richards says of demons: 'Christ is their Lord as well as ours, and they have to obey him for no other reason than for what he is.'[68]

Demons are believed by some charismatics to reside most frequently in the lower abdomen.[69] Others regard them more like leeches which cling to the body and need to be plucked off.[70] The manner in which the exorcism is carried out varies a good deal. Those from Catholic backgrounds often use crucifixes,[71] holy water[72] and even relics.[73] Graham Dow recalled, for example, that the first time he threw holy water over a lunchtime congregation, five spirits immediately manifested.[74] Nigel Wright, on the other hand, found his Protestant tenticles stiffening over some of these issues. 'The use of holy water, crosses, sacred objects, Communion wine, anointing oil or the Lord's Prayer in this context,' he wrote, 'should be discouraged.'[75]

An interesting practice which seems to be commended by many charismatics including the late John Wimber is that of self-deliverance. The Hammonds, for example, make suggestions as follows: 'Pick out an area in your life where you know demons are troubling you, and command them to come out in Jesus' name.'[76] Graham and Shirley Powell in their book entitled *Christian Set Yourself Free* advise that 'once you are adept in self-deliverance, you can be setting yourself free no matter where you are – kneeling in prayer, walking, working or driving.'[77]

The Pros and Cons of Charismatic Warfare

As we reflect on some of these aspects of charismatic spiritual warfare it is immediately apparent that there is again a mixture of the good, the bad and the indifferent. Some charismatics have become almost obsessive about demons and the way in which they can either influence or take hold of people's lives. It is quite possible that such people come largely from Protestant backgrounds and have had strong teaching on the necessity of keeping themselves separate or cut of from the world. This doctrine of 'contamination' was proclaimed very forcefully by John Nelson Darby, the founder of the Plymouth Brethren in the early part of the nineteenth century. Many people who came from strict Open Brethren or free evangelical backgrounds are similarly still overly fearful of the harmful influence of objects and activities which are not, in their view, specifically Christian. Ron Trudinger of Basingstoke wrote, 'If we as a church send anyone into countries like Nepal, we assiduously warn them not to enter Hindu or Buddhist temples or touch or buy religious objects.'[78] Two other charismatics discovered 'a big, stuffed toy frog' had the capacity to attract evil spirits into the bedroom of a nine-year-old girl, causing her sleep to be disturbed'.[79] Once it was removed the parents reported their daughter slept soundly.

A similar kind of paranoia towards the demonic is reflected in some of the teaching emanating out of Ellel Grange. Peter Horrobin, for example, taught on the dangers of taking off your shoes and going in to visit the temple of a religion other than Christianity. When Moses took off his shoes at the burning bush he acknowledged God's presence. 'So,' he continued,

> If you take off your shoes you're actually saying that the demon over the temple is God so it's idolatry and ultimately worship of Satan. Now you may never have thought that taking your shoes off could be worship of Satan but ultimately that's what it is . . . now let's just see how many of you . . . have entered temples . . .[80]

This kind of teaching goes well beyond the teaching and principles of Exodus 3. In reality, taking shoes off probably conveys no more than the respect shown when a man takes off his hat on entering a church or a public building. Such an emphasis can create an unhealthy apprehension about the material aspects of God's created world. If we started to extend this principle, Christians might never go to a cinema for fear that the demon over the local Odeon might get them. Equally they might never eat another curry at their local Indian restaurant for fear it has been offered to Vishnu before it was brought out and put on the table! The New Testament establishes a clear principle that 'an idol is nothing at all'.[81] In fact the same passage even suggests that it is perfectly possible to eat food from an idol's temple.[82] When the apostle Paul found himself in Athens he walked around the city and visited their places of worship seemingly without any worries.[83] He also expressed no apprehension when he later travelled on a ship which had been dedicated to the Roman gods Castor and Pollux. Some charismatics need a wholesome reminder that by his death on the cross Christ has crushed the powers of evil[84] and that he 'has rescued us from the dominion of darkness'.[85] There is a danger of reaching the point where individuals have more faith in the ability of demons to damage them than Jesus' ability to protect them.

Sometimes what are merely natural physical traits or positive human attributes are also put down to the demonic. A number of charismatics, and indeed evangelicals, seem to recoil in horror at any feelings of attraction to the opposite sex. There is an unhealthy tendency to put down masturbation[86] or lust as demons instead of recognising that they are an aspect of a natural God-created mechanism. Steve Chalke, a well-know Baptist charismatic, speaks rather more wholesomely on the matter:

> I have been married for fourteen years and I have found other people attractive. Temptation is part of life. You cannot take cold showers to get rid of these feelings. I live with the danger of adultery and temptation. I would be a very foolish fellow if I sat here and said I know I will never commit adultery. But I don't ever want to be unfaithful. The guy who tells his wife that he will never even look at someone else is a fool. My wife is 38 and she was not born yesterday.[87]

Some charismatics need to take fuller account of the fact that the Bible identifies three sources of temptation: the world, the flesh and the devil. Probably this order indicates a rightful balance. Justice must be done to human nature or the 'flesh' as the New Testament terms it, as a source of temptation. The Old Testament view was that 'the heart is deceitful above all things and desperately wicked'.[88] Jesus endorsed this understanding. 'Out of the heart,' he said, 'keeps coming evil thoughts, murder, theft, hatred and adultery.'[89] What Jesus was doing was stressing human responsibility to grapple with the temptation which may come through our own sinful nature as much as from the devil or a demonic spirit.

In some charismatic circles too many crises are put down to the influence of the devil or evil spirits. The point was well illustrated for me when I watched a TV documentary entitled 'The Exorcist of Wood Green'. It showed the Wood Green Community Church in north London driving to a 'Glories Meeting' in Nottingham. Halfway on their journey they sustained a flat tyre. Several of the party leapt out of the van and started praying against Satan for opposing God's work. But the incident raised an important question: Was it really Satan or could it have been their own careless preparation in taking the van out on the road with a poor tyre and without a spare wheel and, as the police discovered when they arrived, without a valid tax disc?

There is a tendency in some charismatic circles to fall into a 'reds under the bed' mentality and to imagine there are demons lurking behind every quirk of circumstances or minor human problem. In the words of one writer, 'Demons have become the grid through which personal problems are viewed.'[90] An instance of this is a woman 'who got delivered of the fear of lumpy custard' at Ellel Grange.[91] She was made to eat very lumpy custard with her spotted dick pudding when she was at school. The result was 'fear came in and that fear associated itself with lumpy custard'.[92] This extraordinary state of affairs is surely really a matter of taste or preference? It's to do with the way in which we're made. Jack Spratt could eat no fat, his wife could eat no lean! There's surely nothing abnormal about a revulsion for lumpy porridge – or semolina or tapioca for that matter.

In some circles a mentality has developed where demons are thought to be in anything from Grecian wood carvings to the toy frog in the little girl's bedroom. Such notions do not resonate with the apostle Paul's emphatic statement that we know an idol is nothing (1 Cor 8:4).

There are one or two other areas where the charismatic approach to evil needs to be questioned. There is the danger that if too much is attributed to evil spirits or evil forces, individual human responsibility will be undermined. It is a not uncommon experience for people who have been delivered or exorcised of demons to think that everything necessary has been done. As a result they may sink back into a passive mindset and fail to grasp the importance of taking themselves in hand. It is crucial that such people maintain their deliverance by developing a positive outlook, and cultivate the presence of Christ by praying and actively living by the promises of God. We are commanded to 'crucify the old nature'; we can never cast it out!

There is also a danger of too much battle imagery in some charismatic worship, teaching and writing although this diminished somewhat in the 1990s. The New Testament is insistent that Jesus has already won the victory over the forces of evil. He has disarmed the principalities and powers and triumphed over them on his cross. The pages of Paul's writings are full of assertions that Jesus has overcome sin and death and evil and darkness. The emphasis is on thanking God who 'gives us the victory', who always 'causes us to triumph' and who makes us 'more than conquerors'. To constantly be singing warfare songs and battle hymns has a tendency to undermine what Jesus accomplished by his cross. Despite many problems being encountered in churches like those in Galatia and Corinth, there is not a great deal of stress on struggling with demonic influence in Paul's letters to them.

There is a further problem, that the exorcism and deliverance ministry can become a power trip for some. It frequently happens that people who are not good at handling power develop a taste for it in prayer counselling situations. They may also use the alleged presence of demon as the reason for their lack of success in ministry. To take one instance, Rebecca H. whom I know personally, visited a New Frontiers church in the South of England in 1990 together with her sister. She had recently been in a serious car accident and was wearing a neck collar because of bad whiplash. At the end of the service anyone in need of healing was invited to come to the front. Rebecca, coming from a Brethren background, was fairly unfamiliar with this kind of procedure. The pastor came up to her and said: 'When I saw you come into the building God told me you would be healed tonight.' Some fairly enthusiastic ministry commenced but nothing appeared to happen! Eventually they stopped and she was informed that no healing was taking place because she had evil spirits in her and needed to be delivered. She felt trapped and unable to escape while this next phase was initiated. Eventually she was made to take off her neck support but left feeling no better, in fact, in her own words, 'spiritually abused'.

In some instances of demonic encounter there has been evidence of delusion and deception. Perhaps this should not surprise us in the way it sometimes does. The devil is, after all, spoken of as the father of lies and a liar from the beginning. The most celebrated case was probably that of Derry Mainwaring Knight. The vicar of a Sussex parish, the Reverend John Baker, supported by his bishop, Peter Ball, sought to help Knight purchase certain items of satanic regalia which when destroyed would release many others from the grip of Satan. Over a period of months, groups of Christians contributed £200,000 which was later found to have been used to support Knight in an extravagance of high living.[93] More recently, there was a similar case involving a wealthy widow who was a member of an Anglican church in Jersey. She fell under the influence of a couple who were engaged in counselling deliverance ministry. They told her she had many demons and needed ministry. In a short space of time she fell completely under the couple's influence. She ended up giving them considerable sums of her personal money.[94]

The Pros of Charismatic Warfare

Despite these acknowledged areas of weakness, the charismatic movement's approach to the whole question of evil has much that is positive. Twenty-five years ago much of what has been discussed in this chapter would have been dismissed as medieval superstition. The charismatic movement has caused the Christian church to re-think and to take the whole question of evil with seriousness and, in most cases, with respect. Most Christian leaders are no longer prepared to simply dismiss evil as having no objective underlying reality. The reality of a personal devil and the possibility of a person being taken over or gripped by evil spiritual forces is now fully entertained by most Christian churches, charismatic or otherwise. The Church of England has in recent years appointed at least one official exorcist in each diocese. Bishops like clergy to keep them informed about exorcism matters. The Church of England General Synod report, *The Charismatic Movement in the Church of England,* referred to 'the renewed awareness of the demonic' which the charismatic movement had achieved.[95]

The charismatic movement has made Christians aware of the fact that the Christian life is a battle, not just against circumstances, but with unseen spiritual forces. Perhaps one of the real strengths is that they've shown people how to put on the armour of God and equip themselves to grapple and come out on top of the evil which confronts them in their outward circumstances. They have also demonstrated the way in which it is possible to overcome with good the evil they know and experience within themselves. John Wimber and others have very helpfully shown some of the ways in which individuals can begin to take personal steps to release themselves from demonic bondages. Such action begins with a conscious commitment of every area of life to the lordship of Christ, followed by confession and renouncing areas of sin and weakness which are a problem. This is followed by a deliberate taking of authority in Jesus' name and the commanding of any demonic presence to leave. At the conclusion it is recommended that all objects associated with sin especially occult artefacts and books are destroyed.

Clearly there have been, and are, a number of unbiblical emphases in charismatic teaching about the spiritual battle. At times the powers of darkness have had more attention than they deserve. It is, however, often the case that it takes an over-emphasis on a particular issue in one area to draw attention to a lack of emphasis in another. It is my perception that the heightened stress of the charismatic movement on the demonic in individual lives has altered the wider church as a whole to give more adequate attention to the needs of the individual. Many churches now have trained counsellors and offer proper consultation and prayer. In this gradually changing environment, many charismatic churches have themselves come to a more balanced and biblical perspective in this whole area.

Jesus in Luke 10 verse 17 urged the seventy, whom he sent out to assist him in his mission, to focus on their relationship with God and not on their power over the demons. Charismatic Christians whom I encountered in this research struck me as being most concerned with this emphasis, namely to build people up in their relationship with God. Many of the seminars at the New Wine, for example, are focused on topics such as prayer, learning to hear God, spirituality and drawing strength from Scripture. If I had to attempt to sum this matter up, I would venture to suggest that though many lessons have still to be learnt, overall the church is becoming better equipped in this area of work and ministry.

7

PROPHECY

During the middle years of the twentieth century, the historic and mainline churches became progressively more institutionalised and dominated by trained clergy who became an elitist group. Sociologist of religion, Bryan Wilson, wrote:

> There is a tendency for all established and traditional religions to institutionalise their arrangements, and for their activities to become ossified . . . Tradition becomes the touchstone, ensuring the wisdom and safety of particular arrangements.[1]

In an already rationalist sceptical age and against this kind of ecclesiastical rigor mortis, it is not surprising that prophecy remained in the back seat. However, with the emergence of the charismatic movement, prophecy has come from nowhere to occupy a noticeable place in many churches and fellowships.[2] Very recent world events of cataclysmic proportions have also stimulated a desire for prophecy. When situations become desperate in places like Ethiopia, Rwanda and the Balkans, people are driven to hear God. Just recently, an influential man in Ethiopia told me how in his homeland at the present time, many go out into the countryside to hear the monks of the Orthodox Church prophesy into their situations. Clifford Hill wrote: 'In a world of violence, of rapid social, economic and political change, when man's grasp of technology outstrips his wisdom in using it, there is a desperate need for divine guidance that could literally mean the difference between annihilation of mankind and man's salvation'.[3] It is in this setting that leading politicians or their wives have sought the help of mediums and spiritualist counsellors. It is the threat of imminent destruction of the entire planet that has led others into a variety of forms of New Age spirituality. It is the need to know the future in a totally uncertain world which accounts for the fascination with individuals such as Nostradamus or Jeanne Dixon. Dixon correctly prophesied many things, such as the assassination of Jacqueline Kennedy's first husband, the United States' President.

The charismatic movement emphasises the gifts of the Holy Spirit and one of the important gifts which features in the New Testament lists of gifts is prophecy (see Rom 12:6; 1 Cor 12:8; 1 Cor 14:1–5; Eph 4:11). In fact Paul clearly valued it highly and urged the Christians to whom he wrote to seek it and practise it.

One of those who began to take the Pauline injunction seriously was John Wimber and his Vineyard Fellowship International. After encountering people with strong prophetic ministries in Kansas City in 1988, Wimber began to change his somewhat sceptical stance to the prophetic. He wrote of seeing 'prophetic ministries operate at a level I never imagined possible'. He was particularly impressed by 'incredible words of knowledge' and the fact that 'their messages never contradict scripture'.[4]

John Wimber wrote in 1990, 'Prophecy is now assuming centre stage in the Vineyard – as we have done in the past with other moves of God – it is almost all that is talked about.'[5] Bishop David Pytches wrote in the introduction to his detailed study *Prophecy in the Local Church*: 'Our congregations certainly need a dynamic communication from God today, for knowing and doing his will. The prophetic voice of the Lord is available to those God knows will listen and obey.'[6] One of the most popular UK Christian periodicals is *Prophecy Today*. Even though many of its excellent articles deal with world events and the prophecy of yesterday, the magazine's popularity illustrates people's hunger for the prophetic.[7]

At the same time this new enthusiasm also birthed a 'looney' fringe with its clutch of extremists. In the later 1980s a number of prophetic schools began to emerge in America. The Bernard Johnson School of Prophets, for example, took full-page adverts in *Ministries Today*.[8] In the spring of 1990, *Renewal* magazine counselled its readers to be wary of the 'dial-a-prophecy' ministries which were springing up in many places.[9] Mary Relfe announced that she had come in the role of a New Testament prophet. In her bestselling paperback, *When Your Money Fails,* she declared that all the inhabitants of the west European nations were going to be issued with plastic credit cards stamped with 666.

Despite this kind of extravagant musing by the fringe element, Christian leaders did not succumb to the temptation to pull down the shutters. Clifford Hill, editor-in-chief of *Prophecy Today,* wrote:

> The existence of false prophets and teachers of cults and spurious prophecy, is not a valid reason for rejecting divine revelation. The opposite of false prophecy is not no prophecy, but carefully weighed and tested prophecy.[10]

David Pytches wrote similarly that 'while there are dangers of false revelations, there are the more serious dangers of no revelation at all'.[11]

Towards a Definition of Prophecy

Recent studies such as those by Hill, Pytches and others, have done a good deal to help clarify some of the confusion surrounding the nature of prophecy. One of the key questions has been how prophecy should be defined. Related to this is the matter of how it differs from other spoken gifts and what authority it should be given.

Most writers define prophecy as some form of immediate and direct communication from God to his people. Thus Hill analysed prophecy as 'the discerning and declaring of the word of God in the contemporary situation'.[12] David Pytches takes a similar stance. Prophecy, he wrote, 'is an oracle (message) from God through an individual; God's direct response to the human situation'.[13] Clearly both these definitions could equally refer to preaching. Pytches does in fact point out that preaching is a category of prophecy.[14] Hill stresses the point that 'prophecy is God's direct word of response to man's situation'.[15] In other words, there is an element of immediacy in prophecy which is only rarely, if ever, present in preaching. Most sermons result from reflection and preparation. Prophecy is distinguished from preaching by its ex tempore aspect. This, says Hill, is the standpoint taken throughout his study.[16] Peter Wagner also stressed the element of immediacy in his definition of prophecy. 'Prophecy,' he wrote, 'is the special ability that God gives to members of the body of Christ to receive and communicate an immediate message from God to his gathered people.'[17]

H. E. Ward, an English Baptist Union minister, elucidated the matter very clearly. He wrote:

> Preaching differs from prophesying in that preaching is preceded by and is usually the outcome of study and preparation whereas prophecy is the sudden overwhelming urge coming upon a person by the Holy Spirit to proclaim an utterance without any previous thought or preparation.[18]

Ward's distinction is clearly endorsed by Scripture which uses different terms for prophecy and preaching (see Acts 13:1; 1 Cor 12:28; Eph 4:11).

It sometimes happens that the gift of 'prophecy' overplays with the gift of knowledge (see 1 Cor 13:2). This was the gift Jesus exercised when he knew that the woman who sat with him at the well in Samaria had had five husbands and was living with a man to whom she was not married. It would seem that the gift of knowledge involves a fairly high degree of certainty. The person exercising the gift often also knows the application of their words. In prophecy there is often a degree of uncertainty. Prophets frequently do not fully understand the content of their message and often they are not able to discern its application (see 1 Pet 1:10–12).

The biblical direction of prophecy is always from God to man. As Paul puts it in 1 Corinthians 14 verses 2–3, 'he who speaks in a tongue speaks to God, but he who prophesies speaks to men.' Robert Warren and Chris Brain made this point clear. 'Prophets,' they argued, 'are given to enable the church to see itself and its surrounding culture from God's perspective.'[19] Charles Hummel in his study wrote similarly that prophecy 'evaluates the present situation from God's perspective'.[20]

Differing types of prophecy are found in the Old and New Testaments. It is necessary to recognise that each carries a different weight in importance and authority. In the first place there is 'canonical prophecy'. This is prophecy which has been committed to writing and is now included in the accepted canon or collection of inspired Scripture which makes up the Old and New Testaments. Some canonical prophecies are of major significance in that they foretold the coming of Christ and have already been fulfilled. Others foretold events concerning the end times which are clearly of paramount importance. Over against these, were individuals, both men and women, and bands of prophets whose prophecies were clearly of only small value by comparison. David Pytches helpfully distinguished between these two categories with the terms 'high level prophecy' and 'low level prophecy'.[21] Elsewhere he has stated that 'high level prophecies carry divine authority within scripture'.[22]

Wayne Grudem's comprehensive study, *The Gift of Prophecy in the New Testament and Today*, draws a similar kind of distinction between what he terms 'canonical prophecy' and 'congregational prophecy'.[23] Grudem regards the Old Testament prophets and the apostolic authors of the New Testament only as carrying an authority altogether superior to other New Testament prophets. Their utterances could with justification be prefaced with a 'thus saith the Lord', whereas other New Testament prophecy and current prophecy cannot, and must therefore be weighed and tested (1 Cor 14:29).[24]

Grudem's distinction between Old and New Testament prophecy is clearly an important one in terms of assessing modern prophecy within the charismatic movement. If today's prophets are accorded the same weight of authority as those of the Old Testament their utterances will be regarded as above judgement. Clifford Hill and David Pytches have also helpfully underlined some of the ways in which New Testament and contemporary prophecy differs from that of the Old Testament. For instance, Old Testament prophecy was frequently directional. In the words of Hill 'it was prophecy to guide Israel'. Again he wrote that it 'was given by God for the specific purpose of guiding the nation, particularly in times of crisis, so that they would fulfil the purposes of God'.[25]

Old Testament prophecy was a gifting to certain individuals only. It was given by God to a select few outstanding individuals. In the New Testament, Hill, Pytches and others point out that the gift was for all Christian believers.[26]

Old Testament prophecy had a specific function to prepare

people for the coming of the Messiah and to make them aware of aspects of God's salvation. David Pytches points out with firmness that New Testament prophecy did not have the function of bringing a revelation of new truth. Rather its function was, and is, he intimates, to bring fresh revelation on old truths.[27] This has been a very necessary emphasis where in some charismatic circles prophetic teaching has claimed to reveal new details about God's character, about the nature of man and about the end times.[28] It is also a helpful corrective in that it sets recent and contemporary Christian prophecy apart from that which is promoted by groups such as the Seventh Day Adventists and the Church of the Latter Day Saints. Both the SDA and the LDS believe that God has revealed major new doctrine to their respective founders, Mrs Ellen White and Joseph Smith, about salvation and the end times. The Christian churches, including the charismatic movement, believe that there will be no major new truth about the nature of salvation beyond what Jesus and his apostles taught and is written down in the New Testament.

A point which has been carefully stressed in recent writing by charismatic teachers is that Old Testament prophecy was quite largely predictive. In contrast, New Testament prophecy is very largely inspirational, with the aim of building up, encouraging and equipping the people of God. Pytches points out that there are occasional examples of 'directional prophecy' both in the New Testament and at present, although it is capable of being greatly abused. 'It needs treating with great care,' he says, 'and should certainly be tested with the leadership present.'[29] Again, David Pytches is categorical: 'We should never act on any prophecy until the Lord has clearly confirmed it from a completely different source.'[30]

Leaders in the present charismatic movement have also emphasised the distinction between the gift of prophecy and the office of a prophet in the New Testament. All Christians are potentially able to bring an inspirational prophetic word at a church gathering. As house church leader, Wally North, put it: 'Prophecy should be . . . the basic utterance among the children of God when gathered for worship or ministry.'[31] Having made this point, charismatic leaders have been quick to point out 'the distinction between the ministry of the prophet and the gift of prophecy'.[32] Peter Wagner wrote: 'God gives much prophecy through the mouths of ordinary Christians anointed by the Spirit. The office and ministry of the prophet is much more specific.'[33] Hill points out that the failure to make this distinction 'has resulted in many people imagining of themselves to be prophets'. Even new believers within a few months of their conversion have come to this conviction and the result has been great pain and confusion.[34]

The man or woman who has the office of a prophet will consistently give messages which are clearly for the whole church body. They will be relevant and sometimes directional. Their utterances will be recognised as being on a very different level from the short inspirational words contributed by individual members of the congregation during worship. Those who have the office of a prophet will be formally recognised by the whole church and authorised into such a role. For example,in 1991 Mrs Kris Smith was recognised in this way to minister at St Thomas Crookes in Sheffield.

New Testament and Modern Day Prophets of the Charismatic Movement

Charismatics try to ensure that the gift of prophecy and the ministry of the prophet as they exercise it are rooted in New Testament teaching. There is a unanimous view that they will continue to be in evidence in the Christian church until the close of history and the return of Christ. Many fundamentalists and some conservatives have maintained that when God gave the church the completed New Testament canon of Scripture, there was no longer any need for spiritual gifts and they were therefore withdrawn. Many of them maintain that a scriptural warrant for this view is found in 1 Corinthians 13 verse 10: 'when that which is perfect has come, then what is imperfect', spiritual gifts including prophecy as they see it, 'will pass away'. Charismatics take the view however that 'the perfect' is Christ and that the 'coming' refers to his second and final return at the end of the historical age. Until that event takes place, the gifts of the Holy Spirit, including prophecy, will, they contend, continue to be necessary. The fundamentalists and conservatives believe that prophecy and the other gifts were in evidence during the lifetime of the apostles to support the truth of their message. The apostles then left a full and complete account of all that Jesus did and taught so that in effect God stopped speaking anything new from that time. In short, if you want to know what God thinks about anything you read his book! Charismatic Christians maintain that God has continued to speak directly through the mouths of his people. Always, however, such speaking will be in keeping with what is taught in the New Testament.

Charismatic Christians also argue for the continuance of prophecy and prophets up to the present time on the basis of Ephesians 4 verses 11–13. Christ gave both apostles and prophets 'until we all reach unity in the faith and in the knowledge of the Son of God and become mature, attaining to the whole measure of the fulness of Christ'. Since that process (of 'maturing') is still going on, 'apostles and prophets', wrote a prominent house church leader, 'are still with us'.[35]

Charismatics understand the function of New Testament prophecy to be largely in terms of inspiration. It is to build up and to encourage Christian believers. This therefore forms the predominant thrust of charismatic prophecy. Hugh Thompson, who was associated with Bryn Jones, wrote an article in the early days of the Restoration movement entitled, 'You may all prophesy'. In it he commented that 'only a few' are called to 'the ministry of the prophet'. Because these prophets may give 'weighty messages' we must limit their utterances to two or three at the most in one meeting of the local church (1 Cor 14:29–30). 'But by contrast,' he wrote, 'no numerical limit is set on the number of simple prophetic sayings or songs which we may all contribute – so long as they continue to build up the saints.'[36]

Houston is of the opinion that the 'prophecy' referred to by Paul in 1 Corinthians 14 verse 3 can be a blessing and encouragement to God's people (an inspiration)'.[37] Teddy Saunders, well-known for his wide ministry over the years and then more recently for leading many clergy retreats, wrote of the encouragement which he had derived from inspirational prophecy given at charismatic conferences and places of worship.

> I have learnt from the charismatics that New Testament prophecy is for the edification of the church and it will always be positive and consistent with scripture. I have experienced it often and even practised it myself occasionally. On the whole it's pretty innocuous and encouraging.[38]

Charles Schmidt saw three major aspects to New Testament prophecy: 'building up, stirring up, and clearing up'! One comment I heard passed on Clifford Hill's magazine, *Prophecy Today*, was that it tended to deal too much in the gloom and doom. Contrast that with Mike Bickle's words. Inspirational prophecy, he says, 'evokes refreshing, encouragement, exhortation, motivation, comfort, joy, reverence and the like responses from God's people'.[39]

Although modern prophecy is most frequently inspirational in nature, charismatics do believe that it can, on occasion, be legitimately directional. Hummel, for instance, suggested that prophecy in the book of Acts 'is not doctrinal but directional'.[40] He followed this assertion with a discussion of Agabus's prediction of a famine in Acts 11 verse 28. North also noted that Paul often travelled with a prophet on his missionary journeys.[41] Presumably this was so that he could receive both encouragement and also directional input. Again, Mike Bickle noted that prophecy may include 'elements of new direction'.[42]

New Testament and modern prophecy may also be personal, that is directed to one particular individual in a particular context or set of circumstances. David Pytches cites some examples[43] but warns, however, that such prophecy needs very careful handling and needs to be tested with the leadership present.[44]

Controversy in Kansas

John Wimber who did a great deal to put prophecy higher up on the charismatic agenda, was awakened to this gift by meeting with a group of prophets in Kansas City. This small clutch of seers were under the leadership of Mike Bickle, the senior pastor of what was then Kansas City Fellowship. Their prophecies both attracted and astounded many Christians including Wimber himself. He later commented that although he did not believe their ministry to be perfect 'they have brought great blessing to me, and I welcome them into the Vineyard family'.[45] This association which began in 1990 developed quickly and John Wimber introduced the Kansas men to English Christian leaders.

Their profile in England was raised considerably by the publication of Bishop David Pytches' book *Some Said it Thundered* and Clifford Hill's somewhat vitriolic and extended review of it in his *Prophecy Today* magazine (Vol 6, no. 4). Pytches wanted simply to tell the story like it was, warts and all. Hill, perhaps because he lives partly by prophecy, felt the book to be 'dangerous and potentially damaging'.[46] Hill felt that Pytches should have provided a biblical basis for the recognition of genuine prophecy. He wanted an explanation as to why prophecy was being restored in the church today. He also felt that the questionable backgrounds and behaviour of Paul Cain and Bob Jones should have been rigorously scrutinised along with some of their rather more extravagant utterances.

Reflecting back on these events it seems as though Clifford Hill at that moment in time was in the business of producing an articulate apologetic for prophecy. Pytches, on the other hand, had an eye for a good story and is always ready to tell things as they really are, openly and honestly with no holds barred! Nonetheless, one can readily understand why John Wimber had his hesitations about the publication of this book. In fact, Teddy Saunders, his own colleague from Chorleywood, followed suit and initially 'remonstrated' with him not to publish.[47] Saunders later changed his mind after Bob Jones prophesied over him in the early hours of a September morning at Anaheim in 1989. Despite his 'funny language' and 'rather ludicrous idioms', 'he got it right and that's what matters'.[48]

A number of criticisms were levelled at the Kansas City prophets. The backgrounds of some of their number have caused raised eyebrows, not to say outright condemnation on the part of the upright and orthodox. Jones came from a dissolute background of 'alcoholism, violence, fornication and drug abuse'.[49] His prophecies were also said to be laced with occult techniques.[50] Prior to associating with KCF, Paul Cain had been out of high profile ministry for twenty-seven years. He had trawled the American evangelical waters looking for a sponsor before he finally came to dock in Kansas. Furthermore, Cain had earlier been bonded for life to William Branham, an Independent Baptist pastor, who had enjoyed considerable notoriety in the 1930s and 40s. Branham had exercised a high profile signs and wonders ministry but was later dismissed for preaching Arianism.

Some other questionable practices were raised by Paul Thigpen in an article in *Charisma Magazine*. 'Jones,' he claimed, 'lays hands on people so that he can "feel what they feel".' Jones also claims that the presence of the Lord often 'smells to him like roses'. Certain kinds of sin such as witchcraft, he claims, have distinctive smells.[51] The Vineyard, in fact, issued a statement listing twelve areas of KCF which needed correction. These included predictions of natural disasters, lack of accountability and the use of types and allegories to establish doctrine.

Critics also condemned the Kansas men for trivialising prophecy. On one occasion Paul Cain called up Mike Bickle on the phone. After the opening exchange of greetings, Cain said: 'Mike you've got a bit of a sniffle and you are all wet. Your hair is standing up on the left of your head.' Bickle summoned his wife Diana to give him the once over. 'Sweetheart, Paul says I have a "sniffle", I am all wet and my hair is standing up on one side. Am I all wet?' 'Yes,' she said, 'you've just come out of the shower!' 'And is my hair standing up on one side?' 'Yes,' she replied, 'on the left side!' Paul Cain calls these strange experiences 'little tokens that the line is still open with the Lord'.[52]

Clifford Hill also condemned Paul Cain for the dysfunctional incidents which resulted from his ministry. When he speaks 'fuses blow in the meeting hall, telephone lines burn out and fire alarms are triggered, which is more like the powers of magicians and witch-doctors than a prophet of God'.[53] The Vineyard also criticised Cain for the way in which, on occasion, he delivered personal public rebukes to individuals at meetings. On one occasion he pointed to a man in the auditorium and said: 'You old hypocrite, how can you stand there and have anything to do with what's going on at this meeting . . . you are planning to go off with that lady over there (he was pointing directly at her) at the end of the week and to leave your wife'.[54] At the same meeting Cain pointed to another lady in the crowd and said: 'And you, lady, if you don't repent I'm going to tell everyone what you've been doing in room number 202 in your motel today'.[55] Clifford Hill condemned this procedure arguing that such situations should be dealt with in private. 'Surely,' commented Rebecca Pike, 'no person should be condemned to public humiliation.'[56]

Of all the attacks which were levelled at the Kansas City prophets the most vehement were against Bob Jones. He was reported to have engaged in bizarre practices whilst under the auspices of KCF. Once a year for example, on the Day of Atonement, he conducted the ceremony of 'passing under the rod'. He held out a shepherd's rod and everyone in the congregation was required to pass underneath it. This rod of judgement was used as a means of 'cleansing the camp'. If people were felt to be not right with God, Bob Jones would call out their sins with warnings to repent. Occasionally, death threats were uttered if they were deemed to be necessary.[57]

Ernest Gruen of Kansas denied that Bob Jones was a prophet of God. He also doubted the validity of Jones' numerous visions, angelic visitations and out-of-body experiences which totalled 'to more supernatural experiences than those of all the men of the Bible put together'. 'There is,' Gruen concluded, 'something SERIOUSLY WRONG HERE.'[58]

Notwithstanding these deficiencies, many charismatic leaders seemed more than happy to endorse the validity of the Kansas prophets. Dr John White, the Canadian psychiatrist, rated them highly. 'No charge of sexual misconduct or acquisitiveness or arrogance,' he wrote, 'can truly be laid at their doors.'[59] Following ministry by Paul Cain, Bob Jones and John Paul Jackson, a number of prominent English charismatics issued a statement of public support for their ministry. It was published in *Renewal* magazine in October 1990.

> We believe they are true servants of God, men of sound character, humility and evident integrity . . . We observed their radical commitment to the word of God . . . We have no doubt about the validity of their ministry . . . and encourage as many as possible to attend the conferences to be held in Edinburgh, Harrogate and London in the autumn this year, at which they will be ministering.[60]

Signatories included Gerald Coates (Pioneer), Graham Cray (St Michael-le-Belfrey), Roger Forster (Ichthus), Lynn Green (YWAM), David MacInnes (Oxford), Sandy Millar (HTB), John Mumford (South West London Vineyard), Bishop David Pytches, Bishop Brian Skinner, Teddy Saunders, Barry Kissell (St Andrew's Chorleywood), Terry Virgo (Clarendon Church and New Frontiers International), Anne Watson (Belfrey Trust), Rick Williams (Riverside Vineyard, Teddington).

Yet less than a year later, Mike Bickle stood alongside John Wimber at a leaders' conference in London while John read out a statement of apology.[61] Bob Jones was later removed from his ministry because of 'serious sin'. The allegations included 'using the gifts to manipulate people for his personal desires, sexual misconduct, rebelling against pastoral authority, slandering leaders and the promotion of bitterness within the body of Christ'.[62] Moriarty noted that a 'detailed six-page time line of Jones' moral failure was sent to various church leaders and Christian media around the world'.[63]

Was the affair of Kansas another instance of the English church succumbing to the latest fad from America? It certainly does seem that a number of prominent Christian leaders were flying in the face of evidence that had clearly been in front of them for some time. In her account of John's life, Carol Wimber wrote in 1999 that in their introduction to the prophetic 'we went overboard a bit'. She continued: 'We foolishly bought the whole lot of them [Kansas City Prophets] as a package. Bob Jones' eccentricities were merely charming to us rather than alarming as maybe they should have been.'[64]

Weighing Up Prophecy

'Of all nonsense,' said the Scottish poet, Robbie Burns, 'religious nonsense is the most nonsensical.' There is certainly plenty of truth in this remark when it comes to assessing some of the prophecies of the charismatic movement. Wynne Lewis remarked:

> As I travel around the world I have fun and I have heartache when I look at the exercise of spiritual gifts. I am not prepared to have any of this yea, yea, yea, hearken

unto me thus saith the Lord three bags full . . . I don't want that rubbish. Most of the vocal gifts are nonsense. I am sorry.[65]

Certainly there are some bizarre contributions from the floor of the house in charismatic church services. One such was reported to me by two members of the English YWAM central leadership team. At the start of the service one member of the congregation stood up and said: 'Rooty toot toot, thus saith the Lord, I am not here!' At the end of the worship the same individual stood up once more and said with emphasis: 'Rooty toot toot, thus saith the Lord, I am still not here!'[66] One 'prophecy' I heard in an Anglican church in Gloucestershire went something like this: 'My people, when I say unto you "walk", walk. When I say unto you, "run", run. And when I say unto you, "jump", jump.' Some of the prophecies which do the charismatic circuits don't appear to amount to very much in the last analysis. An example would be the 'Diana Prophecy' given on 18 May 1997 which alluded to the death of Diana, Princess of Wales in August of that year which declared, 'I am on the move, says the Lord. And I am on the move in the cities of this nation and where flowers are laid my Spirit will be moving faster than where flowers are removed.'

Although these kinds of contribution are fairly trite and innocuous they do nevertheless trivialise and debase the seriousness of Christian worship. Probably in the long run, however, no greater harm is caused than that done by a soporific evensong in an archaic country church.

Failed Prophecy/Found Wanting!

One area where damage does often result is in the matter of unfulfilled prophecy. In 1973 David Wilkerson, author of *The Cross and the Switchblade,* and one of the prominent leaders of the earlier phase of the charismatic movement, was invited to address a large Lutheran conference. Instead of giving the teaching he gave a lengthy prophecy which took up the whole of his allotted time. The anti-Roman Catholic content caused a particular stir. Wilkerson announced that the Pope was going to speak out against the charismatic movement. In fact the reverse proved to be the case. Less than two years later Pope Paul VI gave the movement full backing in an address in St Peter's, Rome.[67]

The ageing William Branham made a series of startling predictions including a warning that Los Angeles was about to go beneath the ocean and that the destruction of the United States would begin in the year 1977.[68] At the beginning of the following year Clifford Hill announced that in Britain 'three things were about to happen'. One of them was 'economic collapse'. 'I advise Christians not to put their trust in investments but urgently to seek the Lord for guidance in preparation for the coming days.' As it happened, it was three years before the recession began to bite and it never reached what could be termed economic collapse.[69] In 1988 Bob Jones and John Paul Jackson both warned of financial collapse. Despite a recorded plunge in the stock market there was, according to Gruen, no financial collapse![70] Others might have seen it differently. Kenneth Copeland is remembered in Britain as the one who gave a false prophecy at a Full Gospel Businessmen's conference in 1982. He proclaimed that a revival would break out in the UK in September, 1983.[71] Paul Cain gave a prophecy which later caused great confusion and a fair amount of disillusionment among many thousands of Christians in Britain. He declared that revival would break out in London in October 1990.[72] The prophecy was given at a pastors' conference at Denver in August 1989, and at the 'holiness' conference in Anaheim in February 1990. Here it was heard by over 9,000 people from all over the world. Cain said: 'The first shot [of revival] is going to be fired when John [Wimber] comes to England the next time.'[73] The Docklands gathering didn't meet peoples' expectations. Many were left sceptical or disappointed. It was some considerable length of time before any apology or retraction was forthcoming; by which time most of the damage had been done. Finally, John Wimber in an article in *Equipping the Saints,* apologised for misleading the public because he had misunderstood Paul Cain who prophesied 'tokens of revival' as implying something of much greater proportions. Commenting on Cain's failed prophecy, Roland Howard stated:

The effect of creating such false expectations among Charismatic Christians might be expected to generate disillusionment. However (and perhaps this is more telling), the predominant tendency is to forget and to continue until the next big name, offering Charismatic experience or portents of revival comes to town.[74]

It was later asserted that John Wimber rejected the prophetic, but his wife, Carol, subsequently set the record straight. 'He attempted to discipline Bob Jones,' she wrote, 'but he didn't reject the prophetic gifts'.[75]

The following year Charles and Joyce Sibthorpe affirmed their belief that 'we are on the brink of the greatest revival the church has ever known and every part of the body of Christ needs to be prepared and ready for action'.[76] Three years later and there was little sign of any fulfilment of their widely publicised prediction. Gerald Coates, while on a visit to New Zealand in 1989, prophesied that a volcano would erupt in that country in November 1991. It didn't happen. New Zealand's leading Christian newspaper *Challenge Weekly* carried a page one headline, 'Prophet affirms quake prediction'. Gerald's prophecy which, according to the paper, was 'emotionally traumatic to receive', was that an earthquake would take place in November 1991 centring on Taupo.[77] Coates reaffirmed the prophecy during his next visit a year later in 1990. According to the paper, Peter Lyne of Bridge Ministries who brought Coates to New Zealand was adamant that Coates' prophecy be rigorously tested. 'A very clear word has been given with a very specific message. If it doesn't come to pass, we will need to face it and, if needed, report of that word.'[78]

This rather lengthy list of failed prophecies may appear to be carping on a bit. I want it to be of sufficient length to indicate that prophecy needs to be carefully scrutinised and judged. It is often the case that prophecies and prophetic words given by prominent charismatic leaders are taken without question because it is felt that such people must be right. I myself have encountered a Christian business which continued to trade when the financial evidence was against it because of a prophetic word given specifically by a national charismatic preacher. Gerald Coates professed himself deeply disturbed by speakers and writers who are not accountable to any local church. He discovered that many international prophetic ministers 'relate to absolutely nobody!' Such people, he said, either operate on the basis of an 'I have heard it from the Lord' or they surround themselves with 'little people' who 'are about as prophetic as the proverbial plank'.[79] Roland Howard in his book *Charismania,* stated, 'It is very rare for prophets to be publicly confronted with their errors. This may be because a sort of blurring of boundaries occurs in which people speak prophetically without actually calling it a prophecy'.[80] It was with a view to countering the errors of individual prophets that Barry Kissell started a School of Prophecy in 1998. It was established so that a large group of fifty or more could listen and reflect together on what they felt God was saying.

Another area where the downside of charismatic prophecy is frequently visible is in the personalised messages which are brought to individuals. Sometimes this is done in the context of a public gathering or conference. On other occasions they are given in smaller or even private contexts. John Wimber himself warned of the danger of the 'dial-a-prophecy' in which people phone prophets regularly to receive personal guidance. 'We should be wary,' he writes, 'of frequently asking them for information that would normally come to us from God through scripture, prayer, dreams, counsel and other direct means of communication.'[81]

Prophecy has a history of being used as a means of control. Joseph Smith, the founder of the Latter Day Saints, used prophecy as a means of authenticating his proposals. Chris Brain began prophesying as a means of controlling his leadership team who he felt were undermining him. Sometimes his prophecies came in the form of pictures. On one occasion he had an image of himself on a throne with all his leaders trying to climb over him. Brain used this to denounce them as scheming and ambitious and ordered them to look up to him as God's sole appointed leader.[82]

A frequent danger in the giving of private prophecy is the prefixing of the phrase 'thus saith the Lord' or 'this is what the Lord says to you'. A 'thus saith the Lord' doesn't give the hearer much room for manoeuvre nor does it give an adequate opportunity for the prophecy to be judged, even in a congregational context. There is a potential for spiritual and emotional blackmail where a prophecy is given to an individual with only one or two others present. Individual prophecies should always be submitted with utmost humility and the person left with plenty of time to discuss it and test it out. Often this is not the case and it is not unknown for people to be manipulated into situations from which it is difficult for them to escape. Jennifer began to have serious doubts about whether Charlie was right for her. During a vibrant knees-up at their charismatic church the pastor came down into the congregation and to Jennifer's horror prophesied in a spontaneous voice: 'Thus saith the Lord, I have brought you two together and have ordained it that you will be married . . . Surely this will come to pass, for I have arranged it, saith the Lord.'[83]

Fortunately, the girl had her wits about her and was able to get adequate counsel and break the engagement.[84] Grudem understands prophecy as human words which have been inspired by God. A 'thus saith the Lord formula', he considers, 'can be very misleading'. He prefers a more tentative alternative, such as 'I think the Lord is suggesting'.[85]

An associated danger is that charismatic conferences often generate an uncritical atmosphere. This is particularly the case of those where signs and wonders are strongly in evidence. To be critical is tantamount to expressing a lack of faith or seen as a sign of being unspiritual. For these reasons Rebecca Pike states that 'charismatic churches and conferences where signs and wonders are openly displayed tend to carry along with them a somewhat uncritical atmosphere'.[86]

Getting it Right is no Guarantee of a True Prophet

Many charismatics are impressed by the accuracy of some of the prophecies which they hear or receive. David Pytches was impressed by Bob Jones' 'weather predictions' and particularly his declaration that there would be three months' drought ending with rain on the 23 August. At six o'clock on that day it rained. 'And did it rain? It poured! No man could have manipulated that. It just had to be God!'[87] Teddy Saunders was likewise impressed on a visit to Anaheim at the degree of accuracy demonstrated by the Kansas prophets. Commenting on Bob Jones' utterances over him he said: 'He got it right and that is what matters.'[88] Clearly accuracy is important. No one will take note of a prophet who constantly gets it wrong; on the other hand, getting it right is no guarantee of a genuine prophet. Jesus declared that in the last days many would prophesy many wonderful things in his name, and he would have to say to them 'I never knew you' (Mt 7:23). Jesus emphatically stressed that the all-important criteria is that of person's character. He said it is 'by their fruits you shall know them'. By this he meant the fruits of the Holy Spirit as listed in Galations 5 verses 22–23. At the beginning of the second century when prophets were prominent in the churches it became necessary to test their genuineness. One of the early Christian writingss entitled *The Didache*, meaning 'The Teaching', listed some of the tests by which a genuine prophet could be known. These included sensitivity to people, not sponging hospitality, not greedy for money, and humility. True prophets may not always get things exactly correct but they will have the grace and the humility to admit their mistakes and, where necessary, to apologise for them. Such humility will also enable the prophet to submit messages to the judgement of the congregation.

Graham Brown of Cornerstone laid a number of positive tests by which to assess prophecy.[89] Is the person rooted in the local church? Does the message build up, encourage and clarify God's word? What is the spirit behind the message? Does the message conform to Scriptures? Does the message glorify the Lord Jesus? Does it inspire confidence, joy, renewal and releasing of the potential of others or is it manipulative and/or controlling?

Positive Aspects of Prophecy

Although prophecy is clearly not without its problems and difficulties, it has many positive aspects. On occasion it is accurate, helpful and upbuilding. John Widdas related the case of Frances, a member of his parish in Tamworth, Staffordshire. She correctly predicted to the day, exactly three weeks later, an earthquake in Mexico City. Some months later she proclaimed another quake, this time near the Italian–Yugoslav border. It would be once again in three weeks' time on Christmas Day. Widdas wrote to the Italian consulate warning of the impending danger. On Christmas Day that year Mount Etna erupted on the island of Sicily. Devastation followed. One man who had not taken notice of the local warnings was killed. This time Frances had got the right day, the right area of the globe but she was several hundred miles away from the precise area of the blast. Although Frances was not 'spot on' correct, John Widdas recalled the 'awesome effect' that Frances' prophecy had brought to the church prayer and study groups.[90]

There are numerous similar instances which could be cited. For example, Clifford Hill felt God prompting him to take off his clerical collar at a meeting in Central Hall, Westminster. He tore it in half and prophesied that that was what God would do to the Church of England unless there was a repentance from unbelief and other offensive practices.[91] All this was well before the divisive debate about women's ordination, the misappropriation of funds by the church commissioners, the crisis over the monarch as head of the church, and the future surrounding Michael Turnbull's translation to the bishopric of Durham.

Tony Higton preached the evening sermon at Hawkwell Parish Church on Sunday 8 July 1984. It was two days after the consecration of David Jenkins as Bishop of Durham. In his sermon he said: 'God is judging those who should know better.' Within a matter of hours of his sermon being preached York Minster had been struck by a bolt of lightning.[92] Higton also reflected on the Queen's unwillingness to come out against multi-faith worship,[93] and Prince Charles' failure to come clean about his alleged adultery with Camilla Parker-Bowles.[94] He said there seems little doubt, 'that the royal family is under judgement'. 'The church,' he urges, 'must be prophetic about such things and call the nation back to God and his word.'[95] Clifford Hill endorsed this role of prophecy 'discerning and forthrightly declaring the word of God for our times'.[96]

Paul Cain fulfilled a positive role for the Vineyard by calling them out from loose living to discipline, purity and holiness.[97] His prophecy had a remarkable affect on the life of the Vineyard. As Wimber put it: 'We have experienced a quantum leap in holiness and righteousness. God is rooting out all kinds of sin and creating in us a higher commitment to Christ.'[98]

Robert Warren and Chris Brain saw an important but more general role for prophecy. It gives a 'wide angle lens' view of life which can enable Christians to interpret God's purposes in the great movements of history.[99] 'Prophets,' they argued, 'enable the church to see itself and its surrounding culture from God's perspective, so that it can be faithful to God, and, in its turn, prophetic to the community around'.[100] This kind of prophecy is often reflective in nature. We see it in the writings of individuals such as Bishop Lesslie Newbigin who was able to pinpoint the direction in which the church and the Christian faith was moving in the last quarter of the nineteenth century. We see it in some of the writings of David Pawson. He attempted in his book *Fourth Wave* to assess what God may be wanting of charismatic Christians in their relationship with non-charismatic evangelicals.

Charismatic prophecy also operates at a more domestic and localised level. Frequently during a time of worship in charismatic churches there will be brief 'words' from members of the congregation. These will be generally in keeping with Paul's exhortation to the church at Corinth to prophesy words which 'strengthen, encourage and comfort' (1 Cor 14:3).

Such prophecies, if they are to comply with Paul's words, will be thoroughly positive. They may urge a congregation to stand firm in a time of trial or to be faithful in prayer. They may strengthen them in their faith by reminding them of God's love, care and promises. On occasion, there may be a message of comfort. This might perhaps be that God is refining Christian character through a period of difficulty or trial or that the wells of God's Spirit are open in times of drought and difficulty.

It inevitably happens that, on occasion, mistakes are made or people talk in religious jargon or speak out without having been genuinely prompted by the Holy Spirit. This aside, however, many people find that worship is brought to life and made encouraging by the exercise of prophecy. To hear a relevant, gently and graciously put, prophetic message prefaced by 'I think the Lord may be saying something like this . . .' can be a very heart-warming experience. It makes people aware that God knows their situation and that he still speaks in a living and active way. It is the prophetic aspect of the charismatic movement which has restored theism (the belief that God intervenes on behalf of his people) back into the Christian faith. Gerald Coates related how on a visit to Uganda he received a vision of an impending coup. At the time he was sitting in the home of the new minister of State to the President's Office and Chief of Security.

There had been no hint of any disturbance or rival factions in Kampala for years although there was some sporadic fighting in the north of Uganda. The streets of Kampala were safe even in the late evening. Children played without fear of abuse or kidnap.

Gerald Coates very cautiously shared his observations with this Christian man. Several weeks later 600 armed troops stormed these buildings but Dr Dalaki Kyria and his forces were prepared. Gerald later heard that this incident, among other things, was a 'contributory factor to the President recommitting his life to Christ'. In December 1991, President Masevini hosted a national prayer breakfast and sent Gerald Coates a handwritten invitation.[101]

In conclusion, the encouragement which can be derived from a prophetic word is well illustrated by the following instance. This message was given to Helenor Birt, a close friend of our youngest daughter. It was spoken by Charles Slagle whose prophetic ministry, along with his wife Paula, is well known. It was given in Grace Church, Liverpool, on 15 October, 1992 and tape recorded. I have abridged it.

> The Lord . . . wants me to tell you that there's been a painful separation and you're going through another one but he's going to be with you in it all . . . Your tears go right into his heart and he stores them up and they're precious to him . . . The Lord says 'I'm giving you wholeness and healing right now my daughter, and you are being set completely free . . . It's been a left ovary that's been a problem so the Lord says I'm giving you a new one and everything is going to ovulate right . . . fever will not dog your tracks any more. And there's been a problem too and kidney infections . . . the Lord just said he wanted to tell you it's bound off OK.

Helenor wrote the following which she enclosed with the tape.

> The separation discussed was the start of my parents' divorce which of course was very painful. Philip [her boyfriend] had also just left for Germany, and up to this time was a great emotional support regarding my parent. The healing: always had a fear of not being able to have chil-

dren. Kidneys – had had a lot of infection. I had never met Charles and Paula Slagle before, and no-one knew about my parents' divorce at church, or my fears about children.[102]

For Helenor and for others like her who have been on the receiving end of a message of this kind, this was a moment of great encouragement. It left her with a deep sense of God's presence with her and the knowledge that he knew and understood her situation intimately.

8

HEALING

Today health has almost become a cult phenomenon. We live in a world of fitness clinics, in-shape centres and health farms. On almost every stretch of road there are joggers, some of them puffing their way along in the hopes that they will one day be able to see their feet. 'Keep Fit', judo and yoga classes seem to be springing up in almost every village hall and community centre. More people than ever are consciously avoiding fatty foods and products with chemical preservatives and 'E' colourings. Others are majoring on unpolished rice, muesli, bran, wholemeal bread, fruit juices and raw vegetables. Healing has come to have a significant place in New Age thinking and practice. Aromatherapy, acupuncture and healing crystals are highly recommended by 'new agers'. In an uncertain world health has become, to the majority of people, the all-important thing. 'As long as I have my health I'll be OK,' is a view not infrequently expressed.

Against this background it is not surprising that the Christian churches should have found themselves reawakened to their long held healing resources. In 1904 The Guild of Health was formed under the inspiration of Percy Dearmer and Conrad Noel, two Anglo-Catholic priests with a strong social conscience. Its clearly defined objective was 'to restore the healing ministry of Christ in and through his church' and 1915 saw the founding of the specifically Anglican Guild of St Raphael which set out to restore the ministry of healing as part of the ongoing life of the parish church. The Guild promoted prayer for healing and aimed 'to guide the sick and those who care for them to Christ, the source of healing'. In addition to these two organisations there were a small number of individuals who engaged in the ministry of healing, among them Dorothy Kerin (1889–1963) and J. Cameron Peddie (1904–   ) who established a house of healing at Burrswood near Tunbridge Wells in Kent. Nevertheless, for the most part, healing was not high on the churches' agendas or seen as an essential aspect of Jesus' commission to all his followers. It wasn't until the rise of the charismatic movement that there was a real re-kindling of concern for the healing ministry in the UK churches. Writing in 1986 John Gunstone wrote that 'the ministry of healing has spread with the new pentecostal movement'.[1] The earlier General Synod report *The Charismatic Movement in the Church of England* acknowledged 'the new emphasis upon healing and the undoubted glorious healings which have occurred as a result of the charismatic renewal'.[2]

Some Instances of Healing

Examples of the 'glorious healings' to which the report refers are not difficult to find. Chantalle Rowland was firmly in the grip of anorexia. 'Mealtimes were a nightmare,' she said, 'as the problem was really playing havoc with our family in many ways.'[3] For eighteen months the family had not been able to mention food without Chantalle losing her temper. She lost a lot of weight and was eventually hospitalised by the psychiatrist who was treating her. In the summer of 1993 Chantalle attended the Bognor Bible Week with her family. There the leader of the 'Live Set' teenagers meeting asked if he could pray for her. 'As he prayed,' she recalled, 'it felt as if something inside broke, and I began to cry.' She continued:

> I realised that I needed to eat to live and that I had a problem. I have been totally healed by the Lord Jesus. People had tried everything to cure my anorexia, but there was no answer, and there still would not be if it were not for Jesus Christ.[4]

Two-year-old Andrew was born with a condition called Hypospadias which requires an operation, which his doctor said was needed urgently. Andrew was prayed for at the church's Easter Guest Service. The vicar, Tony Higton, recalled that 'he was not very happy about it and yelled a good deal while his father held him'. However, just four days after the prayer he was seen by the consultant who said 'There isn't anything wrong here . . . certainly an operation is out of the question'.[5]

Roger and Faith Forster, the leaders of Ichthus in south west London, saw their fifteen-year-old son miraculously healed through prayer and the laying on of hands. His sudden recovery proved to be a major step forward in the life of their fellowship, coming as it did in a period of intense spiritual stress and conflict. An anonymous curse was daubed on their church wall and signed 'son of Satan' and very shortly afterwards their son started to experience acute breathlessness and was rushed to Guys Hospital. He was diagnosed as suffering from a rapidly growing leukaemic cancer which had already spread throughout the lymphatic system and had entered the spinal fluid. The whole fellowship was called to a day of prayer and fasting and others at Spring Harvest stood with them. By the following day all symptoms had gone and no cancer has since been found in his body.[6]

Peter Lawrence was the vicar of a Birmingham parish in the 1980s. He laid on hands and prayed for many sick people 'many of whom died, and none of them was physically healed'. 'And then at last,' he wrote, 'after fourteen years of trying I got one!' At the close of a time of worship Peter had the word 'waterworks' and gave it out. It was claimed by Mary, a seventy-four-year-old, who had suffered with a bladder complaint for thirty years. Peter laid hands on her head and prayed for her. 'She was healed from that moment and has not been troubled since. To God be the glory!'[7]

Jennifer Rees Larcombe contracted encephalitis in 1982. It attacked her brain and nervous system and nearly proved fatal. For eight years she was like a broken floppy doll, wheelchair-bound and totally dependent on her family and carers. In June 1990 Jennifer went to speak at a church near Guildford on the subject of suffering. Immediately before the lunch break a young mum who had only been a Christian a matter of months said to her shyly: 'I've only been a Christian a few months and this kind of thing has never happened to me before, but I feel God is saying he wants to heal you.'

Later in the afternoon Jennifer asked the young woman to pray for her. She was diffident, claiming she didn't have the gift of healing and wouldn't know what to say! A crowd of people clustered about the wheelchair. The young woman didn't do anything the books on healing suggest, she 'simply asked Jesus to heal me and he did!' There was no falling in the Spirit or warmth or excitement, but Jennifer stood up straight and pain-free and walked off to the loo. Later that evening she returned to her bemused family. The day following was her daughter Naomi's birthday. She iced a cake, the first in eight years, and blew up balloons.[8]

Olive Allison had fallen from a beam in the school gymnasium and ruptured a disc in her spine. From that point on she was in constant pain, although at the time of her marriage in 1959 she could walk freely. During pregnancy, however, Olive's back deteriorated and she spent most of it in a surgical corset and then in a plaster jacket. In the years that followed she spent months at a time in bed, sometimes in a plaster jacket. To get about she normally used electric buggies or a wheelchair. To combat all the intense pain she had spinal injections and ate pills till she rattled.

After twenty-five years, the situation was desperate and Olive was beginning to despair. In December 1985 her consultant suggested she might go for healing at his church. She was introduced to Bishop Banit Chui, a retired Bishop of Singapore. He led her through a series of prayers of repentance, anointed her with oil and laid his hands on her head praying for the forgiveness of her sins and for the Holy Spirit to come and minister healing. Olive felt the pain going from her legs, arms, head and back up out to Bishop Chui's hands. The pain was gone but she was still unable to walk. Later, after further counselling and asking the Lord to forgive her 'for calling on evil spirits' in time past, she was able to put aside her crutches. To her husband Kevin's amazement she dispensed with the chair lift and went up and down the stairs with ease.[9]

Prayer for healing has become one of the identifying features of charismatic churches. In most instances it will be visible at Sunday services probably at least once a month. In many charismatic churches there will be opportunity for prayer for healing every week. Most often this will be at the close of worship. People will come forward and stand at the front of the church building or they may come and kneel at the Communion rail.

Many charismatic churches have ministry teams who work in pairs and are ready to step out and pray for those who come forward. Some have specifically designated healing services, perhaps on a weekday morning or evening. In general, there is a great diversity of practice in the matter even within one church. As one charismatic Baptist pastor put it: 'We do it with laying on of hands, with oil, without laying on of hands. I will pray from the platform for people to be healed without them coming to the front, all sorts of ways I guess.'[10]

The General Synod report of 1981 also noted the great variety of approaches to healing among charismatic churches.

> The ministry of healing is fulfilled amongst charismatics not only by the elders (which James 5 would suggest), but also with a 'gift' of healing (1 Corinthians 12:9, 28). The ministry may be exercised in public worship or privately, and is almost invariably done by laying on of hands, often by several people. The eucharist has become for many a central focus for this ministry. Anointing seems to have been less used by charismatics perhaps because of the reliance on the 'gift' basis for ministry (ie from 1 Corinthians 12–14) rather than on the 'eldership' basis, from James 5.[11]

The Meaning of Healing

An issue which needs clarification is what precisely is meant by the terms 'disease' and 'healing'? At the fundamentalist end of the charismatic spectrum 'disease' seems to be perceived in almost entirely physical or organic terms. By the same token, healing is understood very largely as the restoration from a physical or organic ailment. This approach to healing, if it stops at the level of mere physical or bodily well-being and enjoyment, is shallow and superficial. Health in the full sense of the word is total well-being and wholeness not only of the body but also the mind and the spirit. Many charismatics have extended their understanding of healing to these areas. Some like Kenneth McCall have devoted their ministry to healing of memories and the healing of the family tree. This often involves grieving and prayer for children lost in miscarriage and abortion. Holy Communion services are held during which the family tree is laid on the altar. Prayer is then offered for cutting away of harmful memories, hurts and pain which has been inherited through the generations. Others have also concentrated on praying for the Holy Spirit to touch areas of emotional hurt. Release has been seen to come through tears and crying out. There has been a growing recognition on the part of charismatics that the body must not be seen in isolation from the mind and the spirit. Often physical pain and suffering is the external symptom of some deeper or underlying emotional or spiritual pain.

Charismatic Christians have come increasingly to recognise that the greatest disease is unease with God and that this is caused by our own individual selfishness and wrong. Ben Davies, pastor of a New Frontiers church in Bracknell, put it this way: 'Behind every sickness is sin, Adamic sin. We sinned with Adam, we inherited Adam's nature, one of the results of the fall is sickness, and one of the results of the fall is that one day we're going to die.'[12]

Tom Smail made the same point in a *Renewal* article, 'Sickness has come upon us because of the sin of the world'. 'It is,' he continued, 'a setting loose of destructiveness through the whole area of human life because man has fallen away from his origin in God.'[13] For most charismatics, it is in the death of Christ on the cross that the root of sickness is dealt with. This means that the cross of Christ is the point where all healing begins. It is the means whereby our unease with God is righted. It is the place where mental anguish and suffering were overcome and it is therefore to the cross that emotional pain and hurt and unforgiveness must be taken. Some charismatics have tended to lose sight of this crucial fact and to focus their energies almost exclusively on prayer and the invocation of the Holy Spirit. The majority share Tom Smail's conviction that, 'in the death of Christ is the means for us to be made whole and in his suffering is the way to our healing'.[14]

Another issue which needs clarification is whether 'healing' means making 'completely new' or simply putting back into good working order. Put another way, is it a brand new part or a reconditioned one? Some charismatics, such as Roberts Liardon, contend it is the former. The problem with this kind of contention is that it doesn't take adequate account of the biblical process of ageing and dying. The Christian tradition commends old age as something fine and good. The book of Leviticus urges that people rise in the presence of the aged and show respect for the elderly (Lev 19:32). The Gospels introduce individuals such as Simeon and Anna in such a way as to underline the wisdom and godliness which has come with their advancing years. Charismatic churches which are often quite largely filled with younger people have tended to overlook the fact that ageing is a part of the divine pattern. It is God's purpose that the human frame wears out and the pace of life necessarily slows down. All of this is beautifully expressed in the poetic lines of Psalm 90. John Noble of Pioneer underlined the reality of the situation. 'Don't forget,' he wrote, 'that even those Jesus healed eventually died.'[15]

Charismatic Approaches to Healing

Part of the richness of the charismatic movement is its variety. Perhaps this is nowhere better seen than in the differing approaches to healing within the movement. Often as a prelude to healing ministry 'words of knowledge' from a prayer team are given out or, in some instances, invited from members of the congregation. 'Words of knowledge' generally come as people wait quietly in the presence of God. They may come in the form of passing thoughts, momentary pictures or sometimes feelings. A sudden pain in an arm for example may be taken as a word of knowledge that someone present has that condition and that it is God's purpose to bring healing to them through prayer.

Many charismatics see satanic or demonic interference as lying at the root of some sickness and illness. The way in which healing is then ministered is by breaking the influence of the demonic or, in extreme cases, casting out a demon. Clearly there is biblical precedent for such diagnoses. Jesus, for example, spoke concerning a woman who 'had an evil spirit that made her ill for eighteen years' (Lk 13:11). On another occasion, Matthew records that some people brought to Jesus a man who could not talk because he had a demon (Mt 9:32). On the basis of this strand of biblical teaching many charismatics teach and practise healing through deliverance. The Reverend Andy Arbuthnot and his wife, Audrey, who directed the London Healing Mission, on occasion found that sickness resulted from demonisation. Andy instanced 'a demon of alcohol entering a person who was deliberately drinking to excess'. The need in such a case is to get that person to repent of their sin and to receive the forgiveness of Jesus. Then, and only then, will healing begin to be a possibility. The Arbuthnots carefully distinguish between the deliverance ministry and the healing ministry. Other charismatics show less inclination to do so. Peter Horrobin, the director of Ellel Grange, is rather more confident that greater blame can be attached to the demonic for the sickness and ailments of those who attend his conferences. In his book *Healing Through Deliverance* he wrote:

> Whilst not all sickness is demonic, however, there are far more demonically induced symptoms around than the church would readily admit. And one of the reasons why some people are not healed is because the demonic dimension is not being discerned, even by those who believe in and use the gifts of the Holy Spirit.[16]

Such demonic influences are dealt with in the name of Jesus and by the power of the cross. Some charismatics seem to specialise in a ministry of 'cutting people off' from family curses in the generation line. Their theology is often not altogether very sharply articulated. It's frequently unclear whether the demons are travelling down the generation lines or if it's merely a curse or genetic weakness that's being dealt with. Some charismatics maintain that damaging parental influences can be quite extensive. Ron Trudinger of 'Salt and Light' for example expressed his conviction that

> Any person who has come from non-believing parentage or background will be liable to suffer from spiritual attacks: the enemy latching on to hereditary defects or early experiences. And when such a person is transferred from the domain of darkness to the kingdom of His beloved Son there will always be a need for cutting off and release.[17]

Some of the more upfront charismatic healing evangelists look for instantaneous results. The expectation is that there will be immediate healings details of which can be relayed back to others in their meetings and later sent out in letter form to their financial supporters. This will then increase the faith levels of those who are part of their audience and no doubt raise their financial contributions into the bargain. However, for many charismatics, healing is often seen as occurring gradually over a period of time. Francis MacNutt gave the proportion of instantaneous healings as one in twenty-five. Colin Urquhart mentions in one of his books that he noticed a marked improvement in the health of those he had prayed for and ministered to on five occasions or more. Charismatic centres for healing such as the London Healing Mission and the Harnhill Centre for Christian Healing in Gloucestershire encourage people to attend healing services frequently and to soak themselves in an atmosphere of faith and expectancy. John Wimber underlined the fact that 'most of the healings in the New Testament were immediate, though not all'. He instanced the gradual healing of a blind man in Mark 8 verses 22–26.[18]

Weaknesses and Strengths: Money and Glitz

Possibly in the popular mind it is the 'bad' which is most often at the forefront. Healing immediately conjures up for many images of glitzy extroverts imploring God in frenzied outbursts to 'heeeeal!!' Others have in the back of their minds memories of faith healers sending out anointed cloths and prayed-over handkerchiefs. One practitioner sent out special cloths with advice to 'put it under your pillow and sleep on it tonight'. There was further instruction: 'Do not keep this prayer cloth, return it to me. I will take it and pray over it all night. Miracle power will flow like a river.'[19] Kenneth Hagin recounted one healer who'd spit on every person he prayed for: 'He'd spit in his hand and rub it on them. That's the way he ministered . . . If there was something wrong with your head, he'd spit in his hand and rub it on your forehead.'[20] At the very time in which I wrote the first edition of this book (October 1994), one of the leaders of the church I belong to, Arthur Champion, showed me a letter he'd received out of the blue from healing evangelist, Maurice Cerullo. Headed 'Receive it!', it announced a unique 'End Time Financial Anointing for Your Life' to donors who would give £63 in celebration of his sixty-third birthday, and in thankfulness for each year of his life and for the forty-four years of his ministry. Here is a short extract.

26th September 1994

Arthur Champion
Andoversford
Cheltenham
Glos. GL54 4LG

Dear Arthur
God often moves in very unusual ways. Arthur, I tremble as I write this . . . God has told me to release His End Time Financial Anointing. Do you want it?

Arthur, on my 63rd birthday, and entering my 44th year of ministry, I am facing the most massive financial ministry challenges ever . . .

Never in my 44 years of ministry has God released me to do this. But I must obey his timing.

In honour of my 63rd birthday, please pray about stretching your faith and give £63 which is £1 for each year. I wouldn't ask if I didn't know God was going to abundantly RETURN IT TO YOU.

Don't delay. Do it *deliberately*. Do it *spiritually*. Do it *immediately* . . . and *I will agree in the Spirit over your seed, praying and speaking through the gift of tongues for your need.*

Arthur, don't wait . . . ACTivate your faith now by returning the enclosed End Time Financial Anointing form.

God's faithful servant
Maurice Cerullo[21]

This letter comes close to being a Protestant version of selling Indulgence certificates of pardon. This was a practice which caused Martin Luther to challenge the Papacy in 1517 when he nailed his 95 Theses to the door of the Castle Church in Wittenberg. More serious, this letter and others like it are nothing short of emotional blackmail. Weak people with only a nominal faith in Christ could easily fear that by rejecting Cerullo's advances they are offending God. In this way they get steamrolled into making a 'positive' response. It is also a trifle ironic, to say the least, that a leading evangelist who was himself in substantial debt should have been chosen by God to release an 'end time financial accounting'! Two years later Cerullo, who believes he is called to proclaim the gospel to the British people, followed his birthday anointing with an offer of air miles for every pound donated to his 'Billion Souls Crusade'. An initial payment of £65 secured membership of the 'Eagles Club', a slogan taken from the book of Isaiah: 'They shall mount up as eagles.' Cerullo saw the scheme as 'a spiritual breakthrough in his ministry' allowing participants 'to come alongside me' – to travel with me anywhere in the world – at no cost to you'.[22]

An issue which has concerned many who are actively concerned and involved in the ministry of healing is the seeming inability to produce the same level of result which Jesus and the apostolic churches appeared to achieve. Did not Jesus say to his followers that they would achieve greater results than he had (Jn 14:12)? Yet, somehow, the evidence doesn't seem to be there. As the Church of England working party put it more starkly in 1981:

> Has God commissioned his church to perform miracles of healing? or, in other words, can we say to the paralysed man 'Arise, take up your bed and walk'? The dilemma is that, even for the very high-profile charismatics, there are not the same level of results as were seen in New Testament times . . .[23]

John Wimber and the Vineyard movement have certainly fostered and encouraged many churches in the ministry of healing. Wimber's book *Power Healing* has been a valuable guide and source of inspiration to many. Yet even he found it difficult to demonstrate this in any widespread manner. In a discussion with church leaders in Sydney, Australia, he stated that blindness has a success rate of 3–8 per cent depending on the cause. He himself claimed to have prayed over more than two hundred children with Down's Syndrome. To his great disappointment only one of the two hundred revealed any sign of healing. According to Philip D. Jensen of Sydney, 'the healing rate, then, for Down's Syndrome is 0.5 per cent, and the healing that did take place was only partial (unlike Jesus' healings)'.[24]

There is no doubt that some remarkable healings have taken place under John Wimber's ministry but it has also been hard to get at the concrete evidence. The failure to provide any Christian doctors with verifiable cases of healing at the Sydney 'Signs and Wonders' conference, for example, contributed to the doubts about genuine miracles having occurred. Peter May, an English Christian doctor, has also challenged what he maintains are unwarranted claims by the Vineyard 'Signs and Wonders' movement.[25] While May's biblical analysis of power healing and the miraculous is clearly flawed[26] and has been challenged, it has to be said that medically verifiable physical healings of the kind which would convince a sceptic are hard to locate. There is clear evidence that lasting healings, both physical and emotional, do occur as a result of prayer and laying on of hands. In a random sample of sixty people taken at New Wine 94, twenty-nine were able to pinpoint some definite healing as a result of prayer. The majority of these were emotional rather than physical.

Hard and fast X-ray and clinical evidence of physical and organic healings is not substantial or widespread. My view of the matter is that some charismatics are in danger of making more claims about such healings than the evidence will sustain. Clearly it is right that churches should pray for the sick, as Jesus enjoined, but care must be taken not to raise people's hopes in a wrong way by implying that healing will undoubtedly follow if they have faith.

Danger: Charismatic Healers at Work

A danger which arises out of some charismatic healing ministries is 'triumphalism' or the 'name it and claim it' approach. This kind of teaching was developed initially by the faith charismatics such as Kenneth Hagin and Kenneth Copeland in the late 1960s and 1970s. It was in part a reaction to the negativity, which had been resulting from evangelical teaching on putting to death the self and the old nature. It had resulted in people with very low self-images and discouraged individuals who found it difficult to be positive about anything very much. In rightly countering this negativity, charismatic healers in particular pushed to the opposite extreme to a point where people were encouraged to make positive affirmations even when they hadn't the faith or it was totally unrealistic to do so. The Arbuthnots, for example, related the case of a wheelchair-bound woman about whom they had heard from a friend. She was 'ministered to' by a small group who then exhorted her: 'Stand up now and claim your healing! We have prayed for you and you must be healed.' The woman apparently struggled to her feet, but, to the horror of those by her, her shin bones broke with the unaccustomed weight of her body. She sank back into her chair in agony and screaming with pain. Similar accounts of individuals claiming their healings, though thankfully with less damaging consequences, are frequently recounted in the aftermath of rallies and healing campaigns. Tom Smail counselled against these dangers in one of his six starter tapes on healing today. 'My rule in healing ministry,' he says, 'is to start with no promises at all.' His suggestion is simply to say:

> Well, here is Jesus, in all his ability, able to meet your need, and here are you, in your great need, and what we are going to do by this prayer is to bring him to you and you to him. As we do that, perhaps we shall begin to get some discernment about where God wants to start his healing process in your life. Does he want to bring physical relief or do something about your relationship with him, or does he want you to learn to glorify him in your suffering.[27]

This procedure is clearly safer pastorally in most cases but it doesn't eliminate all the problems. Most obviously, it doesn't explain why, if Jesus touched 'all who came to him' in the days of his earthly ministry, he wouldn't want to do the same today! Some healers have taught, and Wimber among them, that Jesus only did what he saw his Father doing. Because he knew that his Father was about to heal a particular group or individual he prayed for healing in that moment. Inevitably this means that individual Christians cannot expect to achieve the same level of results that Jesus did. Jesus had total discernment of a person's sickness and needs, Christians do not. Jesus' closeness to his Father was clearly on another level when compared with that of his followers' relationship with God. His knowledge of God's working in a particular situation meant that he knew when to pray in a way that the members of the church do not. Care must therefore be exercised that churches approach the healing ministry with realistic expectations.

The Need to Face Reality

A related problem which often stems from the 'name it and claim it' approach to healing is what has sometimes been termed 'believism'. Believism is people pretending or trying to believe that they're healed when plainly they're not. Instances of it are sometimes encountered when people have prayer for their eyes and then break their glasses in faith! One young lady did this at the end of a meeting and then got into her car only to discover the visibility was somewhat hazy! Eventually her passengers were able to reason some sense into her. There is a definite need to be wary of the 'Positive Faith' charismatic teachings which offer guaranteed health. Kenneth Hagin said on one occasion, 'I never talk sickness. I don't believe in sickness. I talk health. I believe in healing. I believe in health. I never talk sickness. I never talk disease. I talk healing.'[28] MacArthur cited the example of a young pastor and his wife who were having difficulty in conceiving so they were exhorted by an enthusiastic member of their church to 'confess their pregnancy' by purchasing a pushchair and walking down the street with it! At root the concept of having faith and trying to develop a positive mindset had a valid point to make. It is often the case that sick people, particularly those attending places of healing, have become very 'passive' in their stance and attitude. There is a tendency in this sort of situation for people to sink back feeling their situation is helpless and beyond hope. Sick people often do need help to take up a more positive attitude to their condition. The Bible has a good deal to say about thinking positively and taking ourselves in hand and constantly reminding ourselves that God is with us and able to do beyond what we ourselves ask or think.

The problem with this line of teaching, as I said before, is that it may reach a point where individuals are asked to believe things they simply haven't the faith for or told to imagine something has happened when it manifestly has not. As one known charismatic healer instructs his patients, 'Believe in spite of the symptoms!' Some charismatics are very real and down to earth in this kind of area. Others are not and need to be encouraged to be so. David Mansell wrote an article in *Restoration* magazine in September 1977 entitled 'What if no healing takes place?' In it, amongst other things, he advised total honesty.

> Firstly, don't panic, and secondly don't pretend . . . If the person seeking healing really is seeking the kingdom of God, then we say nothing has happened and seek God to know by which door he wants the kingdom to come into that person's life.

Countering the Accusation of Hypnosis

At this point it is important to note Philip Foster's critique of Vineyard ministry meetings. Foster, who is himself a charismatic Church of England clergyman, compared Vineyard guidelines for conducting ministry meetings with stage hypnotism. He argued that much of the ministry which is taking place on these occasions is 'hypnotism' which he judges to be unbiblical on the basis that 'charming' is forbidden in the Old Testament, notably in Jeremiah 8 verse 17 and Deuteronomy 18 verses 10–11.[29] Foster continues:

> People such as Kenneth Copeland, Kenneth Hagin Jnr, Rodney Howard-Browne, Benny Hinn, John Arnott, together with Sandy Millar and David Pytches and many others may be practising hypnotism at their meetings. On seeing the video material of their activities, anyone professionally familiar with stage hypnotism will tell you that that is what is going on.[30]

For this reason, he writes, 'many so-called healings don't last'.[31] In response to Foster, two things can be said. First, it is apparently very difficult to hypnotise large numbers of people so there is no reason to be unduly alarmed by accusations of widespread hypnotism. Second, there is nothing intrinsically wrong with hypnotism of itself. It is certainly not what the Old Testament means in its denunciation of 'charming' which relates to spiritism and mediumistic practice. I have known a Christian doctor and a Christian dentist who have both used hypnotism on their patients with very positive results. The key factor is the person doing the hypnotising. This includes their motivation, their procedures and their accountability checks.

Having said that, I think it's not impossible that a few people may, on occasion, experience something akin to a light hypnosis or altered state of consciousness during times of Christian worship. Doctors and medical practitioners with whom I have spoken achieve hypnosis by bringing the person into a safe place. This is often done by playing gentle music and taking the individual back in their imagination to secure and happy moments in their past. Public Christian worship, particularly where there is gentle worshipful singing, can also become a safe place for some people. For this reason, as Foster suggested, great care is needed on the part of the person leading a time of ministry not to engage in extended platform rhetoric which could soften or control the more suggestive members of a congregation. The same also holds good for those involved in individual prayer ministry. They need to avoid intrusive questions or directional prayers. In these 'safe' situations some worshippers may want to 'rest' in the presence of God, either prostrated or seated. John Wimber always emphasised the dignity of the individual and discouraged any kind of manipulation. It is my perception that generally speaking those sections of the charismatic church which share the Vineyard values are given careful instructions to simply bless what God is doing and to allow the Holy Spirit to have his way. This is certainly the case at New Wine and Soul Survivor and their network churches. John Wimber allowed people to be unafraid, to let go, to cry or to give play to their emotions. As a result of these releases there is a catharsis and sense of well-being through which many thousands progressed to receive degrees of wholeness and healing.

What About Unhealed Healers

An issue which has raised concern on occasion is the fact that some healers are themselves unhealed. Indeed, some of them have and do suffer from major illnesses. Other prominent individuals in the Christian world such as David Watson and Roy Castle were prayed for by many people but found no healing in their pain and suffering. John Wimber wrote very humbly and honestly about his own condition in his book *Power Healing*. Returning to Yorba Linda from Brighton in October 1985 a cardiologist's diagnosis confirmed his worst fears, 'I had damaged my heart'.[32] His doctors informed him that if he didn't cut back on his schedule, begin walking daily and lose weight he would most likely die from the results of stress. He responded to the advice he'd been given and his condition improved. Sadly, John Wimber was subsequently diagnosed as suffering from cancer in his nasal cavity in 1993. This necessitated massive proton and radiation therapy. The treatment proved successful but John then suffered a stroke in 1995. Later in the summer of 1997 he underwent a triple by-pass heart operation. He was recovering when he had a fall which resulted in a brain haemorrhage. He died peacefully on 17 November 1997.[33]

Canon David Watson was the best known evangelist in the Church of England in the 1970s. He was a lucid preacher, an able writer and gifted communicator. In the early 1980s he was diagnosed as having cancer and all around the world Christians began to pray for his healing. In December 1983 Teddy and Margaret Saunders took David Watson to the Wimbers' home in Yorba Linda for an eight-day visit. During the course of his stay teams of people from the Anaheim Vineyard prayed for David almost round the clock. In fact he was prayed for hours at a time. Notwithstanding all of this the fluids continued to collect in his body. Wimber said to him, 'David, you're a dying man, and you're denying it . . . unless God sovereignly intervenes you will die, go home and get your affairs in good order.'[34] David died in February 1984. Ten years later, the English entertainer Roy Castle died of lung cancer caused, it was said, by passive smoking in the night clubs and theatres where he had performed in his earlier days. As with David Watson, so had many people prayed for Roy Castle's healing, including many Christians at Spring Harvest in 1992.

Why were these men of God not healed in response to prayer? Why are others like them prayed for over extended periods yet without seemingly positive results? In *Power Healing* Wimber gave a number of reasons why people are not healed. These include not enough faith in God for healing, personal unconfessed sin, sin and unbelief in the bodies of believers and families, incorrect diagnosis of the problem or poor prayer method.[35] A little further on in the same chapter Wimber also wrote: 'There is another reason – I believe the most fundamental reason why people are not healed when prayed for today.

We do not seek God as wholeheartedly as we should'.[36] None of these reasons it seems to me, however, could be identified as applicable in the cases of the three individuals we have been discussing.

Towards a Theology of Suffering

Perhaps what all this is saying is that charismatics in general need to develop a more detailed theology of sickness and suffering. Martin Percy has argued that Wimber's view of God's power 'would not permit him to see God revealing himself (equally) in failure, sickness or powerlessness'.[37] Percy is probably correct in his interpretation of Wimber. Indeed Percy's view is clearly based on the evidence of the Gospels. What Percy failed to do, however, was to give Wimber the credit for highlighting the fact that not everyone is healed. Wimber in fact raised the case of four who were not healed: Epaphroditus (Phil 2:27), Timothy (1 Tim 5:23), Trophimus (Acts 20:4) and Paul himself (Gal 4:13–14). Explanations such as personal sin, defective faith or ignorance in those who were sick or those who prayed for their healing were not plausible in these cases.[38] On this evidence Wimber stated categorically that not all those who were prayed for by the disciples were healed. Furthermore, Wimber advised that it is important to consider carefully whether or not it is a very sick person's appointed time to die. If such is the case 'we should release him or her to God'. 'We can offer the terminally ill a great gift of comfort and courage. One key to offering comfort and courage is our own freedom from anxiety about death, which begins with being rightly related to God.'[39]

Clearly this is an area where charismatic Christians who are active in the healing ministry need to do some more thinking and develop some careful teaching on some of the points which John Wimber made. There needs to be a greater recognition of the fact that God is sovereign. Christians have no automatic right to presume or to assume that because they have prayed he will therefore automatically take action. Charismatics rightly emphasise that God is a God who intervenes in the affairs of his people. If, however, God was for ever intervening to heal in every situation then the human race would no longer be individuals with a freedom of choice, but mere automatons. There perhaps needs to be a greater recognition of the fallenness of the creation and of the human race. Men and women are part of a beautiful but nevertheless defective and imperfect world. They are themselves flawed, not because of their actions but by virtue of being born. They are part of a human race which is tainted and to some extent activated by evil and selfishness. All sickness and suffering ultimately has its roots in this fact. At the most basic level, therefore, it can be said that sickness exists because we live in a sinful, fallen world. Sickness will not finally and permanently be eradicated until the Lord returns and takes total possession of this world order. Charismatics need to recognise that while it's not God's will that there should be natural disasters or accidents, these things are nevertheless the way things are. Any biblical approach to the healing ministry must take full note of this fact.

It also needs to be recognised more fully by some charismatics that on occasion sickness is allowed by God for particular purposes. This is clearly taught in the book of Job and there are glimpses of it in the book of Exodus. In Exodus 4 verse 11, for example, the Lord said to Moses: 'Who gave man his mouth? Who makes him deaf or dumb? Who gives him sight or makes him blind? Is it not I, the Lord?' C. S. Lewis in a classic passage spoke of suffering and sickness as 'God's megaphone in a deaf world'. Often sickness or enforced rest is the only way in which God can get through to his people. Psalm 107, for example, is a meditation on how God's people drifted from him. Then, as a result, they experienced sickness and suffering (see verses 5, 10, 18, 26) through which they were brought back into relationship with God.

Clearly sickness is, in a good many instances, the result of some form of human sinfulness. It may be overeating, overworking, lack of exercise, lack of sleep, poor diet or the breaking of God's commandments. Charismatic healers have a tendency to pass over these more natural causes of sickness. In such cases repentance and forgiveness are going to be the *sine qua non* of any physical and lasting healing. A retired Christian consultant surgeon whom I know well went and visited all the Christian centres of healing and deliverance in the country. One of the things which struck him most forcibly was the fact that the cross seemed to feature very little in their prayer and counselling ministry. It is my perception that in more recent days some charismatics have begun to make repentance and forgiveness more central in their theologies of healing. In 1985 John Gunstone wrote an article for *Renewal* magazine entitled 'Forgiveness is healing'. In it he spoke of the value of open confession. 'Confession to one another acknowledges that our sins do not only break our relationship with God, they also break our relationships with the rest of the Christian community.'[40] Gunstone pointed out that we have to forgive those who have hurt us in the past before we ourselves can receive and experience God's forgiveness. Only then will we be able 'through the sacrifice of Jesus Christ' to know that we are really restored to the status of God's sons and daughters.[41]

Tony Higton in a section on healing in his forthright and uncompromising book *Our God Reigns*, underlined the importance of repentance and forgiveness as a basis for any true healing. Remarking on the question of AIDS he underlined the necessity of true repentance. 'Jesus,' he reminded his readers, 'gave the paralytic absolution before healing him physically' (Mk 2:1–12). He continued:

> It is not loving to the practising homosexual and especially to the AIDS sufferer who contracted the disease through homosexual activity, sexual promiscuity or drug abuse to omit dealing sensitively and lovingly but definitely with the sin involved. The need to encourage penitence and then declare God's forgiveness is just as necessary in a loving ministry to the AIDS sufferer as is healing, acceptance and practical support.[42]

A problem which frequently arises in churches where there is regular prayer for healing is the danger of attracting neurotics, the inadequate and the difficult. In one sense the needy are of course to be welcomed in the way that Jesus welcomed them, but this inevitably leads to difficulties of various kinds. Such individuals can easily swamp and absorb the emotional energy and attention of the church's leadership. They can also monopolise the congregation and be a drain on the time of the ministry team or prayer group. Too much repeated ministry to these kinds of people is in the long run of little value. It becomes a kind of spiritual dram drinking and it can often leave the recipients with a very passive attitude. Such people need to be encouraged to stand up on their own two feet and to make an active effort to contribute to their own healing. Too much prayer and ministry in too short a time can also result in leadership dependency.

As we have already noted in this chapter, many charismatic churches and centres of Christian healing make use of 'words of knowledge' as a means of encouraging faith. For an individual to hear their specific condition or problem spoken out can act as a strong stimulus to ask for prayer. In some churches these 'words' are received by a prayer team or praying group before the worship. In other places, the congregation as a whole is invited to offer such words. In this case, as a precaution, usually only regular members of the congregation are invited to contribute. Typical contributions would be someone with a pain in their right shoulder area, someone with a swollen ankle, a man with severe heartburn, someone with deafness in the left ear, someone with a fear of cancer and so forth. One danger with this kind of procedure is that in some charismatic churches these words are spoken to the congregation as coming directly from God. Care needs to be taken to underline the fact that this is what members have felt, heard in their spirit and that it is up to congregational members to then think it over carefully and assess whether or not they are from God and valid for individual circumstances. On some occasions such words are used in very damaging ways, to drag members of the audience or congregation to identify themselves publicly and come out and be prayed for. These kinds of words of knowledge may also be spoken out by the worship leader. People are then invited to indicate by raising a hand that they have the particular conditions which have been mentioned. They are then asked to come to the front of the church building or meeting hall for prayer. Suddenly to have to go public in this way can be quite an unnerving experience for some people. Charismatics need at all times to respect individuals' right to privacy and to decide whether or not they wish to respond.

Words of knowledge have been criticised on the ground that people's response to them is little more than one would expect from statistical probability. Some are so generalised as to be bound to strike a winner! A woman in her thirties, for example, whose Christian name begins with 'M' with a headache or severe period problems could hardly miss in a audience of several hundred. Nevertheless, the fact remains that in many instances words of knowledge are claimed by someone present in the congregation. In the church to which I belong in Cheltenham, one of the leaders, Frank Booth, kept a written record for a number of months of all the words which were given out each Sunday and tried to keep a check on how many were claimed and by whom. On most Sundays seventy-five per cent or more of the words were claimed by members of the congregation. They generated faith and expectancy of healing on the part of both the praying group and their subjects.

Interestingly, a study of the words of knowledge given at the Signs and Wonders conference at Sheffield in 1984 was carried out by Dr David C. Lewis of the Religious Experience Research Project at Nottingham University. He was clear that the 'words of knowledge' spoken out at this conference posed 'one of the more difficult problems for rational explanation'.[43] Lewis was of the opinion that such words could not have come from ESP, telepathy or clairvoyance. One reason for this was the specificity of some of the words. For example, Wimber claimed that there was someone present with cracked ribs. They 'fell last winter on snow or ice and the ribs haven't healed properly. The left foot slipped. It hurts right through the left side . . . [pause] . . . It was February this year on slushy, icy stuff – hit on the ground . . . [longer pause] . . . your name is George'.[44]

It is well known, according to Lewis, that in spiritualist circles mediums travel round the circuit and get to know individual church members and their conditions. In the case of Sheffield, however, Wimber and his associates had flown in directly from America. They didn't know people in the audience, let alone their medical histories. Many of the words which were spoken out at the conference, according to Lewis, were more detailed even than his pronouncements about George. Lewis also demonstrated that the probability which he witnessed at Sheffield of identifying a particular age group and a particular limb was of the order of 0.2 per cent. Again, this, he felt, defied rational explanation. Overall, Dr Lewis was not a little impressed by his scrutiny of words of knowledge at Sheffield.

The Positive Side of Charismatic Healing

Despite the fact that there are negative aspects to the healing ministry of charismatic churches right across the denominational spectrum, the overall impact has a great deal that's positive. Perhaps most important is the fact that the charismatic movement has helped to recall the churches to Jesus' commission to preach the good news, heal the sick and cast our demons (Lk 9:1–2). Healing the sick was Jesus' commission to the twelve and later to the seventy-two (Lk 10:17). It was a call which extended into the apostolic church and beyond into the early Catholic period. The New Testament plainly enjoins the sick to request for prayer and anointing with oil by the church leaders. The gift of healing is clearly included among the New Testament gifts of the Holy Spirit. There seems to be no good reason why the gift of healing and not some of the other gifts should be withdrawn from the church. There is a problem in that some people are healed in response to prayer while others are not. Nevertheless it has to be said that this is no greater difficulty than the fact that some people respond to the gospel message when it is preached and are converted and others do not. This can be put another way. The fact that people don't immediately and, perhaps never, become Christians when the Christian message is proclaimed doesn't cause preachers to stop preaching. Equally, the fact that people don't immediately, and perhaps never, get healed when prayer for healing with laying on of hands is offered, is no reason to stop doing it.

It is thanks to the charismatic movement that so many churches and chapels across the United Kingdom now have a ministry of healing in which prayer is offered on a regular basis to members of the congregation. The charismatic movement has helped to extend the healing ministry from largely formal sacramental priestly locations to other more informal locations. There is associated with this a much greater willingness on the part of individual Christians to be open about their needs and concerns and to pray for one another both informally in a home setting as well as within a more formal church system.

Of great importance is the fact that many ordinary people testify to having been healed over the last two decades in which the charismatic movement has been in evidence. The 1981 report, *The Charismatic Movement in the Church of England*, acknowledged 'both the new emphasis upon healing and the undoubted glorious healings which have occurred'.[45] It also observed the fact that 'no longer does miraculous healing need explaining – now it is non-healing which has to be explained!'[46] The report continues 'God is expected to be at work in power, and the spate of charismatic books of recent years fills to overflowing with the record of how God both met and exceeded their expectations'.[47] The later Doctrine Commission of the Church of England report, *We Believe in the Holy Spirit,* also noted: 'There is today a great deal of literature about healings and a large corpus of healings actually recorded'.[48]

The charismatic movement has helped the whole church to put healing high on its agenda. It has brought Christians back to the realisation that 'health and wholeness' are an integral part of the ministry of salvation. We live in a world in which 'brokenness' is all about us in almost every situation we care to view. We see it in our inner cities, in our work places, and in our homes and families. If the Christian message is to have wide appeal it has got to address this most basic aspect of people's lives.

The ministry of healing must therefore be a central aspect of the Christian message and Christian ministry. Charismatics have taught and encouraged the wider church a great deal in the matter of healing. They have also learned and developed many practical and helpful insights themselves, which need to be followed and further developed. One of these is the importance of careful and wise counselling alongside prayer for healing so that any roots which may lie behind some sickness can be discerned and attended to. Another aspect is that people who are prayed for need to be carefully prepared beforehand to ensure that their expectations are not unrealistic and that they won't be devastated if the healing they have set their heart on doesn't materialise. All ministry needs to be conducted with gentleness and sensitivity so that the people receiving it are comfortable and affirmed and damaging incidents such as those reported by the Arbuthnots are avoided. With these provisos the ministry of healing will be an important aspect of the church's mission in the new millennium.

9

SIGNS AND WONDERS

In the 1980s the British charismatic movement began to be reinvigorated by new influences emanating from California. It started to be called the Third Wave, a term coined by Peter Wagner who was Dean of the Fuller School of World Mission in Pasadena, California. Wagner defined the Third Wave as 'a new moving of the Holy Spirit among evangelicals who, for one reason or another, have chosen not to identify with either Pentecostals or the Charismatics'.[1] He saw the Third Wave as distinct from, but at the same time very similar to, the first and second waves. The Third Wave was seen as more 'laid back' in style and it involved the whole people of God, not just the clergy and leadership, in ministry in the Holy Spirit.

This movement had its beginnings in the mid 1970s when John Wimber enrolled in Wagner's church growth course at the Fuller. The two fast became friends and Wagner's book *Look out! The Pentecostals are coming*[2] became a significant influence on him. Wimber, who at that time held a cessationist view of the gifts, was mesmerised by the vivid contemporary accounts of healing and deliverance from evil spirits in South America. He started to read avidly the books by the English Pentecostal, Donald Gee (1891–1966), and the American Episcopalian, Morton Kelsey. As he began to study the Gospels from this very different standpoint, Wimber recognised that Jesus always combined the preaching of the kingdom with a demonstration of its power, such as healing the sick, feeding the hungry, casting out demons and raising the dead. The words and the works of Jesus were completely intertwined. Wimber became convinced that the key to effective preaching was demonstration. He made a distinction between traditional 'programme evangelism' and what he termed 'power evangelism'.

The distinctive ingredient in 'power evangelism' was the 'Signs and Wonders' element. John Wimber began to feel increasingly convinced that the signs and wonders which fostered such rapid church growth in the developing nations could be a model for the United States. This led him to resign from his work at Fuller and devote his energies to pastoring the church which was meeting in their home.

John Wimber the Man

John Wimber was born in the American mid-west in 1934. His father left home soon after he was born and this absence was a crucial factor in his early years. His mother remarried seven years later. None of his immediate family circle was a Christian so there was little church or religious influence in his formative years.

The family moved to Orange County California in 1946. As a youngster John began to learn the saxophone and several other musical instruments. From his teenage years he was a member of various local jazz bands and instrumental groups. On leaving school he became a professional musician playing and orchestrating a wide variety of music. His career as a musician reached its zenith when he helped to form a Las Vegas based band called The Righteous Brothers who gained international acclaim.

In 1955 Wimber married Carol who was a non-practising Roman Catholic. The ceremony took place in a Baptist church. Things did not prove too easy for the marriage, however, and the relationship 'deteriorated badly'. In 1961 Carol phoned him and suggested: 'I looked into a sixty-day, Las Vegas "no fault" divorce.'[3] After a period of desolation Wimber began to pray and he and Carol were reconciled and subsequently renewed their marriage vows in the Roman Catholic Church.[4]

John and Carol Wimber were both converted in 1963 and joined a small independent Quaker Congregation at Yorba Linda. John gradually detached himself from the musical industry and between 1970 and 1973 he studied at the Azusa Pacific College and graduated with a degree in Biblical Studies. During this time he served as co-pastor of their church.

Two years later Wimber ended his pastorate and joined with Wagner. During this period Wimber began to change his attitude towards things Pentecostal and charismatic. Among other things his wife Carol received the gift of 'speaking in tongues' and started to organise a prayer group in their house. John was apprehensive, but when he eventually attended he found himself captivated. The Yorba Linda friends were unsympathetic and the new group were ousted, pastorless. They invited Wimber to be their leader and after some initial wavering he resigned from the Fuller and took the oversight of the forty or so people who met in his home.

The new church grew rapidly, moving to Canyon High School in 1978. The music was 'soft-rock', the worship contemporary and the atmosphere laid back. In 1981 the congregation witnessed an extraordinary experience of corporate renewal when a young man who had given testimony invoked the Holy Spirit with the words 'Come Holy Spirit'. The young people, about four hundred of them, fell to the floor, weeping, wailing and speaking in tongues. Congregational growth was explosive. In 1983 Wimber moved his congregation's affiliation to a small network of six churches called Vineyards led by Ken Gulliksen.[5] By this point Wimber's church was about 5,000 members and meeting in a large warehouse complex in Anaheim. 'Vineyard Ministries International' (VMI) was set up as a renewal organisation to organise and sponsor Wimber's growing worldwide ministry and conference programme. With the passing of time Ken Gulliksen handed the movement over to Wimber who commented 'and God told me he was right in doing so'.[6]

By the early 1980s the number of Vineyards was growing rapidly and the Association of Vineyard Churches (AVC) was formed 'for church planting and to provide oversight'.[7] In the words of John Wimber, 'The Association of Vineyard Churches – for better or worse – is a denomination'.[8]

John Wimber's career as a world leader and speaker on the charismatic stage burgeoned in the mid 1980s. There were, as has been noted, moments of hotly-debated controversy. These included his association with the Kansas City prophets and the dismissal of some of his closer leaders and followers for sexual impropriety.[9] Concern was also expressed over some financial issues including conference funding and payments.[10]

John Wimber in England

John Wimber first came to England as a result of having met David Watson at Fuller Seminary in California in 1981. David then invited him to St Michael-le-Belfrey and David Pytches, learning of his intended visit, invited him to come to St Andrew's Chorleywood. He duly arrived at the latter venue with a twenty-nine-strong team and taught on 'Equipping the Saints for the work of the Ministry'. Later in October 1984 a 'Third Way' conference was held by the Vineyard in Westminster Central Hall and others followed in succeeding years at St Albans and Sheffield. Wimber's emphasis soon became apparent in the life of quite a number of Church of England and Restoration churches including St Thomas Crookes in Sheffield, Holy Trinity Brompton and its associated churches in South West London, St John's Harborne, Canford Magna. For these churches and many others besides, both Anglican and non-conformist, John demonstrated how to welcome the Holy Spirit and release individual congregation members in ministry.

The number of Vineyard churches in the Association reached the 500 mark by 1995. By 1997 there were more than 700 Vineyards worldwide and 49 in England.[11] By the close of 1999 the number of English Vineyards had increased to 59.[12]

Martin Percy in an extensive study interpreted John Wimber as a fundamentalist holding rigorously to the doctrine of scriptural inerrancy. He saw Wimber as primarily engaged 'in his own particular holy war with weak, powerless or dead churches'.[13] Percy noted that like many fundamentalists Wimber did not engage in dialogue. In his case however this was not because he believed he had a monopoly hold on truth but simply as a way of conserving energy. There are, it should be noted, many fundamentalists, particularly in America, who disliked Wimber's style and his emphasis on spiritual gifts, sign and wonders, healing, prophecy, deliverance and speaking in tongues. Noting that 'power' is a theme or term which ran right through Wimber's teaching and ministry, Martin Percy set up a critical analysis of Wimber from the standpoint of power. He believes that Wimber viewed everything through the grid of power and powerlessness. The result of this, he suggested, is that Wimber's teachings about Jesus, salvation and the church is deficient. In particular, he maintained that Wimber had little place for weakness, and no adequate theology of suffering and sickness. The end result of this was a juxtaposing of power and love. Because Wimber was so set on emphasising the power of Jesus and other related power concepts in evangelism and healing he had no place for a gospel which is purely love but with no power.[14] Obviously this view needs closer scrutiny and we shall return to it later in this chapter. For the moment, however, this motif will serve as a lead in to consider the main aspect of this chapter which is Wimber's power evangelism or 'signs and wonders teaching'.

Power Evangelism

Although John Wimber returned to the pastorate in a full-time capacity he nevertheless continued his association with Fuller and lectured on an occasional basis. In January 1982 the new School of World Mission Catalogue announced MC 510, 'The miraculous and Church Growth' taught by adjunct professor John Wimber. The first run of the course was held on Monday evenings with a class of about 130 students. The teaching material dealt with the theory and practice of the miraculous in the proclamation of the gospel. Two hours were given to lecture input and discussion. This was followed by a practical laboratory session in which students put into practice what they had learned. Gradually over the duration of the course scepticism receded and many of the students began to pray for healing outside the classroom and in their home churches.

Peter Wagner attended one of the early classes as a spectator with no thought of becoming involved. All that changed, however, when at the end of one of the sessions Wimber asked if anyone present needed prayer for physical healing. At the time Wagner has been taking daily medication for high blood pressure and so he responded. Wagner perched on a stool out in front of the class and John Wimber prayed for him. As he did so he was enveloped by a great sense of peace. After about ten minutes Wimber stated that God was ministering to him but he shouldn't quit his medicine until the doctors gave the go ahead. A few days later Wagner's physician was delighted to observe that his blood pressure was considerably improved. A few months later his condition was normal. Popularly called 'Signs and Wonders' the MC 510 course broke all enrolment records at Fuller.

Wimber's concern was that Western Christians divide their lives up into separate categories: the ordinary or everyday or 'natural', and 'the religious or supernatural'. In theory they believe that God is able to intervene in the world in their everyday affairs but in practice he doesn't. They believe in the miracles of rebirth and changed character but not in healing, deliverance or other signs and wonders. Wimber observed this to be the view of many mainstream evangelists. In his study manual, *Signs and Wonders and Church Growth*, he analysed the book of Acts and in a detailed chart indicated that there are twenty-seven occasions in which church growth was directly related to signs and wonders. Only once is church growth attributed to preaching alone. Wimber commented: 'It seems clear from this survey of Acts that signs and wonders played a vital and integral part in the spread of the gospel. Has this stopped being the case? Surely NOT!'[15] As far as Wimber was concerned 'Power Evangelism' is distinctly evangelical. Unlike many renewal movements where the focus is on the church itself power evangelism 'subordinates' the gift to fulfilling the great commission.

As John Wimber read and re-read the New Testament and reflected on the state of the contemporary Church, he realised that the element which was missing was a 'mighty Jesus' who moved with such power. He taught his disciples to do the works that he did and greater. He empowered them to expel the demons, heal the sick, feed the hungry and set the captives free. Wimber was quite influenced in this early formative period of his thinking by the writings of Dr George Ladd. For example, he quoted him with approval in his *Signs and Wonders* manual: 'The exorcism of demons is proof that the Kingdom of God is at work among men. The casting out of demons is itself a work of the Kingdom.'[16] Wimber came to the view that the churches had excluded God and his power from our theology and practice because it's too difficult to handle. 'We have said,' he wrote, 'it simply does not exist.'[17]

Wimber felt strongly that the church at large had needed to recover a powerful Jesus who could intervene in people's lives and transform their situations. Only when people outside the church began to catch glimpses of such a Jesus would they come to accept the message which was being preached to them. This led Wimber to develop what he termed as 'Power Evangelism'. The heart of this concept is that believers are to expect and to allow Jesus to move in power through them to others and to their situations. It was this power which was 'imparted to the church at Pentecost'. It is this power, he argued, which will persuasively confirm the preaching.

It is at this point that Wimber parted company with many fundamentalists and conservative evangelicals such as the 'Proclamation Trust' in the UK or the Southern Baptists in America. They argue that God has chosen to reveal himself in the Scripture alone. This conviction goes back to the great assertion of Martin Luther and the sixteenth-century Protestant reformers. It is the Scripture alone which God has infused with transforming power. Wimber, while holding firmly to the supremacy of the Scriptures, nevertheless maintained that God also reveals himself in signs, wonders, healings miracles and church growth.

The problem is that Western culture has become so taken over with rationalistic materialism that all possibility of supernatural activity or encounters is more or less ruled out of court by most Christians. Wimber nevertheless remained adamant that in order to grow the church must engage in signs and wonders. This is 'power evangelism'. Wimber maintained that while programme evangelism is effective in a limited way, 'power evangelism' has been, and still is, the best means of growth! Power evangelism, Wimber readily pointed out, is 'best developed in a climate of risk taking and willingness to fail'.[18] People need to be exposed to a model where they can 'see it', 'hear it', and then 'try it'. They can then 'think about it', have it 'reinforced' and 'try it again'. Finally. they will 'be it' and 'do it' for the rest of their lives.[19] All of this can be considerably more daunting and demanding particularly in the early stages, nevertheless this is what works.

Whatever views churches and individual Christians may hold regarding Wimber's teaching few could deny the effectiveness of his ministry. His own Vineyard Association has emerged from a small cluster of churches mostly in the southern USA in the early 1980s to more than 700 worldwide in the later 1990s. They do seem to have a particular capacity to reach the young and unchurched in a way that the historic churches do not. In the UK most of the main denominations have been profoundly and lastingly influenced by Vineyard values, music and ethos. Michael Wood reported that most of the Baptist Union pastors with whom he had spoken acknowledged that 'exposure to the Wimber factor has been helpful and positive. Many people have been helped and changed.'[20] Michael Mitton, formerly of Anglican Renewal Ministries, spoke with immense gratitude for the input which John Wimber has brought to many Church of England parishes.[21] Don Double of Good News Crusade wrote warmly of the way in which John Wimber's 'intellectual emphasis' has brought this ministry in the Holy Spirit 'to a wider audience, particularly to men in the ministry'.[22] During the 1990s Theological Colleges such as St John's College, Nottingham taught their students to minister in the Holy Spirit using the Wimber model.

A Middle Class Phenomenon

Steve Hunt in an extended essay entitled 'Doing the Stuff'[23] has argued forcibly that the Vineyard is essentially a middle class movement where members are 'highly educated, economically secure, with an over-representation of people in management or the professions'. He cited a survey by R. D. Perrin which indicated that 74 per cent were aged between twenty-three and forty-two years old, with the membership comprising 59 per cent females and 41 per cent males.[24] Hunt also observed that one appeal to the middle class made by the Vineyard was that of 'belonging to a successful church caught up in a significant tide of evangelism, without great commitment to the church itself'.[25] Another attracting feature, according to Hunt, are the Vineyard conferences with their 'therapeutic techniques' which offer 'emotional healing'. Additionally, Hunt noted the drawing power of a continually changing menu with offerings of healing, deliverance, prophecy, territorial spirits or revival.[26]

All this is not to say that Wimber was without his critics both in England and America. In the States fundamentalists such as John MacArthur and CRI members, Elliot Miller and Robert Bowman junior, lambasted the 'Third Wave' and all it represents.[27] Other critics include Phillip Jensen, rector of St Matthias Church in Sydney, Australia who published a harsh critique entitled *Wimber Friend or Foe?*[28] and the English Proclamation Trust whose members speak of him as 'a dangerous man from America'.

Wimber's Critics

The main area of attack on Wimber has been on his power concept. His opponents say that he made overmuch use of the concept and motifs of power. All the talk, so it is said, is of 'power healing', 'power evangelism', 'power ministry', 'the dynamics of spiritual life' and so on. There is, his critics say, insufficient attempt to entertain the other side of the Christian message, such themes as suffering, cross bearing, trials and testing and the day of small things. For instance, it has been suggested that in his analysis of church history he selectively instanced signs and wonders in four periods: patristic, medieval, Reformation, modern and twentieth century.[29] There is no doubt that this assertion is correct as a glance at sections 6 and 7 of his work manual *Signs and Wonders and Church Growth* demonstrates.[30] However, it needs to be noted that the instances are substantial and run into sixty A4 pages of closely printed typeface. Wimber was simply pointing out that there is evidence of Signs and Wonders throughout Christian history for those who care to look for it.

Martin Percy has argued strongly that John Wimber's use of 'power stories' and powerful personalities, together with other power metaphors may be 'alienating the sick, the poor, the helpless and the handicapped from the church'.[31] He points out that when the apostle Paul was with the weak he became weak.[32] Not so, by implication, John Wimber. Wimber's church too, Percy maintains, is portrayed as a 'powerful body'. It is a mighty army and the agent of God's power'. Its role is strongly fortified by success-orientated spiritual warfare songs which proclaim that we are the army of the Lord.[33] In answer to Percy, it needs to be said that John Wimber did exhibit a particular concern for the weak and the alienated. He established Vineyards in places like Soweto where there has been a real witness against racism. Many of the American Vineyards continue to show a deep concern for the needs of the poor and demonstrate very practical help on behalf of those who are hungry and homeless. Articles on social justice have also been a feature of

Wimber's magazine *Equipping the Saints*.

Percy's most strident criticism is that Wimber saw Jesus only in terms of 'power'. He is seen almost exclusively in the words of one of the songs as 'mighty mighty Saviour, mighty mighty Lord'. This means that his theology of Jesus' cross and the significance of his death are treated inadequately. Phillip Jensen also referred to the 'striking absence of the cross or repentance' in Wimber's preaching.[34] The accusation here was that Wimber failed to see the life of Jesus as a sharing in weakness or defeat. 'The ultimate function of Christ's death was, therefore, the release of power.'[35] All of this may well exclude the powerless and the disadvantaged. It also, he suggests, holds out little for those who are not healed and who remained wheelchair bound, crippled or impaired in some aspect of their living. My own opinion is that Percy is offering a one-sided account of Wimber in order to sustain the argument of his thesis. It seems to me that there is also plenty of evidence of the centrality of the cross both in Wimber's songs and in his books and his preaching and teaching. Indeed at one point he called the Vineyard song writers together and gave each one a copy of Dr Martyn Lloyd-Jones' book *The Cross*. He encouraged them to study its meaning in the Scriptures. A number of songs which focused on the cross flowed directly from that meeting. These included 'It's Your Blood That Cleanses Me', 'You Gave Your Body', 'At the Cross', 'The Blood of Jesus' and many more.[36]

Wimber had to face criticism in the matter of leadership. His brief encounter and involvement with the Kansas City prophets caused considerable alarm, particularly in the UK where it caused a split among his supporters. Bob Jones, one of the prophets, was dismissed for immoral behaviour. On the other hand, doubting eyebrows were raised when it was revealed that an angel appeared to Paul Cain in his youth and told him that God was jealous of his girlfriend and he must now remain pure. 'From that day on he has experienced no erotic thought.'[37] Blain Cook, described by Percy as 'Wimber's deputy and heir-apparent', was dismissed from his pastorate in 1988 for unwise behaviour towards the opposite sex.[38] Sam and Gloria Thompson and Paul Cain also left the Vineyard for reasons connected with unity and Jack Deare, a prominent leader, left the movement in 1992.[39] In the light of this, it has been suggested that Wimber was not a good judge of people's character and abilities. In reply it could be said that his judgement was certainly no worse than the Church of England which in the same period produced Bishop Peter Ball, Chris Brain and a steady stream of immoral and badly behaved vicars.

John Wimber's overall leadership was high profile. He continued as executive director of almost all Vineyard organisations until 1996 and he was always billed as the chief speaker and chairperson of all the major conferences. There was a danger here, so his questioners maintained, that too much was hanging on one man and that all the power was being gathered in one pair of hands. Everyone is well aware of the old maxim that 'power corrupts and absolute power corrupts absolutely'. At the very heart it is the case that the more dominant a particular leader seems the more dependent the following becomes on him or her. Total leadership dependency has the potential to turn a religious movement from a sect to a cult. It is also the case that the more decisions any one leader is called upon to make, the more inadequate the decisions will prove to be. An article by Mike Wood in *Mainstream* highlighted the dangers of conference Christianity. He pointed out that the special event conference heightened expectation levels. It also served to enhance the image of the leader/speaker, in this case Wimber, and so raise his authority and status over the movement. In the case of Vineyard Conferences there was also the danger of living from one conference to the next and assessing them on the basis of how much phenomena was in evidence. Thus 'a good conference is one in which there's a good ministry time' 'with lots of power around',[40] with signs and wonders prominent and people being significantly touched or falling. The danger is that a surfeit of conferences will lead people to live from one gathering to the next and fail to engage in the realities of daily living.

It has been suggested that the Vineyard leadership shelter themselves from criticism by warning questioning congregational members of the fate of Ananias and Sapphira. Followers who resist or lie to leaders are held to be resisting or lying to God and are therefore liable to his judgement in the same way that Ananias and Sapphira were (see Acts 5:1-11). An illustration of this was seen in Paul Cain's teaching that 'criticism or judgement of himself or Wimber will open the individual to a lot of judgement and severity' (from God). This severity might include hardship or sickness. At one point, he says that 'those who oppose the prophetic will die'.[41] Comments such as this amount to psychological manipulation of individuals to keep their silence. They border on the persuasion techniques used by groups such as the 'Children of God' and the 'Branch Davidians' and should be challenged as such.

Another area of criticism has been the over-emphasis on the demonology of the signs and wonders charismatics. Wimber's teaching that anyone, including Spirit-filled believers, can be demonised (not demon possessed) is no longer just confined to Vineyard.[42] Such views are now more commonplace among other charismatic groups. Wimber identified 'entry points' through which demons can gain access into individual lives. 'These include sinning, traumas, abuse and revenge. 'The prime objective of demons, according to Wimber, is to possess a body.[43]

> There are many demons that don't have a body. Having a body (for a demon) is like having a car. They want to have a car so they can get around; if they don't have a body, they're a second-class demon. They're not first class. I'm not kidding you. That's the way it works. And so (to them) having a body is a big deal. That's why they don't give it up.[44]

Martin Percy writes that 'Wimber needs Satan'. The reason for this need, he says, is that when the 'power' proclamation appears to fail, it can be accounted for in a concrete way: there is a power cut or a break in the circuit brought about by the adversary. Thus, for example, when David Watson contracted cancer of the liver and prayer was unanswered, 'Satan murdered him'.[45] On another occasion when two prominent Vineyard pastors were dismissed for sexual misconduct the explanation was 'Satan entered into them'.[46] If Percy's thesis on Wimber is correct, it could perhaps be said that he needs Satan. However if one doesn't fully buy into his power interpretation, Satan becomes less of a necessity. Having said that I find it hard myself to accept the view that Satan 'murdered' David Watson or that he was solely responsible for the sexual misconduct among the Vineyard leaders.

Wimber's healing ministry also came under questioning in some quarters. For example, Phillip Jensen was critical of both the extent and the technique of Wimber's healing ministry.[47] Jensen considered 'the placebo effect' – where the sufferer takes what they believe to be a cure for their problem (but which is actually a sugar pill) and then improves. 'The evidence so far,' says Jensen, 'suggests that John Wimber heals in the sugar pill area.'[48] Moriarty in the *New Charismatics* pointed out the pastoral dangers which can occur when the anticipated miracles do not occur. The individuals may come to question and doubt not only God's power but even his love. Moriarty appears to suffer from doublethink however because he then endorses the view that if there were too many miracles they would lose their drawing power![49] Nigel Wright in his very sympathetic observation of the signs and wonders ministry noted 'the relative absence of organic healings'. He commented: 'I have been amazed at the gaps between the rhetoric and reality in the area of significant organic healing.'[50] Nigel Wright also observed that some recipients of power ministry became 'superspiritual' and others 'preoccupied with unusual phenomena which has pushed them into themselves and not out into service'.[51]

One area of Wimber's ministry which came under scrutiny was his conferences. Questions were raised following the 1987 Brighton conference. It was estimated that around £230,000 was generated by the four-day event. Fees for the hire of the Brighton Pavilion are waived to certain charitable organisations because of business generated for the tourist industry. Both Vineyard Ministries International and New Frontiers, the conference organisers, refused to comment on the size of the profits. Similar questions were raised following the 1990 London Docklands Conference. The Baptist Union magazine, *Mainstream*, commented that all 'Americans are brilliant at marketing'[52] and that 'mammon lurks in the background when it comes to selling the books and the tapes of the conferences'.[53] At the Vineyard leadership Conference held at the Wembley Grand Hall in September 1994 criticisms were levelled at the visiting team, and even English band members, being billeted at the London Hilton at a discounted £75 per night per head. It seems to me, however, that no concrete evidence of the misappropriation of funds or what could be termed as excessive expenditure ever come to light. It is nevertheless the case that in the contemporary secular world conferences are the name of the game and are known to be potential big money spinners. Many institutions and companies put on conferences solely as an income generating activity and there's always going to be a similar temptation to run Christian conferences to bless people, of course, but also with the underriding aim of making money for the Lord. If such is the motivation in the end it will prove counterproductive.

The Strengths of John Wimber

My own view is that there probably was an element of truth in Percy's assertion that John Wimber was overly focused on 'power themes', but that this was a feature of his earlier years. Later emphases included holiness, prophecy, worship and emotional hurts. Wimber's association with the Kansas City prophets didn't add significantly to Vineyard strategy and direction. In fact the relationship was costly in time and emotional energy and created an unfortunate backlash of public opinion. I see a certain validity in Mike Wood's concern at the surfeit of Vineyard Conferences. Leaving aside the money aspects, they can hinder people from learning to stand on their own feet.

Despite these criticisms and others which were levelled at John Wimber, there can be no doubting that he brought a great deal to the English churches. His input injected a new dimension and fresh sense of purpose and motivation to the charismatic movement. This came at a point when charismatic Christianity was perceived by some to be running out of steam. Wimber also brought together the Restoration and Renewal strands of the charismatic movement at a time when Restoration was beginning to lose its way on hyped-up worship.

One of the most positive aspects of John Wimber's ministry was his stress on intimacy in worship and his emphasis on an experiential personal relationship with Jesus. Wimber certainly did a very great deal to bring a new dimension to evangelical worship. Many charismatic churches who have taken on board his insights testify to a greater reality in their Sunday services. The Vineyard teaching understands the word 'worship' to be a wide-ranging term, but it rightly stresses that the central or core aspect of it is an intimate meeting with God. This is clearly conveyed by the meaning of the Greek word *proskuneo*. Worship leaders were seen by John to have a key task to lead worshippers into this close personal meeting with God. Many of Wimber's songs are intimate in character, using the personal pronouns 'I' and 'You'. They are not hymns about God but hymns to God. This fact is well illustrated by *Songs of the Vineyard, Volume 1*, in which just under half the songs are distinctly 'personal' with the word 'I' appearing in the first line.[54] Many of the lyrics focus on the love, beauty and power of God. There is frequently an element of repetition and echo which enables worshippers to direct their focus on the Lord. It also makes the songs very easy to pick up and their words more memorable. Typical examples of repetition and echoing are:

Hold me Lord, hold me Lord
In your arms, in your arms
Fill me Lord, fill me Lord etc . . .

Isn't He isn't He
Beautiful, *Beautiful,*
Beautiful, *Beautiful,*
Isn't He isn't He
Prince of Peace
Son of God, isn't He.

The atmosphere of Wimber's music is for the most part 'soft rock' which is well suited to the mood and content of the lyrics. The intimacy of worship is seen as the basis of the 'power ministry'. It is as individuals come into close touch with God that they are empowered for ministry. In fact one familiar Vineyard song links the theme of intimacy with that of power. 'More love, more power, more of you in my life.' Peter Wagner pointed out in an article in *Renewal* that Wimber saw intimacy with God as 'the primary goal of the Christian life'.[55] Why so? His answer is that only in maintaining a close relationship with God can we hear his voice, know his will, understand his heart.[56] Although Percy argues that this intimacy with God was the source of power for Wimber, it does not seem to be an obvious interpretation. A stress on tenderness, gentleness and close personal meeting doesn't fit comfortably with images of strength, battle warfare and power.

Closely related to this emphasis on an intimate relationship with God is the raising of people's levels of expectation of what God can do both in them and through them. It has been said that preparation leads to expectation. Wimber saw as the results of intimate worship that 'the expectation of believers is raised: God is no longer distant, but very present, involved in ordinary life and able to transform situations'.[57] He also taught the churches the need for training its members for Christian service and ministry. He published *Equipping the Saints*, an attractively produced bi-monthly magazine, with clear relevant teaching on the practical aspects of Christian living and outreach. Often one issue was devoted to a single theme such as prayer, spiritual warfare, developing Christian character, worship, social justice or concern for the poor. Wimber's Vineyard ran frequent conferences which gave practical hands-on training in these key areas. No one could accuse John Wimber of being in any sense a theorist. His stress was always on persuading people to be 'doers of the word and not hearers only'. For this reason Vineyarders often speak of 'doing the stuff', the stuff being the things which Jesus urged his followers to 'do' (see Mk 16:15–18). The 'Kinship' groups, more recently re-named housegroups, enable people to test things out in an environment where they are free to make mistakes. By these means Wimber helped to make the New Testament concept of the priesthood of all believers into a reality for many more church members. He also released congregational members into active ministry. It is all too easy to sit back with our arms folded and take the passive role of spectator or critic. Wimber demonstrated the way in which sideline lookers on can be converted into active participants.

Two areas where Wimber was criticised, were his Christology and Soteriology. Percy commented that 'Wimber's Christology is essentially subordinationist'. By this he means that he treated the person of Jesus as though he were not equal in every way with the Father. However, Percy gave no concrete evidence or examples to support his contention. 'Jesus is subordinate,' he says, 'both to the will of the Father and the power of the Spirit.'[58] I cannot myself profess to have made an extensive study of the audio tapes of Wimber's teaching, but a cursory glance through the 1990 edition of *Worship Songs of Vineyard* revealed a significant number of songs which express a very high and exalted view of Jesus' person. The following are a few instances: 'Lord of all', 'Messiah', 'Holy one', 'The Universe is in his hands', 'His name is high above all others', and 'Jesus you are Lord and King'.[59] In all of these songs there is not the slightest suggestion that Jesus is in any way less than the complete and full revelation of the God of the Old Testament.

In his book, *The Dynamics of Spiritual Growth*, John Wimber included a chapter about Jesus entitled 'Fully God'. It begins as follows:

> What does God's word say about Who Jesus is? First and foremost, it says that Jesus is fully God. This is clearly stated in many passages . . . On many occasions Jesus himself claimed to be God . . . In the account of the rigged trial in front of the Sanhedrin . . . Not only does Jesus claim Messiahship, but the way he answers makes it clear that he thinks the Messiah is God . . . Jesus not only claimed to be like God, he acted like God.[60]

Percy and others like him also attacked Wimber's soteriology. They asserted that the cross is *not* central in his teaching. The cross, Percy asserted, is almost absent in Wimber's songs replaced by an emphasis on the majesty and closeness of God.[61] Here Percy may be on slightly stronger ground. Of 160 songs in *Worship Songs of the Vineyard, Volume 1*, there are eleven which make some reference to Jesus' substitutionary death and atonement. Familiar examples include: 'It's your blood which cleanses me' (No 74), 'Lord, you gave your life for me' (No 56) and 'Worthy is the Lamb' by John Wimber (No 147).

> Worthy is the Lamb
> Worthy is the Lamb
> Worthy is the Lamb that was slain
> Honoured and adored, exalted evermore
> Worthy is the Lamb that was slain.[62]

This may not be a high percentage of the total, but in many standard hymnbooks the section on atonement is small. Alister McGrath also wrote of Wimber's 'presenting the gospel in terms which make no reference to repentance or forgiveness'; such charges, he comments, 'were pressed particularly forcibly in 1990 at Sydney'.[63] Again it has to be said, this is not the total picture. For example, reflecting personally, Wimber wrote: 'Without knowledge of Jesus Christ's victory over sin and Satan at the cross, Carol and I would have been conscious of our need of salvation – but we would have had no hope of attaining it.'[64] In one of his books Wimber has chapters entitled 'The Father's Sacrificial Love' and 'Under the Blood'. Commenting on God's answer to the dilemma of human sin he wrote:

> The solution is forgiveness. God no longer holds our sins against us, making it possible for him to initiate a relationship with us without violating his holy nature. The key is that Christ uniquely takes our place, he is our substitute (John 11:50; 1 Tim 2:6), enduring God's wrath for us. Jesus also represents us on the cross (2 Cor 5:14), so that as we identify with him, the benefits of his death are applied to us.[65]

Percy is on decidedly weak ground when he suggests that John Wimber 'takes little interest in social responsibility and issues of social injustice' and again, 'actual concern for social justice and for the needs of others outside the gathered congregation is rare'.[66] Wimber has written on the importance of caring for the poor. 'Social justice,' he stated, 'is at the heart of the gospel.' Again he commented that God's kingdom is one in which 'justice rolls on like a river, and righteousness like a never-failing stream' (Am 5:24), a kingdom that upholds the cause of the oppressed and gives food to the hungry and sets prisoners free (Ps 146). An entire issue of *Equipping the Saints* was devoted to the issue of social justice. One subtitle stated, 'Jesus calls us into a spiritual warfare that will profoundly impact the social order on every conceivable level'. Other articles included Graham Cray on the 'Kingdom of God and Social Justice' and Ronald Sider on 'Social Justice and the Evangelicals'. Wimber himself wrote on the need for righteousness and justice. Only those who practise these two qualities, he asserted, 'are fit for the wedding feast of the lamb'.[67] From what I have been able to observe of the Vineyard movement in England and in the United States and Canada there is a genuine concern for the needs of the local community and for the wider poor. South West London Vineyard, for example, are involved in prison work, the homeless and in distributing food, clothes and first aid in the London Embankment area through their 'King's Table' ministry. Similar concerns are also featured in the life of the St Albans and Riverside Vineyards.

John Wimber without doubt reinvigorated the charismatic movement at a point in time when it was beginning to wane. His laid-back style was much more appealing than some of the earlier 'hype'. He particularly endeared himself to the Church of England and some of the other historic churches. Many Christians who were influenced by him came for the first time to have a real experience of the Trinity in their lives. Many more had their first taste of being able to pray and minister to others. This came about because John Wimber offered simple workable models with which individuals were and are comfortable. His teaching that ministry is essentially blessing what God is doing rather than doing and then asking God to bless it, made the whole thing more relaxed and much more possible.

John Wimber was at heart a humble and godly person. He did not fall victim to the temptations of money and publicity in the way that other American Christian leaders have done. He still lived in the same house which he occupied when the Vineyard movement first began and while he received expenses, he accepted no regular salary from the organisation.[68] Those who knew him well speak of his humility, his compassionate spirit and godly character. He was never critical of others.

Wimber's 'Signs and Wonders' emphasis clearly met genuine emotional and spiritual needs. He helped churches to grow, many others beside his own. Power, it could be argued, is not an inappropriate metaphor for today. Wimber helped to empower powerless churches and broken and powerless people from among the liminal elements of society in some of the poorest parts of the world.

There can be no doubting that John Wimber brought a fresh injection of life into the British charismatic movement when it was beginning to run out of steam. His relaxed and laid-back style endeared the charismatic experience to a wider spectrum of middle-class people. His ministry also demonstrated that hype isn't necessary to generate spiritual power.

Wimber made a very significant contribution to worship, particularly at the level of it being a personal encounter with God. Much worship in evangelical churches, especially the singing, was overly theological, cerebral and impersonal in its emphasis. The worship of many charismatic churches was largely a diet of triumphalist praise. Vineyard music has taught the churches the importance of singing to God using personal word forms as opposed to only singing about God. In the quieter moments of reflective, intimate singing, many testify to knowing the nearness of God and to being released of pains and hurts through pictures, visions or tears.

John Wimber was quite obviously a unique leader who was revered and spoken of with bated breath in every Vineyard Church and Kinship. One suspects, however, that the movement will suffer a down turn now that he has died. The Vineyard denomination is a very American outfit and this is one of its strengths, but this has also been a hindrance to its taking widespread roots in British culture. In fact many of the Vineyard leaders in England, Canada and America have been syphoned off from other denominations attracted by John Wimber's leadership and covering. The commitment of many of them may well be diminished in this new millennium now that his successor is in place.

The church as a whole, in this twenty-first century, will without doubt, have benefited from John Wimber's ministry. Not only did he help to raise the level of people's expectancy, his insights and teaching in the areas of ministry, worship and service will prove to have been seminal.

10

REVIVALISM

A number of charismatic leaders, John Wimber among them, have been and are strongly committed to working and praying for revival. 'Revival' is not an easy phenomenon to define. In fact it is not a major biblical concept, although the word 'revive' does occur in one or two places in the Psalms and in the prophecy of Hosea. Jonathan Edwards (1703–58), the Presbyterian minister of Northampton, Massachusetts from 1729 to 1751 and later first president of Princeton, wrote extensively on the subject. In his classic text *The Distinguishing Marks of a Work of the Spirit of God*, first published in 1741, Edwards set out what he considered to be the essential characteristics of a 'revival'. These were that it 'raises the esteem of Jesus', it 'operates against Satan's kingdom', it causes 'greater regard for the Holy Scriptures', it 'removes our darkness' and it 'promotes love of God and Man'.[1]

In more recent times Canon Max Warren, using the work of Dr Edwin Orr an American church historian and researcher, tried to clarify what is meant by the term 'revival'. A particular difficulty is the need to distinguish between widespread effective evangelism, outpourings of the Holy Spirit and charismatic phenomena and revival. Warren eventually asserted that 'any precise definition is impossible. By our human reckoning the Holy Spirit is untidy and unpredictable.'[2] He did agree with Orr that 'revival' brings about 'a revival of New Testament Christianity in the Church of Christ and its related community'. Warren also observed 'the pre-eminent and prevenient part played by prayer'. 'Revivals,' he also noted, are 'spontaneous in character' and he endorsed Orr's view that revivals always evidence 'some repetition of the phenomena of the Acts of the Apostles'. Importantly, they always issue in social transformation and new social initiatives. Most revivals, or revivalistic movements, are accompanied by Spirit phenomena. While the phenomena in themselves are no guarantee that what is being observed is a revival, few revivals occur without them! Obvious examples include falling to the ground, weeping, crying out, shaking and sometimes laughter. All of these were observed in the Methodist revivals under John Wesley in eighteenth-century England. Many of them re-appeared among the revivalistic Primitive Methodists and the Bible Christians in the nineteenth century. Early Salvation Army revival meetings witnessed somersaulting and holy rolling. Other phenomena recorded in nineteenth-century revivals included jerking, jumping, barking and roaring. Some of these phenomena were also noted in the great Welsh revival of 1904–1905, particularly weeping and falling.

The present charismatic movement has from its beginnings in the early 1960s to the present, periodically displayed revivalistic phenomena, particularly shaking, falling and weeping. However, after May 1994 there were a number of intensified movements of the Holy Spirit right across the UK (and indeed across the entire globe) which covered virtually the entire denominational spectrum. It has been popularly, if mistakenly, called the 'Toronto Blessing'. The 'blessing', so-called, originated in other cities in the United States but the major world focus centred on the Airport Vineyard Church (subsequently Toronto Airport Christian Fellowship) on the outskirts of metropolitan Toronto.

Toronto

Much of what has happened in Toronto is traceable to the ministry of Rodney Howard-Browne. For a number of years, Howard-Browne (b 1961) was active in Kenneth Hagin's Rhema Ministries in South Africa. He was associate pastor with Ray MacCauley at the Rhema Mega Church in Johannesburg. In 1987 he felt called to take up residence in the United States. Rodney, like many of the big name charismatics, claimed that he received the call to be the instrument of the 'last days outpouring of God's Holy Spirit' when God appeared to him personally. He wrote of his encounter as follows: 'It felt like liquid fire – like someone poured gasoline over me and set me on fire – the best way I can describe it is that it was as shocking as if I had unscrewed a light bulb from a lamp and put my finger in the socket. I knew it was God.'[3]

By any standards Rodney's ministry must be termed remarkable. He travelled extensively in the United States during the course of 1993 and attracted large audiences which he would 'bring under the power'.[4] In a manner not dissimilar to Benny Hinn, whole sections of his congregations fall to the ground as a result of his blowing on them. He often does this when he walks down among his audiences. According to Clifford Hill, Rodney's particular speciality 'is to have those who fall down begin to laugh uncontrollably, supposedly with the joy of the Lord'.[5] Rodney was apparently bemused himself on one occasion as people laughed while he spoke on hell. Some of those who are smitten down are apparently unable to get up for some time and describe their condition as feeling 'like a block of cement'. Rodney calls people to immerse themselves in the life of Jesus. He urges his hearers to increase God's presence in their lives by spending 'much time reading the gospels and following closely the ministry of Jesus'. The reason that many do not receive more power from God is because 'their thought-life is far from Him'.

One of those who was touched by Rodney's meetings in Tulsa, Oklahoma, was Randy Clarke, the leader of the Vineyard Church at St Louis, Missouri. 'A move of God's Spirit' was soon in evidence at St Louis and Randy's ministry began to move in many of the same phenomena. It was this sudden outbreak of renewal which led John Arnott to invite him to come to Toronto for a conference from Thursday 20 to Sunday 23 January 1994. It was here that the remarkable Toronto phenomena began. Six nights every week since 20 January (there were no meetings on Monday evenings) and still continuing on into 1996, the revival services continued with unabated expectancy and enthusiasm.

Some have understandably asked why Toronto and why 1994? It could be said with some justification that at that point in time the charismatic movement was beginning once again to run out of steam. The 'third wave' initiated by John Wimber had come and had started to ossify into a routine. Charismatic Christianity already had a history of sustaining its following by looking ahead to the next new day or the next new thing God was going to do. By 1994 many were ready for a fresh injection of charisma. Philip Richter suggested that the Toronto Blessing could be understood as 'a psychosomatic response to the failure of Charismatic Renewal to become a truly universal phenomenon with appeal to the wider world'.[6] That its focus was in Toronto should not altogether surprise us. Toronto is in the centre of North America. It has a major international airport and is a city with a burgeoning multi-racial population.

Journeying home from a family wedding in the United States, my wife I were able to be present at the Airport Vineyard in August 1994 at the 250th consecutive revival service. Along with many others from the UK we checked in at the Monte Carlo Inn which gave excellent value at $49 for a double en suite room with breakfast. Mississauga township which encompasses it doesn't provide a particularly inspiring backcloth. However, if you enjoy aircraft you can sit in your motel window and watch the planes taking off. The Airport Vineyard could hardly be more appropriately named. It is literally perched a few hundred yards from the end of one of the main runways of Toronto's Lester Pierson International Airport. Visitors are able to watch jumbo jets and other long haul aircraft lifting their wheels as they take off over the building.

The Monte Carlo Inn did well by the revival since they were provided with a steady flood of overseas guests. They offered 10 per cent discount to those booking through the Vineyard! Having checked into our room we set off in plenty of time and joined the queue for the revival service. Queuing had featured every night since the beginning and we were fortunate enough to get a seat in the main auditorium.

From the outside, the concrete building had the appearance of a small warehouse complex such as one might find on the outskirts of an average English town. The worship area was carpeted throughout with a raised platform across one corner. The chairs were of the comfortable stacking variety. At one end, doors opened into a glass-fronted creche area, church offices and a book and tape store. At the other end was a hot dog, muffin and coffee place.

The services were standard Vineyard fare starting with a forty-five minute worship time with a continuous flow of Vineyard songs. This was followed by notices and greetings.

Visitors were asked to indicate which countries they had come from. There were about thirty-five from the UK, and smaller numbers from France, Belgium, Holland, Germany, South Africa and elsewhere. Next came a protracted and sound sermon which was too long by half. Then came the ministry time. The leader, Carl Nelson, a visiting Vineyard pastor, invited the Holy Spirit to come. Soon there was the sound of gentle thuds as people sank to the ground. Others laughed joyously and some raucously, and some wept. Several pounded the ground with the palms of their hands. Some roared and growled. A lady near us appeared to be doing a combination of dance and mime. As the ministry time continued on, those of us who had come from overseas were invited to come forward for prayer. Most I think found the experience peaceful. Many were overcome by the Holy Spirit and were gently laid out to rest on the floor by ministry team members. By about eleven o'clock we joined the animated crush in the adjoining muffin house for some coffee and plain sustenance. We were lucky enough to find two people from South West London Vineyard with a hired car who kindly took us back to the motel.

Several things impressed themselves on us about the Toronto Airport Vineyard. Perhaps most important, it ran on prayer. There were gatherings for intercession on Monday to Thursday afternoons from 1.30–3.30 pm and on Saturdays and Sundays from 6.00–7.00 pm. At the meeting we attended, the first fifty minutes were spent waiting on God and asking him what he wanted us to bring to him in prayer. Some of those who prayed were literally trembling and wincing under the presence of the Holy Spirit. From time to time the leader stood up in the middle of the group and engaged in a little 'wafting'. This practice in which individuals gently swing their arms forward from a downward position to about waist height was a fairly common procedure. By means of this prayerful and symbolic action the aim is to invoke the Spirit to move in people's lives. Our leader reminded us at one point that the heart of the Christian life is simply learning to 'yield' to Jesus at each step. A carpenter doesn't make a whole piece overnight, we were told, he does it little by little. In a similar way, we have to yield at each stage to Jesus and 'it hurts'.

Some of those attending the Toronto meetings had little difficulty in 'receiving'. They came 'open' and some of the manifestations were immediately apparent in them. The most common was 'resting in the Spirit'. The talk tended not to be of being 'slain' in the Spirit, but rather 'resting'. People either fell or were laid down on the floor. They were conscious and could be engaged in conversation, but they were overwhelmed by a deep sense of well-being and refreshment. For others, the experience was different. It was observed that a number of visitors gradually entered into the blessing over a period of several days. It was as if they arrived like a parched dry ground. As each day they sought to be 'open to God' the level of the Holy Spirit in them extended like the rise of the water table with the coming of rain. By the close of their week they were completely saturated and the familiar manifestations were activated in them. There were some who left Toronto disappointed, feeling that they hadn't experienced any of the manifestations and feeling that God had passed them by. John Arnott and the other leaders however were quick to point out that faith is the one essential ingredient. God, he stressed, may well have touched our lives in a significant manner even though there were no obvious outward manifestations. We learned of a small group of UK pastors who left for home discouraged that they had spent time in Toronto and had felt nothing. But on arrival back in England they prayed for their congregations with powerful effects and saw many of the same manifestations which they'd observed but not experienced at the Airport Vineyard.

For most who went to Toronto between 1994 and 1997 the heart of the blessing was a much deeper consciousness and awareness of the presence of Jesus in their lives. Their walk with him was no longer just a cerebral affair, there is a genuine experiential dimension. For many their level of expectancy and confidence in the ability of Jesus to help them in their situation was raised.

A New Pentecost, May 1994

The *Baptist Times* reported that a foretaste of what was to come in England was seen at a service at Queen's Road Baptist Church in Wimbledon. The pastor, the Reverend Norman Moss, noticed a girl in the congregation weeping in repentance. He called her out and on discovering that she was having a vision of people repenting, he got the church to act out her vision.[7] Familiar by this time with the Toronto scene, Norman and his wife travelled to Canada on 14 May, and stayed until Friday 20. While they were there, Eleanor Mumford, a friend and the wife of the leader of the local South West London Vineyard church, joined them in Toronto.

On their return to England, they both spoke and invited the Holy Spirit to come on their respective congregations. Sunday 22 May proved to be a Pentecost in every sense of the word. People fell to the ground with weeping and in some cases spontaneous uncontrollable laughter. At South West London Vineyard other more unusual phenomena were observed. People were seen running on the spot, pogoing, marching and making reaping actions. Some people were lying on the floor for upwards of an hour shaking and weeping. On the morning of Tuesday 24 May, Eleanor Mumford arranged a meeting to share the Toronto experience with a small number of friends and leaders of some other churches in the area. One of them was Nicky Gumbel, the curate of Holy Trinity Brompton and now internationally known through Alpha. He rushed back to a lunchtime staff meeting just in time to be invited to pray a closing prayer. Remarkable scenes followed and all present were profoundly touched. Prayer was still continuing at 5 pm. Eleanor Mumford was invited to preach at Holy Trinity Brompton both morning and evening on Sunday 29 May. When she asked the Holy Spirit to come there was spontaneous laughter and other manifestations.

News of what had happened travelled rapidly. Pastors and clergy in the South West London area had been meeting together on Tuesday mornings for some months. Now numbers began to swell from twenty to forty and to eighty. Similar experiences were reported at Lewin Road Baptist Church, Streatham, pastored by the Reverend Mike Wood and at Bookham Baptist Church under the ministry of Ian McFarlane. A number of prominent Christian leaders experienced a fresh touch from God. Among them was R.T. Kendall, the Minister of Westminster Chapel and a gifted Bible teacher. R.T. was prayed for by Sandy Millar and some of the Holy Trinity Brompton staff. He had an experience akin to when he 'had sodium pentathol years ago when undergoing major surgery'. He felt 'humbled by the Holy Spirit'.

The leaders at South West London Vineyard prayed for the leadership at St Paul's, Onslow Square and took a ministry team with them to address a Sunday morning service. The blessing spread rapidly 'like the Beijing flu, by contact from person to person', according to Nicki Lee, the congregational leader. Within a matter of days other Church of England leaders were boarding planes for Toronto, among them Sandy Millar, vicar of the fashionable Holy Trinity Brompton, affectionately known as the 'Cathedral of the Charismatics'. He flew out on 31 May with the church's Pastoral Director, Jeremy Jennings. Bishop David Pytches from St Andrew's, Chorleywood also went and was reported by John Arnott as 'down here on the floor roaring like a lion'.[8] Other prominent Anglican charismatics, including Barry Kissell, John Hughes, vicar of St John's, Harborne and Bishop Graham Dow, also made the journey to see for themselves at first hand what God was doing.

The 'blessing', it seems, was transferred to the English churches in two significant ways, from Toronto itself and also directly from the ministry of Rodney Howard-Browne. On their return from Toronto, David Pytches and Sandy Millar organised a series of meetings at HTB for clergy and church leaders who wanted 'to get things going' in their own churches. These were held on 30 June and 14 July, and were intended for clergy in the London area. However, word travelled quickly and at the July meeting the ground floor of the church was packed with church leaders from all over England and Wales! Many clergy and pastors who attended these gatherings were able to initiate things in their own congregations.

Rodney Howard-Browne at Large

At about the same time that things were happening under the auspices of HTB and St Andrew's, Chorleywood, there were parallel movements in the Midlands. Mike Price hosted a series of meetings at Woodgate Church in Birmingham led by Rodney Howard-Browne who had come over from the States. These took place each day and evening from 13 to 17 of June. They were very widely attended with daily coach loads of clergy and church leaders arriving from the south east of England and places to the north from Liverpool and beyond. As at the HTB meetings, dog-collared clergy were to be seen collapsed in laughter on the floor and in one case running in the aisles. Rodney Howard-Browne believes that the 'anointing' which is released at his meetings is 'transferable'. He is always slow to place his hands on people in prayer. He sees this not just as a symbolic action but a means by which 'the life of God on the inside of you flows out into them'. He finds scriptural backing for this in such passages as 1 Timothy 4 verse 14 where Paul speaks of the gift that was given to Timothy when the body of elders laid hands on him. Rodney revealed moments of practical wisdom. He warned against church leaders who 'have no relationship with anyone' or are surrounded by 'yes' people who are unable to see things objectively or question any course of action.

Among those who attended the Howard-Browne meetings were Bryn Jones and other prominent leaders of Covenant Ministries now based at Nettlehill near Birmingham. The Sunday following, 19 June, proved to be an exciting day for a number of Covenant churches and particularly the one in Nottingham where the Holy Spirit came powerfully. The following Wednesday 22 June all the elders of the Covenant churches were brought together by Bryn Jones to share and learn and experience the new move. Since that time the Covenant churches succeeded in running with the new move. Every subsequent Wednesday and Sunday evening for a number of months there were open meetings attended by six or seven hundred people. The entire summer issue of *Covenant* was devoted to reporting on the new moves of the Holy Spirit, particularly as it has impacted Covenant Ministry churches. Bryn wrote in his editorial: 'It is refreshing. It is festive – the cry is "drink, drink, drink!" and everyone is getting drunk. Not with Tetley's Best Bitter or Carling Black Label, but with the Holy Spirit. A giant party is taking place!'[9]

The Covenant church in Cardiff reported many people 'drunk in the Spirit' and 'having to be carried to their cars'. At Leeds City Church 'many people have had to be carried out of the meetings'. At one gathering of the Wirral Community Church, senior elder, Hugh Thompson, laid his 'hands lightly on about forty-five people, who all fell to the ground under the power of the Spirit'. At Manchester 'over three hundred people gathered at short notice just to wait on God for his refreshing'. So the journal continued over several pages.[10]

Another who was present at the Woodgate meetings was Derek Brown, the leader of the King's Church at Aldershot. He was touched himself and was able to spread the experience among the twenty or twenty-five churches who related to him. Derek later produced a small pamphlet entitled 'What's happening in the church?' He also distributed a broadsheet entitled 'A season of glorious disorder'. In it he wrote as follows: 'On Sunday 19th June, 1994, the Spirit of God fell upon the church and now we are in that season of glorious disorder. This is not unique to us but part of a move of God that is happening worldwide.'

One of the most active cluster of newer churches at the time was the New Frontiers network spearheaded by Terry Virgo. The headquarters of the group is located at the 'Church of Christ the King' in Hove. The senior elder, Alan Preston, went out to Toronto at the end of April and returned and spoke at Christ the King on Sunday 1 May. He shared and ministered what he had experienced in Toronto, with the thousand-strong congregation. Major manifestations of joy, weeping and laughter followed.

Shortly after this, Terry Virgo came across from the States having already been prayed for by Rodney Howard-Browne. He gathered together the New Frontiers senior elders on the 12 to the 13 May to share his experiences with them. Two further days of prayer, fasting and sharing were held for all NFI leaders and pastors on 17 and 18 May. Those who were present at these gatherings for leaders from virtually all the ninety New Frontiers congregations began to experience the new waves of the Holy Spirit's activities. Terry Virgo also preached at Christ the King on Sunday 15 May. Remarkable scenes followed, as people wept, laughed and slipped to the floor.

Over a period of several weeks in the latter part of the spring, Gerald Coates, the leader of Pioneer, began to notice that the power of the Spirit in his ministry intensified. In April 1994 he was present at a meeting in Dublin where he saw 'hundreds, confessing and laughing'. At his home fellowship in Cobham he saw thirty or so people coming to Christ over a period of just a few days. At this same point he received a video of Rodney

Howard-Browne's ministry which helped him to focus into what God was doing.

Roger Stevenson of the Tooting Pioneer Congregation was among those who were blessed early on through the meetings at Queens Road Baptist Church in the latter part of June and early July. Gerald Coates encouraged him to visit all the Pioneer churches in the home counties and to pass on what he had received. In this way the move spread rapidly among the Pioneer people in the Greater London area.[11]

A number of other Pioneer churches were deeply affected. Stuart Bell was reported as 'powerfully used' in the Lincoln area. From Sunday 11 to Sunday 25 September Gerald Coates' Cobham-based fellowship rented a thousand-seater marquee for what they styled 'Event in a Tent'. John Wimber was present on Sunday 18 and ministered with extraordinary power. A feature of these meetings was the ministry of children assisting the adults. Peter Birch of the Platt Christian Centre, Putney, was prayed for by a small girl on the Sunday. He found himself lying on the floor of the tent six rows further back! He then had to sit still for about twenty minutes before he could get up. Small wonder, perhaps, that the *Surrey Advertiser* reported 'religious enthusiasm is sweeping across Surrey with waves of extraordinary phenomena'.[12] The *Leatherhead Advertiser* also noted that 'an outbreak of spiritual activity . . . has left people laughing, crying, appearing to be drunk and falling to the floor as though in a faint'.[13]

On 3 and 4 June all the churches linked to Ichthus participated in a conference at Westminster Chapel. Sandy Millar addressed the final celebration following which things began to happen. From that point the Ichthus network of churches began to be strongly affected. From Monday 20 June Ichthus started to hold 'receiving meetings' every week night for two weeks. This was repeated later in July.

The Toronto experience was no respecter of denominations and individuals and churches right across the spectrum were touched. Daniel Payne and Sheila O'Donnell, the leaders of the Roman Catholic 'upper room' in St Albans, went to Toronto in August on behalf of the community. Following their return members experienced the laughter and the tears and other aspects of the 'blessing'. The 'Cor Lumen Christi' (With the light of Christ) Community at Epsom were also touched with Toronto as were the House of the Open Door near Broadway. The latter community, which included several Roman Catholics, ran regular weekly meetings for refreshment. The St Albans and Epsom communities also organised similar activities on a monthly basis. Tears, laughter and roaring were all in evidence.[14]

Strangely perhaps, the Methodists, whose founders inspired such revivalism in the eighteenth century, were little touched by Toronto. One leading Methodist churchman somewhat dejectedly commented to me that few Methodist ministers 'go with the flow' these days.

The Toronto wave was reinforced for many Christians and churches at some of the summer conferences. At the New Frontiers International Conference at Stoneleigh in Warwickshire the whole adult celebration dissolved into helpless happy laughter during the first main Sunday evening celebration. Terry Virgo made the theme of his main address what was happening at Toronto. Seminars were also held for leaders to discuss what God was doing and to give instruction on how to receive. New Wine 94, hosted by David and Mary Pytches and Barry and Mary Kissell, followed a similar pattern. On several evenings the entire adult celebration broke with spontaneous joy and laughing. Seminars were held on the Toronto Blessing led by Bishop Pytches and Eleanor Mumford. Eli also gave one of the main celebration addresses.

Hitting the Headlines

It was inevitable that these goings-on would reach the national press sooner or later, particularly as some well-known Church of England churches were getting involved. The *Independent* on 21 June 1994 carried the headline 'The Holy Spirit hits South Kensington'. The paper's Andrew Brown, visiting St Paul's, Onslow Square, reported 'in front of me a tanned blonde in a blue dress suddenly went down sideways and was helped to the floor, where she wept in heart-rending abandon'. Brown also observed six individuals 'just roaring with laughter, rolling on the floor over and over, holding their sides as if they would really burst'. Others who were lying on the floor made a sound 'like the noise that rabbits make to warn one another'. Some could not walk for laughter and these, mind, are 'sensible, normal people,' commented a bemused Andrew Brown.

The *Daily Telegraph* carried a report under the title 'Faithful fall for the power of the Spirit', which included an interview with John Arnott, the Airport Vineyard's senior pastor.[15] The report was for the most part fair and objective. Ruth Gledhill of *The Times* recounted her visit to the South West London Vineyard on the last Sunday in June. In her Saturday column entitled, 'At your service', she offered a fairly factual account of the 'laughing, weeping and shaking as if in delirium tremens'. She gave a two-star rating to Mr Mumford for his sermon on 'marriage, divorce and the death of love', a three for the music and a five-star mark for the after service care ('climb over prostrate bodies to reach tea and coffee').[16]

Whilst at Toronto at the end of August, we were informed that there had been forty reports on the blessing in the Canadian daily press, all of them positive. The British press were a little more mixed. A later edition of the *Daily Telegraph* gave details of the Toronto Blessing affecting more than 1,000 children at New Wine. A somewhat onesided view was proferred and children were reported as 'sad or frightened'.[17] The matter, however, was in fact discussed with parents and those responsible, beforehand. Most were more than happy to allow their children to be ministered to. The paper gave no hint of this fact. The *Daily Mail* of 3 September carried a very hostile and critical article entitled 'A dangerous emptiness'. It was written by Paul Johnson, said to be an historian. He, however, showed no evidence of having witnessed at first hand any of the present phenomena he described. Certainly there was no reference to any meetings, churches or individuals. He could see no positive outcome from the eighteenth-century Methodist revival under John Wesley. The only consequence of the first great awakening in the American colonies his preconceived notion of revival allowed him to see was the Revolutionary War of Independence!

In surveying the way in which the Toronto Blessing was appropriated in the UK, it's clear that it was the newer churches in particular which have picked up on what had been happening. This was particularly seen in the total responses on the part of the Covenant, Pioneer and New Frontiers groups. It was also true of some of the smaller clusters, such as the King's Churches and UK Vineyards. In a sense this was predictable because it was this section of the church which embraced the charismatic movement most wholeheartedly in the early 1970s. It was also this group which had begun to recognise in Gerald Coates' words, 'the first plateauing' of charismatic experience and influence. As one cynic put it, the charismatic movement had begun to run out of steam and it was this section of the Church which was most deeply a part of it. Clearly many other churches of all denominations also opened themselves to what was coming out of Canada. An announcement was made while we were in Toronto in August 1994 that they now had received visitors from more than 1,500 UK churches. Anglicans and Baptists appeared to be the most enthusiastic of the historic denominations and the Methodists the least responsive.

Assessing Toronto

All of this raises the question, how are we as Christians to evaluate these Toronto phenomena? Clearly we have been given minds by God to use both in our worship of him and in all other aspects of our daily living. We are urged in the New Testament to test every spirit to ascertain whether they're from God (1 Jn 4:1 and 1 Thess 5:21). It is perfectly right and proper that Christians should try to assess whether an experience has both a rational and a solid biblical foundation. The early Christians at Berea were commended because they combed the Scriptures every day to check out whether what Paul was saying was correct (Acts 17:11). A sound approach is to keep an open mind, questioning what we see but at the same time remaining open to the possibility that this was a genuine move of God's Spirit. Within the confines of this short chapter, any assessment is necessarily limited in scope. I have attempted it from five perspectives: historical, biblical, consequential, psychological and rational.

An Historical Perspective

A number of writers and preachers attempted to validate the Toronto experience by comparing some of its more significant phenomena with that which was observed in other earlier revivals. This kind of endeavour needs to be engaged in with care. In the first place, it is necessary to assess whether the earlier revivals used in comparison, had a positive and lasting impact. Were the churches significantly enlarged and was the level of their spiritual life raised? Were the earlier revivals instrumental in bringing about social improvement, grappling with injustice and generating necessary reform? Such questions are obvious and crucial.

The phenomena of revival, particularly those which are bizarre or extreme in character are not easy to assess from any perspective. Jonathan Edwards astutely pointed out after his experiences in Northampton, that 'not all manifestations have express biblical warrants'. He also stressed the fact that ecstatic behaviour is not an argument against a movement being a genuine work of the Spirit of God.[18] Nor, he wrote, is the fact that human effort has been invested in a work an argument against its being a move of God. Equally, the fact that manifestations occasion a great deal of talk or opposition is no reason to doubt their genuineness.[19]

What historical research does show is that most of the prominent aspects of the 'Toronto Blessing' can be documented in earlier 'revivals' which have been adjudged to be clear workings of God's Spirit. The most obvious phenomena are people falling to the ground, spontaneous laughter, weeping, roaring and shaking. There were a host of less widespread phenomena which made an impact on others attending meetings. These include pogoing, jumping, marching, running, waving, wafting, jerking, threshing and reaping actions, pounding the floor and snaking.

A cursory examination of some revivals in the pre-Constantine church and in England and America in the eighteenth and nineteenth century makes it clear that few, if any, of the Toronto phenomena are new in themselves. For example, Hilary of Poitiers (c.315–367) described the experience of being filled by the Holy Spirit in baptism. 'We who have been reborn through the sacrament of baptism experience intense joy (*maximum gaudium*) when we feel the first stirrings of the Holy Spirit'. In another place Hilary wrote: 'Among us there is no one who, from time to time, does not feel the gift of the grace of the Spirit.' 'We begin,' he says, 'to have insight into the mysteries of faith, we are able to prophesy and to speak with wisdom. We become steadfast in hope and receive gifts of healing.'[20]

John Wesley (1703–91) was a Church of England clergyman who had a dramatic experience of God at a little chapel at Aldersgate Street in the East End of London in May 1738. He later wrote: 'I felt my heart strangely warmed. I felt I did trust in Christ alone, for salvation; and an assurance was given me, that he had taken away my sins, even mine, and saved me from the law of sin and death.' There has been some debate among historians as to whether this was a conversion experience or a subsequent re-affirmation of his previous commitment to Christ. However, all that need concern us is that from that moment in time, Wesley was a changed man. He preached everywhere, taking to the fields and declaring 'the world is my parish'. As he did so, many of his hearers were affected in ways not dissimilar to the Toronto experience.

In 1739, Wesley attended a meeting in London. His brother Charles and George Whitefield were also present. He recorded the experience in his *Journal*.

About three in the morning, as we were continuing instant in prayer, the power of God came mightily upon us, in so much that many cried out for exceeding joy, and many fell to the ground. As soon as we recovered, a little from the awe and amazement at the presence of his majesty, we broke out with one voice, 'We praise thee, O God, we acknowledge thee to be the Lord'.[21]

A little later the same year, Wesley was preaching at the Weavers Hall in Bristol when 'a young man was suddenly seized with a violent trembling all over, and, in a few minutes, the sorrows of his heart being enlarged, sank down to the ground'. In a short while he had found peace. It frequently happened that Wesley's hearers would cry aloud or fall down as if dead. On another occasion, on 25 April, while Wesley was preaching, 'Immediately one, and another, and another sank to the earth; they dropped on every side as if thunderstruck'. On another occasion Wesley reported: 'My voice could scarce be heard amidst the groanings of some, and the cries of others, calling aloud to "him that is mighty to save".' Wesley reported the conclusion of a prayer meeting which he attended: 'Just as we rose from giving thanks, another person reeled (drunkenness) four or five steps, and then dropped down.' It seems that almost everywhere Wesley went people were stricken down. During one of his periods in London he preached at Wapping, and 'twenty-six people were stricken down under conviction of sin'. 'Some sunk down and there remained no strength in them . . . others exceedingly trembled and quaked; some were torn with a kind of compulsive motion in every part of their bodies'.[22] During another preachment at Baldwin Street, Wesley reported that two persons were seized with strong pain, and constrained to 'roar for the disquietness of their hearts'.[23]

For the most part, Wesley was not disturbed by these occurrences which he took to be from God. He usually responded by praying himself for the persons concerned or by requesting similar help from his lay assistants. The outcome was usually positive. At Wapping, for example, he responded immediately with prayer. The Wesleys also experienced laughter. In his *Journal* for May 1740 Wesley reported that just as he and his brother Charles were about to sing psalms together 'he burst out in a loud laughter'. Wesley continues: 'I asked him if he were distracted; and began to be very angry and presently after began to laugh as loud as he. Nor could we possibly refrain, though we were ready to tear ourselves in pieces, but we were forced to go home without singing another line.'

At the same time that Wesley was experiencing and promoting revival in England, Jonathan Edwards was witnessing similar occurrences in America. In his classic account of *The Revival of Religion in Northampton 1740–42* and in his other writings, Edwards also makes it clear that many of these same phenomena were present in the revival of religion that took place under his ministry. Reporting on the year 1741 he wrote:

> The months of August and September were the most remarkable of any this year for . . . great revivings . . . and for extraordinary external effects of these things. It was a very frequent thing to see a house full of outcries, faintings, convulsions, and such like, both with distress and also with admiration and joy. It was not the manner here to hold meetings all night, as in some places, nor was it common to continue them till late in the night; but it was pretty often so, that there were some that were so affected,

and their bodies so overcome, that they could not go home, but were obliged to stay all night where they were.[24]

At the beginning of 1742 Mr Buell, another preacher from the locality, came to the town and the people 'were exceedingly moved'. There were, Edwards related, some instances of persons 'lying in a sort of trance, remaining perhaps for a whole twenty-four hours motionless, and with their senses locked up; but in the mean time under strong imaginations, as though they went to heaven and had there a vision of glorious and delightful objects'.[25] Summarising the situation as it appeared to him a year later, Edwards wrote:

> Some that have had very great raptures of joy, and have been extraordinarily filled (as the vulgar phrase is), and have had their bodies overcome, and that very often, have manifested far less of the temper of Christians in their conduct since, than some others that have been still and have made no great outward show.[26]

One other revival which has received much attention from historians is the Cumberland Revival which took place in the upper part of Kentucky somewhere between 1800 and 1801. It was here that the celebrated Cane Ridge Camp meeting took place. The meeting was protracted for three weeks and kept up day and night. It is reckoned at times that from 12,000 to 25,000 people were in attendance. Hundreds fell prostrate under the power of God, giving the appearance of men slain on a battle field. A prominent phenomenon at Cane Ridge was an exercise known as 'jerking'. Individuals would be seized 'as by a strange power' which caused them to jerk. Cartwright recalled that the jerks were so spontaneous that young men and women's hats would fly.

A number of people at Toronto and those influenced by it experienced the 'jerks'. As I participated in a prayer group at the Airport Vineyard, a number of people were unable to stop themselves from jerking. Cartwright regarded 'the jerks' as a genuine manifestation of God's Spirit. He wrote: 'I always looked upon the jerks as a judgement sent from God, first to bring sinners to repentance; and, secondly, to show professors that God could work with or without means'.[27] Cartwright related the instance of one man at Cane Ridge who, when taken with 'jerking', swore he would drink them off. As he attempted to raise a whiskey bottle to his lips he jerked so violently that his neck was broken. The incident, Cartwright recalled, brought great conviction of sin on the people.

A Biblical Perspective

Many seeking to make sense of the Toronto experience rightly attempted to reflect biblically on the more significant phenomena. However, simply finding biblical references for 'laughter' or 'heavy breathing', for example, should not be taken as automatic endorsements of their Toronto counterparts. The context of the biblical phenomena is crucially important and must obviously be carefully scrutinised. For instance, if laughter is being considered, we must ask was the biblical instance cited spontaneous or was it evoked by external circumstances? Was such laughter controlled or raucous and totally out of hand? Did the biblical writer endorse or commend the phenomena or was she/he indifferent or condemnatory? For example, Vivien Calver in his chapter in *The Mark of the Spirit? A Charismatic Critique of the Toronto Blessing* made an extended study of laughter in the Old and New Testaments. Many of the references to laughter, he observed, were to 'mocking laughter'. The only verse in the whole Bible, in his view, which predicated the laughter of Christians is Luke 6 verse 21.[28]

One of the more common Toronto manifestations is 'drunkenness'. Ruth Meaden of HTB, for example, commented on her first Sunday in church following her summer holiday, 'I spent over an hour rolling on the floor hysterically crying and laughing. When I left I was so drunk! I couldn't get into the car. I had to be put in.'[29] Presumably she was driven home by someone else. Eli Mumford related that after one of the meetings which she addressed at a fashionable London church, one young man was so drunk that the only way his friends could get him home was in a supermarket shopping trolley![30] Jeff Lucas, Vice-President of the Evangelical Alliance, attended a meeting with his wife Kay. They were apparently intoxicated to the point where they were completely incapacitated. Unable to drive or walk they had to be carried by friends to the car and later to their house!

This phenomenon was widespread and commonplace in churches which were moving with the Toronto Blessing. I myself witnessed it at South West London Vineyard, St Andrew's, Chorleywood, HTB, Queens Road Baptist Church, New Wine 94, New Frontiers Stoneleigh Conference, and Pioneer's 'Event in a Tent'. There seems little doubt that it was something akin to this that the crowds witnessed when the Holy Spirit came on the disciples on the Day of Pentecost (Acts 2:13–16). Paul later urged Christians at Ephesus not to get drunk with wine but rather with God's Spirit (Eph 5:18).

Closely related to drunkenness is falling! The two clearly go hand in hand and doubtless did so on the Day of Pentecost. Falling was commonplace in the Toronto experience. The *Baptist Times* reported over 200 people lying on the floor of Queens Road Baptist Church, Wimbledon. At a meeting for clergy and church leaders at HTB on 30 June there must have been close on 100 prostrate bodies laid out, most resting peacefully. In the early phases of the charismatic movement the talk was of being 'slain in the Spirit'. Following the incipient phase of Toronto the talk was more of 'resting in the spirit'. Those who went down were clearly conscious, and could be engaged in conversation. At the same time many felt a heaviness on them and sensed it would be a struggle to get up. Scriptural precedents which affirm falling might include the following. Saul fell when he met the risen Jesus on the road to Damascus (Acts 9:4). The disciples fell down on the Mount of Transfiguration before the glorified Jesus (Mt 17:6–7) and the apostle John fell as though dead before the risen Jesus (Rev 1:17). All three biblical instances indicate that falling to the ground can certainly result from a personal encounter with Jesus.

Shaking was common at Toronto-style meetings. It varied in intensity; sometimes it was just people's arms and hands which shook or trembled. On other occasions, the whole body was shaken with an intensity which was quite violent. There are some clear positive scriptural endorsements for such trembling and shaking. The phenomenon seems often to have indicated that God was powerfully present or about to act decisively. 'The LORD reigns, let earth shake,' said the psalmist. The prophet Jeremiah declared that all his bones 'trembled' because of the

Lord (Jer 23:9). Other relevant biblical material includes Psalm 114 verse 7, Daniel 10 verse 7 and Habakkuk 3 verse 16. The prophet Habakkuk in fact prophesied that the last days would witness the shaking not only of the nations but of the whole earth.

Many people who fell found themselves crying and weeping. In fact, it seems to have been the case that many more wept than laughed. Some shed tears as their experience of the Holy Spirit released them from pain and emotional hurts. Others wept over their past sins and a number cried tears of repentance and mourning for their generation and nation. I witnessed people crying out of sorrow for the sins of their generation. It is clear enough from both Old and New Testaments that tears are a sign of the Holy Spirit's working. The prophet Joel marked out weeping as a sign of genuine repentance (Joel 2:13). When the people of God heard Ezra read from the Book of the Law they also wept (Neh 8:9) in repentance.

The manifestation most highlighted in the Toronto experience would seem to be laughter. Frequently this was accompanied by falling to the ground. On other occasions those who laughed were in a variety of postures, often sitting, sometimes standing. Observers were understandably disturbed that in some instances the laughter appeared to be hysterical or even maniacal in character. Laughter is certainly depicted in Scripture as an expression of release (Ps 126:2) and joy (Gen 21:8, Job 8:21). Joy is also a fruit of the Spirit and 'joy' and 'rejoicing' are among the most frequently used words in the Bible describing the character of God's people. In his first letter, the apostle Peter referred to the 'inexpressible and glorious joy' experienced by the persecuted and suffering Christians to whom he wrote. The problem which many observers felt regarding a good deal of the laughter associated with the Toronto Blessing revolved largely around its inappropriateness and uncontrollable character. There clearly are times when it is right and good to laugh, but laughter during the reading of Scripture or in moments when a congregation are being directed to reverence the majesty and holiness of God cannot be seen as appropriate, right or prompted by the Holy Spirit. It needs always to be remembered – self-control is a fruit of the Holy Spirit.

Other so-called Toronto manifestations which were

observed included the following. Some of these have biblical though not necessarily positive endorsing precedents, as indicated by the bracketed references: roaring like a lion (Rev 10:3, Hos 11:10), groaning (Rom 8:22–23, 2 Cor 5:4), spontaneous clapping (Is 42:13), running (Is 40:31; 52:7), jerking/trembling (Ps 2:11, Dan 10:10), jumping (Is 35:6, Mal 4:2, Lk 6:23), snaking/writhing prostrate on the ground (Dan 10:9; Ez 4:4–8), making threshing actions and waving the arms. Many of those who observed these phenomena, such as Bishop David Pytches, believed that they were symbolic actions or signs of what God was doing or about to do. The Old Testament prophets often acted out the purposes of God in a dramatic form. Thus roaring like a lion at the Toronto Vineyard was seen as a declaration of impending judgement, groaning as a form of crying out to God for mercy and marching a sign that God was on the move. Jerking and trembling were felt by some to be indicative of God's judgement, snaking or writhing on the ground as a symbolic plea for penitence, while jumping and the waving arms were seen as natural expressions of joy and welcome at what God was doing.

A Consequential Perspective

A number of observers have contended that some of the results of the Toronto experience are 'dysfunctional'. Critics maintain that some of the phenomena were excesses of emotionalism and, in some cases, forms of hysteria. Professor Arthur Pollard, by his own admission a biblical conservative and Protestant fundamentalist, wrote in the *Church of England Newspaper*, 'There should be no place for mass emotionalism, rolling in the aisles and mindless laughter, the sort of exhibitionism we have been hearing about lately'. Alan Morrison, a Baptist minister, wrote of thousands 'being hoodwinked by psycho-religious phenomena'.[31]

The laughter associated with the Toronto Blessing was one of the main focal points of criticism. The *Daily Telegraph* of 18 June highlighted the fact that a Communion service at HTB had had to be cancelled amid 'unprecedented scenes of ecstasy'. Tony Haynes wrote poignantly to the *Baptist Times* under the title 'The "Toronto Blessing": Whatever Happened to Self-Control?'. 'Self-control,' he pointed out, 'is one ninth of the

Spirit's fruit (Galatians 5:23) . . . so where do people . . . being convulsed by uncontrollable laughter fit in?' Clifford Hill similarly expressed his concern that the laughter was 'often hysterical and even maniacal'.[32] Hysterical laughter, he suggested, is an excess which the believer ought to be able to control out of courtesy for others.[33] Andrew Walker suggested that in the *Philokalia* the Desert Fathers see laughter – and certainly mockery and out-of-control laughter – as demonic, at worst; and they are very keen to stress the importance of sobriety as a means by which we are able to discern truth from falsehood.[34] I listened to and witnessed at close quarters Toronto Blessing laughter on at least twenty different occasions. It seemed to me that there was some validity in the comments of Haynes and Hill and others like them. Some I saw were 'resting in the Spirit' laughing heartily and joyously. In other cases there was raucousness to a point where there was potential for 'busting a gut'. In the long run, however, it is doubtful, as I heard Gerald Coates point out, if a season of laughter is any much more damaging than the dull ministry of monotonous church services. Also, Tony Haynes perhaps needs to reflect that if he pressed his point too strongly, the Day of Pentecost would have to go down as uncontrolled and therefore not of God.

In times past, and at the present moment, individuals have questioned the practice of invoking the Spirit to come with the formula 'Come Holy Spirit'. Clifford Hill wrote: 'It is never right to pray "Come Holy Spirit"! Prayer should be addressed either to the Father or to the Son.'[35] Professor Colin Gunton writing on God the Holy Spirit warned of the charismatic movement's 'tendency to depersonalise the Holy Spirit'.[36] What Hill suggests may be a good general guideline but it needs to be recognised that Jesus told the disciples to wait for the Holy Spirit to come and to be filled with him. Furthermore, there is a very early tradition of the Christian church invoking the Holy Spirit on the bread and wine of Communion and on the communicants themselves. One of the most ancient Christian hymns dating back to the second century is 'Come, Holy Ghost, eternal God, proceeding from above'.[37]

Just as the first Pentecost led to repentance, so the Toronto experience was to some extent characterised by a spirit of repentance. Dave Roberts, editor of *Alpha* magazine, wrote that 'from the very start there has been a note of repentance in the testimony of many churches and individuals'.[38] Gerald Coates, leader of Pioneer, commented, 'I have never had so many confessions of sin, letters of apology and acts of reconciliation'.[39] Clifford Hill noted that repentance featured in the preaching at churches where the blessing is evidenced.[40]

In a number of places people who experienced the Toronto Blessing gained an increased desire for holiness. The *Baptist Times* observed that as a result of these manifestations there was 'an accelerated growth in sanctification or holiness'.[41] People also spoke of a stronger appetite for prayer and study of the Bible.

Among other fruits of the Toronto Blessing there have been many instances of physical healings.[42] I heard several testimonies of healing at Cobham on the evening of 22 September 1994, including the lifting of depression and the reconciliation of broken relationships. Commenting on what was happening in the Covenant churches it was reported that 'Christians young and old were finding a new dynamism in reaching out to others with the gospel, and people are turning to the Lord'. Eli Mumford said it for many on her return from Canada: a day or so after getting back she found herself talking quite spontaneously to a group of women about recent events and reflected that this 'was evangelism and it didn't even hurt!'[43] For many there was this same boldness to launch out and a new appetite to be involved in God's work.[4]

Psychological Perspective

A great deal of entertaining fare could be written about the psychological aspects of Toronto. Doubtless if William James or William Sargant had been resurrected they could have found plenty to get their teeth into![44] As it happened critics were not slow to come forward. One of the foremost critics was Alan Morrison, a Baptist pastor for Crick in Derbyshire. He published two pamphlets *Falling for the Lie: Questions and Answers on Charismatic Deception,* and *We All Fall Down: An Investigation into the Experience known as 'Slain in the Spirit'*. In the first of these he argued that the disciples on the Day of Pentecost were not mocked as drunks because they were 'falling to the floor, or laughing hysterically, or grinning inanely, or uttering gibberish, or crowing like cockerels, or roaring like lions, or waving their arms in the air, or holding their quaking hands out in front of them, such as happens with the so called "Toronto Blessing".' This kind of phenomena, according to Morrison, has only ever been practised among mystery religions, mystical orders, shamanistic cults and pagan sects. 'The phenomena we're seeing in the times of refreshing are at best,' he asserted, 'the outworkings of a childish and hysterical mimicry; at worst, they are the result of something far more sinister.'

In his second piece, Morrison suggested that the phenomenon of 'falling in the Spirit' was in fact a form of hypnotism such as was practised by Maria Woodworth-Etter, a nineteenth-century holiness preacher, and by Franz Anton Mesmer, an Austrian physician, who lived a little earlier. 'It is,' Morrison asserted, 'Mesmer's crude form of manipulative hypnotherapy which is being practised by the Pentecostal–charismatic movement, through which the strong suggestions and even the mere touch of a powerful teacher can turn the lives of the gullible inside out.' Morrison concluded his second pamphlet by declaring that charismatic churches are not producing disciples of Christ. Rather they are grooming a new generation of spirit mediums. Nigel Wright suggested that many of the phenomena witnessed in the Vineyard and more particularly in the Toronto Blessing had been partially generated by a 'psychic' stream. He spoke of 'psychic phenomena in the Wimber movement'. Wright also maintained that the use of teams was an important factor in this process because they 'catalyse' religious phenomena. Conversely, when the teams leave, the intensity of the phenomena is diminished.[45] Professor Andrew Walker also saw revivalism as 'some sort of psychological phenomenon due to some stimulus external to the people concerned, such as a group response to hypnotic suggestion'.[46] My own feeling is that the phenomena emerging out of Toronto were for the most part a mixture of the divine and the human. The leaders of the Toronto Airport Church understood the phenomena to be human responses to the divine presence of God. But it does seem to me that there is evidence that some of the phenomena could be understood as responses to psychological pressure rather than the divine presence. Nevertheless, despite what many took to be excessive emotionalism or worse, many testified to feeling of well-being and wholeness. People who experienced the laughter felt so much better for it. Indeed laughter is known to be therapeutic. Dr Patrick Dixon, a well-known physician, wrote at some length on the Toronto phenomenon of laughter. He observed that many who have laughed for long periods reported an overwhelming sense of God's love and of relief, as if 'a massive weight of cares had been lifted away'. This fact caused him to do a computer trawl of the literature on the subject of laughter. He pointed out that laughter is a powerful means of reducing tension and that the mere action of laughing is therapeutic. Laughter also increases our level of contentment and alertness. More significant, laughter shuts down the harmful hormones which are released into the body when we are under stress. In short, laughter is a relaxing emotion.

Regardless of what we view as the origin or source of such laughter, and Dixon was open to the possibility of it coming from a purely human or psychological root, it is nevertheless wholesome and to be commended.[47] Dixon recounted his own experience which was very positive, in some detail. He was prayed for at the Pioneer leaders' day on 4 July at Fairmile Court.

In twenty-five years of being a Christian I have never experienced anything like it, and have tended to distrust such feelings in others as largely emotionalism. I was so curious to know whether hyperventilation could possibly be the explanation for what I was feeling that I consciously restricted my breathing until it became impossible to do so anymore – and still the sensations continued. I am certain that hyperventilation had nothing whatever to do with it . . . I laughed until my body was more than half off the floor and then some more until it hurt and I started to wheeze . . . lying there it felt like sunbathing or perhaps that should be 'Son bathing', being washed in the presence of God. A joyful, peaceful, refreshing wonderful, thing.[48]

For Dixon the impact of this personal experience was totally positive. Reflecting on it two months later he recognised that the most significant thing had been the conviction of sin, recognising that wrong attitudes and feelings had crept imperceptibly into his life. He also found himself to be more confident and assertive in sharing his faith with others.

Whilst in Toronto with my wife we had occasion to meet a Canadian medical doctor who was engaged in (secular) counselling people with emotional stress and hurt. She had been interested to read reports of the Airport Church in the Toronto daily press (about forty different reports between January and August 1994). She commented on how important it is to get people to laugh as a form of release. 'I always try to get my patients to laugh,' she said.

During our discussion she related how she put her patients into a mild hypnosis. When they were securely 'resting' in that state she asked them if there was a particular memory or area of stress or hurt they would like to examine. Gradually through counselling it becomes possible for the individual to allow the pain to come to the surface and to come to terms with it. From what she had read and heard of the goings-on at the Airport Vineyard she felt that through the worship and the experience of 'resting in the Spirit' people were being released in a similar kind of way from emotional wounds and scars.

People experiencing the blessing in England testified to this kind of release. One young woman at South West London Vineyard stood for an hour at the end of the evening worship, then she was down on the floor for a further hour. She commented later, 'I felt as though I had been washed inside from all the stains of the past ten years.' Another lady, herself a counsellor, who was 'touched' at Queens Road Baptist Church said that the release she experienced would have taken ten or eleven months of counselling to accomplish. It is for this kind of reason that Dr Simon Wessley, senior lecturer at Kings College School of Medicine in London, commented in the *Observer*, 4 September 1994, that 'this religious experience appears to be cathartic'.

A Rational and Cumulative Perspective

One further attempt to assess the religious experience of Toronto is that attempted by David Middlemiss in his *Interpreting Charismatic Experience*. He endorses the views of John Locke that reason is a God-given faculty which must be used to scrutinize both revelation and experience. In

Middlemiss's own words, 'The final decision on whether any particular claim should be considered as true revelation can only be made in the end by reason. It is reason that requires adequate evidence if it is to give assent.'[49]

The difficulty which arises from the assertion of reason as the final arbiter is whose reason or which reason are we talking about? Our own or someone else's? One person's reason would tell them Toronto laughter is uncontrolled and therefore not of God's Spirit. In contrast, another individual may decide that this is no more uncontrollable than the behaviour of the crowds in Jerusalem on the Day of Pentecost and is therefore probably of God. It has to be recognised, as Lesslie Newbigin so clearly pointed out, that 'there are no "truths of reason" except those that have been developed in a historical tradition'.[50] In other words, all reason is conditioned by the tradition from which it has emerged. This being so, the Christian can only aim to make use of a reason which has been informed by the Judeo–Christian tradition and a knowledge of Jesus. Yet even this is no easy matter which is why Middlemiss suggests that a reason needs to be supplemented by other assessment criteria. He points out, for example, that in order to assess Christian belief and experience, the apostle John did not give one answer 'but offered a combination of factors: moral behaviour, doctrinal correctness (particularly about the person of Jesus), love for others in the fellowship, humility, an awareness of sin, a desire to be holy, a practical Christianity – and an internal conviction which gives confidence to approach God'.[51] A little later Middlemiss also suggests other additional means of assessment using the disciplines of sociology, psychology, church history and medicine.[52] Only in this 'cumulative way' can a wide-ranging, many-faceted experience such as the Toronto Blessing or other revivalistic phenomena be authentically assessed.

Denouement

What are we to say in conclusion? Clearly the revivalism advocated with Toronto has had an impact that is both dysfunctional and positive. On the downside there was and continues to be in some places an over-prizing of religious phenomena. Too many people were travelling from place to place to experience the next piece of powerful ministry. Indeed the feeling still persists that if people shake, cry or fall it's 'powerful'. It needs to be recognised that spirit phenomena are no necessary guarantee of genuine spirituality. In fact psychic or religious phenomena can readily occur without any prompting of the Spirit of God at all.

It has to be said that the Toronto Blessing does not appear to have significantly increased the membership of UK churches as a whole although some individual congregations such as Holy Trinity, Brompton and Holy Trinity, Cheltenham, did see significant growth in its wake. The Toronto Blessing in fact had a divisive effect on the charismatic section of the church. Some charismatics clearly embraced the phenomena, others stood out strongly against it.[53] Since Toronto, two distinct strands of charismatic Christianity seem to have emerged. One continues to have its roots in the earlier emphasis of the Fountain Trust and stands aloof from Toronto. This group might be termed 'Renewal charismatics'. The other, which embraces the Toronto Blessing and its associated phenomena and continues to talk up revival, might be categorised as 'Revivalist charismatics'.

There is little doubt that the Toronto Blessing and its associated phenomena led large sections of the charismatic churches to eschew the term 'charismatic' and identify themselves with the mainstream evangelicals. A typical instance of this was the case of Peter Fenwick, a prominent charismatic church leader in Sheffield. Peter had started a meeting of charismatic leaders in the city, but with the onset of Toronto had with others to quit his own initiative.

Clearly it is possible to argue that some instances of falling had been a form of something akin to hypnotism brought about by soft music and quiet repetitive singing. This however is not a sufficient explanation for the world-wide spread of what was focused at Toronto. Hysteria, as suggested by Alan Morrison and others, is less likely since it is normally generated by fervour and hype. In fact many of the Toronto Blessing meetings were laid back and low key in style. On some occasions manifestations took place after an extended period of quiet sometimes of more than half an hour's duration. It is obvious that a great many churches in the UK were 'touched'. In fact within a year it was estimated that as many as 3,000 UK churches were experiencing the 'Toronto Blessing'.

In retrospect, what came out of Toronto is probably best

described as 'a time of refreshing'. The phrase is taken from the book of Acts chapter 3 verse 19. The apostle Peter urged the people to whom he preached to repent that 'times of refreshing may come from the presence of the Lord'. Many people who experienced these phenomena, particularly the falling, the laughter and the weeping, testified at the time that their relationship with God had been renewed. They felt heightened consciousness of the presence of Jesus in their lives. For significant numbers there was a release from burdens, pains, sickness and emotional hurt. For them it seems therefore appropriate to term this experience as a time of 'refreshment'.

The Toronto 'manifestations' or phenomena certainly featured in most of the so-called 'great revivals' in the history of the Christian Church. Alone and of themselves they do not, however, constitute a revival, but there have been few revivals without them. For a move of God to be designated as 'revival', there will need to be an accompanying impact on people outside the churches and on the wider society. This would include movements of social reform and social justice together with compassionate care for the disadvantaged. If revival is a biblical category, it is the reviving of the individual, the revival of the Church and the revival of the nation. It is ultimately about the 'healing of the land' (2 Chron 7:14) and this must include issues of justice, law and politics. The only revival in the United Kingdom which has begun to impact the land in this way was the Methodist revival under the Wesleys and Whitefield in the mid-eighteenth century. In view of this it does not seem appropriate to speak of the Toronto occurrences as a 'revival'. Overall, however, there were a number of positive results of the 'Toronto Blessing'. It was a common testimony on the part of many that they had been left with a greater sense of the presence of Jesus in their lives. Peter Nodding wrote in the *Baptist Times* of recipients having 'a far greater passion for Jesus'.[54] Sandy Millar, vicar of HTB wrote, 'People are experiencing a tremendous new love for Jesus.' Ashley Meaney, one of his congregation, reported, 'I have walked round in a funk . . . I have a much greater sense of the presence of the Lord as a result of what has been happening.' Tuana Tan commented similarly: 'I just felt so good! It has strengthened my faith even more. I know God will always be with me if I invite him.'[55] Accounts such as these were legion and could be replicated from the 1994 summer editions of *Covenant, Frontline, Pioneer, Direction* and other magazines. A significant aspect of this was the response on the part of children and young people. At the Toronto Vineyard many younger children were actively involved helping their parents to pray for others. At Soul Survivor 94 hundreds of teenagers found themselves deeply touched by the new move of God's Spirit. Many spoke of having found healing and the release from pain and abuse. Some national papers printed factually incorrect scare stories about children being disturbed at the New Wine Summer Conference. My own limited observations there, at the South West London Vineyard and at Gerald Coates' Event in a Tent left me with the impression that the children and young people were reacting very positively. All this is clearly important as the churches set out in this new millennium. It is the present generation of teenagers who are going to be at the forefront of Christian mission in the next two decades.

On the downside, the Toronto Blessing clearly had a divisive effect on both charismatics and the church as a whole. There were numbers who left the church altogether and significant groups of churches who disowned the term 'charismatic' as a result. My own view is that the Toronto phenomena was probably a mixture of the Divine, the human and the psychologically-induced. John Wimber wisely perceived the danger that this heightened concern with phenomena was detracting from evangelism and asked the Airport Vineyard to withdraw from his denomination.[56]

If this move had impacted the ways of God on the life of this nation as a whole, then we might perhaps have been permitted to regard 'Toronto' as a prelude to what later became a revival. As things turned out the impetus of Toronto had begun to diminish by the end of 1996. The leaders were running out of steam and the rhetoric could no longer be sustained. In sociological terms the charisma was 'evaporating'. Having said this much, however, perhaps two things can be added. First, it is clear from both the Old and New Testaments that in God's economy there were often 'seasons' or periods of new spiritual life in the experience of God's people. Jesus himself spoke of God's times and seasons (Acts 1:7) and the book of Acts and the history of the Christian church in the early Catholic period also bear witness to localised periods of intensive and vigorous new life. Second, in the wake of the Toronto Blessing, the Alpha course took off in a way which has been beyond all expectation. Indeed at the beginning of the year 2000 the number of churches running Alpha courses was still rising.

11

CHURCH PLANTING

During the past two decades attendance at the historic churches declined steadily. This is well illustrated by the following statistics taken from denominational yearbooks.[1]

	1969	1991	1995	1997
Anglican	1,795,000*	1,481,000	1,445,000	1,171,000
Baptist Union	275,000	160,000	150,900	139,650
Methodist	651,139	431,549**	380,269	353,330***
Congrega-tionalist/ URC		114,692	103,000	93,665***
Pentecostal	168,337	161,251	188,420	350,000****

In 1989 it was reported that 91 per cent of the population had no regular church allegiance or contact. Of the 9 per cent who supposedly did, many would have had only a nominal allegiance.[2] During the 1980s the number of active Anglicans in England declined by 16 per cent.[3] Between the Pastoral Measure of 1968 and 1994, 1,397 Church of England places of worship were closed.[4] This figure slowed in the period 1994–1998 when only 122 places of worship were closed. In my own diocese of Gloucester, eighteen Church of England churches were closed in the same period.[5]

The Church of England presents a particularly bleak picture. The number of infant baptisms has declined from 554 per 1,000 live births in England 1960, to 272 per 1,000 in 1991 to 228 per

1,000 in 1997. The number of Easter Communicants has plummeted from 2,159,000 in 1960 to 1,481,000 in 1991 to 1,171,600 in 1997. Electoral rolls fell from 1,912,000 in 1975 to 1,540,000 in 1990 to 1,483,000 in 1992 to 1,324,700 in 1997. Some have estimated the loss at 300 members every week for the past ten years. Occasionally the odd bishop has tried to delude us by announcing that more people are attending Holy Communion on Sundays than was previously the norm. The fact of the matter, however, is simply that most churches are holding more Communion services than was previously the case. It needs to be noted that some sociologists interpret this and heightened sacramentalism in general as a sign of introversionism and secularisation.[6] Mike Hill, former Archdeacon of Berkshire, sounded a similar note when he declared: 'The Church of England is in danger of becoming a eucharistic sect – simply a club for those with a religious interest, instead of having a mindset geared to winning others for Christ'.[7] He also underlined the fact that the establishment is geared to maintenance rather than mission. This is evidenced, he said, by its resistance to change, its obsession with buildings, its concern with internal detail, its suspicion of numerical growth, its lack of concern for unbelievers and an absence of biblical doctrine.[8] Bryan Wilson commented that the ritualistic and liturgical emphases in both Catholicism and Anglicanism in the earlier part of this century 'can be seen to have been no more than passing and perhaps misplaced reactions against the dominant long-term secularising trend in Western society'.[9]

Perhaps the demise of denominational religion is nowhere more forcefully illustrated than in twentieth-century English Methodism. In 1932, the main branches of Methodism came together in what ecumenists enthusiastically heralded as the panacea for a vibrant advancing of the kingdom of God. 'The whole Methodist church will enter upon a new era of extension which will rival the early days,'[10] said one leading Wesleyan churchman. In fact Methodism continued in steep decline throughout the following decade in which it is estimated more than 2,000 church and chapel buildings were closed.

Baptist churches in particular have suffered decline in membership numbers. Forty-eight per cent of Baptist churches in 1983 were reported as having less than fifty-one members. In the same year, three-quarters of all Baptist Union churches were listed as having less than one hundred members.[11] Clearly here is evidence that historic traditional Christianity is in decline.

Charismatic Impetus to Church Planting

Against the background of this general decline in the older denominational churches there has been a marked rise in the number of charismatic Christians in the UK in recent years. In 1989, charismatic evangelicals were estimated at 425,000 with mainstream evangelicals at 262,000 and broad evangelicals numbering 340,000. In 1991, evangelicals were 27 per cent of all UK churchgoers including Roman Catholics. If current trends continue, charismatics will increase to 47 per cent of that total by the year 2000.[12] Alongside this the older Pentecostal churches have continued to grow in numerical strength. The Elim church membership in the UK numbered 23,303 in 1983 and 47,618 in 1993. By 1998 it had further increased to 62,000.[13] Similarly the Assemblies of God numbered 35,000 in 1979, but had increased to 54,000 in 1993 and 58,500 in 1998.[14] In the history of British Pentecostalism, 1998 was a very significant year. In that year nine classic Pentecostal churches came together to form the Pentecostal Churches of the United Kingdom (PCUK). They were: Assemblies of God, Apostolic Church, Elim, New Testament Church of God, Church of God of Prophecy, New Testament Assemblies, The Redeemed Church of God, Connections and The Centre for Black and White Partnerships. Their combined membership is 350,000. It is, however, the new or house churches which are fully charismatic which have displayed spectacular church growth. Starting virtually from nothing in the early 1970s they now have around 2,000 congregations with an estimated membership of about 125,000.[15]

While it is obviously the case that there are a range of influences which have motivated church planting, it is clear that the rise of the charismatic movement has been an important factor. In particular its doctrine of ministry has been crucial. The historic mainline churches have laid stress on priesthood and the ministerial office. In contrast, charismatics in general, but particularly those from the new churches, have emphasised the priesthood of all believers. This has without doubt been a major contributor to their success and ability to plant new churches.

Ellis and Mitchell in their much acclaimed *Radical Church Planting* underlined this point.

> Planting and church growth at the level we need will not be achieved by a church adhering to a professional or elitist approach to ministry and serving God. The concept of clergy and laity (priest and congregation) will need to be discarded from our thinking if we are to move forward.[16]

Charismatics have been able to demonstrate to the wider churches that planting new congregations is the effective way to evangelise. Peter Wagner studied church growth in a world-wide context. His dictum that 'the most effective means of growing churches today is planting churches'[17] has gained wide recognition. Others have begun to echo his findings. Roger Forster of Ichthus, for example, stated: 'It is now widely recognised by Christians around the world that the most effective way to evangelise, or re-evangelise, a society is by planting churches.'[18] Sandy Millar has helpfully pinpointed the fact that the basic philosophy behind this is that the more churches there are in an area 'the easier and more successful the total effect of those churches will be'.[19] Sadly, the Church of England as a whole seems to take the reverse view despite the fact that the evidence is against it. Starting in 1987, St Barnabas Church, Cheltenham, planned over a two-year period to establish a new overflow congregation. A variety of locations were suggested and discussed with the then Archdeacon of Cheltenham, John Lewis, and the rural dean. These included the possibility of the vicar, the Revd Peter Sibley, being appointed to the vacant living at Emmanuel Church and taking two large house groups from St Barnabas with him. Later establishing a congregation at St James's Church in the centre of town was proposed. St James, a former evangelical congregation had been closed in 1961 but its building was still in good order. Always the fear the church hierarchy had was that the new plant would be a threat. It would draw away members from the nearby parish churches or create too much evangelical or charismatic influence.

Another later example was the Oaktree Fellowship established in Acton by St Barnabas, Kensington. Although supported initially by the area bishop, Graham Dow, the congregation was vehemently opposed by the prejudiced clergy of the local deanery.

Generally speaking, it has been the charismatics who were the pioneers and the thinkers behind the church planting movement of the past two decades. Terry Virgo who has been one of the most significant strategists wrote in 1985 that 'we need to plant a great number of new churches if we are going to see the tide turn in the nation – churches that are healthy, powerful communities built firmly on the word of God and relevant to modern society'.[20]

Charismatic leaders have developed what is generally termed a 'new wine skin' theology of church planting. This initially emerged amongst the new churches in the 1970s. The early first recipients of renewal waited patiently. They hoped that their denominational churches would be prepared to allow a greater freedom for the Holy Spirit in their worship and structures. In the event, however, their hopes were dashed because many of the denominations were overseen by anti-evangelical and anti-charismatic people. So the new wineskin theology began to evolve with the plea of 'new wineskins for new wine'. Thus the first independent churches were born. To take one example, a small group of Christians who worshipped at Ian Barclay's church, St Luke's, Hove, experienced renewal in the Holy Spirit. They tried for a time to find ways to express the new touch they felt God had given them but in the end left frustrated. Together with others they formed the Clarendon Fellowship which has since become the Church of Christ the King, one of the largest congregations in the UK. Peter Fenwick, who is now a leader and respected elder statesman in the new churches, was converted in the Church of England in Sheffield. After completing a degree in law and economics, he and his wife Rita, started a young people's coffee bar in the city centre. As the months passed his vicar at St John's Church urged him to integrate these teenagers into the worshipping life of the church. On the few occasions when the attempt was made the youngsters who attended were overcome by the awesome building and uncomfortable with the formality of the worship.

Peter's vicar eventually informed him that the church had decided to cut the coffee bar work loose. Peter, who had no formal biblical training, was left isolated and rejected. He did, however, find support from several local men and his youth congregation soon reached 250 members. In time another five plants came into being and eventually an association of some forty-five fellowships emerged under the title Network. What an encouragement such a group could have proved to the diocese if its clerical officialdom could have been a little less rigid and more open to embrace what God was so obviously doing.[21]

Two Anglican bishops, David Pytches and Brian Skinner later took up the plea for 'new wine skins' for the Church of England in a book of the same title. As Virgo and Coates before them had done, they pointed out clearly that 'as Jesus says, the new wine will burst the old wineskins and the old wine will be lost, as indeed will the new wine also'.[22] They pointed out, for example, that the old structures are not necessarily wrong: 'We must respect the old wineskins, and love the old wine which some say is better.'[23] On the other hand, they urged that those who are 'used to the old structures' should bless the new wine skins. In that process their hope was that they 'will be blessed themselves'. Their book which was irenical in tone and the epitome of graciousness was, sadly, greeted with a storm of prejudice and horror on the part of many diocesan bishops. They retreated to the age-old position that the parish is a spiritual 'closed shop'. Even though planters may have tried to negotiate for several years with diocesan authorities, woe betide anyone who 'unilaterally decides to muscle in on another parish'.[24]

Charismatics not only theorised about the need for new wineskins, they have demonstrated a great ability to initiate them. In this, variety and informality have been key factors. Whereas the Church of England and other historic denominations have displayed a seemingly endless capacity to clone daughter churches, charismatic church planters have fostered a rich diversity with informality being the key. Recent literature such as Roger Forster's *Ten New Churches* (Marc Europe, 1985), Bob Hopkins' *Church Planting: Models for Mission in the Church of England* (Grove, 1989) and *Planting New Churches* (1992), Roger Ellis and Roger Mitchell's *Radical Church Planting* (Crossway, 1992), Derek Allan's *Planted to Grow* (Baptist Union, 1994) and Nigel Scotland's *Recovering the Ground* (Kingdom Power Trust Publications, 1995) also indicate a variety of strategic models on which the new wine skins can be based. These include the Mass

Evangelism Plant where new converts are formed into a new church immediately as on the Day of Pentecost (Acts 2). Similar is the Mega Church Plant which establishes smaller fellowships in outlying areas. From time to time these are gathered in for large celebrations and corporate teaching. Another model is the Mobile Plant where a small group or team uproot and move to another area or location, establish a church and then move on. Closely related is the Mini-mission Church Plant where a small team or group move to another location and settle there permanently to establish a church. An example of this was when the Cobham Pioneer Fellowship planted a church in Tooting. Twenty-six people moved from the leafy suburbs into a deprived inner city area. This move was inevitably at considerable cost to the families concerned, affecting their children's education and environment. Within eighteen months, however, the church grew to 100 people. By the end of three years they numbered 150 and planted a further congregation. The 'mother church' plant method is one where a large central church establishes daughters in the surrounding locations. It seems to have been the case that a number of New Testament churches were spawned from Ephesus in all probability including Colossae, Hierapolis and Laodicea. These later would have become separate entities. This was the method adopted by Ichthus. Initially the 'baby' church remains a part of the mother's body. Later it becomes a separate entity but still dependent on the mother to some extent. Eventually it becomes totally independent of the mother. Ichthus began as one congregation in the South East corner of London, and remained like that for eight years. After a further nine years it had spawned forty congregations. Another strategy which has been utilised a good deal, particularly by the Vineyard groups in the UK is the multi-cell church plant. This is found in Acts 28 where even before Paul arrived in Rome there were already at least five small groups established in the city (see Rom 16).

The English Vineyard denomination plant new churches by first establishing cell groups, called Kinships until the mid-1990s, in other new towns or cities. St Albans Vineyard, for example, established such a group in Hull and the Oxford Vineyard did the same in Cheltenham in the mid 1990s. When these are felt to be sufficiently strong, Sunday worship is commenced and a new Vineyard established. This has proved an effective strategy in a number of other locations in London and South East England.

The Vineyard denomination pioneered and led by John Wimber has given major impetus to church planting both internationally and in the British Isles. John Wimber reminded his readers and hearers on a number of occasions that an intimate relationship or experience with God will ultimately lead to numerical church growth. More than that it will result in the establishment of new churches or church plants.[25] In all of this John Wimber was much influenced by Donald McGavran's *Understanding Church Growth* (1970). Crucial to McGavran's thought on this topic was the notion of 'homogenous units' as crucial to church growth. The Christian faith would spread more effectively if each plant carefully targeted its audience and focussed on its needs and cultural identity. McGavran suggested on this basis that in India it would be far more effective if a church were to be established for each particular caste group rather than to have one church for all castes.[26]

It is now the case that almost all denominations are engaged in seeking to plant new churches. Nevertheless, it is the charismatics who have shown a willingness to take the risks and to explore new patterns and new ways of doing things. It is charismatics who pioneered the way, provided the stimulus and the training and motivated and inspired the wider church to the task. Charismatic church plants have achieved success for a number of reasons. In many cases, they have been informal and relaxed in their style and ethos. Not only have they deliberately chosen to worship in secular buildings such as schools, pubs, winebars and community centres, they have avoided a diet of formal liturgical services with lengthy prayers and intellectual sermons. Equally important, many of these newer plants have practised an incarnational theology as they have sought to become Christ to their neighbours. Roger Ellis and Roger Mitchell perceived the vision and the call 'to "flesh out" the life, character and qualities of our Head'.[27] Many charismatic church plants have set a precedent of deep involvement in the societies of which they are a part. Members of Pioneer for example have cleared gardens, decorated rooms, cooked and shopped for social services. Others have got involved in ACET (Aids Care

Education and Training) teams and given AIDS education in schools. The Vineyard churches in London have demonstrated a particular care for the London homeless and the hungry and developed a King's Table ministry to offer them hospitality. Ichthus took a major stand against the positive discrimination in favour of gay and lesbian lifestyle adopted by their local council. New Frontiers churches have been sending teams to India as have the Bristol Christian Fellowship congregations. Prominent charismatic Anglican churches such as St Andrew's, Chorleywood have been linked in actively supporting urban priority parishes in inner London and elsewhere. Many people have been attracted into newer church plants on account of their very genuine 'hands on' practical care.

The criticism has sometimes been made that many of the charismatic church plants grew by syphoning off discontented members from the older denominational churches. Probably, however, it was not so much a case of sheep stealing but rather it was simply a matter of the spiritually hungry looking for better pastures. Nevertheless, it was undoubtedly the case that many charismatic plants particularly in their early days drew in members from already existing churches. Brian and Anne Murgatroyd who were active in the Salt and Light community churches in Oxfordshire reported: 'It was a powerful movement . . . it was drawing everybody with any sort of spiritual knowledge out of every other church. It was emptying Anglican and Baptist churches and anybody with any sort of desire for anything more.'[28]

The King's Church in Aldershot recognised that its early growth in 1974–75 came as a result of the 'transfer of mature Christians from other churches'. However, by 1985 they found that 'the newly converted and those never associated with the church were being added'.[29] The Editorial of *Renewal* for December 1981 reported 'mounting tension' between some of the house churches and those involved in renewal in the historic churches. Michael Harper commented, 'The cry from the Dales Week platform to "come out" has become more strident.'[30] The plea was further reinforced by the publication of Arthur Wallis' book, *The Radical Christian*, with its strong attack on the historic churches. On the other hand, Geoff Crocker , an elder at Agape Christian Fellowship, Leamington Spa, sympathised with 'the initial frustration and subsequent partial eclipse of renewed Christians trying to squeeze the quart of their abundant life and vision into the pint-sized place their church has for them'.[31] At about the same time it was reported that many Christians in the Brighton area were coming out of the mainline churches and joining a Restoration church based in Hove.[32] Sociologist of religion, Professor Andrew Walker, found himelf writing in 1985 that 'Restorationists have yet to prove that they can recruit from secular society in any significant numbers'.[33] Reflecting fifteen years further on, we can now see clearly that the church plants established by the newer charismatic churches are not only well established but drawing in unchurched people in significant numbers.

One other fact which remains clear is that in all church groupings, the mainline denominations included, the charismatics are continuing to make a major impact in the area of church planting. This can be seen by a cursory survey of the major groupings which make up the Christian Church in the British Isles.

Charismatic Anglican Church Planting

Some writers have questioned whether or not the Church of England really engages in church planting at all. Barry Roche pointed out very sharply that in actual fact the Church of England engages not in church planting, but for the most part in 'mission hall evangelism'. Most of what *Breaking New Ground* enthusiastically described as church plants are based on the strawberry runner model. They are attached by a runner either to the sending parish or the runner is attached to the church of the receiving parish. Rarely is a completely new independent self-governing, self-sustaining and self-propagating plant established. As any good gardener will know, a new plant will only grow vigorously and mature fully if it is severed from the parent plant. To take another analogy, children will never become fully mature adults until they become independent of their parents. Church of England planters seem not to have imbibed this fundamental point in the way that the newer churches and some other older denominations, such as the Baptists, have done. Even Archbishop Carey seemed not to have grasped the matter fully. He declared: 'Church planting is a tool of mission, not the final purpose of mission. It is not a replacement for the parish, but an extension of its life. That is why I strongly encourage all parishes of moderate size to consider church planting.'

Archbishop Carey suggested two things here. First, church planting is 'but an extension of the parish church'. Second, the ultimate in mission is 'the parish church'. Most charismatics and indeed non-charismatic church planters from other denominations would profoundly disagree with both of his contentions. In the first place, to have as the ultimate goal of mission a 'spiritual closed shop' can only be a recipe for stagnation and decline. It cannot be healthy to allow the parochial incumbent to sit entrenched behind his boundaries in this way. It seems strange to allow other denominations to come into the parish and set up what churches they like while at the same time shooting on sight any fellow Anglicans who dare to even contemplate the possibility of establishing Sunday worship.

What church planters have learned is that variety is the spice of life and that different expressions of Christian worship are necessary for different people groups. To allow only one expression of Church of England worship in a geographical parochial area means that, at best, only about a tenth of the people's emotional and spiritual needs are catered for. Canon law requires that the Church of England clergyman attend to the spiritual needs of all within his charge. Such a canon law is impossible to fulfil when territorial boundaries are so rigorously enforced.

A cursory glance at the 1993 *Anglican Church Planting Initiative List* showed that a total of 192 new congregations had been established since 1970. The vast majority (about 95 per cent) of these are either still attached to the sending church or to the parish church where they were established. Very few indeed have become healthy independent plants. This fact was made abundantly clear in the Church of England report, *Breaking New Ground*.[34] It pointed out that the most common type of church plant is where a new congregation is created in a location within the parish boundaries with a leadership team from the parish. There were 177 known instances of this type. Less common was where a planting team came from an outside parish (either in junior or equal partnership) with the objective of bolstering up its mission. There were twenty-seven examples of this type.

Hopkins and Lings have noted a growing diversity of plants

in the last decade of the twentieth century. A number of new congregations were planted on the cell church model and these were harder to quantify. Cell churches are not beefed-up house groups. In very general terms they are seen to be based around four pillars, welcome, worship, word and witness.[35] By the close of 1999, some fifty to sixty Anglican churches were known to have started to develop cells based on these principles.[36] In addition to the cell churches there are well over a hundred youth church plants, many of which are charismatic in their theology and worship. Obvious examples would be Soul Survivor, Watford with a congregation of about 300, pastored by Mike Pilavachi, and Soul Survivor Harrow.

A more recent list held on a data base at the Sheffield Centre revealed that there were 155 new Church of England church plants between 1992 and 1999. Of these only 144 gave details of their churchmanship. The most significant affiliations were central, thirty-six, evangelical, thirty-nine and charismatic, sixty-five. Of the sixty-five, fifty-two described themselves as 'charismatic evangelical', ten as simply 'charismatic', two as 'Catholic charismatic' and one as 'Catholic, evangelical and charismatic'.[37] What these figures indicate is that charismatic influence is still the most significant motivational factor in Church of England church planting.

Of the 192 Church of England plants on the 1993 list it was possible to identify sixty-five as being founded by charismatics and having a charismatic ethos. This list did not include a number of plants made outside the parish by charismatic churches such as Holy Trinity Brompton and St Andrew's, Chorleywood.

Generally speaking, charismatic church plants are less formal in style than plants from other sections of the Church of England. Some are lay led, robes are not often worn and the music and songs tend to be less traditional. Quite often there is a family service or part of the worship is given an all-age emphasis. The liturgy is not followed slavishly and there is a good deal of opportunity for individual members of the congregation to participate in prayers and readings and to contribute impromptu words of encouragement or testimony.

The Problem of Parish Boundaries

The real problem where Anglican church planting is concerned is the matter of parish boundaries. In fact the parish boundary system has rightly been termed the 'contraceptive of the decade of evangelism'. It is the boundary lines which have prevented the coming into birth of separate new independent congregations which can mature and grow in their own right. The Church of England is full of reactionary clerics who are ever ready to defend the ancient customs, rights and privileges of the established Church. Philip King, for example, the secretary to the House of Bishops Working Party, wrote in the *Church of England Newspaper* in defence of parochial boundaries. 'Boundaries,' he urged, 'can now be changed in a matter of weeks (did he mean years or perhaps decades!) if interested parties agree.' Again, he commented, 'the problem lies not in the boundaries themselves but in the need for getting agreement'.[38]

Church of England charismatics tend to disagree strongly with King's position. Bishops Pytches and Skinner for example wrote:

> The parish system is neither sacrosanct nor carved in stone. Since the late 1950s it has been seriously challenged for its inappropriateness as a matrix. It was never part of British church life before Theodore of Tarsus, the then Archbishop of Canterbury, who laid the foundations for it between the years AD 669–690.[39]

They continue by asserting that parish boundaries 'must be seen as transient structures, which admirably suited the needs of a previous age, but in many if not most places, actually inhibit the life of the church today'.[40] Sandy Millar wrote in 1992 that 'every recent church report has recognised that the parish is no longer the appropriate geographical area with which to work'.[41] In 1993 George Lings wrote of 'the heavily defended citadel of territorial parochial boundaries'. Bob Hopkins noted that the parish boundary 'has been described at its worst, as operating in some situations as "a line drawn around thousands of people" to protect them from hearing the gospel'. 'The challenge to the present system,' he also wrote, 'is to change from an outdated monument to maintenance into a facilitating agent . . . for mission and evangelism.'[42]

It is very difficult to understand why the Church of England has to cling so tightly to a parochial system which was virtually obsolete in almost all large towns and cities by the end of Queen Victoria's reign. At the beginning of the nineteenth century the parish had six functions: Poor Law (social security) administration, registration of births and baptisms, the conduct of marriage, collecting a church rate for the maintenance of the parish church, burials and the management of local government including public health, roads and policing.

By the New Poor Law Act of 1834 Poor Law Unions replaced the parish as the unit for administering social relief. By the Registration Act of 1836 secular registration was established and Non-conformist and Roman Catholic places could be licensed for marriages. By the 1868 Compulsary Rate Abolition Act, compulsary church rates were abolished and the parish vestry ceased to have any significance. By the Burials Act of 1880 Non-conformists were given the right to conduct a funeral service in the parish burial ground. By the Local Government Act of 1894 the secular parish was separated from the Church parish so that the clergyman was no longer automatically chairman of the parish council and neither he nor the wardens had any oversight of social or community issues such as sanitation, vagrancy, policing, education or transport.

For all intents and purposes, therefore, by the close of 1894, the parish system had ceased to fulfil any of the functions for which it was designed. For the past one hundred years it has continued to drag on as a kind of ecclesiastical closed-shop whereby the incumbent has the sole control of all Church of England worship within its bounds.

As early as 1987 Canon John Gunstone reflected on the 'growing interest in church planting in the country'. He highlighted the charismatic movement as one of the significant influences behind this. In the same article he went on to warn of the dangers the Church of England would face if it continued its slavish adherence to parish boundaries.

It is no exaggeration to say that Anglicans are faced in many places with the choice of maintaining the boundaries and continuing to decline, or of declaring (in co-operation with other denominations) that certain neighbourhoods are 'mission areas' where any growing congregation will be welcomed to plant.[43]

The Church of England is probably the most moribund of all the denominations in England. Almost everything has fallen into the control of the bishops, Church House and the diocesan authorities. It is, in short, as church planters along with many others have discovered, a bureaucratic nightmare. One reason why so many bishops cling so rigidly to the parochial system is because it is an easy way to keep tight control over the Church and its finances. The established Church is, as Michael Mitton put it, 'a tired old lady' or as Archbishop Carey earlier stated in a less-carefully drawn metaphor 'a toothless old woman'. The Revd Teddy Saunders who was involved in a number of church planting initiatives commented that 'the Church of England, to which I belong . . . is now reduced to a pitiful minority, not only in the community as a whole but even among practising Christians'.[44] Clifford Longley put the matter even more starkly in a letter to *The Times* in December 1987. He wrote as follows:

> The marginalisation of the Church of England is not easy to contradict . . . its decline could well be the single most important thing that has happened to the English this century. And the strangest thing is that by and large the church itself does not realise it . . .[45]

During the 1980s, the number of active Anglicans in England declined by 16 per cent while in the same period the membership of the new churches grew by 85 per cent.[46] Some charismatics are expressing the fear that if the Church of England doesn't do something radical soon to start planting vigorous new congregations, it may well lose some of the most vibrant ones which are still at present within its ranks. In 1994, Michael Mitton, the former director of Anglican Renewal Ministries, reported that a number of vitally alive charismatic Anglican congregations were 'hanging on to the Church of England by the skin of their teeth'. Were there to be any further pressure on their finances, worship or their desire to reach out in evangelism in their local areas, they would probably leave en bloc and affiliate elsewhere.[47]

One of the few genuine initiatives in radical charismatic

planting was the initiative of bishops David Pytches and Brian Skinner in forming the Federation of Independent Anglican Churches in February 1992. This sought to provide an umbrella organisation for cross-boundary church plants which wanted to remain Anglican but have been excluded from the Church of England by the parish system. The Federation's 'Faith and Order Statement' is as follows: 'The Bible is the Word of God and the three historic creeds are to be recognised as an orthodox summary of its principal teachings. We value the doctrines expressed in the Thirty-Nine Articles of the Church of England.' Each congregation is run 'in accordance with generally accepted Church of England teaching and practice'.[48] Congregations function much in the way that Church of England proprietary chapels are organised. Several of the congregations are located in Hertfordshire near to Chorleywood but there were others in places as far away as Farnham and Cheltenham. It is felt by some that the Federation could prove an ideal base for Church of England congregations who want to plant outside their parish area but for one reason or another cannot achieve agreement with the local diocesan bishop, deanery or parish authorities. FIAC church plants which are Anglican, though not Church of England, have a number of aspects which could be seen as attractive. For example, they are not dependent on any diocesan funding, they can be led by ordained or suitable lay people, their ethos is informal and flexible and their worship is not required to adhere to Canon Law. FIAC churches, like Church of England proprietary chapels and Forward in Faith churches, seek to relate to appropriate episcopal supervision. They represent genuine independent attempts at church planting as opposed to daughter church clones and mission hall evangelism. Church of England daughter churches and mission halls are not churches in the full sense. They are not what Henry Venn, the nineteenth-century mission strategist strove for, namely churches which would be 'self-sustaining, self-governing and self-propagating'. Sadly, most bishops expressed vehement hostility to David Pytches and Brian Skinner's bold initiative. It is a damning reflection on the present state of the Church of England that a priest can deny that Jesus is the Son of God and remain in post or be convicted of an act of gross indecency and be a diocesan bishop. Equally he or she can live in a sexual relationship in the vicarage with a partner of the same sex, but plant a new congregation the wrong side of an imaginary line and their license to minister will be taken away forthwith.[49]

Baptist Church Plants

Generally speaking, Baptists have been much more active in church planting than the Church of England. While the established church planted 270 plants between 1970 and 1994, Baptist churches planted 200 new congregations between 1980 and 1990. An article in the January 1991 edition of *Mainstream* anounced: 'Church planting is happening. It's happening all over the UK. It's probably happening near you! It's happening among Baptists. In fact it's happening especially among Baptists!'[50]

In fact the Mainstream group of Baptists who are active in charismatic renewal have also been most active in the Baptist Union in promoting and encouraging church planting. In the early part of 1991, Mainstream called on the denominational offices at Didcot to initiate Baptist church planting. Their statement was as follows: 'We invite our national leaders to set an ambitious national growth target for Baptists in the coming decade.'[51] Noting the Dawn 2000 project's aim for one congregation for every five hundred people, Mainstream made a further plea. They called for 'a bold target for the number of new congregations we want to establish by the end of the century'.[52]

Derek Allan produced an excellent slim volume entitled *Planted to Grow* which was published by the Baptist Union in 1994. It was a study of Baptist church plants made over the previous ten years or so in England, north of London and the M4.[53] The author noted that 'Church planting now appears on agendas at all levels of Baptist life and the past ten years have seen dozens of new Baptist churches coming into being'.[54] Of the forty-eight plants surveyed in this study, eighteen, just over one third, identified themselves as 'charismatic'.[55] Twenty-nine churches of the other thirty termed themselves 'relaxed Baptists'. Allan noted that his 'examination of comments and personal interviews indicated that the line between "relaxed Baptists" and "charismatic" is often crossed'.[56]

Another Baptist, the Revd John Roberts of New Milton, conducted a similar survey in part of the Southern Baptist

Association. All of the church plants in his survey were situated south of the M4 motorway. He investigated a total of eighteen plants in all. Of these, six had decidedly charismatic input and ethos and a further five fitted the 'relaxed Baptist' category. The remainder were either traditional or reformed Baptist. All of this indicates that the charismatic movement has had a considerable effect in motivating Baptist churches to engage in church planting initiatives. According to the Baptist Union there have been approximately twelve Baptist church plants each year during the period 1995–1999. Although specific statistics are not available there is general perception that the charismatic churches have been a significant influence in these plants.[57]

Other Denominations and Church Planting

Probably it's true to say that all the older historic churches are demonstrating some sort of concern to plant new churches. The Methodist churches, for example, planted thirty new congregations between 1989 and 1994.[58] The Annnual Methodist Conference of 1992 called upon every circuit in the connection 'seriously and prayerfully . . . to explore in co-operation with its ecumenical partners the possibility of planting at least one new congregation by the year 2000'.[59] The extent of the charismatic influence in recent Methodist church planting is hard to gauge because circuits are the planting body. However, Brian Hoare of the Methodist Home Mission department, hazarded a hunch that the worship style of the majority would be untraditional and that there would be input from the more charismatic element of Methodism.[60]

The United Reformed Church has also planted some new congregations in recent years. At its 1992 General Assembly it underlined its previous policy 'to promote church extension within the local area and to submit proposals to the Synod for establishing new causes'.[61] Resolution 40 at the 1993 General Assembly was much more detailed:

> The Assembly recognising the increasing interest and commitment to church planting calls upon every district council of the United Reformed Church to engage with ecumenical partners in research aimed at placing a body of Christian people in every locality and to set up new

Mission Projects for congregations where appropriate. The Assembly recommends the DAWN principles for responsible church planting.[62]

Generally speaking, it is the case that the majority of the other older denominations have only been touched in marginal ways by charismatic experience or church planting concerns. Those who have, however, been most significantly influenced by both charismatic experience and the desire to plant new congregations are what sociologists term the 'new churches'. These groups and strands all have the planting of new churches as a specific aspect of their vision. It is and has been a constant item on their leadership agendas and in their annual conferences.

The New Churches and Church Planting

In the early days of the house church movement in the 1970s a number of the early congregations contained significant numbers of charismatic Christians who had become disillusioned with the old wine skins and were looking for forms of worship in which they could express themselves more freely. It is clear, however, that by the mid 1980s substantial numbers of unchurched people were being recruited. People were attracted by the less imposing environment of schools, community halls and public houses. The worship was more vibrant and informal in style. Above all, people felt their spirits were being touched.

In these early days there was a good deal of jealousy and rivalry among the major groupings led by Bryn Jones, Barney Coombs, Terry Virgo and Gerald Coates. Members of the Salt and Light community churches in Oxfordshire and Gloucestershire with whom I spoke recalled that there was a highly competitive spirit abroad between the different groups in the matter of church planting.

The most powerful force in the early days of the Restoration house church movement was Bryn Jones whose headquarters were in Bradford. Bryn's driving temperament and uncompromising leadership soon resulted in plans to establish a new church in Leeds. By 1989 this church had grown to an adult membership of 350. The Leeds congregation in turn planted thriving communities in Wakefield and York. Later a Keighley church of 200 members was also birthed from Bradford. They in turn started another church in Skipton. Other plantings led to strong churches in Halifax and Huddersfield. Further groups of Christians moved out from Bradford to start other congregations in the Midlands and further south.[63] In 1989, fifty-five churches were reported as being 'in close relationship with Bryn and Keri and their apostolic team'. The spring 1994 list of Covenant churches which now have their headquarters at Nettlehill near Coventry , showed only fifty fellowships. Of these, thirty were located in the Midlands and the north of England. Some of the present congregations are quite large with Leicester having between 450 and 500 members and Bradford 600. Others such as Bath and Manchester also have a Sunday attendance of around the 500 mark.[64] David Matthew reported that the majority of congregations probably run out at between 100–200. This means that in 1995 Covenant membership was probably in the order of 10,000–15,000. By 1999 this figure was considerably diminished as Bryn Jones commissioned a number of his co-leaders to start smaller networks of their own. Church planting continues to be on the Covenant agenda but its profile is no longer as high as in the earlier days.

Church planting has retained a high profile among the Pioneer churches which relate to Gerald Coates. In 1987 they launched TIE Teams – 'TIE' standing for 'training in evangelism'. Each year hundreds of people spend their summer holidays, or even up to one year, engaged in evangelism and church planting.[65] Gerald Coates is still totally committed to evangelism by planting new congregations. He was an active supporter of the DAWN challenge to plant 20,000 by the year 2000. He expressed his conviction as follows:

We will never reach our nation hoping we can do it through the mass media. The Kingdom of God and the Church of Christ are relational. The media is not . . . That is why I am fully committed to evangelise and church plant to reach every people group in England and beyond.[66]

In the summer of 1994 there were sixty-four Pioneer churches, only seven of which were north of the London area. By 1999 this figure had risen substantially to ninety-six. In addition, some of these churches such as the Bristol Christian Fellowship have clusters of satellite congregations.[67]

New Frontiers, led by Terry Virgo from its Brighton head-quarters at the Church of Christ the King, continues to give a high priority to church planting. It had ninety-five related UK churches in 1993 about half of which were situated in the London area or the south and west of England. Their 1993 official brochure gave details of seven new churches which were in process of formation. Some of them were formed with quite small planting teams of between twenty and thirty individuals. The financial statement for the year ending 31st December 1992 indicated that £230,000 had been set aside for church planting acitivities. New Frontiers had a membership in 1994 of about 15,000. Some of its churches had large congregations with the Church of Christ the King numbering 750 and Woking and Bracknell about 700. By the close of 1999, New Frontiers International had increased to 142 congregations.[68] The Salt and Light churches led by Barney Coombs have kept a modest public profile over recent years. Nevertheless, in recent years church planting has been high on their agenda. The mother congregation in Basingstoke which began in 1977 had grown to eleven congregations by 1995 and spread over a wide area. A number of new congregations were planted in the 1990s in Oxfordshire and Gloucestershire.

Other smaller new church groups who are active in church planting include Ichthus in the south London area with about forty congregations, the Bristol Christian Fellowship with eleven congregations and the Vineyard.

The Charismatic Contribution to Church Planting
Clearly, on any showing, charismatic Christianity has given a major boost both to church planting and evangelism. On the face of it, one would expect charismatic worship to have inbuilt 'introversionist' tendencies. Lengthy sessions of fervent choruses, people might feel, would be off-putting to those who are strangers to the Christian faith. In fact, the statistics and the evidence tell another story. Intimacy in worship, as John Wimber long maintained, does in fact generate an impulse to reach out to others with the gospel message.

Charismatics have come to recognise that church planting is

a most effective method of evangelism. It's a practice which they see as clearly outlined in the evangelistic strategies of the book of Acts. Charismatics have also learned that where more churches are planted in a particular area the overall impact of the gospel message is increased rather than diminished. It seems to be the case that increased numbers of new churches can saturate an area with faith and expectancy. This opens the way for the kingdom of God to be extended. As more congregations are established in an area there is increased prayer for its needs and people and a greater receptivity for the Christian message is created.

One note of hope on which to end is the fact that there is now much less competitiveness between planting groups. Charismatics right across the board are learning to work together in partnership in the matter of church planting. Gerald Coates made the point clearly in his Foreword to *Radical Church Planting*. 'Our framework,' he suggested, must emphasise 'a policy of cooperation'.[69]

Charismatics, and particularly those from the new or house churches, have demonstrated to the wider church of all denominations the extent of what can be achieved by planting new congregations. Not only have their churches survived for fifteen or twenty years, and in some cases thirty years, they have grown in numbers and matured in leadership and teaching. Most of them now have competent, full-time pastors whom they pay well above Church of England and denominational rates of pay.

In the early days, the criticism was levelled at the new churches that they were simply syphoning the discontented away from the older denominations. This is an accusation which it would be hard to substantiate at the present time. The newer churches have demonstrated that church planting is in fact a most effective means of evangelism and reaching unchurched groups of people.

It is clear from the overall figures which have been considered in this chapter that the level of church planting plateaued in the 1990s. The reasons for this were twofold. First, most of the churches that were in a position to plant did so in the 1980s and most hadn't sufficiently recovered by the 1990s to plant again. Second, those churches which were planted in the 1990s didn't grow sufficiently fast enough to enable them to plant again. Nevertheless, it is clear that it is the charismatic congregations in the majority of denominations who have been most active in church planting.

It is because of the impact of charismatic church planters, especially those of the new churches, that church planting is now on the agenda of every major denomination in the United Kingdom. As the church progresses into the third millennium we can anticipate the establishment of many more congregations with an ethos and strategy appropriate to individual localities and housing areas.

12

CHARISMATICS AND THEOLOGY

David Tracy, in *The Analogical Imagination: Christian Theology and the Culture of Pluralism,* suggested that the theologian has three distinct audiences: society, the academy and the church.[1] Society includes technological and economic structures, social justice and power, and culture which is largely, but not solely, art and religion. The academy is the secular university. The church which is composed of communities of believers also includes the seminary and the Christian university. This categorisation is helpful to our present purpose since it enables us to identify more clearly the nature of charismatic theology.

In any kind of discussion, it has to be recognized that charismatic Christians are a diverse grouping. As we have noted, they belong to a variety of strands and denominations each with their own nuances and agendas. But having said that, from any general survey of the writings of British charismatics, two things are clear. First, only a small percentage of their number engage in theological writing. Second, what little theology there is, is largely addressed to the church. In broad terms, charismatic theology is what might be termed as 'pastoral' rather than 'academic'. By this is meant that it focuses on issues such as the kingdom, prophecy, healing, the demonic and revival rather than major credal concerns such as creation, sin, redemption and Christology. Additionally, most charismatic theology makes little use of critical rational and intellectual procedures.

Tom Smail recalled that Dr J.I. Packer once described the charismatic renewal as being 'a movement looking for a theology'. Smail continued, 'If he had said that it was a movement in need of a theology, I would have agreed with him straight away – but looking for a theology, how I wish it were true!'[2] Smail went on to recall how in his earlier days at the Fountain Trust,

274

if the word 'theology' was mentioned at gatherings of charismatic clergy, the chief reaction was 'a scornful titter'.[3] What such church leaders were saying in effect was, now that we know it we don't need to think about it or question it any further.

This lack of interest in theology among charismatics in general should not surprise us, however, since charismatic religion is by its very nature intuitive rather than rational, and experienced-based rather than text-based. That is, it is preoccupied with the satisfaction of emotional and spiritual needs. Its central concerns are with personal well-being, feelings, therapies and empowerment. In this it is what Andrew Walker has termed a 'thoroughly modern' movement.[4] There is nothing intrinsically wrong with any of these foci but the inherent danger is always that charismatic religion will become decontextualised or cut loose from its biblical moorings. As Martin Percy put it in a somewhat over-generalised comment: 'It is playfully ambiguous in its treatment of absolute values, tending towards pneumatological situationalism in moral and theological questions.'[5]

The basic non-rational element inherent in charismatic religion has led to a tendency to attempt a theological endorsement of the latest new wave, be it tongues, prophecy, praising God for all things, words of knowledge, kingdom power over the demons, healing, revival, the Toronto Blessing or holy molars. Often this is done in an uncritical way by producing Bible verses which on the face of it might seem to offer some kind of supporting basis. This procedure was epitomised by Guy Chevreau of the Airport Vineyard as it then was. In a talk to visiting pilgrims, he explained the fact that 'God is laying out lots of his leaders' on the basis of Psalm 23 verse 2, 'he makes me lie down'.[6] In a similar vein others supported the alleged instant gold filling of believers' teeth at Gerald Coates' Pioneer churches in June 1999 on the basis of Psalm 81 verse 10: 'Open your mouth wide and I will fill it.'[7] In general terms there is a hankering among certain charismatics to provide some kind of biblical underpinning for the latest success story whether it be the new phenomenon, the new technique or an empowerment story. Care, however, must be taken not to imagine that just because something is successful it is therefore of God. On the one hand, success can of course be positive and the Church, of all institutions, needs good news. But the other side of the coin is that it must deal in the truth. This means that when things fail or go wrong or disappoint, there needs to be a careful rational and biblically-based assessment. Too often unrealized hopes are met with explanations as to why the word of knowledge, the healing, prophecy or revival didn't happen, when what was needed was humility, reflection and a revision of opinion.

It has been suggested, and with a certain amount of good reason, that faith in the charismatic circles isn't so much a reasoned questioning which includes an element of doubt but rather a psychological state in which individuals 'psych' themselves up into a particular state of mind that such and such is the case. As one charismatic healer put it, 'You keep believing in spite of the symptoms.' Indeed, as another cynic put it: 'If you can believe something for no reason whatsoever, your faith has reached the top level.' Such 'faith', it must be said, doesn't resonate with the New Testament understanding, where faith is seen as a rational holding on and standing firm in times of doubt or spiritual conflict. It was for these kinds of reason that David Middlemiss designated charismatic Christianity as 'enthusiasm'. He wrote: 'By definition, enthusiasm begins when experience is given priority over reason as the basis of truth.'[8] He pinpointed the contrast between enthusiasm and mainstream religion in the following lines:

> The traditional Christian writes books on doctrine which seek to understand God through reasoned analysis of the Bible (Systematic theology and objective truth). The enthusiast, however, writes numerous books of 'testimonies' about experience, and then seeks to justify these claims so that others can share the same experience.[9]

It could of course be countered that the traditional academic theologian, when he or she uses the New Testament, is still dealing with experience, only in this case the systematized experience of the first Christian churches. The difference, however, is that the mainstream theologian relates his or her present experiences in a reasoned and critical way to the foundational experiences of Apostolic Christianity.

Charismatic Academic Theologians

In *Historical Theology*, Alister McGrath has a small section on 'Charismatic Theologians'.[10] This should not, however, be taken to imply that charismatic Christianity in the UK has not produced any academic theologians. It certainly has. Indeed there is a small but growing cluster of charismatics who are doing theology in an academic context. Among them are Tom Smail, Andrew Walker and Nigel Wright who produced *Charismatic Renewal: The Search for Theology* (SPCK, 1995). In addition, others include Professor Max Turner of the London Bible College who worships at St Andrew's, Chorleywood, Christopher Cocksworth, Director of the Southern Theological Education and Training Scheme and Mark Stibbe who formerly taught Biblical Studies at Sheffield University.

Smail, Walker and Wright all share the charismatic experience and although their theological understanding and churchmanships have changed, they all endorse and value their initial experience of the Holy Spirit. In three memorable weeks in November, 1965, Tom Smail, now living in retirement, had 'the only major religious crisis I have ever experienced' in which his relationship with God was dramatically changed.[11] His relationship to God was renewed, he found a new closeness with other people, there was a new spirit of prayer and he spoke with tongues.[12] Nigel Wright, sometimes known as 'the thinking man's charismatic', discovered the gift of tongues in a sound-proofed language laboratory in the basement of a modern languages building at his university. He was later impacted by the ministry of John Wimber and Lonnie Frisbee in June 1982.[13] For Wright, the early years of enthusiasm for things charismatic have been followed by a period of reflection, but he still affirms the value of his experience pointing as it does 'to the Lord and giver of life, of whom we shall always stand in constant need'.[14] Andrew Walker grew up the son of an Elim Pentecostal minister, but discovered the meaning of Pentecost as a fourteen-year-old in Neath Apostolic Church. When the pastor prayed over him at the end of the service he recalled 'tongues rushed out and I felt good but strange, and a little frightened'.[15] Although during his university years Walker moved on and embraced the Russian Orthodox Church in 1973, he later wrote in 1995: 'I have never, however, reneged on my past experience, even though I would have to say unequivocally that my Churchmanship, Theology and Spirituality are Orthodox.'[16]

Working from within the movement, as it were, Tom Smail, Nigel Wright and Andrew Walker have between them produced some serious theological reflection and critiques of controversial and key aspects of charismatic renewal. Nigel Wright contributed a careful analysis of 'Signs and Wonders' in which he examined John Wimber's theology and approach to healing. He interpreted the spiritual phenomena as essentially 'varied human responses to the approach of the transcendent God'.[17] Andrew Walker offered a wise balance in his assessment of 'Demonology and the Charismatic Movement'.[18] He rightly pointed out that unless we are 'prepared to override the biblical witness, it is difficult to reject completely the devil and the notion of a spiritual war between the forces of good and evil'. However, he went on to describe much of modern-day charismatic spiritual warfare as 'paranoia'. Paranoid people are those who see their enemies lurking at every corner and forever out to get them. He argued that it was in the 1980s and largely through the influence of Bill Subritzky and Derek Prince, that demons began to come out from beneath the beds as in *Gremlins 2: The New Batch*.[19] He further contended that there is far too much focus on demonic entry points which is matched by an equal fascination with their exit through vomiting, spitting, foaming, coughing and yawning. He quoted Subritzky who said, 'Sometimes particular demons cause people to sleep during meetings, particularly when the gospel is being preached.'[20] Walker pointed out that there is little material and a lack of fascination with the demonic in the Acts of the Apostles and the Pauline letters. His conclusion is judicious in that demon possession is a reality but none the less rare.

Reflecting on charismatic worship, Tom Smail expressed his conviction that it has made 'valuable contributions and indeed corrections'.[21] In particular it has underlined the importance of 'songs of intimacy' and 'hushed reverence'. It has also drawn the churches into 'deeply and engrossingly praiseful worship'. Where it tends to lack is in a strong focus on the work of Jesus at Calvary, the sacrament of the Lord's Supper and intercession. Authentic worship, Smail rightly reminded his readers, is 'in truth' as well as 'in spirit'. 'The task of the Church,' according to Smail, 'is to discover a new and creative relationship between liturgical tradition and charismatic tradition.'[22]

In a brief examination of the rise of the prophetic, Wright made the point that a distinction needs to be drawn between it and extended words of knowledge. Some of John Wimber's earlier prophetic associates such as Paul Cain, were 'astonishingly accurate in their knowledge of individual circumstances' but inaccurate in their prophetic utterances. Wright underscored a widely recognised fact that prophetically gifted people frequently fall victim to unorthodox theology, not to mention, on occasion, unorthodox behaviour. The prophetic, Nigel Wright stressed, is an area where the church needs to make 'careful theological, pastoral and political reflection'.[23]

In a concluding essay, Andrew Walker engaged with 'Miracles, Strange Phenomena and Holiness'. In upholding the view that there is no reason for the miracles of the New Testament to have ceased, Walker maintained that charismatics 'have the logic of the gospels on their side'.[24] However, he warned that miracles are crowd-pullers and that charismatic Christianity can easily be taken over by itinerant fraudsters who feed congregations with hearsay stories and conjecture. What appear to be miraculous occurrences can be psycho-social constructions. In an important postscript, Walker urged that the presence of God provokes wonder and holiness and suggested that where genuine miracles occur they engender reverence and an overwhelming sense of God's presence.[25]

Perhaps the most significant contribution in this volume is Tom Smail's model of renewal.[26] He suggested that there are two basic models, the Pentecostal and the Paschal. Smail prefers the latter for reasons which will shortly become clear. The Pentecost model sees what happened on the Day of Pentecost as 'the second of the great New Testament beginnings'. The first stage is the work of Jesus which climaxed at the cross. The second stage is seen as an advance upon and 'superior to the first'.[27] This model, he suggested, is prominent in Luke. The Paschal model, according to Smail, is more prominent in John where the coming of the Spirit is linked with the going of Jesus to the cross. The Paschal model is Smail's preferred option because he sees it as being less triumphalist. Jesus didn't attack evil 'smashing it by laser beams of supernatural force', but rather 'by taking it on himself and letting it do its worst to him'.[28] 'Our ultimate victory,' he urges, 'comes not from escaping evil but from being given the ability to endure and bear it.'[29] However, if a brief interjection might be permitted at this point, a case might be made for combining these two models which to some extent counterbalance each other. On the one hand, a constant focus on the cross as the central act of salvation and the example of sacrifice and humility which it provides is the *sine qua non* of Christian theology. The flip side, however, is that there are times when God's people need empowerment and there are a number of instances of this in the book of Acts. It may well be that the Salvation Army with its motto of 'Blood and Fire' has struck the right emphasis.

It obviously is not possible within the confines of one chapter to give consideration to all the contributions made by theologians from the charismatic wing of the Church. However, the writings of Max Turner and Christopher Cocksworth are of particular importance since they concern the Holy Spirit and the Trinity and are therefore at the heart of the charismatic agenda.

Max Turner published two substantial scholarly volumes both in 1996, *The Holy Spirit and Spiritual Gifts Then and Now* and *Power from on High: The Spirit in Israel's Restoration and Witness in Luke–Acts*.[30] In the first of these two books, Turner examined the development of the New Testament doctrine of the Holy Spirit against the background of Judaism. He demonstrated how later Judaism, particularly in the intertestamental period, anticipated gifts from the Spirit including charismatic revelation, charismatic wisdom and invasive charismatic speech but above all 'the spirit of prophecy'.[31] He underlined the primary roles of the Spirit in Old Testament Judaism as being God in action, ethical transformation and inspired speech. In the New Testament, first through the claims of Jesus and then the outpouring of the Holy Spirit on the Day of Pentecost, there are disclosures of the Trinity.[32] Turner also decisively dismissed cessationism, the view that spiritual gifts ceased at the conclusion of the Apostolic era. Turner asserted that 'nothing in the New Testament suggests that healings would cease',[33] and he pointed out that the gift of the Spirit which Peter promised on the Day of Pentecost was to all who call on the name of the Lord – even the bearers' children's children.[34] Additionally, Turner shows clearly that there is plenty of evidence in the history of the early church that miraculous gifts continued into the second and third centuries.[35] Unlike many conservative and evangelical theologians, Turner does not attempt to put the Holy Spirit into a straitjacket. He noted, for example, that the gift of tongues had an evangelistic function on the Day of Pentecost but elsewhere it is presented as 'a gift mainly (but not exclusively) for private worship'.[36]

Turner's *Power from on High: The Spirit in Israel's Restoration and Witness in Luke–Acts* is an extensive study of Lukan pneumatology which presents a real challenge to the Non-Pentecostal/non-charismatic sectors of the church. Turner demonstrates that the book of Acts represents the Spirit as 'the transcendence of God over and through the Church'.[37] For example, he is the Spirit who comes with the noise of wind, who shakes the house, who plucks up and transports the evangelist and who reveals God's power in 'signs and wonders' and in 'the invasive praise of glossolalia'.[38] This stands in contrast to those non-charismatics who tend to 'over-formalise' and 'over-institutionalise' the divine presence. They see the work of the Spirit as primarily located in the preaching, in the ordained ministry, in the corporate worship of the church and in the sacrament. On this understanding there is a danger of 'reducing the Spirit' to the immanence of God. Luke's presentation of the Holy Spirit also challenges us to an ongoing spirituality and the goal of not relying on a past baptism of the Spirit but 'living in the fullness of the Spirit'.[39]

Christopher Cocksworth, in his book *Holy, Holy, Holy, Worshipping the Trinitarian God*[40] examines the Trinity through the lens of worship and worship through the lens of the Trinity. He demonstrates that it was as the early Christians worshipped God that the Trinitarian pattern of their experience of salvation came into focus. Cocksworth shows how prayer to God is also prayer to Jesus[41] and praise and worship of the one God came to include worship of Jesus.[42] Using the writings of the early church leaders known as 'the Fathers', Cocksworth goes on to show how the doctrine of the Trinity developed in the second and third centuries. He shows how they spoke of the inter-relatedness of the persons of the Godhead and crafted prayers in their liturgical services which were Trinitarian in character.[43] The later Church Fathers, he demonstrates, recognized the mystery of God's unity that 'the Godhead is . . . undivided in separate persons'. It was the Fathers of the Cappadocian Churches in Asia Minor who came to emphasise the Lordship of the Holy Spirit and so ensured that the full divinity of the Spirit was defined at the Council of Constantinople in 381. In the second part of the book there is an extended study of the Glory or face of God which is reflected both by Christ 'as the Lord of Glory' (1 Cor 2:8)[44] and the Holy Spirit who is 'the Spirit of Glory, which is the Spirit of God, resting on [us]' (1 Pet 4:14).[45] The Trinity, Christopher Cocksworth concludes, is a model of relational unity and as such prompts us to acknowledge the dignity of our fellow human beings and to work for justice.[46] It is also the worship of the Trinitarian God which sends us out unto the world to live and speak the good news of the Kingdom.[47]

Other writers who have allowed their experience of the Spirit to impact their writing include John McKay and Mark Stibbe. McKay produced a four-volume charismatic theology, *The Way of the Spirit*.[48] McKay who was formerly a lecturer in Old Testament at the University of Hull entitled his volumes: *The Call of the Cross, Times of Refreshing, Heirs of the Prophets*, and *My Lord and My God*. In general terms McKay worked through the biblical material and developed a theology of the Spirit's working. Stibbe has offered many relevant insights, particularly in the realm of hermeneutics, revival and creation. Regarding the last issue Stibbe argued that charismatics should by virtue of their experience of the Spirit have a 'sympathetic attitude' to the creation. He demonstrated how Paul understands the Holy Spirit 'as the suffering presence of God in creation'. He wrote: 'The Christian who has grasped the deep teaching about the suffering presence of the Holy Spirit in creation (Romans 8) knows that s/he stands with creation, not against it. The Christian disciple stands in a relationship of solidity with the universe.'[49]

Further Reflection on Aspects of Charismatic Theology

Throughout the course of this book an effort has been made to offer theological and practical consideration of the themes which have been raised. This penultimate chapter now attempts some further reflection on the seminal aspects of charismatic practice and theology. What are taken to be positive developments will be highlighted while areas for concern will be identified. In this exercise a wide divergence of opinion will inevitably be observed at some points in the approach of those charismatics who are attempting to do academic theology and those who are essentially pastors and preachers whose audience is the faithful who are clamouring for the latest book or anointed teaching tape.

Authority and Revelation

The New Testament is the principal source for Christian doctrine and any scrutiny of charismatic theology must begin at this point. The majority of English charismatics would seem to come from a Protestant evangelical background. For such it is axiomatic that Scripture is coherent. That is, while there may be different perspectives between the authors, essentially the biblical books tell one story and do not contain unresolvable contradictions. The available evidence suggests that most UK charismatics do take their stand on Martin Luther's 'Sola Scriptura' principle. This contention can readily be gauged by the fact most of our historic Christian churches adhere to the Catholic creeds, and denominations such as the Church of England and the Presbyterians have their own additional bases of faith in statements such as the Thirty-Nine Articles or the Westminster Catechism. Restoration charismatics and those from the new churches either have their own formularies which express their commitment to the supreme authority of the Bible or they are affiliated to the Evangelical Alliance whose doctrinal basis declares: 'The divine inspiration of Holy Scripture and its consequent entire trustworthiness and supreme authority in all matters of faith and practice.'

Academic theologians who are charismatics, such as Smail, Wright, Cocksworth and Turner,[50] clearly adhere to this foundational basis. They and others would subscribe to the conviction expressed by Smail in his book, *Once and For All A Confession of the Cross*:

> My primary contact with Christ is through the scriptures of the New Testament in which the person and culminating event of his life and their significance is presented to me . . . My personal idiosyncrasies and my cultural presuppositions have alike to be submitted to the judgement of the written word of God, because it is only through the written word that I have contact with the living Word who died on Calvary.[51]

Having an agreed basis of authority and source for theology is one thing. Where, however, divergence begins to be more apparent is in the matter of hermeneutics or how that source is interpreted. It is the case that some non-academic charismatics incline to what has been termed the 'hermeneutic of immediacy'. The emphasis of this is on what is God saying today through a particular verse or passage, regardless of what it might have meant to the original hearers. Clearly this can lead to speculative interpretations. Thus, for example, 'Come out from among them and be separate' can be taken as God saying that charismatic Christians should leave their denominational churches and join one of the new churches. The prevention of God's messenger, by 'the Prince of Persia', from reaching Daniel for twenty-one days (Dan 10:13) was taken as God's warning that there are strong demonic over-lords over every city in the British Isles and God's immediate call to engage in spiritual warfare. The locust plagues of Joel 2 are God's army and that army is his Spirit-filled people of the 1990s who have been raised up for the end times. Equally, Hosea's prophecy that the Lord would heal and revive the injured people of Israel (6:1) was the Lord saying he would revive the flagging charismatic section of his church in the early 1990s. 'Behold I am doing a new thing says the Lord' (Is 42:9) has been taken as God's imprimatur on almost every fresh wave of revival since the 1970s and his endorsement of each new enthusiasm from spiritual warfare, high praise and prophecy to holy molars and gold dust. The added difficulty here is that there comes a limit to how many 'new things' this one particular text can be made to sustain.

Closely related to the 'hermeneutic of immediacy' is Mark Stibbe's 'this is that' hermeneutic. This is based on Peter's use of the prophet Joel during his sermon on the Day of Pentecost (see Acts 2:16). An obvious example of how it works out in practice is found in Mark Stibbe's book *Times of Refreshing: A Practical Theology of Revival Today*. Stibbe considers the description of the river flowing out from Israel's temple in Ezekiel 47. Near the temple precinct the water is shallow but as it progresses it becomes first of all knee-deep, then waist-deep and finally too deep to stand in at all. These four varying levels, Stibbe suggests, represent a four-staged pattern of revival which can be applied to the twentieth century. Stibbe then proposed the following thesis: 'that in the twentieth century, we can speak of four main movements of God's Holy Spirit, and that these four "waves" represent a THIS which corresponds to the THAT which we find in Ezekiel 47:1–12.' The first wave was the emergence of Pentecostalism in 1906 followed secondly by the charismatic renewal of the 1960s and then by what he calls the 'Protestant Evangelical Renewal' energised by John Wimber in the 1980s. The fourth wave was beginning its arrival with the Toronto Blessing in 1995.[52]

At the outset, Stibbe's proposal raises the question of whether 1906 can fairly be described as a 'revival' since crime, drunkenness and church attendance in South Wales soon returned to their pre-1906 levels. Additionally, was the Toronto Blessing really the precursor of a major revival? Leaving these two issues aside however, Stibbe's interpretation of Ezekiel 47 raises some further crucial questions of biblical interpretation. In particular, did the prophet really intend the four water levels to indicate a recurring four separate stage pattern of spiritual revival and how important is the original meaning of the text? These are major considerations which fall beyond the scope of this chapter. Suffice it to say, however, that if the original meaning for the writer and his original hearers is regarded as only of secondary importance, then Christian living, worship and experience will become decontextualised and subjective. Indeed, it might come to the point where two entirely different 'this is thats' are being based on the same text. Clearly it is important that the Holy Spirit illuminate our understanding but if he is the Spirit of truth then the context, historical setting and obvious meaning must be taken seriously. Always we have to take note of Augustine's point that the human mind is part of the image of God in humanity. Rationality is therefore a God-given faculty with which 'spiritual' needs to be assessed.

Some charismatics incline to a fundamentalist hermeneutic, others go even further and indulge what might be regarded as a 'gnostic hermeneutic'. The fundamentalist hermeneutic is perhaps most visible in the patriarchal views of Bryn Jones and Covenant Ministries. It is seen in all male 'apostolic covering' and congregational leadership, strict tithing and the refusal to allow women to teach or preach at the Sunday worship services. Glimmers of it are also discernible in Bill Subritzky's contention that demons can be distinguished from angels because 'angels usually have wings'[53] and the insistence of the Jesus Army that women should wear their hair long and be in submission to men.[54]

Gnostic hermeneutics are at their most visible at the extreme ends of the charismatic movement. Here the interpretation extends beyond even a rigid fundamentalist reading of a text. Additional insights come from private revelation or creative imagination and go beyond any detail provided by canonical Scripture. For example, Kenneth Copeland tells us that God is '. . . very much like you and me. A being that stands somewhere around 6'2" 6'3", that weighs somewhere in the neighbourhood of a couple of hundred pounds, little better, [and] has a [hand] span of nine inches across.'[55] Smail, Walker and Wright have argued convincingly that a good deal of faith teaching goes beyond what Scripture can sustain, particularly in the area of healing and material prosperity. They point out a fundamental flaw in the faith movement's understanding of humankind which they illustrate from Kenneth Hagin's writing. Hagin sees us as essentially spiritual beings clothed with a body of flesh. 'Man,' according to him, 'is a spirit who possesses a soul and lives in a body . . . Man at physical death, leaves his body. Yet he is no less man than he was when he had his body.'[56] This leads logically to a faith charismatic healer telling people to believe for their healing in spite of the fact that their symptoms tell them otherwise. The thinking here is perfectly logical because on their understanding, which is almost the same as that of Christian Science, human flesh isn't the 'reality' of our fundamental nature. We are, according to Hagin, spirit. This means, faith charismatics say, we can reject the 'natural' and believe in the 'spiritual'. The problem here is that this is not the biblical understanding of man. We are equally body, mind and spirit which of course is why Jesus came in human flesh and suffered and died in human flesh.

A further aspect of the gnostic hermeneutics of faith charismatics is seen in Hagin's claim that he received his four principles not from Scripture but directly in a vision from Jesus.[57] The four principles, as was noted in Chapter 2, are (1) say it, (2) do it, (3) receive it and (4) tell it. At root, this kind of faith really amounts to 'positive thinking' rather than an active trust and personal reliance on the person of Jesus which is at the heart of New Testament believing.

Gnostic hermeneutics are also seen in much of the charismatic teaching on the whole area of spiritual transference. The warning that sins will be punished to the third and fourth generation has been made the basis of teaching that demonic spirits are passed down from parent to child through sexual intercourse. Old Testament teaching on defilement has been used to support the notion that if you listen to or receive ministry from someone who is demonically influenced, you yourself become demonically influenced. All of this, it seems to me, is reading too much out of the texts of Scripture.

Despite these and other obvious weaknesses of the charismatic approach to Scripture there are some very clear strengths. Charismatics come to the Bible not simply to learn about God and increase their knowledge of God, they come to its pages to encounter God. The Bible for them is a living book. It is the Spirit's sword and they come to it expecting that God will speak to them personally from its pages. Stibbe explains that in the 'this is that' approach we allow 'the Holy Spirit to lead us to Bible texts'.[58] Provided this approach does not result in passages being taken out of context or detached from their genre, this involvement of the Spirit must be seen to be positive.

The Holy Spirit

The doctrine of the Holy Spirit is central to charismatic experience and theology. Charismatics, as we have seen, lay particular stress on an invasive felt experience of the Holy Spirit. This is something which happens either at conversion or subsequently and then needs to be sustained thereafter. Despite the fact that this 'filling' has brought a new dimension to many Christian lives it has also raised a number of questions in people's minds.

Perhaps most obvious is the danger among charismatic Christians of separating the Holy Spirit and Jesus at the very least in people's thinking. At times, there seems to be an over stress on 'the anointing', 'anointed ministries', and invocations of the Holy Spirit, with little or no reference to Jesus. It needs to be remembered that the Spirit is the Spirit of Jesus, that Jesus sent the Spirit and that the Spirit's function is to glorify Jesus. It would be helpful, one feels on occasion, for the Spirit to be invited to come and reveal or glorify Jesus. On the other hand, if the work of the Spirit is seen as solely to apply the benefits of Jesus to the believer there is a danger that the Spirit may come to be regarded as subordinate to Jesus.

Professor Colin Gunton who is sympathetic in his observations of what he terms 'the charismatic movement', wrote that 'there is sometimes a tendency to depersonalise the Spirit'.[59] It seems to me that certain techniques such as hand wafting or shaking or impersonal invocations of 'More power', or 'Let the power come' need to be used carefully together with other personal forms of address. A wife possibly wouldn't be too pleased if at the end of a nice meal her husband held up his hand and said, 'More food', 'Jemima, let the food come'. Hopefully, in such circumstances there would also be expressions of warm gratitude and a gracious request for further sustenance. Perhaps it was for these kinds of reason that Andrew Walker wrote that 'throughout the renewal movement you tend to get the idea that the Holy Spirit is the power of Jesus, but not really personal – that he is not a hypostasis, in theological language'.[60] He related how his pilgrimage took him from Elim Pentecostalism to the Russian Orthodox Church where he learned from his new tradition that the Holy Spirit is a person not a power.[61]

There has been a good deal of debate over the procession of the Holy Spirit between Western Catholicism and the Eastern Orthodox Churches. The Orthodox tradition has been that the Holy Spirit proceeds from the Father and the Western Church adds 'and the Son'. This is known as the filioque clause. A mediating alternative which has been suggested by some charismatics is that the Spirit proceeds from the Father through the Son.

This formula has the merit of not implying that the eternal sending of the Holy Spirit followed the generation of the Son. It therefore avoids the suggestion that the Spirit is less than the son.

Charismatic Christians have made a significant contribution to the theology of the Holy Spirit. There has been a strong tendency in conservative evangelicalism to limit the role of the Holy Spirit to making Jesus' saving work real in the life of the believer and convicting individuals of sin, righteousness and judgement. Clearly, charismatic Christianity has given a much wider biblical perspective to the person and work of the Holy Spirit. Historically down through the centuries the institutional church has sought to keep a tight control on the Spirit. In the last quarter of the twentieth century charismatic Christianity sought to allow the Holy Spirit greater freedom to inspire less rigid forms of liturgy, music, prayer and church leadership.

Professor Colin Gunton has suggested that 'the whole Christian tradition in its entirety may be at fault in over-playing the immanence of the Spirit'.[62] Here once again it can be contended that charismatic Christianity has helped the church to recover and recognise the lordship of the Spirit. Clearly the Holy Spirit is active in the world but he is also over the world because in the words of the Nicene Creed, he is also 'the Lord and giver of life'.

The rediscovery of the Holy Spirit as both person and Lord has led on to a rediscovery of the Trinity both in terms of experience and as a model for mission. Christopher Cocksworth has demonstrated both these aspects very fully in his study.[63] Others have pointed out the fact that love limited to only two persons is incomplete and self-gratifying, but that the introduction of a third party enables that love to reach beyond itself. The Holy Spirit is therefore the perfecter of God's love and enables the Godhead to reach out to others. In this way the Holy Spirit is both the model and the motivator of mission.

The Trinity is a Trinity in unity and so is an exemplar and inspirer of Christian unity. This point was earlier made by Friedrich Schleiermacher who contended that religion could be located in feeling and institution, not just in credal formulae and that the doctrine of the Trinity could be regarded as a 'coping stone' binding the two walls together and protecting them.[64] It seems to me that charismatic Christians have remained solid in their adherence to essential first order Christian doctrine and that there is a growing development of cross-denominational ties and fellowship among them. Martin Percy interprets the charismatic world as being in a state of continual fracturing.[65] My perception is different and is that at grass roots level charismatic Christians move freely between charismatic churches and fellowships of every denomination and that there is a growing coming together in movements such as Spring Harvest, Stoneleigh Bible Week and New Wine.

Spiritual Gifts

Closely related to the person and work of the Holy Spirit is the whole area of spiritual gifts. Charismatic Christianity has certainly brought the question of spiritual gifts to the fore. Scholars such as Max Turner have convinced even non-charismatic conservative evangelicals that healing and other spiritual gifts did not cease with the closing of the Apostolic age. Andrew Walker commented forcibly:

> John 14:12 for example, does not say that the wonders of Christ will disappear with his passing. On the contrary, it says: Most assuredly, I say to you, he who believes in Me, the works that I do he will do also; and greater works than these he will do because I go to my Father.[66]

To maintain that all spiritual gifts ceased after the passing of the last apostle would require an end of all authentic claims to their use in the second century. The reality of the situation is, however, that there is fulsome evidence of spiritual gifts in the church down to the time of Athanasius (c.296–377) in the late fourth century and beyond. We have evidence of tongues and prophecy at the time of Tertullian (c.155–220) in the early third century and conflict with the demonic in the life of Antony (251–356) the hermit. Irenaeus (c.115–190) writing about AD 170, tells us that 'exorcisms, healings and even the raising of the dead took place in the name of Jesus'. He further related how people received words of knowledge, visions, prophecy and a multitude of other gifts through the name of Christ.[67]

It is the case that some charismatics have overplayed the use of spiritual gifts or utilized them in extreme ways. Others have trivialized miracles down to the level of 'God healed my headache' or made the bus late so that I could catch it and be in time for work. It has to be remembered that miraculous gifts are always a strong crowd-puller as Jesus himself was aware and he warned that it is an evil generation which seeks for signs as ends in themselves. There has been a tendency in certain circles to play hard on signs and wonders and promote healing services as a way of getting new people in. The end result of this kind of misplaced emphasis has often been disillusionment and loss of faith. Some of this has been reflected in the not inconsiderable numbers of people who left charismatic churches in the aftermath of the Toronto Blessing.

It is probably in the area of the gift of healing that most difficulties occur. There has been tendency in charismatic approaches to healing to downplay or completely pass over the natural roots of pain and sickness. These could include bad relationships, working over-long hours, poor diet, lack of exercise and fresh air and a generally unbalanced lifestyle. It doesn't make sense to bind a sickness or rebuke a fever when its possible root causes are altogether ignored. Too often the rhetoric on healing is much greater than the reality. Clearly there are some remarkable genuine and lasting healings which have taken place in response to prayer. On the other hand, when one tries to quantify healings the numbers of very obvious instances are often relatively small. The late John Wimber was one of the few charismatics who did in fact address this point indicating the selectiveness of God's healing.[68]

A problem which relates to those who are not healed is an inability to face up to the reality of the situation. This is particularly true in the case of faith charismatics who tend to look for explanations as to why people have not been healed. They didn't pray enough, there was hidden sin in their life, they lacked faith or there was demonic influence which hadn't been adequately dealt with. Any explanation seems to do other than to question or doubt the efficacy of those doing the praying. However, the fact has to be faced in the end that in the New Testament only those who are doing the praying are ever reprimanded for their lack of faith and in no case is the sick person ever condemned for their insufficient believing.

Another spiritual gift which is cause for serious concern is that of prophecy. As has been noted, prophecy is important in the church's life and the apostle Paul urges Christians to pursue and grow in their practice of it. Nevertheless some major problems have resulted particularly stemming from unfulfilled public predictions. For example, the same prophecy concerning Westminster Chapel was given twice by Gerald Coates first at Spring Harvest on 25 April 1995 and repeated a second time on 2 October 1995 in the church itself. His prediction was as follows:

> The Spirit of the Lord will come upon you with increasing power. But you need to understand that over these next eighteen months although many attacks will come, that if you are faithful to your brothers, and not seek to achieve in human strength what only God can achieve by His Holy Spirit, in eighteen months from this month, eighteen months from April 1995, your Church, Westminster Chapel, will be unrecognizable . . . in eighteen months, the Spirit of God will come among many who live in that area . . . many . . . taxi drivers would get out of their taxis because the Spirit of God is so strong in that place.[69]

Here was an unequivocal announcement of a revival beginning at Westminster Chapel and its environs eighteen months from April, 1995. In short, in October 1996 the entire aspect of both the congregation and the locality would be completely changed. In a public statement made on Sunday morning 27 October 1996 R.T. Kendall stated bluntly: 'It didn't happen. I promised not to rationalise or explain it away – it did not happen.' Kendall went on to affirm, 'Gerald is a good man' and that some of the other words of the prophecy 'have blessed and comforted me . . . have helped me no end.' There seems no question, as Kendall underlined, that Coates is a person of integrity and no one is going to get it right all the time. The problem, as I understood it from conversations with members of the Westminster Chapel congregation, is that the matter was largely swept under the carpet. Some left disillusioned, others are hanging on in the hopes that the date may have been wrong. Inevitably, genuine prophets will occasionally prophesy error, just as gifted preachers will preach it, but the key issue is how the aftermath is dealt with. Clearly there needs to be a theology which addresses not only what prophecy is but considers the nature of the prophetic office and ministry and the ways in which prophecy should be handled and actioned. A member of Cornerstone, Graham Cook, himself a prophet and the author of a solid book on prophecy,[70] has warned that there are too many loose prophetic cannons who travel the world ministering but who are not rooted in a local church and are answerable to no one for the prophecies they give.

Prophecy, as was noted earlier, also needs to be distinguished from 'words of knowledge'. Some of the late twentieth and early twenty-first-century prophets deal in extended words of knowledge revealing details of individuals' past lives and experiences and giving them encouragement or direction for the future. Often in these circumstances there are insufficient safeguards or pastoral oversight to ensure the individual can adequately assess what has been said and make a balanced judgement.

Having said all this, it remains the case that the charismatic emphasis on spiritual gifts in the church has brought many positive benefits. It has helped to recreate the local church as a body in which all the members have an active role or function to play in one of the gifts of healing, helping or speaking. Every-member ministry has contributed to laicisation of the church in what is essentially an anti-clerical age in which vocations to the ordained ministry continue to decline steeply. All this has further helped individuals to develop and mature as people both within the Christian fellowship and beyond as they learn to transfer their newly developing skills into their work stations and local communities.

The Kingdom

Since the inception of the charismatic movement in the late 1960s and early 1970s, the Kingdom of God has been a central focus. The Kingdom was proclaimed as operating in any place where the evidence of the rule of Christ the King was clearly visible. In the early 1970s, and still for the majority of present charismatics, the Kingdom has been seen in largely quasi-spiritual terms. Only in the later 1990s did some begin to see the

Kingdom as embracing the whole of life including its social and economic dimensions in the way that Frederick Denison Maurice and Charles Kingsley had done in the early 1850s.

The great turning point in charismatic Kingdom theology was brought about by Arthur Wallis. Coming from a Brethren background he had been schooled, like most evangelicals, in a Pre-millennialism which asserted that the world situation would gradually deteriorate and the Man of Lawlessness would be unloosed. Then Christ would return 'pre' or before the inauguration of a millennial or thousand-year period of bliss on earth. Wallis exchanged this position for the post-millennial teaching of the Wesleys and the earlier Puritans. On this view the world situation was going to rapidly improve as the revived end-time, Spirit-filled church, led by restored apostles, would usher in a world-wide revival which in turn would embrace the Millennium and be followed by Jesus' return. This end-time post-millennial view has remained strong in charismatic circles and has prompted urgent prayer for the revival which it is believed will herald the start of the last days. Many charismatic leaders for this reason continue to be upbeat and to talk up the prospect of a revival. For example, speaking at Grapevine in August 1996 Gerald Coates declared:

> I don't want to be a part of the 'Oh no people. Oh no, we can't see our Royal Family changed. Oh no, we can't see the House of Lords changed. Oh no, it's too late we can't see the Welfare State changed. Oh no, we can't see the Church changed. I don't want to be one of those sitting in their offices and writing desperately gloomy prophetic magazines, telling us it's going to be worse. No, the glory of the Lord is going to fill the earth as the water covers the sea.

This stress on the post-millennial Kingdom and Kingdom theology in general has had some positive spin-offs for contemporary Christianity. Perhaps most significantly, it has helped believers to see beyond the confines of their local church or fellowship to something which is much broader and wider. The mission of God's people is seen as not merely to promote the Church but to proclaim the Kingdom of God. Kingdom theology has also served to increase Christian concern for the world beyond the community of faith. It is a fact that in the last two decades of the twentieth century many charismatic Christians became much more actively involved in local and national issues, particularly through the work of Care which has been mobilized under the leadership of Lyndon Bowring. This concern focused predominantly on pro-life issues, the family and education but it also extended to prison aftercare and concern over the impact of the media. The Evangelical Alliance with which many charismatic churches are affiliated also involved itself with social issues such as homelessness and drug related crime.

In the past, evangelical social work has been criticized for treating the symptoms of poverty but not really concerning itself with the underlying structures which generate poverty. It seems now to be the case that by beginning to concern themselves with issues such as the family, homelessness and unemployment charismatic Christians are starting to grapple with poverty at the base level. Although there is an urgent need for theology to concern itself in depth with issues of social justice the case can be made that in general charismatic churches do as much, and probably more, in this area than most other sectors of the Christian Church.

Dominion Theology

This stress on a Kingdom of God which can be partially experienced in the present has led to a preoccupation with 'dominion theology' which is concerned with asserting Jesus' dominion over Satan, who is the 'Prince of this World'. Dominion theology has reference to the dominion of individuals, institutions and the land in the name of God. As John Wimber saw it, the Kingdom of God is a realm of power in which Satan is ousted from control. This happens as Christians engage in 'power' evangelism, 'power' healing and particularly in spiritual warfare as they cast out the demon emissaries of Satan's kingdom.

The notion of spiritual warfare has led many charismatic Christians into an unhealthy dualism in which the whole of life is perceived as an intensive battle between the forces of light and the forces of darkness. It has led to what Andrew Walker termed the 'paranoid universe' in which the world is seen as infested with demons which cling to people like flies and enter into their bodies through their eyes, mouths and other points. This in turn has generated some extreme and horrendous exorcism procedures in which individuals have been plunged into baths of holy water and had their breasts and genitalia anointed with sacred wine. In short, charismatics need to find a more balanced theology of the devil. Such will take more seriously the fact that Jesus did not see the world as being overrun by demonic forces. It will avoid investing the enemy of souls with overmuch power and it will recognise that there are three factors which cause us to do evil, namely the world, the flesh and the devil.

On the plus side, charismatics have helped to retain belief in a personal eevil being at a time when some conservative theologians are referring to the devil as a 'principle' rather than a person. Nevertheless, it is important that the devil is not accredited with more power than is his by right. It needs always to be remembered that Jesus gave authority to his followers 'to overcome all the power of the enemy' so that 'nothing would harm them'.[71]

Eschatology and Ecclesiology

Charismatic Kingdom theology with its emphasis on a post-millennial period of bliss has to some extent re-focused the whole issue of the eschatological debate. A number of conservative New Testament theologians, and notably Tom Wright,[72] have recently argued that the coming of the Son of Man which Jesus predicted would take place, was fulfilled in the events surrounding the destruction of Jerusalem by the Roman armies in AD 70. On this understanding, the Son of Man's coming as depicted in the Gospel passages, has already been realised. For writers such as Wright the one significant event which remains to be fulfilled is the final judgement. In contrast, most charismatics are still looking towards a future Millennium which will either precede or be followed by a literal personal and bodily return of the Lord. In the mind of many, such a future second coming of Christ clearly meshed with charismatic phenomena since the biblical record stated that in the last days the Lord would pour out his Holy Spirit on all flesh. Related to this in the earlier phases of the charismatic movement, there was a strong emphasis on the Church as 'the New Israel' who would be instrumental in bringing in this end time. By the later 1990s, however, many charismatics, prompted by the growth of messianic Judaism and the return of large numbers of Jews to Israel, had dispensed with replacement theology. The majority view had now become that it was the restored nation of Israel which would herald the revival and final aspects of the eschaton.

One of the more dysfunctional aspects of charismatic eschatology has been its strong emphasis on revivals and revivalism which are seen as the concrete evidence of the end-time outpouring of the Spirit. Clearly, all sections of the 'One Holy Catholic and Apostolic Church' recognize the need for some kind of worldwide revitalisation of the Christian faith, but too great an emphasis on revival can, and has had, a debilitating effect on the quality and effectiveness of Christian living and commitment. It has led to extremes of failed prophecy and a constant endeavour by books and conferences to talk up revival in the hope of generating it. After nearly a decade, there are signs of a resultant growing disillusionment and lapsing of faith. This was brought home to me when I recently heard a man of about forty expressing deep cynicism about his own local charismatic church. He said that for twenty years they'd preached the anointing with revival just around the corner and in all that time nothing had changed. In short, it was just boring and he had left it.

Charismatics, and indeed church historians in general, need to produce a credible theory of revival. In particular, work needs to be done to formulate an agreed or working definition of revival. It seems to me that many who pray earnestly for revival and attend revival conferences have very little notion of what it is they're praying for and what revival will be like on the ground when it occurs. Most have some vague notion that all the churches will be full to bursting on Sundays and that vicars and pastors will be strolling around blessing what God is doing and singing new selections of Vineyard choruses. It needs to be recognized however that quite probably when revival does come many of those who have prayed for it, won't recognize it or accept it. Any definition of revival must surely also embrace not only the spiritual revival of the individual and the church but also the social, economic and political structures of the nation. Indeed there is stress in the Old Testament tradition of renewal about the healing of the land. This was actually one of the significant features of the Wesleyan revival which profoundly impacted British social, political and economic structures. This included such things as the abolition of slave trade, educational advances, Sunday legislation, factory reform, societies to meet the needs of the poor, attacks on the National Lottery and its eventual abolition, the condemnation of child labour and excessive working hours and attacks on pornography and vice. It was for this reason that historians have described the aftermath of the Wesleyan revival as 'the Age of Reform'. On this understanding any future revival is most likely to culminate through the work of organisations such as Care, the Evangelical Alliance, Tear Fund and the Jubilee Trust.

It is arguable that this strong futurist eschatology with its continued emphasis on revivalism has led to a distinctive charismatic ecclesiology. The way this was reasoned out was that a revived church is a 'pure church', a vigorous spotless bride and not a limping old-age pensioner beset with corruption and compromise. Indeed Peter Hocken[73] has shown how the ecclesiology of the Plymouth Brethren impacted on the early phase of the charismatic movement. In particular, both David Lillie and Arthur Wallis, two early Restoration leaders, came from Brethren backgrounds. They followed the convictions of John Nelson Darby, the Brethren founder, who called Christians to recognize the ruin of the established churches.[74] In the first phase of the charismatic movement this led Restoration house fellowships to call those who had been renewed to leave their established denominational churches. Even now when the competitive element among charismatics has diminished there is still a general tendency either to be suspicious of denominational and catholic traditions or to sit lightly on them. By the same token there is much less stress on the ministerial office and the sacramental understanding of Holy Communion. The flip side of this, however, is that charismatics in general fostered a growing degree of cross-denominational co-operation in the 1990s. Nowhere was this more clearly observed than in the take-up of Alpha courses by churches of every denomination.

It is significant that many of the former house churches now generally designated 'new churches' which were once so hostile to the historic churches are now developing strong denominational structures. Even more recent groupings such as the Vineyard are now emerging with hierarchies of area superintendents, senior pastors, music pastors and youth pastors.

Denouement

In general terms it is true to say that charismatics have remained strongly attached to the credal formulae of the Catholic faith. It could reasonably be claimed that British charismatics have adhered as firmly to orthodox Christian doctrine as any other section of the Church. Indeed the vast majority of UK charismatic churches have established their credentials by affiliating with the Evangelical Alliance and therefore subscribe to the cardinal aspects of Protestantism. It clearly is the case that the bulk of charismatic theology is pastoral in nature but it is manifestly incorrect to suggest that the charismatic section of the church lacks any theology or has no serious academic theologians. The fact is that there is a small but increasing number of university and college-based charismatic Christians who are engaging in the scholarly disciplines of theology.[75] In addition, there are a growing number of PhD theses being produced by Pentecostal and charismatic students and scholarly periodicals such as the *Journal of Pentecostal Theology* and its monograph series, published by Sheffield Academic Press, give a taste of further developments to come. In summation the prospects for charismatics and theology are moving in an increasingly positive direction.

CHARISMATICS AND
THE THIRD MILLENNIUM

Some recent voices have suggested that the charismatic movement in the United Kingdom is passing through difficult
straits. Nick Cuthbert, for example, in his book *Charismatics in
Crisis* wrote: 'We would have to say in the midst of all this [the
charismatic movement] that we have barely touched the
world.'[1] Again, he added: 'We have failed to allow the Holy
Spirit to achieve what he wanted, and have instead turned his
work in upon ourselves.'[2]

Charismatic Routinisation
Some critics of the charismatic renewal want to argue that the
movement as a whole is running out of steam. They want to say
that charismatics, along with their older classical Pentecostal
brothers and sisters, have lost their earlier sharp cutting edge
and sectarian radicalism. This is seen in the steadily emerging
middle-classness of charismatic circles right across the denominational spectrum. Andrew Walker observed that
'Restorationists (both R1 and R2) have already scored over their
classical elder brothers and sisters in their inroads into the middle classes.[3] Walker took Gerald Coates' Cobham group in
Surrey to be 'almost exclusively middle class, whilst every
Restoration church and fellowship has a high proportion of professional members'.[4]

It could well be that something of the charismatic appeal to
the middle classes has had to do with its business-like ethos.
Their efficient hierarchical line management system of pastoral
care running from apostles through elders to pastors and house
group leaders was very much like the line management busi-

ness systems of the early 1980s. In general terms the new churches then demonstrated a capacity to move with the mood of the age. As management styles began to change from hierarchies to flat teams in the later 1980s, the charismatic networks followed suit. The whole ethos started to become relational rather than controlling. The talk was no longer, 'Which apostle are you under?' but, 'Who do you relate to?' Glossy magazines like *Restoration* and *Pioneer* have the look of a company magazine about them.

The new church leaders, it is argued, have made the passage from sectarian men of 'charisma' to the appearance of slick middle-class business executives. From humble uncultured positions many of them began to live in considerable comfort replete with the latest desk-top hardware. They have learned a good deal about business management and not a few of them earn executive salaries which they show a great reluctance to disclose.

If the charismatic leaders of the newer churches show a tendency to move away from their initial enthusiasm, the same is true of some of those in the denominational churches. Here there seems to be a growing tendency to encapsulate the earlier vigorous 'charisma' in intellectual aesthetic spiritualities. Ignatian and Celtic varieties seem to be favoured by Anglicans in particular. The danger here is that the whole charismatic experience could become 'routinised' in a sedate and sophisticated cultural ethos based on bookish middle-class disciplines. All of this looks like a classic illustration of Richard Niebuhr's theory that vital 'charisma' experiences and charismatic sectarian groups run down into 'church-type' communities in one generation. Vance Havner of Wheaton College, Illinois, plotted this process in four stages. First there is a 'man', the charismatic leader. Then he generates a 'movement', in this case the charismatic movement. There follows a 'method' – new forms of spirituality which keep it all in tabs. Finally, there is only a 'movement' – tongues ceased here! The fire fell in 1985 or whatever.

In fact one of the weaknesses of the charismatic movement is that by and large it has failed to renew the structures of the historic churches. In the case of the Church of England this has been in spite of the bold stands which were taken by Tony Higton and ABWON. The charismatic movement has impacted

Baptist and Church of England worship. It has, however, failed to put even a dent into Anglican bureaucracy, centralisation and cumbersome diocesan machinery. Thus in the words of Martin Percy, 'instead of displacing the liberal hierarchy, it finds itself placed within it – just another "also ran" '.[5] The inflexibility of the parochial boundary system, the power of the bishops and the rigidity of diocesan bureaucracies remain as tight as before. Church of England clergy with a vision for church planting have left to form Vineyards or throw in their lot with New Frontiers, Ichthus or Salt and Light. Renewal in an Anglican context may thus be seen as renewal of the individual and of corporate worship but not of the structures. Still the overriding view of ministry in the Church of England and in others of the historic denominations is of the one man priesthood. Large sections of the established church are still deeply wedded to post-Constantinian Catholicism with its priestly buildings, ecclesiastical officials, altars, vestments and staid liturgical services. Small wonder therefore that the Church Commissioners reported that 1,544 Church of England churches had been made redundant in the period 1969–98.[6] Such historic denominational organisations which are still rigidly attached to the 'old wineskins' need to heed Roger Forster's words:

> A church that has lost elasticity in its structures through age-long, undisturbed traditions is to be sympathised with, not condemned; but it must recognise the necessity for younger congregations to do what the older ones must admit to themselves they cannot. Such churches which cannot change must not criticise or denigrate those who can, namely the new, but recognise that they have a different part to play.[7]

Peter Hocken rightly stated that the 'astonishing rise' of the independent charismatic churches is a 'chastening reminder to the mainline churches of the insufficiency of their response to the profligacy of God's gift of the Spirit in this century'.[8]

Charismatic Divisiveness

A number of writers have made the point, and with a certain amount of justification, that charismatic churches have been the cause of divisiveness and local unhappiness. Where that is the case, clearly there must be repentance and forgiveness. Against this, however, can be set the fact that charismatic churches have created far more unity than they have displaced. The charismatic movement is essentially 'transdenominational'. It has brought Catholics, Anglicans, Pentecostals and new church leaders together to worship and work in co-operation.

Charismatics from Pentecostal backgrounds have come to appreciate and value aspects of Catholic spirituality, including the eucharist, the daily offices, and the writings of the late medieval mystics. In Northern Ireland, charismatic Catholics and Protestants have joined together in fellowship to work for peace and reconciliation.

Furthermore, before the historic denominations cast too many accusing stones at the charismatics for causing division, they would perhaps do well to reflect on their own early histories! The Church of England was brought into being by an act of open rebellion against the church of Rome by a lecherous monarch who was unable to get a divorce to marry the woman he was having an affair with. The Congregationalists, Baptists and Methodists all repeated the rebellion, in their cases with some justification, and emerged in subsequent splits from the Church of England. Members of the Church of England left the establishment in the late 1820s to form the Brethren. William and Catherine Booth turned their backs on Methodism to start the Salvation Army. No doubt other examples could be added to this selection. Let him who is innocent of 'divisiveness', so-called, cast the first stone.

Despite these criticisms, there is still much, I would suggest, about the charismatic movement which offers hope to the church for the third millennium. In order to point this out, it is necessary to re-visit some of the aspects and themes in the earlier chapters and pages of this book.

Charismatic Experience

To begin at the very beginning it needs to be said that charismatic experience is a very significant factor. Indeed Professor Ninian Smart, Stephen Glock and other sociologists of religion have made the point that experience is an essential dimension of religion. In fact, without it there can be no religion at all.

Professor James Packer underlined the importance of charismatic experience in the following paragraph:

> The charismatic renewal has brought millions of Christians, including many clergy, to a deeper, more exuberant faith in Christ than they had before. It has quickened thousands of congregations, invigorating their worship, making love and fellowship blossom among them, increasing their expectancy and enterprise and giving a stimulus to their evangelism. Charismatic insistence on openness to God has transformed countless lives that previously were not open to him.[9]

One of the key aspects of charismatic experience is its Christocentricity. Jesus becomes a reality in the faith of many charismatic Christians. I attended the Anglican Charismatic Theological Consultation at Ridley Hall in Cambridge in September 1994.[10] One of the papers was read to us by Canon John Gunstone. He began with a personal reflection. After graduating from Durham University he was ordained into the ministry of the Anglican Church and spent some of his early years at Rush Green in Essex. As a good priest in the Catholic wing of the Church he described how he'd spent his first ten years of ministry encouraging his people to be good churchmen and women. He urged them to know their faith, to attend the sacraments regularly and to play their full part in parish life. Then John told us how he was baptised in the Holy Spirit in 1964. It transformed his ministry. It made him 'unhappy with the cult of the priesthood' and 'unhappy to wear a cassock in the street'. He remained appreciative of most of the rest of his Catholic heritage but his goal was now in his own words 'to introduce people to Jesus'. It is my general impression that charismatic Christians are much more ready to speak about Jesus in an easy way than those from other sections of the church.

The early part of the charismatic movement coincided with the rationality of modernism. Theology was sceptical and intellectual and a good deal of official Christianity was correspondingly cerebral, cold and unfeeling. Early charismatic experience was therefore in reaction to this. Since the later 1980s modernism has crumbled with a remarkable suddenness. Now, unexpectedly, experience is seen to be perfectly valid. Indeed, it is even felt to be a valid means of apprehending truth. Truth is no longer regarded solely as a body of doctrine which is appropriated by bending the mind round it. Truth can actually be experienced in ways more akin to Eastern custom and philosophy.

The central aspect of charismatic experience is seen as 'intimacy' with God. This is an emphasis which has featured since the charismatic movement began, although it has been re-emphasised in more recent times by John Wimber and the Vineyard teachers. It's nowhere more apparent than in many of their songs. Here are some familiar examples:

> Within the veil I now would come;
> Into the holy place, to *look upon his face.*

> One thing I ask
> One thing I desire
> Is to *see you*
> Is to *see you.*

> Draw me closer, Lord
> Draw me closer, Lord
> So that I might *touch you*
> So that I might *touch you*
> Lord I want to *touch you.*

> To be *in your presence*
> To sit at your feet
> This is my desire, O Lord
> This is my desire.

Charismatic Christianity has taught its adherents above all else to experience the presence of God in a tangible way. Charismatics, like their mainstream evangelical brothers and sisters, love the Bible and value it as their supreme guide in all matters of faith and practice. They also cry out with the hymn writer: 'Beyond the sacred page, I seek thee, Lord; my spirit longs for thee, the living Word.'

Experience like anything else has potential for danger, though this is more often than not exaggerated by doubters and scaremongering tales. As someone recently said, 'In some quarters, when the Holy Spirit is invited to come, people have more faith in the devil to provide a bad experience than they have in God to give a good experience!' There has been a tendency on the part of some to pray and speak of the Holy Spirit in isolation from the other persons of the Trinity. Nevertheless the fact remains that most charismatics have a working daily experience of the doctrine of the Trinity. This enables them to measure and relate their encounters of the Holy Spirit to their knowledge of God the Father and Jesus, the Son.

The heart ot the Christian faith is a personal relationship between Jesus and the believer. Jesus spent time with his apostles and followers deepening and discipling them in this relationship with himself. What seems to be happening in much of the contemporary church is that people are brought to the start of a personal relationship with Jesus but in many cases it stops there. Instead of discipling them on in that relationship, the churches bombard them with packages. They're processed through beginner courses, committed membership, adult baptism and confirmation. They're encouraged to buy Bible dictionaries and commentaries, to get thoroughly involved in Christian work and even to aquaint themselves with the mysteries of sacred ritual and churchmanship. Is it any wonder that 80 per cent don't stay with it and cease to be active Christians within five years? This is not to say that these things aren't good, clearly most are. The danger is that too much of them detracts from building a daily relationship with Jesus where he is at the centre of their thinking, their consciousness and their activities.

One of the real strengths which the charismatic movement has to bring to the wider church in the third millennium, is its willingness to keep grappling with this central aspect of Christianity. In the pressurised pace of life and the stresses on family relationships, it's only the few who can take in and process yet more information. What people need is something much more basic, a personal relationship with God which is reality.

Charismatic Focus on the Self
Closely allied to charismatic experience is the movement's focus on the self. This might at first sight be felt to be a significant

weakness revealing strongly introspective tendencies. However, it needs to be recognised that no individual is going to be of any use to society until they're fully in touch with and secure with their inner self. The Christian tradition makes it plain that we can only love and serve our neighbour in so far as we love ourselves. We live in an age in which many people cannot face themselves and the thought of contemplating what is within fills them with alarm and horror. The charismatic focus on the inner self is very much addressing the need of the moment.

Almost everywhere we look, the search for self is on. The upwardly-mobile middle class tell us 'I am what I do'. The first question many ask is not 'How are you?' or 'May I know your name?' even, but rather 'What do you do?' My self is identified by what I am capable of, by what I achieve rather than any state of being. In short, this view reduces people to human doings rather than affirming them as human beings.

Another way of identifying self is in terms of possessions. 'I am what I own' is the message that the media, the banks and the magazines are constantly telling us. If they stopped to think about it, they probably don't believe the propaganda they are putting out. They do it nonetheless because their livelihood depends on it. Others think they are the person people tell them they are. 'I am who people say I am' is what many people believe. This is almost as unreal and stressful as the previous notion. People who have such a view are constantly straining to measure up to other people's expectations of themselves. Worse still, they cease to be true to themselves because they are always so busy trying to wear the masks others are attempting to put on them. The discovery and the identity of the true self is a major focus of the post-modern era. The variant solutions are legion. Others which are put forward include 'I am what I feel', and 'I am what circumstances and society have made me'.

The Christian assertion is that we find our true self, our true identity, in the God who made us. St Augustine's frequently quoted lines express the matter perfectly: 'O God our hearts are restless till they find their rest in you.' The French philosopher Blaise Pascale asserted that within every man there is a God-shaped vacuum. This deepest aspect of a human being is spirit. It's that part of us which grieves, hurts, longs, loves, yearns, hopes, elates, fears, cries. The charismatic experience is essentially one which is touching people at this the profoundest level of their being. For many, the charismatic experience of the Holy Spirit conveys release, healing and heightened awareness and consciousness of the presence of Jesus. Through this people are finding self-affirmation and a renewed confidence in themselves and in their situation. Critics of charismatic Christianity have been ready to sneer at it as therapy religion but the fact of the matter is, this is where so many people have genuine needs. The wider church owes a great debt to people such as Mary Pytches who have taught and demonstrated the importance of prayer counselling.

The charismatic experience is corporate as well as being individualistic. For many it is an experience of close personal relationships with others of the community or church. Warm friendships and close associations are what many people most need and are looking for. One American critic of the charismatic movement was honest enough to write that 'charismatics are champions in this area'.[11] Charismatics have recognised the fact that people do not just crave for an intimacy with God, they also look for it with one another. Charismatics have correctly understood that knowledge cannot replace human friendship.

Much traditional religion has been objective, distant and cerebral. The charismatic focus on the needs of the self is one of the movement's major assets as the Church progresses into the third millennium. The signs are that society, and Western society in particular, is going to fragment further and become increasingly pluralistic. In such a situation the cry for identity will become even more insistent. Only those people who can address this need in a positive and vital way will be widely received. Charismatic Christianity has the capacity to give individuals the experience of being loved and affirmed for who they are and as they are. This begins to happen as they are filled with the Holy Spirit in a way which can be felt and which touches their emotions at a deep level. It enables people to feel good about themselves and thus more able to reach out to others in a positive manner.

Identity is also corporate in that it is gained from belonging to and being part of a larger group. It is widely recognised that much of mainline Christianity offers only one basic setting in which people can find an identity. In the main it is based on middle-class culture, discipline and education. It has been said with a certain amount of truth that 'the greater the education, the greater the alienation'. It is a fact that the higher the educative level of congregational worship and activities the more people are for that reason left out and unable to find an identity. Charismatics are showing an increasing capacity to be much more flexible than other sections of the church in attempting to provide a range of different settings in which people can find their identity. There are charismatic churches which meet in a wide range of venues in a diversity of cultural settings and people groups. Such churches meet and worship informally in public house , wine bars, hotel lounges, cinemas, community centres and schools. Some of these are focused on particular age ranges. A number of charismatics have recognised that many young people are entirely alienated from adults and can only be reached for Christ and find their identity in him in a youth setting. A number of charismatic groups have pioneered specific youth churches in places such as Chichester, Swindon and Watford. There are now well over a hundred such youth congregations.

Charismatic Worship

As charismatics see it, worship is central to developing an individual identity in God as well as to deepening their relationships with other Christians. For charismatics, the singing of specifically worship songs is seen as the major means by which God comes near and the Holy Spirit touches their lives in a fresh way.

The worship of many of the historic denominational churches has a richness in terms of its traditions stretching back into the past, its liturgies, creeds and great hymns. It tends, however, to be characterised by anonymity and arid intellectualism. Many people who go to traditional services, do so to be alone and to escape the 'hurly burly' and the pressures of their daily lives. They go to get a bit of peace and to make their private communion with God. This is not to say that charismatics don't value stillness and silence, increasing numbers of them do. Charismatic worship does, however, lay stress on corporate communion and on experiencing God's presence together with others. Charismatic worship is generally much more participatory in style. People are encouraged to be active and to contribute in some or all of the ways which Paul urged the early church at Corinth (see 1 Cor 14). Charismatic worship conveys the sense of the 'nearness of God' and the immediacy of his presence. Generally speaking, worshippers in charismatic churches have a greater anticipation and expectancy that God will act and meet with them in their situation and their needs. In much traditional worship the service is *about* God. The prayers are addressed to a distant God in formal ecclesiastical language. The sermons tend to be *about* God. In charismatic worship the aim is to meet God personally and to experience his very presence. Generally speaking the singing is *to* God rather than about God and the prayers are more personal and less formal. In the preaching, the expectation is that God will speak personally and directly to the congregation. In charismatic churches people tend to dress down and the atmosphere is informal, relaxed, affirming and welcoming.

The Bible and Preaching

The criticism is often made of charismatics that they undervalue good biblical preaching and they don't give proclamation the central place it should have. I can only state that this has certainly not been my personal observation. David Pawson, a leading charismatic, once referred to the place of the Bible in his church in Guildford. He said: 'I want nothing in this church which is not in this book. However, I do want everything that is in this book in this church.'[12] In all the worship in charismatic churches which I have attended there has been good practical, biblical preaching of at least twenty-five minutes in length. I observe that charismatics are increasingly willing to utilise the insights of scholarship in their preaching. Significantly, there are a number of rising theological and biblical scholars who are also charismatics. Among them are Mark Stibbe, John McKay, Professor Max Turner, Christopher Cocksworth and John Goldingay. I have found also that charismatic preaching is able to make the word of God powerfully and authoritatively alive and present.

One of the ways in which charismatics have enhanced preaching is by their particular hermeneutic or interpretation of

Scripture. In a very thoughtful and enlightening paper, *Towards a Charismatic Hermeneutic,* Mark Stibbe has highlighted this in a clear way. He suggested, along with John McKay, that a very large part of current biblical interpretation, whether conservative or liberal, is essentially a case of the natural mind searching for meaning in God's word. This is done by using the common tools of biblical scholarship along with other disciplines including philosophy and critical historical method. Stibbe pointed out that many would concur that 'conservative hermeneutics is a product of the enlightenment'.[13] Whereas liberals deny the reality of miracles in the past and conservatives tend to deny their reality in the present, charismatics see them 'as the record of the same kinds of events which are witnessed today'.[14] The problem with the liberal and conservative approach is that it fails to recognise a dimension which is clearly in the Scripture itself that is what we might term 'the spiritual or charismatic or prophetic dimension'.

The question is, is it legitimate to try and discover a meaning in Scripture which the original authors of Scripture could never have intended? The answer, according to Stibbe, 'has to be a very guarded yes'. He suggests that we examine the way in which the New Testament authors use the Old Testament. They are 'constantly finding meanings in the Old Testament which were not intended by the original authors'.[15] One example which Stibbe cites is Matthew 2 verse 15. Matthew is writing about the flight of Mary and Joseph and the infant Jesus to Egypt where they took refuge until the death of Herod. In explaining their return, Matthew wrote, 'This was to fulfil what the Lord had spoken by the prophet, "Out of Egypt I have called my Son".' The Old Testament text which Matthew is quoting is Hosea 11 verse 1: 'When Israel was a child, I loved him, and out of Egypt I called my Son.' This text, as Hosea used it, referred to God calling Israel in the childhood period of his people, out of slavery in Egypt. Matthew completely passed the original meaning and used it in an altogether different context to do with the boy Jesus' return from Egypt.[16]

Stibbe goes on to point out that charismatic exegesis of Scripture is in fact existential, experiential, spiritual and at best also communal. In regard to the latter point, he indicates that some charismatic fellowships are invited to judge what is taught and to discern whether this is what God is saying to the fellow-ship or church.

One of the strong aspects of charismatic preaching is that it is often very alive and well orientated to the business of everyday living. This aspect is particularly observable in the ministry of many of the leading charismatic preachers of recent years and the present time. It is certainly the case that the charismatic movement has produced a crop of outstanding preachers including such people as David Watson, David Pawson, Clive Calver, Wynne Lewis, Michael Green, David McInnes, Lyndon Bowring, J John, Gerald Coates, R.T. Kendall, Jackie Pullinger, Colin Urquhart and Terry Virgo. Their style, approach and manner has provided an inspiration for younger generations to follow. Not only that, charismatic church groups are becoming increasingly competent at sharing their experiences and training up others. Day conferences run by prominent churches such as Holy Trinity Brompton, St Andrew's, Chorleywood and Westminster Chapel frequently give practical instruction to clergy. Summer teaching events such as New Wine and Stoneleigh offer good seminars to clergy and lay leaders. Groups such as Pioneer and Salt and Light regularly gather their leaders together for training in the various aspects of ministry.

Charismatic Theology

It is a fact, as we noted in the previous chapter, that few charismatics have involved themselves in academic theology particularly in the early years of renewal. However, many charismatics engage in practical theology of the everyday. In this they reveal a further echo of seventeenth-century Puritans who were said to be 'masters of no divinity but practical divinity'.

One of the most distinctive teachings of the Christian faith is the doctrine of the Trinity. Until the charismatic movement was birthed, the Trinity was for most Christians in the British Isles a formula which they knew they were supposed to assent to but found very hard to do. By helping Christians to experience the filling of the Holy Spirit, charismatics enabled them by the same token to discover the reality of the third person of the Trinity in their individual lives. Because of this, increasing numbers of charismatics have developed a renewed interest in Trinitarian theology. This is a matter which has profound implications. The Trinity is a community of persons each in perfect inter-relationship with the others. This has obvious application for the unity of the church, the church as a community and as a caring, relating fellowship. The doctrine of the Trinity also helps to set the right perspective and balance for Christian worship. True worship must be Trinitarian, that is focused on the Father, through the Son and in the Holy Spirit. The same pattern is probably the most healthful in terms of private prayer, devotion and spirituality. It is possible that conservative and evangelical worship was in danger of becoming a little too Christocentric and too much focused on the cross and substitutionary atonement. The Trinity, as has been noted is also an exemplar and an inspirer of mission and evangelism.

The emphasis on the Holy Spirit has also enabled the Christian church to focus outward. Wherever the Holy Spirit is truly empowering he will be thrusting God's people out in mission as happened on the Day of Pentecost. Worldwide, there can be little doubt but that it is the charismatic churches who are reaching out in evangelism and mission. In the United Kingdom the same is becoming increasingly more apparent. A continuing charismatic pneumatology is one which will continue to generate mission in the next millennium.

Charismatics have gradually evolved their own pattern of church extension. It is clearly a network pattern. People are drawn into charismatic churches through the social network in which they operate the other aspects of their daily lives. To some extent this is true of all sections of the church in the British Isles although less so perhaps in the case of Anglicans in the countryside and Roman Catholics. Many charismatics travel quite long distances from their residence to their place of Sunday worship or weeknight housegroup. However, this is no more the case than they might travel to work, or to their local Sainsbury's, doctor's surgery or sports club. Of the specific New Testament models of the church: the fellowship or temple of the Holy Spirit, the people of God, the Family of God, the Body, the Bride, the servant and the vine, it is probably the Body and the Family which are the most widely operated. The Body in particular finds a ready correspondence with the charismatic understanding of every-member ministry. For many, baptism is seen as an ordination or commissioning into the service of the church. There are few 'lay' members in a charismatic church who do not find an active role within it. Every individual receives his or her own particular 'manifestation of the Spirit' and has a service to give to others. Although in earlier days, particularly in the Restoration churches, women had a subservient role, this seems to be changing. There are now women in leadership in Ichthus and Pioneer. One new church which grew out of a youth organisation in Sussex in 1983 had a group of women leaders. They were called 'thunderbirds' because there were five of them!

Late twentieth-century/early twenty-first century society is one in which people are increasingly looking for identity and roles which they can fulfil. Charismatic ecclesiology is set right to enable individuals to fulfil their God-given gifts and abilities in ways which other models of the church would not be able to facilitate. Generally speaking it is the case that where Christians are actively participating in the life of a fellowship and drawing strength and inspiration from it they are more likely to be reaching out to others. Charismatic churches have demonstrated this fact well. They spend a good deal of their time in worshipping and relating to one another, but the statistics demonstrate that they are also among the most effective at reaching unchurched groups.

Charismatic eschatology is an area where some work is undoubtedly needed. It seems to me that far too much stress has been placed on the 'end times'. This was particularly so in the early days of the charismatic movement and among the Restoration churches. There was a strong sense that the church was in the 'end time' era and must purify and prepare itself for the return of Christ, the Bridegroom. This resulted in calls to charismatics to leave the corrupt and compromising denominational churches and join the 'New Israel' which would restore the kingdom and be the instruments of God as the Spirit was poured out in the 'latter days'. All of this led to an intensive introversionism and exclusive and condescending attitudes.

The focus of this kind of eschatology was firmly rooted in the imminent return of Christ and the establishing of a future kingdom. However, as the charismatic movement has extended for ten, twenty and now thirty years, there has been a shift in emphasis away from the future kingdom and the need to make it a reality now in the present as it is in heaven. This change of emphasis has been to some extent reinforced by John Wimber's teaching that the Holy Spirit is moving now among the people of God to create a foretaste of the Kingdom which Jesus will inaugurate at the end time. In the late 1960s and 1970s most charismatics held to a replacement theology in which they, the church, were the 'New Israel' who had displaced the Jewish nation. However, the past decade in particular has witnessed the rise of Messianic Judaism and a new eschatology is emerging which to some extent embraces what is happening in modern Judaism. In short, some charismatics assert that it is those who are Jews by birth, not the church as the 'New Israel', who will be the instuments of God's purposes in the last days. The new churches are now becoming more concerned and involved with the present order of things rather than having their focus on the future and the end time.

Some charismatic theologians are helpfully developing a way forward by highlighting that the Holy Spirit both points the church forward to the future and also brings aspects of the future into the present. James Begbie, for example, pointed out that the Holy Spirit is God present to the world bringing it to the conclusion determined by the Father but also made a present reality by the Son.[17] In many ways as the whole church moves forward in the third millennium it is the charismatic section which is now set fair to make an impact on the wider world. The older denominational churches, in contrast, appear to be rent by internal problems over the ordination of women, homosexuality, the future of marriage, the re-marriage of divorcees in church and inclusive language, not to mention their growing financial crises.

Charismatic Social Activism

This concept of the Spirit moving us outwards and also of drawing the future into the present, leads naturally to the social activism of the charismatic movement. In the same way that their earlier futuristic view of God's Kingdom has gradually been replaced by a more present view of the kingdom, so it has been with social concern. In fact, in 1990, Bryn Jones who fostered very strong introversionist attitudes in his Covenant churches wrote a small book entitled *God's Kingdom – Here and Now*. In it he wrote:

> The gospel of the kingdom isn't an escapist gospel. It is dangerous to open the New Testament if you like to live in a private world. It won't allow you to become cocooned in charismatic culture. In Christ, all privatism that locks out our fellow men and women is condemned.[18]

Taken as a whole, this book demonstrates a profound awareness of the dangers of the church withdrawing from the world. It is also remarkable for its careful footnoting and citations from the *Kairos Document, The Churches Together in Unity* and *Faith in the City*. All of this was a major departure from the earlier days when few Harvestime articles or booklets had references to anything beyond the Bible. Yet even in earlier times Bryn Jones had always been strong in his opposition to apartheid.[19] His remarkably changed attitude to the world beyond Harvestime and Covenant-related activities, fostered no doubt by his graduate degree in peace studies at Bradford University, is reflected in a general widening social concern on the part of charismatic churches in general.

In the summer of 1991, a significant international conference was held at Canterbury, hosted jointly by Anglican Renewal Ministries and SOMA. Forty bishops and people from over fifty countries gathered at the conference. Bishop Peter Lee from South Africa gave a key address on renewal for the world. He made the point that if renewal did not impact the affairs of the world, it was not worth keeping. He asserted that renewal is to do with the place of weeping and bleeding and starving and despairing. 'It is,' he said, 'to do with the God of love and therefore it is to do with the needs of the world.'[20] This growing concern on the part of charismatic leaders and churches to be engaged in social action was put forcibly by Mark Stibbe.

> In the final analysis, any pneumatology or doctrine of the Holy Spirit which is purely concerned with the work of the Spirit in the church, or, worse still, in us as individual Christians, is hopelessly myopic. The Holy Spirit is concerned not only with our own liberation, but also with the

liberation of societies, cultures, nature and indeed the whole cosmos.[21]

Robert Warren has also pointed out the way in which renewed churches can often be 'Places from which committed churchgoers are more involved in social work (Relate, Samaritans, work with the homeless, etc) than non-churchgoers'.[22] Roger Forster, in his survey of new churches, observed that 'Social action is often high on the agenda'. 'Most,' he continued, are concerned 'to relate to the disadvantaged and deprived'.[23] Examples of this which his book instances are schemes for the unemployed at Anfield in Liverpool and in South London with Ichthus. Another aspect of social activism includes education and play schemes. Charismatic churches, particularly new churches, have formed a number of Christian schools which seek to bring Christian principles to bear on both the curriculum and the total school experience. These are open to the children of parents who are not Christians or members of the church. Fees are set on a sliding scale at the level at which parents can afford to pay. Prominent examples are the King's School in Witney, the King's School in Basingstoke, The School of the Lion in Gloucester and the River School in Worcester.

Many renewed congregations have involvement with other less well-endowed churches or with projects overseas. The Bristol Christian Fellowship, for example, have links with Zambia and South Africa. New Frontiers International, spearheaded by Terry Virgo, have congregations and work in India, the Stroud Christian Fellowship which relates to Barney Coombs has established a pregnancy crisis centre. In the late 1980s, Dr Patrick Dixon launched ACET (AIDS, Care, Education and Training) in West London as a Christian response to HIV/AIDS. ACET has a staff of thirty and is caring for more AIDs patients than any other independent agency. Over 60 per cent of ACET's staff are from Pioneer churches, as are the majority of volunteer workers. Two London Vineyard churches have shown a great deal of practical care for the homeless and hungry on the London embankments. St Martha's Anglican Church, Broxstowe in Nottingham have been deeply immersed in their local community. The Courage Trust is a London-based organisation run by charismatic Christians who help to rehabilitate homosexuals who want to change to a heterosexual lifestyle. St Philip and St James Church in Bath has sent mission teams and aid to South Africa, the Middle East, Croatia and Uganda. St Andrew's Church, Chorleywood is active in fund raising and other projects for the homeless in London. Pioneer People in the Wirral are working with a partnership project in Albania. Members of Petersfield Christian Fellowship who have been actively concerned for children in Colombia and South America, have formed a charity known as In Ministry to Children. In 1998 they helped to raise over £45,000 to assist missionaries in the field relieve at least some hardship. Salt and Light Ministries have their own extension arm, CRI (Church Relief International). It channels money and personnel into practical and relief work, worldwide. River Church, which is part of the Pioneer network, purchased a five- or six-bedroom house for the homeless in the early 1990s. Single men between the ages of eighteen and thirty years can be based there, helped and sent out into the community at an appropriate time. Pioneer also established Romania Aid based at Cobham in Surrey. In 1974 Myrtle and Cecil Kerr founded a Christian Renewal Centre at Rostrevor in Northern Ireland. There, a community from different denominations, both Roman Catholic and Protestant, work together for renewal and reconciliation primarily in Ireland but also in a worldwide context. At the 1999 Stoneleigh Bible Week a collection raised £1.2 million, £300,000 of which was set aside to help NFI churches to extend their ministry to the poor. Many charismatic Christians are active supporters of CARE and the Evangelical Alliance. Both of these agencies are deeply involved in the socio-political arena. Significantly their directors, Lyndon Bowring and Joel Edwards are themselves both charismatic Christians. Numbers of charismatic churches have also been active in the Jubilee Campaign to 'Keep Sunday Special' and 'Christmas Cracker' which raises money and sends gifts to poor children in developing war-torn countries. Other congregations have given support to Baroness Cox and Christian Solidarity International. These organisations and initiatives are a representative selection of the social activities in which charismatic Christians are actively involved. They are indicative of the growing social concern for the wider world on the part of charismatic churches.

Charismatic Organisations

Organisations and conferences are major contributing factors to the growing strength of the charismatic movement. They will undoubtedly help equip both individual Christians and the churches as they progress in the third millennium. Charismatic Christians have been very actively involved in the organisation and running of Spring Harvest. This is by far the largest annual Christian gathering in the British Isles and attracted 80,000 mostly middle-class individuals to several centres at Easter 1991. This figure had reduced to 60,000 by 1999 largely, however, on account of the necessity of using smaller sites. Spring Harvest takes the form of an evangelical family holiday with seminars and nightly celebrations at centres such as Skegness, Minehead, Pwllheli and Weymouth. While it is not avowedly charismatic, its worship is charismatic in style and a number of the speakers are charismatic Christians. Significantly, Clive Calver, one of its founders and a leading influence, is a high profile charismatic Christian. In addition, there are a number of other large annual summer events organised by charismatic groups. Among these is Grapevine organised by Stuart Bell and the Ground Level Team. Based at the Lincolnshire Showground, this is the longest running charismatic summer Bible week. It attracts 5,000 people each year. Stoneleigh Bible Week organised by Terry Virgo's New Frontiers International is the biggest of the summer gatherings. In 1994 it attracted some 14,500 people. In 1999 this increased to 21,000 with 3,000 day visitors. In 1994 New Wine, hosted by David and Mary Pytches and Barry and Mary Kissell, drew 8,500 participants. Its related youth conference, Soul Survivor, led by Mike Pilavachi had some 4,000 teenagers. In 1999, New Wine and Soul Survivor, drew 29,500 people. At Soul Survivor some 800 young people made a commitment of their lives to Christ. There are other smaller but equally vibrant groups. These include Don Double's Good News Crusade Family Camp at Malvern Showground attended by about 2,000 and Eagle Camp at Lacock in Wiltshire which is run by Charles and Joyce Sibthorpe with a presence of about 1,000.

The March for Jesus which has been organised by Gerald Coates of Pioneer and Graham Kendrick together with Lynn

Green of YWAM and Roger Forster of Ichthus since 1987 is making a growing impact on the British nation and has evoked positive responses in the national press. Estimates by the media suggested that 250,000 marchers took to the streets of the British Isles in 1990. Numbers continued to grow subsequently and 1994 saw the first worldwide March for Jesus with 177 nations taking part with the estimated number of marchers at between 10 and 12 million. By the close of 1999 it was estimated that nearly 50 million Christians from a 180 nations have praise marched or prayer walked with Global March for Jesus.

Colin Urquhart's Roffey Place and Spirit of Faith Ministries specifically trains students and churches to live in 'revival'. Along with Anglican Renewal Ministries it also provides regular courses and teaching materials on the ministry of the Holy Spirit. Centres of retreat and healing such as Lee Abbey in Devon, Scargill in Yorkshire and the Harnhill Centre for Christian Healing near Cirencester are also doing a great deal to provide an ongoing charismatic ministry of prayer counselling and support. The most significant national course at the present time is 'Alpha' which originated from Holy Trinity Brompton. This provides Christian basics in an informal and relaxed atmosphere. The 'P' in Alpha stands for pasta and the supper forms an essential aspect of the Alpha experience. By the autumn of 1994 some five hundred churches of all denominations were running Alpha courses. By 1998 more than 1.5 million people were believed to have attended Alpha courses, half of them in Britain. From modest beginnings in Holy Trinity Brompton, Alpha is now administered from an office block adjoining the church. It spends upwards of £750,000 producing materials. The Alpha course, which was updated and rewritten by Nicky Gumbel, puts across the Christian message in a simple 'non-church-goer friendly' way. Integral to the ten-session course is a weekend away in which there is both teaching and an opportunity to receive the Holy Spirit.[24] In a period when the church has been losing members at the rate of 1,000 a week, Alpha is one of the most significant movements of the contemporary church. At the close of 1999, Alpha courses were running in 6,500 churches of all traditions in the United Kingdom – 435,980 people attended Alpha courses in 1998.[25] Significantly more than 100 prisons in the UK ran Alpha courses in 1999.

Impacting the New Millennium

As we reflect on the state of the UK at the start of the new millennium it is clear that there is a growing anxiety in many directions. All the signs are that Britain is fast becoming what a former prime minister, Benjamin Disraeli, described as 'Two Nations'. The one half is privileged and prosperous, the other alienated and in a poverty trap. There seems to be a deep-seated brokenness in British society. It is at its most visible in the disintegration of the family unit which is reflected in the broken marriages of the Royal Family. Parliament seems intent on promoting homosexuality in schools and among consenting sixteen-year-olds. The Broadcasting Standards Committee seems incapable of restraining the diet of sex and brutality on the nation's television channels. The level of violent crime, which is undoubtedly related, is still at unaceptably high levels. There were 347,000 reported crimes with violence in 1997. The use of drugs is still widespread among young people. There is acknowledged institutional racism within the nation's police force. The majority of the British people are confused and uncertain about moral values and most lack any sense of purpose or self-worth.

The 'Two Nations' are seen most obviously in the 'haves' who are in work and becoming increasingly wealthy. The ranks of the 'have-nots', on the other hand, remain solid with the unemployed who depend on income support, housing benefits and maintenance payments which often take months to materialise. Many of the 'haves' are gripped by drivenness which is destroying both them and their families. This drivenness has been fuelled by constant goal-setting, attainment targets and the government pressure for performance-related pay in the entire public sector (except politics). All this has led to excessive hours of work way beyond contractual requirements and a huge increase in stress and stress-related illnesses. It has been calculated that one in four people in the UK will suffer from a stress-related illness at some point in their lives. Many executives and middle management officials have forgotten how to relate to anything other than their computer screens. Is it any wonder that family life is being wrecked on a wide scale? Perhaps it's time there was some Sabbath legislation to encourage a regular day of rest.

Alongside this, society has become increasingly pluralistic with the representatives of many world faiths establishing themselves and evangelising strongly. Much of the religion taught in our schools has reinforced this pluralism by suggesting that one faith is as good as another. All of this, on top of an already secularisng trend, has created what sociologists term 'anomie', that is, a condition in which society no longer recognises any universally accepted values, standards or norms.

Against this background, the charismatic movement has the potential to make a really positive and transforming impact on British Society. Much will depend however on its ability to sort itself out, particularly in the areas of leadership, authority and control. Charismatics, like everyone else, make their mistakes but they are at least ready to take the risks. They are open to God and they are not afraid of new experiences of God.

Charismatics are firm in their commitment to biblical standards and values. In fact they show a far greater commitment to the creedal faith than most other sections of the Christian church. It is not without significance that if the BBC is looking for a definite Christian voice to offset the bleatings of a liberal cleric they invariably turn to a charismatic such as Clive Calver, Joel Edwards, Lyndon Bowring, Tony Higton, Michael Green or Gerald Coates. In a confused world in which many are uncertain which path to follow, it is the clarity and definiteness of charismatic preaching and writing which points out the way forward which will attract people to Christ.

Charismatic experience is well equipped to touch people who are carrying emotional hurts and wounds. In particular, speaking in tongues has been shown to have the capacity to release both guilt and pain from the unconscious and subconscious mind. Charismatic worship is also clearly a vehicle for healing. Many relate the ways in which the hurt of mistreatment by others, trauma and disappointment, have been released through tears in extended times of quiet worship. Charismatic experience has been able to touch the lives of young people in a more significant way than any other expressions of Christianity. In fact, charismatic churches have more churchgoers in their twenties than any other section of the church in the British Isles.[26] Charismatic Christianity clearly has a much greater capability of reaching people for Christ who don't come from middle-class backgounds and who have little formal education. This fact is not only readily observable in churches such as Soul Survivor, Watford, Revelation Church, Chichester and St Thomas Crookes in Sheffield, it has been demonstrated by detailed research.

In his book *Post Evangelical*, Dave Tomlinson has a section which he headed 'The Charismaticizing of Mainstream Evangelicalism'.[27] He began the first paragraph by reflecting on the fact that during the late 1960s and early 1970s 'evangelicals' and 'charismatics' were almost totally incompatible. This was partly due to the fact that many evangelicals denounced renewal as the work of the devil. By the later 1970s much of the antipathy was gone and there was a willingness to talk. Fifteen years later Tomlinson observed that 'the situation had changed dramatically' in that the whole centre ground of evangelicalism had become 'charismaticized'. It is now not unusual to go to a mainstream evangelical church and find an atmosphere which is informal, people dressed casually, clergy without robes and the congregation singing Vineyard songs with a worship band. All this is not only a witness to the positive impact which the charismatic movement has made on the wider Church, it has also helped other sections of the church to become more user-friendly and to resonate with their surrounding culture.

Charismatics, as I read it, are now beginning to set their sights increasingly on the broken world around them. As well as preaching the good news they are seeing the need to care practically as a demonstration of the Christian gospel. Even former Restoration church leaders are now speaking of the need for Christians to be 'incarnational', that is, to demonstrate practical love in the way that God did by taking human flesh in the person of Jesus.

One of the great strengths of the charismatic churches at the beginning of this new millennium is in their human resources. People such as Clive Calver, David Pytches, Lyndon Bowring, Wynne Lewis, Colin Dye, Gerald Coates, Sandy Millar, Nicky Gumbel are strong leaders, people who others are prepared to get behind and support. They have also been wise and forward thinking in that they have been quietly training up and putting in place a new and younger generation to succeed them. This point has been particularly well illustrated by the way in which David and Mary Pytches have shared the leadership of New Wine with John and Anne Coles, Mark Melluish, Mike Breen, Mark Bailey and Bruce Collins. Additionally, the New Wine Area Network has been established to embrace, encourage and teach churches who affiliate.

The new generation of charismatic leaders are for the most part theologically conservative, socially concerned, eager to evangelise and concerned to bring biblical values and standards to bear on our national life. It will inevitably take time to heal some of the post-Toronto rifts but the signs are that prominent charismatic leaders are beginning to turn away from their earlier over-preoccupation with future spiritual revival to the business of evangelism, concern for the poor and impacting society with Christian values.

Martin Percy predicted an increasingly fragmented future for the charismatic movement, with six prominent strands emerging: Apocalyptic focusing on the end times, Novel specialising in exotic encounters, Communitarian who will withdraw from the world, Sectarian who will adopt unorthodox beliefs and practices, Political, who will adopt social justice or right wing agendas and Fundamentalists who will rediscover conservative evangelicalism. In one sense it is hard to disagree with Percy since all these strands are already in evidence, indeed they have been present from the early days of the charismatic movement. My sense is that rather than a deepening fragmentation there will be an increasing drawing together of charismatic evangelicals and mainstream evangelicals to the mutual benefit and effectiveness of both groups. Since Toronto there has been a much greater desire on the part of charismatics to be grounded in the word as well as the Spirit. The growing interest in Celtic Spirituality on the part of charismatics also reveals an emerging need to set religious experience in a framework which relates to the business of everyday living. This is a development which can only in the long run have a beneficial outcome.

For these reasons the charismatic movement will be the most growing force and section of the church in the United Kingdom. It also represents the largest group of evangelicals in England.[28] For these reasons it will also make an increasing contribution to the wider Christian church and the universal mission of Jesus in this new millennium.

Bibliography

Books

Allan, D., *Planted to Grow* (Baptist Union of Great Britain, 1990).

Angel, G., *Delusion or Dynamite* (Marc Europe, 1989).

Anon, *Belonging to an Anointed Body* (Biblecraft, 1983).

Baker, J., *Baptised in One Spirit* (The Fountain Trust, 1967).

Brierley, P., *Christian England* (Marc Europe, 1991).

Bugden, V., *The Charismatics and the Word of God* (Evangelical Press, 1985).

Carey, G. & others, *Planting New Churches* (Eagle, 1973).

Carothers, M., *Power in Praise* (Kingsway, 1974).

Cho, P.Y., *Prayer: Key to Revival* (Word Publishing, 1985); *The Holy Spirit My Senior Partner* (Word Publishing, 1989).

Coates, G., *Kingdom Now* (Kingsway, 1993); *What on Earth is this Kingdom?* (Kingsway, 1983).

Cocksworth, C., *Holy Holy Holy: Worshipping the Trinitarian God* (Darton, Longman & Todd, 1997).

Coombs, B., *No Other Way* (Sarum Publications, 1972).

Cooper, S. & Farrant, M., *Fire in Our Hearts* (Kingsway, 1991).

Cornwall, J., *Let Us Praise* (Logos, 1973).

Craston, C. (chairman), *The Charismatic Movement in the Church of England* (CIO Publishing, 1981).

Cuthbert, N., *Charismatics in Crisis* (Kingsway, 1994).

Davies, R., *Methodism* (Penguin Books, 1964).

Dawson, J., *Taking Our Cities for God* (Word UK, 1989).

Deare, J., *Surprised by the Power of the Spirit* (Kingsway, 1993).

Ditchfield, G.M., *The Evangelical Revival* (UCL Press, 1998).

Dixon, P., *Signs of Revival* (Kingsway, 1994).

Dodds, A., *Desert Harvest* (Collectors Books Ltd, 1992).

Edwards, J., *A Narrative of Surprising Conversions, The Distinguishing Marks of a Work of God, An Account of the Revival of Religion in Northampton 1740–1742* (Banner of Truth Trust, 1965).

Ellis, R. and Mitchell, R., *Radical Church Planting* (Crossway Books, 1992).

England, E. (ed), *Living in the Light of Pentecost* (Highland, 1990).

Fiddes, P., *Charismatic Renewal: A Baptist View* (Baptist Publications, 1980).

Forster, R., *Ten New Churches* (Marc Europe, 1986).

Gardner, J., & Tingle, R., *Ticket to Toronto* (Privately published, 1995).

Glennon, J., *Your Healing is Within You* (Hodder & Stoughton, 1979).

Graham, A., *We Believe in the Holy Spirit* (Church House, 1991).

Graham, J., *The Giant Awakes* (Marshalls, 1982).

Green, M., *I Believe in the Holy Spirit* (Hodder & Stoughton, 1975).

Gunstone, J., *Signs and Wonders: the Wimber Phenomenon* (Daybreak, 1989); *The Lord is Our Healer* (Hodder & Stoughton, 1986).

Hammond, F. & I., *Pigs in the Parlour* (New Wine Press, 1992).

Harper, M., *As at the Beginning* (Hodder & Stoughton, 1965); *Spiritual Warfare* (Hodder & Stoughton, 1970); *None Can Guess* (Hodder & Stoughton, 1973).

Harris, P., *Breaking New Ground* (General Synod, 1994).

Harrison, P., *Learning the Way of the Holy Spirit* (Harrison House, 1989).

Higton, T. & Kirby, G., *The Challenge of the House Churches* (Latimer House, 1988); *Our God Reigns* (Hodder & Stoughton, 1988); *That the World May Believe*

(Marshall Pickering, 1988).

Hill, C., *Prophecy Past and Present* (Highland, 1989).

Hill, C., Fenwick, P., Forbes, D., & Noakes, D., *Blessing the Church?* (Eagle, 1995).

Hocken, P., *Streams of Renewal* (Paternoster, 1986); *The Glory and the Shame* (Eagle, 1994); *The Strategy of the Spirit?* (Eagle, 1998).

Hollenweger, W., *The Pentecostals: The Charismatics in the Churches* (SCM, 1966).

Hopkins, B., *Church Planting* (Grove, 1989).

Horrobin, P., *Healing Through Deliverance* (Sovereign World Ltd, 1991).

Houston, *Prophecy: A Gift for Today* (IVP, 1989).

Howard, D., *The Life and Theology of Watchman Nee: Study of the Little Flock Movement* (Boston Spa).

Howard, R., *Charismania* (Mowbray, 1997).

Hummell, C.E., *Fire in the Fireplace: Charismatic Renewal in the Nineties* (IVP, 1993).

Hunt, D. & McMahon, T.A., *The Seduction of Christianity* (Harvestime, 1985).

Hunt, D., *Beyond Seduction: A Return to Biblical Christianity* (Harrison House, 1987).

Hunt, S., Hamilton, M., Walter, T., *Charismatic Christianity: Sociological Perspectives* (MacMillan Press, 1997).

Jensen, P., *John Wimber Friend or Foe?* (St Matthias Press, 1990).

Jones, B., *God's Kingdom – Here and Now* (Harvestime, 1990); *Joined in Covenant* (Harvestime, 1990); *Poverty or Prosperity* (Harvestime, 1990); *The Radical Church* (Design Image Publishers, 1999).

Kelly, J.W., *The Radical Wesley Reconsidered* (Bangor Christian Trust, 1984).

Kerr, J.S., *The Mystery and Magic of the Occult* (SCM Ltd, 1971).

Kew, R. & White, R., *New Millennium and New Church* (Cowley Publications, 1992).

Koch, K., *Between Christ and Satan* (Evangelisation Publishers, 1961).

Kraybill, D., *Kingdom Upside Down* (Herald Press, 1978).

Kuhlman, K., *A Glimpse into Glory* (Logos International, 1979).

Lawrence, P., *The Hot Line* (Kingsway, 1990).

Lawson, J.G., *Deeper Experiences of Famous Christians* (Warner Press, 1970).

Liardon, R., *I Saw Heaven* (Embassy Publishing, 1983).

MacArthur, J.F., *Charismatic Chaos* (Zondervan Publishing House, 1992).

MacNutt, F., *Healing* (Ave Maria Press, 1974).

Mansell, D., *Building* (Springtide Fellowship, 1978); *Staying on Top* (Harvestime, 1990).

Martin, D. & Mullen, P. (eds), *Strange Gifts* (Blackwell, 1984).

Martin, D., *Strange Gifts: A Guide to Charismatic Renewal* (SPCK, 1984).

Masters, P., Whitcomb, J.C., *The Charismatic Phenomenon* (The Wakeman Trust, 1992).

Matthew, D. (ed), *Apostles Today* (Harvestime, 1988); *Church Adrift* (Marshalls, 1985).

Middlemiss, D., *Interpreting Charismatic Experience* (SCM Press Ltd, 1996).

Mills, B., *Preparing for Revival* (Kingsway, 1990).

Moriarty, M., *The New Charismatics* (Zondervan, 1992).

Neill, S., *Christian Missions* (Penguin Books, 1964).

Newbigin, L., *The Gospel in a Pluralist Society* (William B Eerdmans Publishing Company, 1989).

Noble, J., *The Body Book* (Marc Europe, 1993).

North, G.W., *Apostleship* (Exeter, 1988); *Discipleship* (Exeter, 1984); *Eldership* (Exeter, 1979); *Initial Evidence* (Exeter, 1976); *Spiritual Life and Spiritual Gifts* (Exeter, 1976); *The Representative Man* (Horton Trust, 1976).

Pawson, D., *Fourth Wave* (Hodder & Stoughton, 1993); *The Normal Christian Birth* (Hodder & Stoughton, 1989).

Peddie, J. Cameron, *The Forgotten Talent* (Collins Fontana, 1961).

Penn-Lewis, J., *War on the Saints* (The Overcomer Literature Trust, undated).

Percy, M., *Words, Wonders & Power: Understanding Contemporary Christian Fundamentalism and Revivalism* (SPCK, 1996).

Petersen, L. (editor), *The Mark of the Spirit* (Paternoster Press, 1998).

Porter, S.E., & Richter, P.J., *The Toronto Blessing – or Is It?* (Darton, Longman & Todd, 1995).

Powell, G. & S., *Christian Set Yourself Free* (New Wine Press, 1983).

Prince, D., *Uproar in the Church* (Derek Prince Ministries, 1994).

Pulkingham, G., *Renewal: an Emerging Pattern* (Celebration Publishing, 1980).

Pullinger, J., *Chasing the Dragon* (Hodder & Stoughton, 1980).

Pytches, D. & Skinner, B., *New Wine Skins* (Eagle, 1991).

Pytches, D., *Come Holy Spirit* (Hodder & Stoughton, 1985); *Does God Speak Today?* (Hodder & Stoughton, 1989); *Prophecy in the Local Church* (Hodder & Stoughton, 1993); *Some Said it Thundered* (Hodder & Stoughton, 1990); (Editor) *John Wimber, His Influence and Legacy* (Eagle, 1998).

Ramsey, M., *Holy Spirit* (SPCK, 1977).

Richards, J., *But Deliver Us From Evil* (Darton, Longman & Todd, 1980 edition).

Richards, N., *The Worshipping Church* (Pioneer, 1993).

Ridley, G.R., *Towards 2000* (Milton Keynes, 1994).

Roberts, D., *The Toronto Blessing* (Kingsway, 1994).

Sandford, J. & M., *Delivered or Healed* (Marshall Pickering, 1992).

Scotland, A., *The Hallmarks of a Healthy Church* (Lifelink, 1998).

Scotland, N.A.D. (Ed.) *Recovering the Ground* (Kingdom Power Trust, 1995).

Scott, M., *Prophecy in the Church* (Pioneer, 1992).

Shakarian, D., *The Happiest People on Earth* (Hodder & Stoughton, 1973).

Simpson, C., *The Challenge to Care* (Kingsway, 1986).

Smail, T., *Reflected Glory* (Hodder & Stoughton, 1975); *Once and for All* (Darton, Longman & Todd, 1998).

Smail, T., Walker, A., Wright, N., *Charismatic Renewal* (SPCK, 1995).

Sherrill, J.L., *They Speak With Other Tongues* (Spire Books, 1979).

Stibbe, M., *A Kingdom of Priests* (Darton, Longman & Todd, 1994).

Subritzky, B., *Demons Defeated* (Sovereign World, 1982).

Tomlinson, D., *The Post-Evangelical* (Triangle, 1995).

Trudinger, R., *Built to Last* (Kingsway, 1982); *Cells for Life* (Olive Tree Publications, 1979); *Master Plan* (Olive Tree Publications, Basingstoke 1980).

Urquhart, Colin, *Faith for the Future* (Hodder & Stoughton, 1982).

Urquhart, Caroline, *His God My God* (Hodder & Stoughton, 1983).

Virgo, T., *Restoration in the Church* (Kingsway, 1985).

Walker, A., *Restoring the Kingdom* (First edition, Hodder & Stoughton, 1985); *Restoring the Kingdom* (Fully revised and expanded edition, Eagle, 1998).

Wallis, A., *In the Day of Thy Power* (CLC, 1989 edition); *Praying in the Spirit* (Kingsway, 1970); *Rain from Heaven* (Hodder & Stoughton, 1979); *The Radical Christian* (Kingsway, 1981).

Warren, R., *In the Crucible* (Highland Books, 1989); *On the Anvil* (Highland Books, 1990).

Weston, R. & J., *Times of Refreshing* (MFOT Publications, 1994).

White, J., *When the Spirit Comes with Power* (Hodder & Stoughton, 1989).

Wilson, B., *Religion in a Sociological Perspective* (OUP, 1982).

Wimber, C., *John Wimber: The Way it Was* (Hodder & Stoughton, 1999).

Wimber, J., *Holiness Unto the Lord* (Mercy Publishing, 1990); *Kingdom Suffering, Kingdom Fellowship, Kingdom Come, Kingdom Evangelism* (Hodder & Stoughton,

1989); *Power Evangelism: Signs and Wonders for Today* (Hodder & Stoughton, 1985); *Power Healing* (Hodder & Stoughton, 1986); *Riding the Third Wave* (Marshall Pickering, 1981); *Signs and Wonders and Church Growth* (Vineyard International, 1984); *The Dynamics of Spiritual Growth* (Hodder & Stoughton, 1990).
Wright, N., *The Fair Face of Evil* (Marshall Pickering, 1989); *The Radical Kingdom* (Kingsway, 1986).

Newspapers, Magazines and Journals

Alpha News
Anglicans for Renewal
Aware Magazine, October/November 1994
Compass
Dunamis
Encounters on the Edge
Equipped
Equipping the Saints
Fullness
Gloucester Citizen, 21 September 1994
Home and Family Restoration
Mainstream (Baptists for Life and Growth) 1980–1994
News of Liturgy
Prophecy Today
Prophetic Sharing
Renewal
Restoration
Shalom
Shepton Mallet Journal
Skepsis
Spread the Fire
Theological Renewal
The Restorer
Worship Update

Pamphlets

Morrison, A., *Falling for the Lie* (Diakrisis Publications, 1994); *We All Fall Down* (Diakrisis Publications, 1994).

Theses

Haram, A.G., *A Critical Analysis of Pastoral Care in Restoration Churches with Special Reference to Covenant Ministries* (BA Dissertation, Cheltenham & Gloucester College of Higher Education, 1994).
Percy, M., *Signs, Wonders and Church Growth: The Theme of Power in Contemporary Fundamentalism with Special Reference to the Works of John Wimber* (unpublished PhD Thesis, University of London, 1993).
Pike, R., *An Analysis of Prophecy Within the Charismatic Movement* (BA Dissertation, Cheltenham & Gloucester College of Higher Education, 1993).
Thurman, J., *New Wineskins: A Study of the House Church Movement* (Birmingham University Thesis, 1982).
Walters, M., *The Appeal of the House Churches: A Study in the Growth of the Restoration Movement* (BA Dissertation, College of St Paul & St Mary, Cheltenham, 1990).

Articles

Bayes, J., 'The Significance of Restoration: An Alternative View', Haddon Willmer's Response, *The Baptist Quarterly*, July 1988 Vol XXXII No 7.

Hair, J., Francis, L.J., & Robbins, M., 'Personality and Attraction to the Charismatic Movement: a study among Anglican clergy', *Journal of Beliefs and Values* Volume 20, No 2, 1999, pp 239–246.

Harthill, R., 'Front Room Gospel' (Script Library, Radio 4, 28 March 1984).

Hollengweger, W., 'After Twenty Years' Research on Pentecostalism', *Theology*, November 1984; 'The House Church Movement in Great Britain', *Expository Times*, November 1980.

Jones, H., 'Are There Apostles Today?', *Evangelical Review of Theology*, 1985 Vol 9 Part 2, pp 107–116.

McMillon, L.A., 'Alexander Campbell's Early Exposure to Scottish Restorationism 1808–1809', *Restoration Quarterly*, 1988 Vol 30 Part 2-3, pp 105–110.

Turner, M., 'Ecclesiology in the Major "Apostolic" Restorationist Churches in the United Kingdom', *Vox Evangelica*, 1989 Vol 19, pp 83–108.

Walker, A., 'From Revival to Restoration: the Emergence of Britain's New Classical Pentecostalism', *Social Compass: International Review of Socio-Religious Studies*, 1985 Vol 32 Part 2-3, pp 261–271.

Willmer, H., 'The Significance of Restorationism', *The Baptist Quarterly*, January 1987 Vol XXXII No 1.

Wright, N., 'Restoration and the House Church Movement', *Themelios*, January/February 1991 Vol 16 No 2.

Unpublished Papers

Mumford, B., *Memorandum: Public Statement Concerning Discipleship*, 1 November 1989.

Williams, D., 'Committed Membership Churches – One Response to Secular Society', November 1988.

Audio and Video Tapes

Coates, G., Grapevine Tape 1604 24 August, 1996; Westminster Chapel Tape 1473 22 October, 1995.

Horobin, P., Healing Through Deliverance, EME 93/6/C.

Lewis, W., Ministry at the Cotswold Christian Centre 1993, Tapes 1 and 2.

Mumford, B., Setting in the Safety Factors, Tape 1, Oxford Community Churches.

Mumford, E., Toronto Experience, New Wine 1994, Tape Neww1.

Slagle, C. & P., Grace Christian Centre, A Tapes, 15 October 1992.

Notes

Chapter 1
1. See The Biggest Little Church in the World, CVG Television.
2. www.uriel.net/~peggy/page4.html
3. Cited C.E. Hummell, *Fire in the Fireplace* (IVP, 1993) p 21.
4. See P. Brierley, *Christian England* (Marc Europe, 1991) pp 11, 175.
5. Information received from Peter Brierley, interview 23 October, 1999.
6. Andrew Walker, *Charismatic Christianity* (Macmillan Press Ltd, 1997) p 27.
7. Peter Hocken, *Streams of Renewal* (Paternoster, 1997) p 185. Jean Stone was married to an executive of an American airline. She was subsequently divorced and remarried. She is now Jean Williams.
8. For Montanism see D. Aune, *Prophecy in Early Christianity* (Eerdman, 1983).
9. Irenaeus, *Against Heresies*, Chapter 8.
10. Justin Martyr, *Dialogue with Trypho*, Chapter 88.
11. S. Neill, *A History of Christian Missions* (Penguin, 1964) p 53.
12. M. Harper, *As At The Beginning* (Hodder & Stoughton, 1965).
13. D. Christie-Murray, *Voices from the Gods: Speaking with Tongues* (Routledge, 1978) p 47.
14. See S. O'Brien, 'A Transatlantic Community of Saints: The Great Awakening and First Evangelical Network 1735-1755', American History Review, Vol 91 No 4 October 1987.
15. D. Christie-Murray, op. cit., p 50.
16. Ibid., p 5.
17. See A. Dallimore, *The Life of Edward Irving* (Banner of Truth Trust, 1983).
18. See F. Bartlemann, *Azusa Street* (Bridge Publishing, 1980) p ix.
19. C. Whittaker, *Seven Pentecostal Pioneers* (Marshalls, 1983) p 26.
20. Ibid., p 4.
21. See *Restoration*, November/December 1983, p 38.
22. See P. Hocken, *Streams of Renewal: The Origins and Development of the Charismatic Movement in Great Britain* (Paternoster Press, 1986) p 115.
23. See J. and E. Sherrill, *The Happiest People on Earth* (Hodder & Stoughton, 1975).
24. P. Hocken, op. cit., p 118.
25. Ibid., p 86.
26. See M. Harper, Canon Dennis Bennett,

Renewal, No 189, 1992.
27. A. Walker, *Restoring the Kingdom* (Hodder & Stoughton, 1985) p 77ff.
28. Charismatic Renewal, *Where Did It Come From?* (Catholic Charismatic Renewal office, London 1992) p 1.
29. See K. and D. Ranaghan, *Catholic Pentecostals* (Paulist Press, 1969) p 21.
30. 'Catholic Charismatic Renewal in Britain', *Renewal*, No 104, April/May 1983.
31. J. and E. Sherrill, *They Speak With Other Tongues* (Westwood, Spire, 1965) pp 102–103.
32. For Clarke see P. Hocken, 'Charles J. Clarke', *Renewal*, No 190, March 1992.
33. D. McBain, *Charismatic Christianity* (Macmillan Press, Ltd, 1997) p 46.
34. A. Walker, op. cit., p 22. Walker reiterated this distinction in his revised updated edition *Restoring the Kingdom: the Radical Christianity of the House Church Movement* (Eagle, 1998) pp 41ff.
35. See *Restoration*, November/December 1981, p 13.
36. T. Virgo, *Restoration* (Hodder & Stoughton, 1980).
37. A. Walker, *Restoring the Kingdom*, op. cit. p 117.
38. P. Brierley, *UK Christian Handbook: Religious Trends 1998/1999* (Paternoster Press, 1999) p 9.9.
39. *Renewal*, No 185, October 1991, p 5.
40. P. Brierley, *UK Christian Handbook: Religious Trends 1998/1999*, op. cit. p 9.10.
41. Ichthus Christian Fellowship Congregations updated 4 May 1999. *Welcome to Ichthus Christian Fellowship* (Ichthus, London, 1999) p 3.
42. P. Brierley, op. cit. p 9.11.
43. Ibid p 9.9.
44. I. Boston, 'The Controversial Gerald Coates', *Renewal*, No 170 July 1990.
45. *Sunday Telegraph*, 19 June, 1994.
46. This number was given by John Campbell, Jesus Fellowship/Jesus Army Press Officer in writing, 3 June 1999'.
47. *Jesus the Name, Jesus the Foundation*, p 5.
48. Ibid., p 5.
49. I. Katz, 'The Theocrats', *Weekend Guardian*, 6 July 1991, pp 20–21.
50. 'Women in the Church', *Flame Leaflet No. 10*, Texas Fellowship Revised, April 1992.
51. Ibid.
52. *Church Alive*, p 2.

53. S. Cooper and M. Farrant, *Fire in Our Hearts* (Kingsway, 1991).
54. See *Renewal*, No 182, 1991 p 10 and No 157, June 1989 p 21.
55. *Renewal*, No 151 June 1989.
56. *Renewal*, January 1989 Vol 1.152.
57. Ibid., No 189, February 1992 p 27.
58. B. Jones, *The Radical Church* (Destiny Image Publishers, 1999).
59. Ibid., p 36
60. Ibid., p 73
61. Ibid., p 75
62. A. Walker, op. cit., p 161.
63. P. Hocken, *The Glory and the Shame* (Eagle, 1994), see especially pp 62ff.
64. R. Kew and R. White, *New Millennium New Church* (Cowley Publications, 1992) p 19.

Chapter 2

1. J.A.T. Robinson, *Honest to God* (SCM, 1963).
2. P. Hocken, *Renewal*, No 184 September 1991, p 7.
3. Ibid.
4. Ibid.
5. A. Walker, 'From Revival to Restoration: the Emergence of Britain's New Classical Pentecostalism', *Social Compass: International Review of Socio-Religious Studies*, 1985 vol 32 p 263.
6. Ibid.
7. J. Penn Lewis, *War on the Saints* (Overcomer Trust, undated) pp 46–47.
8. P. Hocken, *The Glory and the Shame* (Eagle, 1994) p 36.
9. A. Walker, op. cit., p 261.
10. J.I. Packer in *Renewal*, No 170 July 1990, p 32.
11. C. Craston (ed) *The Charismatic Movement in the Church of England* (CIO, 1981) p 31.
12. Ibid., p 31.
13. J.R.W. Stott, *The Baptism and Fullness of the Holy Spirit* (IVF, 1964).
14. See, for example, P. Hocken, *Streams of Renewal* (Paternoster, 1986) p 107.
15. J.D. Pawson, *The Normal Christian Birth* (Hodder & Stoughton, 1989).
16. J.D. Pawson, *Fourth Wave* (Hodder & Stoughton, 1993) p 92.
17. *Mainstream*, January 1982.
18. *Towards 2000*, ABWON's Radical Anglican Manifesto, p 7.
19. Ibid., p 7.
20. Ibid., p 7.
21. J.D. Pawson, *Fourth Wave*, op. cit. p 91.
22. Tape-recorded interview at ARM HQ in Derby, June 1994.
23. T. Walker, 'Renew Us By Your Spirit', p 41 cited by P. Hocken in *Streams of Renewal* (Paternoster, 1986) p 102.
24. R. Harthill, 'Front Room Gospel' script 28.3.1984.
25. J.F. MacArthur, *Charismatic Chaos* (Zondervan, 1992) pp 125f.
26. J. Smith, *History of the Church* (1870) Vol 1, p 481.
27. V. Bloxham, *Truth will Prevail* p 15.
28. See M. Harper, *As at the Beginning* (Hodder & Stoughton, 1965) pp 102–103.
29. Ibid., p 34.
30. Ibid., p 35.
31. Ibid., p 20
32. The present writer recalls this from going to visit David Pawson at Goldhill Baptist Manse when a student at the London College of Divinity.
33. J.D. Pawson, *Fourth Wave*, op. cit., p 101.
34. Ibid. See also N. Wright, *The Radical Kingdom* (Kingsway, 1986) p 150.
35. D. Pytches, 'Answers to Almost Every Question About the Gift of Tongues', *Renewal*, No 113, 1984 pp 8–11.
36. M. Mitton tape-recorded interview ARM Derby, June 1994.
37. C. Craston (ed), *The Charismatic Movement in the Church of England*, op. cit., p 1.
38. *Anglicans for Renewal*, Vol no 44, Spring 1991 p 1.
39. R. Liardon, *I Saw Heaven* (Embassy Publishing) 10th edition 1983 p 24.
40. Ibid., p 24.
41. Ibid., p 25.
42. Ibid., p 26.
43. Ibid., p 29.
44. Ibid., p 30.
45. Ibid., p 38.
46. Ibid., p 47.
47. H.B. Kendall, *The Origin and History of the Primitive Methodist Church* (London) Vol I p 97; F.W. Bourne, *The Bible Christians* (1905) pp 36–42 cited E.P. Thompson, *The Making of the English Working Class* (Victor Gollancz, 1963) p 419.
48. W.R. Ward, *Religion and Society in England* (Batsford, 1972) p 78.
49. J.S. Werner, *The Primitive Methodist Connexion: Its Background and Early History* (University of Wisconsin Press, 1984) p 78.
50. R. Davies, *Methodism* (Penguin, 1963) p 13.
51. Interview with Dr D. Calcott; David Pawson, *Fourth Wave*, op. cit. (p 68), wisely points out that a person's collapse should not be taken as 'proof' that the

work and the ministy is complete. It may even be an evasion of futher help, especially in the case of the demonised.

52. Structured questionnaire sample.

53. J.D. Pawson, *Fourth Wave*, op. cit., p 157.

54. M. Mitton, op. cit.

55. K. Copeland, *Take Time to Pray*, p 9 cited M.G. Moriarty, *The New Charismatics* (Zondervan, 1992) p 263.

56. W. Lewis, *Ministry at Cotswold Christian Centre*, Autumn 1993.

57. P. Hocken, *The Glory and the Shame*, op. cit. p 70.

58. Ibid., p 72.

59. N. Wright, op. cit., p 148.

60. *Renewal*, No 113 1984 pp 8–11.

61. *Renewal*, No 97 Feb/March 1982.

62. *Renewal*, No 60 December 1975/January 1976.

Chapter 3

1. See for example J. Osborne, *Women in Leadership – A Biblical View*, a paper prepared on behalf of the eldership of the Bristol Christian Fellowship.

2. *Anglicans for Renewal*, Vol 44 Spring 1991.

3. J. Wimber, 'Worship Intimacy With God', *Equipping the Saints*, Vol 1 Number 1, January/February 1987, p 5.

4. D. Pytches, *Come Holy Spirit* (Hodder & Stoughton, 1985) p 260.

5. M. Stibbe, *A Kingdom of Priests* (Darton, Longman & Todd, 1994) p 94 ,

6. Ibid., p 94.

7. R. Hare in *Renewal*, No 70 August/September 1977.

8. Ibid.

9. C. Craston (chair) *The Charismatic Movement in the Church of England* (CIO Publishing 1981) p 36.

10. Ibid., p 37.

11. N. Richards, *The Worshipping Church* (Word Publishing, 1993) p 47.

12. R. Trudinger, *Master Plan* (Basingstoke, 1980) p 36.

13. Ibid., p 36.

14. Cited by J. Coffey, Democracy and Popular Religion: Moody and Sankey's mission to Britain, 1873–1875 in E. Biagini, (editor) *Citizenship and Community* (CUP, 1996) p 93.

15. N.A.D. Scotland, *Methodism and the Revolt of the Field* (Gloucester, 1981) pp 104–105, 177.

16. See N. Richards, *The Worshipping Church*, op. cit., p 46.

17. The phrase is taken from C. Craston (chair) op. cit., p 42.

18. N. Richards, op. cit.

19. D. Watson, *I Believe in the Holy Spirit* (Hodder & Stoughton).

20. J.D. Pawson, *Fourth Wave*, op. cit., p 148.

21. Ibid., p 149.

22. J.R.W. Stott, *Your Mind Matters* (IVP, 1972) p 21.

23. C. Craston (chair) op. cit., p 16.

24. Ibid., p 39.

25. See for example R.T. Kendall cited in *Mainstream*, No 7 April 1981, Anon, *Belonging to an Anointed Body* (Liverpool, undated) p 42; R Forster (ed) *Ten New Churches* (Marc Europe, 1986), p 125; ISCA Christian Fellowship in Exeter. 'We teach our people to tithe and to bring the tithe into the storehouse' (Malachi 3:10).

26. Interview with Malcolm Widdecombe, 25 October 1999.

27. M. Mitton, Interview at Anglican Renewal Ministries, Derby.

28. C. Cocksworth, *The Anglican Tradition in Worship – An Analysis* (an unpublished paper, 1992) p 8.

29. R. Warren, 'Maturing Christian Worship', *Skepsis* p 7.

Chapter 4

1. M. Muggeridge, *Jesus Rediscovered* (Collins, 1969) p 144.

2. Ibid., p 144.

3. *Renewal*, No 69 June/July 1977 p 11.

4. Ibid., No 111 June/July 1984.

5. *Restoration*, July/August 1978 p 11.

6. *Renewal*, No 191, April 1992 p 8.

7. Ibid., p 8.

8. *ABWON News*, February 1994.

9. Ibid.

10. *Mainstream*, April 1982.

11. See A. Walker, *Restoring the Kingdom* (Hodder & Stoughton, 1985) p 59.

12. Ibid., p 61.

13. A. Walker 'From Revival to Restoration', op. cit., p 267.

14. *First Tuesday*, ITV 1987.

15. Keri Jones, Interview, 8 March 1994.

16. G.W. North, *Apostleship* (Exeter, 1988) p 326.

17. Ibid., p 327.

18. *Restoration*, November/December 1981 p 18.

19. Ibid., p 3.

20. Ibid., p 3.

21. Ibid., p 3.

22. Ibid., p 18.

23. Ibid., p 7.

24. Ibid., p 19.

25. Ibid., p 21.

26. Interview with Maurice Smith, 6 July 1994.
27. W. Nee, *Spiritual Authority* (Christian Fellowship Publications, 1972 edition) p 71.
28. E. Baxter, EBI Tape 'The King and His Army'.
29. W. Nee, op. cit., p 71.
30. T. Virgo, 'The Apostle is No Optional Extra', *Restoration,* November/December 1981.
31. Ibid.
32. M. Smith, interview 6 July 1994.
33. *The Apostle and the Prophet,* ITV.
34. Ibid.
35. See for example *The Sun* 11 March, 1993 pp 1, 4–5, 12 March, 1993 p 5.
36. Bill Bates, interview 29 July 1994.
37. T. Higton and G. Kirby, *The Challenge of the House Churches* (Latimer, 1988).
38. Ibid., p 19, citing *Church of England Newspaper* 13 September 1985.
39. Ibid., p 19.
40. Ibid., pp 19–20.
41. *Restoration,* November/December 1981 p 21.
42. T. Virgo, *Restoration in the Church* (Kingsway, 1985) p 139.
43. M. Harper, *Let My People Grow* (Hodder & Stoughton, 1977).
44. D. Pytches, *Come Holy Spirit* (Hodder & Stoughton, 1985).
45. Ibid., p 10.
46. R. Harthill, *Front Room Gospel* (Script Library, Radio 4, 28 March 1984).
47. R. Forster, *Ten New Churches,* op. cit. p 144.
48. A. Walker, 'From Renewal to Restoration', *International Review of Socio-Religious Studies,* p 269.
49. *Pioneer Magazine,* No 11 Summer 1994, p 2.
50. J. Osbourne, *Women in Leadership* (November 1993).
51. Ibid., p 2.
52. Ibid., p 2.
53. Bristol Christian Fellowship Foundation Course.
54. T. Higton, 'Women Priests', *ABWON News,* August 1993.
55. Ibid., p 1.
56. B. Wilson, *Religion in a Sociological Perspective* (OUP, 1982) p 141.
57. T. Saunders and H. Sansom, *David Watson* (Hodder & Stoughton, 1992) p 194.
58. Ibid., pp 197–198.

Chapter 5
1. Personal information.
2. Personal knowledge.
3. Figures taken from T. Higton, *Our God Reigns* (Hodder & Stoughton, 1988).
4. B. Mumford in *Christianity Today,* 19 March 1990 cited M.G. Moriarty, *The New Charismatics* (Zondervan, 1992) p 77.
5. H. Willmer in *Mainstream,* No 12 January 1983.
6. Ibid.
7. See M.G. Moriarty, op. cit., p 78.
8. W. Nee, *The Body of Christ,* p 69.
9. W. Nee, *Spiritual Authority* (New York, 1972) p 71.
10. W. Nee, *Body of Christ,* p 20.
11. Ibid, p 54.
12. M.G. Moriarty, op. cit., p 258.
13. See A. Walker, *Restoring the Kingdom* (Hodder & Stoughton, 1988).
14. A. Walker, *From Revival to Restoration,* op. cit., p 268.
15. D. Tomlinson, 'Is Discipleship Biblical?', *Restoration,* July/August 1980.
16. Ibid., p 2. See also Acts 20:31.
17. Ibid., p 2.
18. Ibid., p 2.
19. Ibid., p 2.
20. Anon, *Belonging to an Anointed Body* (Liverpool, undated) p 24.
21. Brian Murgatroyd, interview at Glenfall House, Charlton Kings, 13 May 1994.
22. Ibid.
23. Keith Fyleman, interview April 1994.
24. S. Harrison, interview 5 July 1994.
25. Information received from Mrs Nicki Harrison, Bath, 29 June 1994.
26. *The Apostle and the Prophet,* ITV Documentary, 1 November 1988.
27. Ibid.
28. Donna Woodman, interview 10 July 1994.
29. S. Cooper and M. Farrant, *Fire in our Hearts* (Kingsway, 1991) p 96.
30. I. Katz, 'The Theocrats', *Weekend Guardian,* 6 July 1991, pp 20–21.
31. F. MacDonald-Smith, 'The Jesus Army Wants You', *Independent Magazine,* 29 April 1995.
32. *Renewal,* No 102 December 1982/January 1983.
33. Jesus the Name, Jesus the Foundation.
34. C. Simpson's, *The Challenge to Care* (Kingsway, 1986) was a clear statement of shepherding principles.
35. See A. Walker, *Restoring the Kingdom,* op. cit., p 172.
36. M.G. Moriarty, op. cit., p 259.

37. G.W. North, *Eldership* (Exeter, 1980) p 87.
38. Ibid., p 87.
39. Ibid., p 86.
40. N. Wright, *The Radical Kingdom* (Kingsway, 1986) p 104.
41. A. Walker, *Restoring the Kingdom* (Eagle, 1998) p 121.
42. B. Murgatroyd, interview.
43. Ibid.
44. M.G. Moriarty, op. cit., p 78.
45. *Christianity Today*, 19 March 1990. See also *Charisma Magazine*, August 1987.
46. Ibid.
47. B. Mumford, *Memorandum: Public Statement Concerning Discipleship*, San Rafael, California, 1 November 1989.
48. R. Forster, *Ten New Churches* (Marc Europe,1986) p 52.
49. Ibid., p 52.
50. *Renewal*, No 152 January 1989 p 14.
51. Bristol Christian Fellowship Foundation Course (1994).
52. Ibid., p 14.
53. Ibid., p 14.
54. *Leading a Church into Restoration Within an Historic Denomination* (ABWON Broadsheet).
55. B. Jones, *Joined in Covenant* (Harvestime, 1990) pp 15f.
56. R. Trudinger, *Master Plan*, p 102.
57. Ibid., p 105.
58. Ibid., p 106.
59. D. Basham, *A Covenant Community* (undated) circulated to members of Salt and Light.
60. R. Trudinger, op. cit., pp 107–108. See A. Walker, *Restoring the Kingdom*, op. cit., p 91.
61. A. Walker, ibid., p 81.
62. A Walker, *Harmful Religion* (1997) p 87.
63. Dave Tomlinson in A. Walker, *Harmful Religion*, ibid.
64. Ibid., pp 41f.
65. A. Haram, interview 9 July 1994. See also A. Haram, *A Critical Analysis of Pastoral Care in Restoration Churches with Special Reference to Covenant Ministries*. (BA Dissertation, 1994) pp 43f.
66. *Church Times*, 1 September 1995.
67. Ibid.
68. Ibid.
69. R. Howard, *The Rise and Fall of the Nine O'Clock Service* (Mowbray, 1996) p 103.
70. *The Times*, 18 September 1995.
71. *The Independent*, 30 June 1994 p 1.
72. C. Craston (chair) *The Charismatic Movement in the Church of England* (CIO, 1981) p 37.
73. *Renewal*, No 66 December 1976/January 1977.

Chapter 6
1. *Renewal*, No 52, August/September 1974.
2. *Sunday Mirror*, 25 March 1990.
3. *The Daily Telegraph*, 9 September 1999.
4. *The Independent on Sunday*, 19 October 1990.
5. Ibid., No 184, September 1991.
6. Interview with Ben Davies 13 July 1994.
7. *News of the World*, 22 February 1998.
8. Symposium.
9. F. and I. Hammond, *Pigs in the Parlour* (New Wine Press, 1992) p 40.
10. *Restoration*, vol 3 No 6 January/February 1978.
11. F. and I. Hammond, op. cit., p 22.
12. *Renewal*, No 170, July 1990.
13. P. Horrobin, 'Angels and Demons are Real', *Renewal*, No 181, June 1991.
14. Ibid.
15. Ibid.
16. F. and I. Hammond, op. cit., pp 145–148.
17. Ibid., pp 145–148.
18. Ibid., p 26.
19. *Restoration*, vol No 3 January/February 1978, p 17.
20. Ibid., vol No 3 January/February 1978.
21. Interview with David Carruthers.
22. B. Subritzky, *Demons Defeated* (Sovereign World, 1985) p 12. There is a large amount of literature on territorial spirits. See for example J. Dawson, *Taking Our Cities For God* (Word Publishing, 1991).
23. G. Dow, *Anchoring the Healing and Deliverance Ministries in the Life of the Local Church*, video tape, Ellel Grange Ministries 1993.
24. G. Dow, *Deliverance* (Sovereign World, 1991) p 22.
25. T. Higton, *Towards 2000 ABWON's Radical Anglican Manifesto* (ABWON, undated).
26. T. Higton, *That the World May Believe* (Marshall Pickering, 1985) p 168.
27. Ibid., p 164.
28. Ibid., p 170.
29. *Renewal*, No 174, November 1990.
30. Ibid.
31. Ibid.
32. G. Kendrick, *Make Way Song Book and Instruction Manual* (Kingsway, 1986) p 3.
33. Ibid., p 3.
34. Ibid.
35. Bede, *Ecclesiastical History* (Penguin edition) Book 4 chapter 28.

36. G. Dow, *Anchoring the Healing and Deliverance Ministries in the Life of the Local Church* (video).
37. G. Cray, 'The Kingdom of God and Social Justice', *Equipping the Saints*, volume 3 number 2 Spring 1989, p 5.
38. J. Cornwall, *Let Us Praise* (Logos, 1973).
39. Origen, *Against Celsus* 1.46,47.
40. See 1549 *Book of Common Prayer*.
41. F. and I. Hammond, op. cit., p 169.
42. G. Dow, *Anchoring the Healing and Deliverance Ministries in the Life of the Local Church*.
43. G. Dow, *Deliverance* (Sovereign World, 1991) p 26.
44. M. Harper, *Spiritual Warfare* (Hodder & Stoughton, 1970) p 110.
45. Ibid., p 110.
46. J. Richards, *But Deliver Us From Evil* (DLT, 1980 ed) p 129.
47. E.M.B. Green, *I Believe in Satan's Downfall* (Hodder & Stoughton, 1981).
48. G. Dow, *Anchoring the Healing and Deliverance Ministries in the Life of the Local Church*.
49. N. Wright, *The Fair Face of Evil* (Marshall Pickering, 1989) pp 126, 114.
50. See ibid., pp 112, 117.
51. G. Dow, *Anchoring the Healing and Deliverance Ministries in the Life of the Local Church*.
52. G. Dow, *Deliverance*, op. cit., pp 30–32.
53. J. Richards, op. cit., pp 150–151.
54. R. Trudinger, *Master Plan* (Basingstoke, 1980) p 131.
55. F. and I. Hammond, op. cit., p 68.
56. G. Dow, *Anchoring the Healing and Deliverance Ministries in the Life of the Local Church*.
57. G. Coates, *Kingdom Now* (Kingsway, 1993) pp 82, 83.
58. Ben Davies, interview 13 July 1994.
59. See P. Horrobin, *Healing Through Deliverance* (Sovereign World Ltd, 1991) p 107.
60. G. Dow, op. cit.
61. G. Dow, op. cit.
62. P.H. Lawrence, *The Hotline* (Kingsway, 1990) p 154.
63. C.J. Wright, *Deliverance* (Printed notes issued at New Wine, 1994) p 2.
64. Ibid., p 2.
65. G. Dow, op. cit., pp 42–44.
66. Ibid., p 45.
67. N. Wright, op. cit., p 127.
68. J. Richards, op. cit., p 162.
69. F. and I. Hammond, op. cit., p 108.
70. B. Subritzky, op. cit., pp 78–79.
71. J. Richards, op. cit., p 224.
72. E.M.B. Green, *I Believe in Satan's Downfall*, op. cit.
73. J. Richards, op. cit., p 224.
74. G. Dow, *Anchoring the Healing and Deliverance Ministries in the Life of the Local Church*.
75. N. Wright, op. cit., p 127.
76. F. and I. Hammond, op. cit., p 23.
77. G. and S. Powell, *Christian Set Yourself Free* (New Wine Press, 1983) p 149.
78. R. Trudinger, Master Plan, op. cit., p 86.
79. F. and I. Hammond, op. cit., p 175.
80. P. Horrobin, *Healing Through Deliverance,* op. cit.
81. 1 Corinthians 8:10. The only exception to this principle is where a Christian of 'weaker' conscience might be offended at seeing a 'stronger' Christian eating food which had been offered to idols.
82. Colossians 1:13.
83. Acts 17:23.
84. Colossians 2:15.
85. Colossians 1:13.
86. See for example B. Subritzky, op. cit. p 110; J. Wimber, *Power Healing* (Hodder & Stoughton, 1986) p 128.
87. Daily Mirror, 11 July 1994.
88. Jeremiah 17:9.
89. Matthew 15:19.
90. N. Wright, op. cit., p 114.
91. P. Horrobin, op. cit., EME 93/6/c Tape 3.
92. Ibid.
93. See M. Barling, 'Satan, the Church and a Con-man', *Renewal*, No 124, August/September 1986.
94. Information by private interview.
95. C. Craston (ed), *The Charismatic Movement in the Church of England* (CIO Publishing 1981) p 37.

Chapter 7

1. B. Wilson, *Religion in a Sociological Perspective* (OUP, 1982) p 125.
2. See *Renewal*, No 112, August/September 1984.
3. C. Hill, *Prophecy Past and Present* (Highland, 1989) p 7.
4. J. Wimber, 'Introducing Prophetic Ministry', *Equipping the Saints*, 1990 p 6.
5. *Renewal*, No 167, April 1990 p 5.
6. D. Pytches, *Prophecy in the Local Church* (Hodder & Stoughton, 1993) p 3.
7. *Prophecy Today* is published bi-monthly by Prophetic Word Ministries.
8. See *Ministries Today*, September/October 1990.

9. *Renewal,* No 167, April 1990 p 5.
10. C. Hill, op. cit., p 5.
11. D. Pytches, op. cit., p 2.
12. C. Hill, op. cit., p 5.
13. D. Pytches, op. cit., p 10.
14. Ibid.
15. C. Hill, op. cit., p 20.
16. Ibid., p 20.
17. *Renewal,* No 167, April 1990 p 39.
18. H.E. Ward, 'Despise not prophesying', *Mainstream,* No 12, January 1983.
19. Ibid, No 179, 1991 p 35.
20. C. Hummel, *Fire in the Fireplace* (IVP, 1993) p 99.
21. D. Pytches, op. cit., pp 14–16.
22. See R. Pike, *An Analysis of Prophecy Within the Charismatic Movement* (BA Dissertation, Cheltenham and Gloucester College of Higher Education, 1993) p 25, based on an interview with Bishop Pytches at Chorleywood on 14 January 1993.
23. W. Grudem, *The Gift of Prophecy in the New Testament and Today* (Crossway Books, 1988) pp 63–64.
24. W. Grudem, cited by M. Bickle in 'Prophecy' *Vineyard Lecture Notes* (Mercy Publishing, 1990) p 24.
25. C. Hill, op. cit., p 172.
26. Ibid., p 174. D. Pytches, op. cit., pp 8–9.
27. D. Pytches, op. cit., p 25.
28. For example, Latter Rain charismatics teach Dominion Theology which emphasises a final surge of power in the last days to prepare saints for the parousia. All children born since 1973 are known as the 'elected seed generation', an 'end time Omega generation superchurch. They will move lightning . . . if a person is an aran it will be instantly created etc . . .' See R. Pike, op. cit., p 35.
29. D. Pytches, op. cit., p 93.
30. Ibid., p 93.
31. W. North, *Spiritual Life and Spiritual Gifts* (1978 edition) p 59.
32. *Renewal,* No 157, June 1989 p 8.
33. Ibid,. No 167, April 1990 p 39.
34. Ibid., No 157, June 1989 p 8.
35. Anon, *Belonging to an Anointed Body* (Liverpool, undated) p 28.
36. H. Thompson, 'You may all prophesy', *Restoration,* Vol 2, No 5, November/December 1976.
37. G. Houston, *Prophecy: A Gift for Today* (IVP, 1989) p 69.
38. *Renewal,* No 168, May 1990 p 18.
39. M. Bickle, 'Prophecy', *Vineyard Lecture Notes,* p 26.
40. C. Hummel, op. cit., p 106.
41. W. North, op. cit., p 65.
42. M. Bickle, op. cit., p 42.
43. D. Pytches, op. cit., p 93.
44. Ibid., p 44.
45. J. Wimber, 'A response to Pastor Ernie Gruen's controversy with KCF', *Equipping the Saints,* special UK edition, Fall 1990 p 28.
46. C. Hill, *Prophecy Today* Vol 6, No 4, July/August 1990 p 5.
47. T. Saunders, *Renewal,* No 168, May 1990 p 18.
48. Ibid.
49. *Prophecy Today,* July/August 1990.
50. M.G. Moriarty, *The New Charismatics* (Zondervan, 1992) p 102.
51. P. Thigpen, 'How is God speaking today?', *Charisma Magazine,* September 1989 pp 53–54.
52. C. Hill, 'Kansas City Prophets', *Prophecy Today* Vol 6, No 4, July/August 1990. See D. Pytches, *Some Said it Thundered* (Hodder & Stoughton, 1990) p 5.
53. C. Hill, op. cit., p 6.
54. D. Pytches, *Some Said it Thundered,* op. cit. p 33.
55. Ibid., p 34.
56. R. Pike, op. cit., p 38.
57. C. Hill, op. cit., p 7.
58. E. Gruen, 'The Kansas City Prophets', p 6, cited by R. Pike, op. cit., p 35.
59. *Renewal,* No 172, 1990.
60. Ibid., No 173, October 1990 p 7.
61. Ibid., No 183, August 1991 p 21.
62. Ibid., No 190, March 1992. See also M.G. Moriarty, op. cit., p 102.
63. Ibid., p 102.
64. C. Wimber, *John Wimber, the Way it Was* (Hodder & Stoughton, 1999) p 179.
65. Wynne Lewis, ministry at the Cotswold Christian Centre, Winchcombe, October 1993.
66. This 'prophecy' was related to me by John and Susi Peachey of YWAM headquarters in Harpenden, Hertfordshire.
67. M. Harper, 'Prophecy the big ones', *Renewal,* No 112, August/September 1984.
68. M.G. Moriarty, op. cit., p 55.
69. C. Hill, '1987 The word of God', *Prophecy Today,* Vol 3, January/February 1987 p 5.
70. E. Gruen, op. cit., p 9, cited by R. Pike, op. cit., p 34.
71. *Prophecy Today,* Vol 4, No 2, March/April 1988.
72. C. Hill in *Prophecy Today,* Vol 9, No 6, p 31.
73. J. Wimber, 'Revival fire', *Renewal,* No 184, September 1991

74. R. Howard, *Charismania* (SPCK, 1997) p 40.
75. Carol Wimber, op. cit. p 181.
76. C. & J. Sibthorpe, 'A new church', *Renewal*, No 178, March 1991.
77. *Challenge Weekly*, October 1991.
78. Ibid.
79. G. Coates, *Kingdom Now* (Kingsway, 1993) p 122.
80. *Charismania*, op. cit.
81. *Renewal*, No 167, April 1990 p 5.
82. R. Howard, *Charismania* (Mowbray, 1997) p 44.
83. M.G. Moriarty, op. cit., p 214.
84. Ibid.
85. W. Grudem, *The Gift of Prophecy* (Kingsway, 1988) p 113.
86. R. Pike, op. cit., p 40.
87. D. Pytches, *Some Said it Thundered* (Hodder 1990), p 90.
88. *Renewal*, No 172, 1990 p 20.
89. See G. Cooke, *Developing your Prophetic Gifting* (Sovereign World, 1994).
90. *Renewal*, No 178, March 1991, p 19.
91. *Prophecy Today*, Vol 9, No 1 p 5.
92. *ABWON News*, February 1993, p 2.
93. Ibid., p 2.
94. Ibid., p 2.
95. Ibid., p 4.
96. *Renewal*, No 173, October 1990 p 7.
97. Ibid., No 172, 1990 p 2.
98. Ibid., p 20.
99. Ibid., No 179, April 1991, p 35.
100. Ibid.
101. G. Coates, op. cit. pp 118–119.
102. Information from Helenor Birt.

Chapter 8
1. J. Gunstone, *The Lord is Our Healer* (Hodder & Stoughton, 1986) p 106.
2. C. Craston, *The Charismatic Movement in the Church of England* (General Synod 1981) p 35.
3. *Direction*, 1994, Vol 5.
4. Ibid.
5. T. Higton, *That the World May Believe* (Marshall Pickering, 1988) p 162.
6. R. Forster, *Ten New Churches* (Marc Europe, 1985) p 67.
7. P. Lawrence, *The Hot Line* (Kingsway, 1990) p 107.
8. *Renewal*, No 173, October 1990.
9. Letters and testimony from Kevin and Olive Allison of Verwood, Dorset.
10. Interview with Ben Davies.
11. C. Craston, op. cit., p 35.
12. Interview with Ben Davies.
13. T. Smail, *Living in the Light of Pentecost* (Highland, 1990) p 274.
14. Ibid., p 274.
15. Ibid., p 300.
16. P.J. Horrobin, *Healing Through Deliverence* (Sovereign World Ltd, 1991) p 142.
17. R. Trudinger, *Master Plan*, op. cit.
18. J. Wimber, *Power Healing* (Hodder & Stoughton, 1986) p 157.
19. J.F. MacArthur, *Charismatic Chaos* (Zondervan, 1992) p 114.
20. Ibid., p 198.
21. Letter from M. Cerullo, *Receive it!* (September 1994).
22. *The Daily Telegraph*, 8 August 1996. See also *The Sunday Telegraph*, 28 July 1996 and *The Daily Telegraph*, 29 July 1996.
23. C. Craston, op. cit., p 34.
24. See P. Jensen, *Wimber, Friend or Foe* (St Matthias Press, 1990) p 7.
25. See P. May in *Focussing on the Eternal* (IVP, 1989) pp 27–45.
26. See C. Hummel, *Fire in the Fireplace*, op. cit., p 152.
27. T. Smail, 'Talks on healing' (tape St John's Nottingham J36) cited *Living in the Light of Pentecost*, pp 275–276.
28. J. MacArthur, *Charismatic Chaos* (Zondervan, 1994) p 282.
29. See P. Glover, ed, *The Signs and Wonders Movement Exposed* (Day One Publications, 1997) pp 61–82.
30. Ibid., p 67.
31. Ibid., p 69.
32. J. Wimber, op. cit., p 159.
33. *Renewal*, January 1998, No 260.
34. J. Wimber, op. cit., pp 14–15.
35. Ibid., p 164.
36. Ibid., p 169.
37. M. Percy, op. cit., p 45.
38. J. Wimber, op. cit., pp 162–163.
39. Ibid, p 176.
40. J. Gunstone in *Living in the Light of Pentecost* (Highland, 1990) p 280.
41. Ibid., p 280.
42. Ibid., p 257.
43. Dr David C. Lewis' research is appended in full at the back of John Wimber's book *Power Healing* (Hodder 1986) pp 252ff.
44. Ibid, p 257.
45. C. Craston, op. cit., p 35.
46. Ibid, p 34.
47. Ibid., p 34.
48. A. Graham (chair), *We Believe in the Holy Spirit* (General Synod, 1991) p 51.

Chapter 9

1. C. Hummell, *Fire in the Fireplace: Charismatic Renewal in the Nineties*, op. cit., p 201.
2. C.P. Wagner, *Look Out! The Pentecostals are coming* (Carol Streams, Creation House, 1973).
3. See J. Wimber, *The Dynamics of Spiritual Growth* (Hodder & Stoughton, 1990) p.17.
4. Ibid., p 23.
5. J. Gunstone, *Signs and Wonders*, op. cit., p 11.
6. Vineyard *Reflections; John Wimber's Leadership letter* Oct-Dec,1993 p 1.
7. Ibid., p1.
8. Ibid., p1.
9. M.W. Percy, *Signs, Wonders and Church Growth: The Theme of Power in Contemporary Christian Fundamentalism with Special Reference to the works of John Wimber* (Unpublished PRD thesis, London University, 1993) p 42.
10. Ibid., p42.
11. D. Pytches, ed. John Wimber: His Influence and Legacy (Eagle, 1998) p 312.
12. Equipped, No 2 May 1999, p 7.
13. Ibid., p 32.
14. Ibid., pp 247–257.
15. J. Wimber, *Signs and Wonders and Church Growth* (VMI, 1984) p 14.
16. Ibid., p 8.
17. Ibid., p 8.
18. Ibid., section 4 p 5.
19. Ibid., p 5.
20. *Mainstream*, No 26, September, 1987.
21. M. Mitton, Interview.
22. *Renewal*, No 124 August/September 1986.
23. S. Hunt, 'Doing the Stuff' in S. Hunt (editor) *Charismatic Christianity* (MacMillan Press, 1997) pp 77–96.
24. Ibid., p 88.
25. Ibid., p 90.
26. Ibid., p 91.
27. See J.F. MacArthur, *Charismatic Chaos* (Zondervan, 1992) pp 146–147.
28. P. Jensen (editor), *John Wimber Friend or Foe?* (St Matthias Press, 1990).
29. M.W. Percy, op. cit., p 70.
30. J. Wimber, op. cit., sections 6 and 7.
31. M.W. Percy, op. cit., p 60.
32. Ibid, p 60.
33. Ibid, pp 167–169.
34. P. Jensen, op. cit., p 10.
35. M.W. Percy, op. cit., p 195.
36. See Carol Wimber, *Wimber, the Way it Was*, op. cit., pp 170–171
37. Ibid., p 125.
38. Ibid., p 125.
39. Ibid., p 237 footnote 3.
40. M. Wood, *Mainstream*, No 27, 1987.
41. M.W. Percy, op. cit., p 62, see footnote 8.
42. J. Wimber, *Power Healing*, op. cit., p 127.
43. Ibid., pp 130–131.
44. J. Wimber, 'Healing Seminar' 3 tapes 1981 edition unpublished, tape 1 cited by J.F. MacArthur, *Charismatic Chaos* (Zondervan, 1992) p 142.
45. M. Percy, op. cit., p 123 footnote 14, tape 7 'On Prayer' Brighton Conference, 1986.
46. Ibid., p 189.
47. P. Jensen, op. cit., p 7.
48. Ibid., p 8.
49. M. Moriarty, *The New Charismatics* (Zondervan, 1992) p 204.
50. *Renewal*, No 153 February, 1989, p 12.
51. Ibid., No 152 January 1989, pp 22–23.
52. *Mainstream*, No 27, September, 1987.
53. *Mainstream*, No 27, September, 1987.
54. M. Percy, op. cit., p 147.
55. *Renewal*, No 192 May 1992, p 24.
56. Ibid, No 192 May 1992, p 24.
57. M. Percy, op. cit., pp 266f.
58. Ibid., p 182.
59. *Worship Songs of the Vineyard* (Revised July 1990, Mercy Publishing).
60. J. Wimber, *The Dynamics of Spiritual Growth*, op. cit., pp 87–88.
61. M. Percy, op. cit., p 147.
62. See *Worship Songs of the Vineyard*, op. cit. Nos 6, 56, 74, 86, 96, 103, 106, 142, 145, 147, and 155.
63. A. McGrath, *Evangelicalism and the Future of Christianity* (Hodder & Stoughton, 1994) pp 65–66.
64. J. Wimber, op. cit., p 22.
65. Ibid., p 108.
66. M. Percy, op. cit., pp 169, 264.
67. See *Equipping the Saints*, Vol 3 No 2/Spring 1989.
68. Information received from Bishop David Pytches.

Chapter 10

1. See J. Edwards, *The Distinguishing Marks of a Work of the Spirit of God* (Banner of Truth, 1991) pp 109f.
2. M. Warren, 'Revivals in Religion', *Churchman*, Vol 91 No 1, pp 6–18.
3. R. Howard-Browne, *Manifesting the Holy Ghost* (RHBE Publications, 1992) p 16.
4. 'Rumour of Revival', *Alpha*, July 1994.
5. *Prophecy Today*, Vol 10, No 5, p 5.
6. P. Richter, 'The Toronto Blessing', in S. Hunt, et al (editor) *Charismatic Christianity*

(Macmillan Press Ltd, 1997) p 116.

7. *Baptist Times*, 30 June 1994.
8. *The Sunday Telegraph*, 19 June 1994.
9. *Covenant*, Summer 1994, p 1.
10. Ibid.
11. Interview Peter Birch, 19 September 1994.
12. *The Surrey Advertiser*, 5 August 1994.
13. *The Leatherhead Advertiser*, 22 June 1994.
14. Interview with Ann Nolan of Catholic Charismatic Renewal Service, 20 September 1994.
15. *The Daily Telegraph*, 19 June 1994.
16. *The Times*, 2 July 1994.
17. *The Daily Telegraph*, 31 August 1994.
18. J. Edwards, op. cit., p 97.
19. Ibid.
20. K. McDonnell and G.T. Montague (editors), *Fanning the Flame* (Michael Glazier Books, 1991), pp 16–17.
21. Wesley, *Journal*, 1 January 1739.
22. J.G. Gilchrist, *Deeper Experiences of Famous Christians* (Warner Press, 1970) pp 122f.
23. Ibid., p 69.
24. J. Edwards, *An Account of the Revival of Religion in Northampton 1740-42* (Northampton, 1743, Banner of Truth 1991) p 151.
25. Ibid., p 154.
26. Ibid., p 159.
27. J.G. Lawson, op. cit. pp 173–174.
28. L. Peterson, (editor) *The Mark of the Spirit? A Charismatic Critique of the Toronto Blessing* (Paternoster Press, 1998) p 78.
29. *HTB in Focus*, 10 July 1994.
30. E. Mumford, *Toronto Experience*, New Wine Audio Tape, August 1994.
31. *The Church of England Newspaper*, 8 July 1994.
32. *Prophecy Today*, Vol 10, No 5, 1994.
33. Ibid.
34. A. Walker, From 'The Toronto Blessing' to Trinitarian Renewal in T. Smail, et al, *Charismatic Renewal* (SPCK, 1945) p 159.
35. *Prophecy Today*, Vol 10, No 5, 1994.
36. C. Gunton, *Theory through the Theologies* (T. & T. Clark, 1996) p 107.
37. D. Pytches, *Come Holy Spirit* (Hodder & Stoughton, 1986) p 144.
38. D. Roberts, *The Toronto Blessing* (Kingsway, 1994) pp 48f.
39. *The Daily Telegraph*, 8 August 1994.
40. *Prophecy Today*, Vol 10, No 5, 1994.
41. *Baptist Times*, 21 July 1994.
42. See *Covenant*, Summer 1994, pp 7, 10.
43. E. Mumford, op. cit.
44. See W. James, *The Varieties of Religious Experience* (Longmans, Greene, Co, 1947);

W. Sargant, *Battle for the Mind: A Physiology of Conversion and Brain Washing* (Heinemann, 1957).
45. N. Wright, *Charismatic Renewal* (SPCK, 1995) pp 83–84.
46. A. Walker, in ibid. p 153.
47. P. Dixon, *Signs and Revival* (Kingsway, 1994).
48. Ibid., pp 282–284.
49. D. Middlemiss, *Interpreting Charismatic Experience* (SCM Press Ltd, 1996) p 74.
50. L. Newbigin, *The Gospel in a Pluralist Society* (William B. Erdmans Publishing Company, 1989) p 57.
51. D. Middlemiss, op.cit., p 234.
52. Ibid., p 238.
53. See for example P. Glover (editor) *The Signs and Wonders Movement Exposed* (Day One, 1997) p 11 and L. Petersen, *The Mark of the Spirit* (Paternoster, 1998) pp 1–5.
54. *Baptist Times*, 21 July 1994.
55. *HTB in Focus*, 10 July 1994.
56. C. Wimber, *John Wimber: The Way it Was*, op. cit., pp 180–181.

Chapter 11

1. See *The Methodist Church Annual Directory, 1999* p 65, *The Church of England Yearbook 1995*, *The Baptist Union Directory 1998–99* p 161, *The United Reformed Church Year Book 1999* p 23 *1968 figure, ** 1989 figure, *** 1998 figure. This figure for Pentecostals increased to 350,000 because in 1998 nine classic Pentecostal churches came together to form The Pentecostal Churches of the United Kingdom (PCUK).
2. *Mainstream*, 30 October 1988, p 3.
3. *ABWON News*, February 1993, p 2.
4. See Church Commissioners, List of Redundant Churches 1968–1993 (Church Commissioners, 1994).
5. Sourced from *UK Christian Handbook 1994/95*.
6. See B. Wilson, *Religion in a Sociological Perspective* (OUP, 1982) p 81.
7. *Church Planting in Oxford Diocese*, Spring 1994.
8. Ibid., p 1.
9. B. Wilson, op. cit., p 81.
10. R. Currie, *Methodism Divided* (Faber, 1968) p 273.
11. *Mainstream*, No 14, September 1983, p 4.
12. Ibid., No 34, October 1989.
13. *Elim Church Conference Agenda and Report 1991* includes a full set of average annual Elim Church attendance figures. *Elim Church Conference Agenda and Report 1999* p 60.

14. P. Brierley, *Marc Europe Report on the Assemblies of God* (unpublished) and information received from David Gill, Assemblies of God Head Office October 1999.
15. This figure is computed on the basis of the 1989 figure for the house churches which was given as 108,000. See 'Anglican Pentecostals', *Economist* 30 March 1991.
16. R. Ellis and R. Mitchell, *Radical Church Planting* (Crossway Books, 1992) p 29.
17. Cited ibid., p 202.
18. Foreword in C. Cleverly, *Church Planting – Our Future Hope* (SU, 1991).
19. R. Ellis and R. Mitchell, op. cit., p 208.
20. *Renewal*, No 118, August/September 1985.
21. B. Hewitt, *Doing a New Thing* (London, Hodder & Stoughton, 1995) pp 160–167 and personal information from Peter Fenwick.
22. D. Pytches and B. Skinner, *New Wineskins* (Eagle, 1991) p 24.
23. Ibid., p 25.
24. R. Hopkins (ed), *Planting New Churches* (Eagle, 1992) p 28.
25. See *God's Heart for Expansion I and II and The Church in the Nineties* (1990) cited by M. Percy, op. cit., p 209.
26. See M. Percy, op. cit., p 92.
27. R. Ellis and R. Mitchell, op. cit., p 92.
28. Interview with Bryan and Anne Murgatroyd.
29. R. Forster (ed), *Ten New Churches* (Marc Europe, 1986) p 137.
30. *Renewal*, No 96, December 1981/January 1982, pp 4–5.
31. Ibid., pp 16–17.
32. Ibid., No 97, February/March 1982.
33. A. Walker, 'Revival to Restoration: the Emergence in Britain of New Classical Pentecostalism', *Review of Socio-Religious Studies, 1985*, Vol 32, Parts 2–3, p 270.
34. *Breaking New Ground* (Church House Publishing, 1994).
35. See 'Has Church Reached its Cell Buy Date?' *Encounters on the Edge*, No 3, p 7.
36. Ibid., p 6.
37. Information received from the data base, Sheffield Centre, 19 October 1999.
38. CEN, 29 July 1994.
39. D. Pytches and B. Skinner, op. cit., p 20.
40. Ibid., p 20.
41. R. Ellis and R. Mitchell, op. cit., p 205.
42. R. Hopkins, *Church Planting: Some Experiences and Challenges* (Grove Books, 1989) p 21.
43. J. Gunstone in *Renewal*, No 170, July 1990, p 26.
44. *Renewal*, No 168, May 1990.
45. *The Times*, 24 December 1987, cited *Prophecy Today*, Vol 4, No 3, p 6.
46. *ABWON News*, February 1993, p 2.
47. Tape-recorded interview with Michael Mitton ARM Office Derby, 7 June 1994.
48. *Federation of Independent Anglican Church Faith and Order Statement* (Chorleywood, 1992).
49. See 'Where is the New Ground?', *Church of England Newspaper*, 1 July 1994.
50. *Mainstream*, No 39, January 1991.
51. Ibid., No 40, April 1991.
52. Ibid., p 1.
53. D. Allan, *Planted to Grow* (Baptist Union, 1994).
54. Ibid., p 1.
55. Ibid., p 20.
56. Ibid., p 20.
57. Interview with Danny Jackson, 26 October, 1999.
58. List and Synopsis of Methodist Church Plants kept at Central Hall, Westminster.
59. Methodist Conference Minutes 1992 Resolutions.
60. Interview with Brian Hoare, 5 October 1994 by phone.
61. Minutes of the General Assembly 1992.
62. Ibid., 1993, Resolution No 40.
63. *Restoration*, March/April 1989, p 31.
64. Interview with David Matthew of Covenant Ministries, Nettlehill by telephone, 5 October 1994.
65. *Renewal*, No 170, July 1990.
66. *Challenge 2000* (Printed leaflet, London 1994).
67. *Directions*, 1999.
68. List supplied by NFI, September 1999.
69. R. Ellis and R. Mitchell, op. cit., pp x–xi.

Chapter 12

1. D. Tracy, *The Analogical Imagination: Christian Theology and the Culture of Pluralism* (SCM Press, 1981) p 5.
2. T. Smail, 'The Cross and the Spirit', essay in T. Smail, A. Walker and N. Wright, *Charismatic Renewal: The Search for a Theology* (SPCK, 1993) p 49.
3. Ibid., p 3.
4. A. Walker, 'Thoroughly Modern: Sociological Reflections on the Charismatic Movement from the End of the Twentieth Century', in S. Hunt, M. Hamilton and T. Walter (eds) *Charismatic Christianity* (Macmillan Press, 1967) pp 17–42.
5. M. Percy, 'City on a Beach', in ibid., p 215.

6. G. Chevreaux, Talk at Toronto Airport Vineyard 25 July 1975.
7. *The Daily Mail* 14 June 1999. See also *The Sunday Telegraph* 13 June 1999.
8. D. Middlemiss, *Interpreting Charismatic Experience* (SCM, 1996) p 66.
9. Ibid., p 62.
10. See A. McGrath, *Historical Theology* (Blackwell, 1998) pp 251-253.
11. T. Smail, in T. Smail, A. Walker and N. Wright, op. cit., p 15.
12. Ibid., pp 17-19.
13. N. Wright, in ibid., pp 24-27.
14. Ibid., p 12.
15. A. Walker, in ibid., p 37.
16. Ibid., p 87.
17. N. Wright, in ibid., p 82.
18. A. Walker, in ibid., pp 86-105.
19. Ibid., p 87.
20. Ibid., p 92.
21. Ibid., p 95.
22. T. Smail in ibid., p 111.
23. Ibid., p 116.
24. Ibid., p 122.
25. A. Walker, in ibid., p 123.
26. Ibid., p 129.
27. See T. Smail in ibid., pp 55-66.
28. Ibid., p 57.
29. Ibid., p 62.
30. See M. Turner, *Power from on High: The Spirit in Israel's Restoration and Witness in Luke-Acts* (Sheffield Academic Press, 1996) and *The Holy Spirit and Spiritual Gifts Then and Now* (Paternoster, 1996).
31. See M. Turner, *The Holy Spirit and Spiritual Gifts Then and Now* (Paternoster, 1996) pp 1-18.
32. Ibid., pp 172-180.
33. Ibid., pp 293.
34. Ibid., p 298.
35. Ibid., pp 298-302.
36. Ibid., p 313.
37. M. Turner, *Power from on High: The Spirit in Israel's Restoration and Witness in Luke-Acts* (Sheffield Academics Press, 1996) p 439.
38. Ibid., p 441.
39. Ibid., p 455.
40. C. Cocksworth, *Holy Holy Holy Worshipping the Trinitarian God* (Darton, Longman & Todd, 1997).
41. Ibid., p 56.
42. Ibid., p 62.
43. Ibid., pp 102-106.
44. Ibid., p 138.
45. Ibid., p 144.
46. Ibid., p 216.

47. Ibid., p 214.
48. J. McKay, *The Way of the Spirit* (Marshall Pickering, 1988-1990).
49. M. Stibbe, 'The Revival of the Harvest: A Charismatic Theology of Creation' *Skepsis*.
50. See for example C. Cocksworth, ibid., pp 3-6, M. Turner, *The Holy Spirit and Spiritual Gifts* (Paternoster, 1996) p 149.
51. T. Smail, *Once and For all: A Confession of the Cross* (Darton, Longman & Todd, 1998) p 14.
52. M. Stibbe, *Times of Refreshing: A Practical Theology of Revival for Today* (Marshall Pickering, 1995).
53. B. Subritzky, *Demons Defeated* (Sovereign World Ltd, 1986) p 65.
54. *Women in the Church*, Flame Leaflet (Jesus Fellowship, Revised, April 1992).
55. H. Hanegaff, *Christianity in Crisis* (Harvest House, 1993) p 85, cited in S. Hunt et al (editors) *Charismatic Renewal*, pp 149-150.
56. Ibid., p 137.
57. Ibid., p 142.
58. M. Stibbe, op. cit., p 5.
59. C. Gunton, *Theology Through the Theologians* (T & T Clark, 1996) p 106.
60. A. Walker, *Charismatic Renewal*, p 165.
61. Ibid., p 42.
62. C. Gunton, op. cit., p 108.
63. See C. Cocksworth, op. cit.
64. M. Percy, *Charismatic Christianity*, p 216.
65. Ibid., p 216.
66. A. Walker, ibid., p 124.
67. Irenaeus, *Against Heresies* 2.32.5.
68. J. Wimber, *Power Healing* (Hodder & Stoughton, 1986) p 164.
69. G. Coates, Westminster Chapel Tape No. 1473, Sunday evening 22 October 1995.
70. C.G. Cooke, *Developing Your Prophetic Gifting* (Sovereign World, 1994).
71. Luke 10:19.
72. See for example T. Wright, *The New Testament and the People of God* (SPCK, 1992) pp 461-462.
73. P. Hocken, *Streams of Renewal* (Paternoster, 1997) pp 201-211.
74. Ibid., p 202.
75. A recent survey revealed at least twenty charismatics who are currently supervising PhD theses in some area of theology in UK universities.

Chapter 13

1. N. Cuthbert, *Charismatics in Crisis* (Kingsway, 1994) p 14.
2. Ibid., p 14.
3. A. Walker, *From Revival to Restoration*, p 266.

4. Ibid.
5. M. Percy, *Charismatic Christianity* (MacMillan Press Ltd, 1997) p 213.
6. The Church Commissioners for England *Annual Report & Accounts 1998* p 19.
7. R. Forster, *Ten New Churches* (Marc Europe, 1985) p 10.
8. P. Hocken, *The Glory and the Shame* (Eagle, 1994) p 135.
9. *Renewal*, No 170, July 1990, p 32.
10. The Anglican Charismatic Theological Consultation was held at Ridley Hall, Cambridge, 12–14 September 1994.
11. M.G. Moriarty, *The New Charismatics* (Zondervan, 1992) p 156.
12. R. Forster (ed), *Ten New Churches* (Marc Europe, 1985) p 156.
13. M. Stibbe, *Towards a Charismatic Hermeneutic* (unpublished paper, Ridley Hall, Cambridge, September 1994) p 4.
14. Ibid., p 6.
15. Ibid., p 7.
16. Ibid., p 8.
17. See J. Begbie 'Who is this God? – Biblical inspiration revisited', *Tyndale Bulletin*, 43.2, 1992, p 281.
18. B. Jones, *God's Kingdom – Here and Now* (Harvestime, 1990) p 29.
19. W. Richards, 'Everything you always wanted to know about Bryn Jones, but were afraid to ask', *Restoration*, March/April 1989, p 28.
20. See *Anglicans for Renewal*, Vol 49, Summer 1992.
21. M. Stibbe, 'The renewal of harvest – a charismatic theology of creation', *Skepsis*, p 6.
22. See R. Warren, 'Maturing Christian worship', *Skepsis*, p 4.
23. R. Forster (ed), op. cit., p 15.
24. *The Independent*, 17 September 1998.
25. *Alpha News*, March–June 1999, No 8.
26. P. Brierley, *Christian England* (Marc Europe, 1991) p 99.
27. D. Tomlinson, *Post Evangelical* (Triangle, 1995) pp 15–17.
28. Ibid., p 211. See also P. Brierley, *UK Christian Handbook: Religious Trends 1998/99* (Paternoster Press, 1999) p 2.17 Table 2.17.2.

Index

RESTORING THE KINGDOM
DR ANDREW WALKER
The radical Christianity of the House Church Movement

The story of the House Church Movement (or Restorationists), Britain's fastest growing churches of the eighties, is documented in this seminal study. *Restoring the Kingdom* provides a historical understanding of the origins of, and influences on, what are often called the 'new churches'. This new edition has been fully revised and contains two new chapters bringing its analysis up-to-date to the end of the Nineties.

With characteristic verve and illuminating detail Andrew Walker offers a standard account of one of the most dynamic of contemporary religious initiatives.

DAVID MARTIN (Emeritus Professor of Sociology,
London School of Economics)

Based on face-to-face interviews, this is the only authoritative and informed book on the mistakes and failures, as well as the incredible growth and influence of the New Church Movement.

GERALD COATES, Pioneer

An extremely useful and informative book, particularly for main-line clergy who need to know what is going on 'down the road'.

COLIN GUNTON, Professor, University of London

DR ANDREW WALKER is the Director for the Centre of Theology and Culture at King's College, University of London. He is the author of *Telling the Story: Gospel, Mission and Culture*, co-editor with Lawrence Osborn of *Harmful Religion: an Exploration of Religious Abuse* and co-editor with James Patrick of *Rumours of Heaven*.

0 86347 160 9
Eagle Publishing

THE GLORY AND THE SHAME

PETER HOCKEN

*Reflections on the 20th century
outpouring of the Holy Spirit*

This book is a comprehensive portrayal of the growth over the
past century of the worldwide charismatic movement. It is
the work of a scholar who has experienced most of what he
writes, and sets the work of the Holy Spirit in the context of
Christian unity and the Second Coming.

Peter Hocken's overview is exciting, demanding, fearless:
God's surprises are emphasised; the link between Pentecost
and the Second Coming is dominant; the pivotal role of
Israel is brought sharply into focus; and the responsibilities
of the worldwide contemporary church are highlighted.

*A real privilege to read . . . I very much enjoyed it . . . although
miles apart in our ecclesiology, we are so close in our common
love for Jesus*
ROGER FORSTER, ICHTHUS FELLOWSHIP

*A masterpiece of careful observation and evaluation . . . His desire
for balance and a clear lucid style make the book attractive.*
CLIVE CALVER, FORMER GENERAL SECRETARY,
EVANGELICAL ALLIANCE

Scholarly, yet accessible, passionate yet balanced.
DR ANDREW WALKER, KINGS COLLEGE, LONDON

0 86347 117 X
Eagle Publishing